The Sociology of
Georg Simmel

TRANSLATED, EDITED, AND WITH AN INTRODUCTION BY

Kurt H. Wolff

THE FREE PRESS, *New York*

COLLIER-MACMILLAN LIMITED, *London*

Printed in the United States of America

FIRST FREE PRESS PAPERBACK EDITION 1964
For information, address:
The Free Press
A Division of The Macmillan Company
60 Fifth Avenue, New York, N.Y., 10011

Collier-Macmillan Canada, Ltd., Toronto, Ontario
DESIGNED BY SIDNEY SOLOMON

Second Printing 1965

Acknowledgements

To Professor Virgil G. Hinshaw, Jr., for closely reading the entire manuscript, for numerous clarifications and improvements of the text, and for philosophical discussions that have left their impact upon the Introduction;

To Professor Arthur Salz for over-all help on text and Introduction, and for biographical and bibliographical information;

To Dr. Else Simmel for biographical and bibliographical information, and for permission to translate and publish a letter from Georg Simmel;

To Professor Albert Salomon for orientation and advice concerning many matters, including selections;

To Professors Everett C. Hughes and Talcott Parsons for general consultation;

To Professor Meno Lovenstein for suggestions regarding the organization and wording of the Introduction;

To Professors John Dewey and Arthur Child for bibliographical additions;

To Professors H. H. Gerth and C. Wright Mills for permission to use their translation of Simmel's *Die Grossstädte und das Geistesleben;*

To my wife for unfailing help, secretarial and otherwise.

—Kurt H. Wolff

Contents

xii *Contents*

PART FIVE: *Faithfulness and Gratitude; Negativity of Collective Behavior; the Stranger; Metropolis*

Introduction

SIMMEL'S READERS MAY well find themselves puzzled once they try to analyze their impression: does it come from an extraordinary mind or from its product, from a process or from an achievement, from an attitude or from the discoveries made by virtue of it? The dichotomies may be clarified by testimonials of Simmel's *hearers*, who "too, helped build"; Simmel took "his students down an oblique pit into the mine"; he was not a teacher, he was an "inciter." "Just about the time when . . . one felt he had reached a conclusion, he had a way of raising his right arm and, with three fingers of his hand, turning the imaginary object so as to exhibit still another facet." [1] A lecture by Simmel was creation-at-the-moment-of-delivery: the essence of Simmel's spell seems to have been the spontaneous exemplification of the creative process.

Who was this man? Does his life give insight into his significance? Is there a relation between a man's biography and his work? What little we know indicates that biography is the less important, the less true to type and the more original the man; but there are certain data we feel relevant in all cases, if only for the contrast between a man and his history to stand out the more clearly: "to be a stranger is . . . a very positive relation; it is a specific form of interaction." [2] And further, once we are aroused to explore a life as a clue to a mind, and the mind as a clue to its work, we become aware of our ignorance. In the case of Simmel, with hardly a biography, no biographical diary, with few letters existing and practically none published,[3] the case is worse; worse still, because what biographical facts are known suggest only the most tenuous hypotheses concerning their relation to his work. We pass them in review quickly, along with what light they may throw on Simmel's mind.

§ 1. *Fragments of Simmel's Life and Mind*

Georg Simmel,[4] the youngest of seven children, was born in Berlin on March 1, 1858. His father, a partner in a well-known chocolate factory, died when Georg was a boy. A friend of the family, the founder of an international music publishing house, was appointed his guardian. He left Simmel a considerable fortune which enabled him to lead the life of a scholar. Simmel's mother was temperamental and domineering.

After graduating from the gymnasium, Simmel entered the University of Berlin at the age of eighteen to study history. Despite Mommsen's impact on him, he soon changed to philosophy. Later, he named Lazarus and Steinthal, the founders of *Völkerpsychologie,* as his most important teachers; but he also studied with Harms and Zeller (philosophy), with Bastian (psychology), with Droysen, Sybel, Treitschke, Grimm, and Jordan (history). As the second "minor" in his doctoral examination, he chose medieval Italian, and made a special study of Petrarch. In 1881, he received his doctor's degree with a dissertation on "The Nature of Matter according to Kant's Physical Monadology." From 1885 to 1900, he was a *Privatdozent* (a lecturer unpaid except for student fees) in philosophy, and for another fourteen years, an *ausserordentlicher Professor* ("professor extraordinary," an honorary, but not a remunerative title)— both at the University of Berlin. In 1914, at the age of 56, four years before his death, he was called to Strasbourg as a full professor (*Ordinarius*). He died on September 26, 1918.

Simmel's slow advancement [5] stood in contrast with his great reputation as a speaker and thinker. But for many, this reputation was that of an exclusively negative and critical spirit; and both Simmel's mind and work were the indirect basis of the judgment. His mind has been characterized as dialectical; there was a preponderance of the logical and epistemological element over the normative; there was his "microscopic method," the absence of the "unerring instinct of the truly artistic man," the overabundance of associations.[6] And in his first books, his power of discrimination was employed critically more than constructively, especially in his "Introduction to Moral Science," a survey of ethical concepts. But unless one is critical of a critical attitude, one must agree with Simmel himself, who wrote (to Max Weber, in connection with an abortive effort to obtain a professorship for him at Heidelberg, March 18, 1908):

"What you write has not surprised me. . . . Only this, briefly: in certain circles the idea exists that I am an exclusively critical, even a destructive spirit, and that my lectures lead one only to negation. Perhaps I don't have to tell you that this is a nasty untruth. My lectures as, for many years, all my work, tend exclusively toward the positive, toward the demonstration of a deeper insight into world and spirit, with complete renunciation of polemics and criticism in regard to divergent conditions and theories. Whoever understands my lectures and books at all, *cannot* understand them in any other way. Nevertheless, that opinion has existed for a long time; it is my kismet; and I am convinced that the minister's 'unfavorable mood' goes back to some such communication . . ." [7]

Simmel lectured on "logic, principles of philosophy, history of philosophy, modern philosophy, Kant, Lotze, Schopenhauer, Darwin, pessimism, ethics, philosophy of religion, philosophy of art, psychology, social psychology, political psychology, and sociology." [8] His writings ranged equally far, and he published much. [9] The areas of his major production may be classified as sociology, philosophy of history, ethics, general philosophy, philosophy of art, philosophy of contemporary civilization, and metaphysics. [10]

Reading Simmel prompts an inquiry into his mind. Simmel often appears as though in the midst of writing he were overwhelmed by an idea, by an avalanche of ideas, and as if he incorporated them without interrupting himself, digesting and assimilating only to the extent granted him by the onrush. This, perhaps, strikes some as personal about his writing, and others as disorganized, even irritating. His few published aphorisms and posthumous fragments [11] suggest that one way in which he developed an essay was to begin with ideas occurring to him as themes that were jotted down for later elaboration and connection.

"The Simmelian order resembles the interrelations in the collection of a real friend of the arts, who has always bought only what excited him and was an experience to him . . . And yet, the collection has a compelling unity, because all its pieces were chosen on the basis of a unique attitude toward art, of a unique view of life and world."

But "sometimes"

"one has the feeling that Simmel . . . insistently prefers Cinderellas among experiences (so to speak), either to reveal, precisely in them, his virtuosity of philosophizing . . . or to show how, even from them, paths lead into ultimate depths." [12]

Simmel's relation to things—"things," "objects," the "objective," "objectivity" occupied him in many of his writings, especially in his "Philosophy of Money" [13]—seems to have been as intimate as his relation to ideas. Wandering through the streets of a city where he had given a lecture, he discovered two black Wedgwood bowls in a cobbler's shop—which was the beginning of a collection. He may have hit upon ideas in a similar fashion, and they, too, were often beginnings of collections, if they did not remain isolated discoveries which he put in his diary or filed away or did not record at all.[14] Perhaps one could make a good case for the proposition that he was most profound in his aphorisms, in his shots into the unknown—or perhaps it is merely that the distance between the allusion and the uncharted (uncharted at least for Simmel) is so much more striking than between the road and the landscape through which it leads. A few samples may clarify the point:

"I don't know which of these two shows man's vulgarity more: when he gets accustomed to ugliness or when he gets accustomed to beauty.

Objectivity toward people often hides the most boundless solipsism.

To treat not only every person, but every thing as if it were its own end: this would be a cosmic ethics.

In comedy, a highly individual fate is fulfilled by typical characters; in tragedy, a general-human fate by individual characters.

All that can be proved can also be disputed. Only the unprovable is indisputable.

We think we actually understand things only when we have traced them back to what we do not understand and cannot understand—to causality, to axioms, to God, to character." [15]

Simmel's attitude toward events and processes during his lifetime is difficult to infer. His writings reveal little, although his interest in certain contemporary literary, philosophical, and artistic phenomena is obvious, and his constitutive function in some of them would reward investigation.[16] But up to the war, he was not interested in following the history of his time. With the outbreak of the war, however, he began to write much in great agitation, and he continued to write and speak until shortly before his death. In the beginning he was swayed, it seems, by the general excitement; and, in a speech on "Germany's Inner Transformation," delivered in Strasbourg in November, 1914, he spoke and then published such phrases as "This is what is so wonderful about this time"; "*history* we are now experiencing"; "I dare say that most of us have only now experienced what may be called an absolute situation"; "I love Germany and therefore want it to live—to hell with all 'objective' justification of this will in terms of culture, ethics, history, or God knows what else"; "Germany . . . again pregnant with a great possibility"; "This war somehow has a significance different from that of other wars"; [17] and the like. But only fourteen months later, in another speech on the "Crisis of Culture," held in Vienna, he said *this* about the war, and published it in the same pamphlet ("The War and the Spiritual Decisions," 1917):

"The most basic formula of a highly developed culture—a formula which transcends all particular contents—may be suggested by designating it as a crisis constantly held back. . . . Insofar as [the war] has any effect at all on these fundamental, inner forms of culture . . . it can merely inaugurate a scene or an act of this endless drama." [18]

And in this vein, as a pointed and passionate analyst of contemporary civilization, he wrote his last comments on the times (especially the speech just quoted, "The Idea of Europe," and "The Conflict of Modern Civilization" [1918]—when he was not the morally outraged critic of misconduct [19] or spoke in the service of charitable organizations, such as the Red Cross, or to soldiers at the front.

Two-and-a-half months before his death, he wrote in a letter:

"There is hardly anything to say about us. We live in the antinomy between the most enormous inner excitements and tensions and a cloisterly secluded, evenly bleak external existence. . . . The conflict over the fact that one is firmly tied to Germany's and Europe's fates and is torn without resistance into all of their turmoil—but that for the very sake of Germany and Europe one must free oneself from this and stand above it in the redeeming sphere of the spirit: this conflict demands, even for the very imperfect measure in which one can bear or solve it from hour to hour, an effort which I don't know how much longer can be sustained." [20]

In the end, Simmel no longer asked about political events. "During his last days," Gertrud Simmel, his wife, wrote shortly after he died, "Georg no longer wanted the paper, and I did not want to bring it uncalled lest I disturb him in his thoughts." [21] And ten years later:

"Before he died, Georg Simmel said emphatically and on more than one occasion that he had done his essential work; that he could merely have applied his way of looking at things farther and farther and to ever new objects—to something really new it would not have come.

And yet, one felt something like a reservation in these utterances; and in fact he once spoke of it by adding: "Unless I had another twenty years of full strength ahead of me, something which in my age is not at all my share." His reservation presumably concerned studies which would have been in the pursuance of the line traced by his last book, *Lebensanschauung* ["View of Life"]—in the pursuance of this line, or perhaps in a new turn." [22]

Simmel seems to have been impressed from the beginning by the relationism of all items (a more suggestive name for much of his "relativism" [23]), which he found to haunt ever new territories—from sociology to history to ethics to epistemology to art. But he appears to have yearned for an Archimedean point; and although he may be said always to have had such a point,[24] he made it explicit (if at all) only in his metaphysics of life, in *Lebensanschauung,* which he found shortly before he died. Most of this was in 1918 when, knowing that he was stricken with cancer of the liver, he went to the Black Forest to finish the book. Those who knew him best agree he was greatest, came into his perfection, during those last months, in his life even more than in the book written out of it—that, clearly, what he once said of a beloved person, applied to him: he was "a flower on the tree of mankind."

"What permitted Simmel to get along with a minimum of personal experiences and to reconstruct and sympathize with the most alien and varied conditions, attitudes, conflicts, sufferings, and happinesses? Was he ultimately a naïve intellect who drew upon the depth and the wealth of his own inner experiences? Or did he have a kind of clairvoyant imagination and the capacity to push this imagination dialectically ever further? Or did the free mobility of his intellect awaken and progressively strengthen, as its own complement, a longing after roots in a firm province, after a home in a circle of ultimate experience? This, too, is possible." [25]

Simmel's conception of philosophy as the expression of a human type [26] raises in a new light the old question of the nature of subject and object and of their relation, most conspicuously perhaps as the connection between attitude and validity (a variant of the question posed earlier here). To focus on this problem, in fact, may *objectively* be the most fruitful attack on the yield of Simmel's work. But it is well to remember a suggestion in regard to a comprehensive study of him, which has to solve two tasks above all:

"first, it must illumine for us Simmel's intellectual existence, as he illumined Goethe's [in his book on Goethe]; that is, his deeds and omissions, his creations and accomplishments, must be understood out of the uniqueness of his personality. And then, his works must be collected, ordered, and minutely indexed, for only then can they become fertile for science . . . , which will be able to change all the gold that glitters and shines in this work into its own coin." [27]

But it would also seem promising to appreciate the matters about which Simmel did *not* write (or hardly wrote), and for what reasons: for instance, language, music, and "human types" other than Rembrandt, Michelangelo, Rodin, Goethe, the "ultimate heightenings of his own self." [28] And what matters did he take for granted? Pointing analysis on such questions might not only lead to formulating his "central attitude," [29] but might also elucidate the objective problem of the relation between attitude and validity, and between subject and object in general. It is hoped that in the last two sections of this introduction studies of this sort are anticipated.

§ 2. *Simmel in America*

In the United States, Simmel never had a great name as a philosopher, but from the turn of the century to the 'twenties he was well known as a sociologist. Between 1893 and 1910, a number of his writings, most of them sociological, appeared in American periodicals,[30] especially in *The American Journal of Sociology,* the majority of them in translations by Albion W. Small. Park and Burgess gave him a prominent position in their classic *Introduction to the Science of Sociology* (1921).[31] Spykman's *The Social Theory of Georg Simmel,* further evidence of his enthusiastic reception, followed shortly (1925), but its author, along with Park, was presently criticized by Sorokin.[32] In the following year, Abel published a new appraisal of Simmel's sociology (1929), and soon afterward (1932) appeared Becker's elaboration of von Wiese's "systematic sociology," a work in which Simmel plays an important role.[33] These few events mark his career in America to date.

Fifty years ago, American sociology was still in the process of emerging from its European influences, especially the German. Many of its best known representatives spent some of their student days in Germany, and numerous products of German sociology, conspicuously among them some of Simmel's, were at once made available to American readers.[34] But with the development of sociology as an empirical and quantitative study, interest in the more theoretical and philosophical European literature receded. The last decade, however, has witnessed a new appeal of selected European contributions, the most important cases in point being Talcott Parsons' *The Structure of Social Action* and the various Max Weber translations.[35]

Translation, of course, is neither a prerequisite nor a guarantee of acquaintance or influence. Some American sociologists are well-versed in European sociology, whether translated or not, and others, perhaps, do not fully utilize what renditions exist. And it is a question whether a translation is as helpful in communicating a thinker's ideas as an appraisal of his thought.[36] It seems obvious, however, that it is the most desirable means of introducing two types of works: those ought to be introduced into American scholarship whose foremost relevance lies in empirical knowledge or methodological acumen not yet surpassed by American achievements (and here Weber and Durkheim would seem to qualify pre-eminently); and those whose greatest importance lies in the exemplification—predominantly, or in addition to the first criterion—of a suggestive intellectual approach. Simmel's work appears best to fit this second category.

§ 3. *The Translations*

The translations contained in this book have been taken from three sources. Part One, "Fundamental Problems of Sociology (Individual and Society)," is a complete rendition of *Grundfragen der Soziologie (Individuum und Gesellschaft)* (1917), Simmel's last comprehensive statement on sociology. Parts Two through Five, Chapter 3, inclusive, are taken from his major work in the field, *Soziologie, Untersuchungen über die Formen der Vergesellschaftung* (1908). (Parts Two through Four are given in the order in which they appear as chapters in that work; Part Five, Chapters 1-3, consists of *"Exkurse"* contained in other chapters of *Soziologie* not included here.) The remaining pages of the volume (Part Five, Chapter 4) are the translation of a lecture, *"Die Grossstädte und das Geistesleben"* (1902-03).[37]

Simmel appended the following note to the table of contents of *Soziologie:*

"Each of these chapters contains many discussions which more or less closely surround its title problem. But they are not only treatments of it: they also are relatively *independent* contributions to the total problem [of the book]. The ultimate intention and the methodological structure of these studies required their arrangement under few central concepts but, at the same time, required great latitude in regard to the particular questions treated under their heads. The chapter headings, therefore, cover the content only quite imperfectly; the content is given in the subject index at the end of the volume." [38]

This suggests that the ten chapters of *Soziologie* might be likened to connected nets which must be opened by those who want to know what they contain. Simmel's short "Preface" to the work gives an important clue to their arrangement:

"If a study is carried on according to the legitimate cognitive purposes and methods of an existing science, the connection with this science determines the place of the study: an introduction to it need not establish the right to this place but can simply claim a right already justified. But if an investigation lacks such a connection (which would, at least, eliminate the need for discussing its right to its specific way of asking questions); if the manner in which the investigation connects phenomena finds no model for its formula in any domain of the recognized disciplines —then, clearly, the determination of its place within the system of the sciences, the discussion of its methods and potential fertilities, is a new task in itself, which requires its solution not in a preface, but as the first part of the very investigation.

This is the situation of the present attempt at giving the fluctuating concept of sociology an unambiguous content, dominated by one, methodologically certain, problem-idea. The request to the reader to hold on, uninterruptedly, to this one method of asking questions, as it is developed in the first chapter (since otherwise these pages might impress him as an accumulation of unrelated facts and reflections)—this request is the only matter which must be mentioned at the head of this book."

The first chapter, on "the problem of sociology," including the epistemological discussion of the question, "How is society possible?" is not contained in the present volume. It is replaced by Simmel's later conception (Part One, Chapter 1, below) according to which there are three kinds of sociology that are exemplified in the remaining three chapters of Part One. The selections making up the remaining four fifths of this book are indeed held together by a "specific way of asking questions," by "one, methodologically certain, problem-idea"; but it is doubtful that Simmel gave as "unambiguous" a formula of it as he seems to have believed he did.

There are perhaps no intrinsic reasons for preferring the passages selected to others; the major reason is that several American sociologists [39] acquainted with Simmel's work, and with the teaching of it, agreed upon their importance (and on that of several others whose inclusion has been prevented only by technical circumstances).

§ 4. *Simmel's "Field of Sociology"*

For reasons of economy, comments on this book will be restricted to its first chapter, an over-all outline of sociology. In contrast to the preceding paragraphs, the following pages thus deal with Simmel's *work*. The treatment, of course, is colored by the earlier statements, with their (not altogether explicit) conception of Simmel. But an interpretation, Simmel wrote, "will always, admittedly or not, also be a confession of the interpreter," [40] and if the interpreter's "involvement" leads to insights not otherwise gained, there is a chance that it becomes an objective example, and thus justified.

Two observations must be made, however, before discussing the "field of sociology." The first, which the reader will make for himself, is that the following comments cannot be understood without a knowledge of their text. Without the second observation explicitly made, the reader may gain a false impression or become confused. The point is that there exists no contradiction between the positive attitude exhibited in many of the preceding pages, and the critical attitude exemplified in the present section. The work commented upon is so important that no human precautions are called for. The general statements on sociology, of which the text discussed is a pre-eminent example, are among the most vulnerable of Simmel's sociological writings, *but for this very reason,* the most profoundly important to historians and philosophers of sociology. Simmel's topical chapters, a good sample of which is offered in this volume, are equally if not more brilliant; and many of them, as the reader will discover, have not been surpassed in their grasp, depth, sensitivity, timeliness. But in these chapters, Simmel is creating, and to watch him at work is a delight. Here, in his methodological and metaphysical concerns, he seems, rather, to be struggling; and the reaction, to the extent he is, is not delight, but sympathy, empathy, awe, concern, participation, involvement. Even here, however, we may be inclined to expose ourselves to that aspect of his mind in which the distinction we are accustomed to make between science and philosophy seems to dim and become precocious and petty, dissolving, as it does, in the crucible of creativity. If it is nevertheless insisted upon in the following pages, this is done in a combined act of daredeviltry and devil's advocacy, in order to clarify the problems which Simmel (it must not be forgotten) has given us, for us to receive and transform.

[a] "SOCIETY" AND "INDIVIDUAL"

In order to delimit the nature of sociology, Simmel criticizes two equally misleading conceptions of its subject matter, "society." One of them minimizes the concept; the other exaggerates it. That is, Simmel suggests, we cannot be satisfied with admitting either that individuals *alone* are "real," or that society *alone* is "real" (merely because all human life occurs in society): we cannot do without either of the two ideas. For, "society" is among the "least dubious and most legitimate contents" of "human knowledge"; and the "individual," though not an ultimate cognitive unit, is a (presumably ineradicable) object "of experience."

Almost three decades earlier (in *Über sociale Differenzierung*), when Simmel faced the individual-society "problem" for the first time, he presented a similar argument. But instead of denying the individual as a *cognitive* object, he insisted upon the *difficulty*, due to our knowledge of evolution, of so conceiving of him: logic (he wrote) leads us to recognize only atoms as the ultimately "real." [41] In *Grundfragen*, however, in his formulation of the individual as a unit of *experience*, he presents a conception very closely related to that of Dilthey, who maintained:

"We know natural objects from without through our senses. . . How different is the way in which mental life is given to us! In contrast to external perception, inner perception rests upon an awareness (*Innewerden*), a lived experience (*Erleben*), it is immediately given." [42]

Yet shortly after calling the individual a unit of experience, Simmel returns to his earlier argument:

"Color molecules, letters, particles of water indeed 'exist'; but the painting, the book, the river are syntheses: they are units that do not exist in objective reality but only in the consciousness which constitutes them. . . . It is perfectly arbitrary to stop the reduction, which leads to ultimately real elements, at the individual. For this reduction is interminable."

But in "Social Differentiation," Simmel recognized atomism as theoretically inescapable, though practically unusable: "The question of how many and which real units we have to fuse into a higher but only subjective unit . . . is only a question of practice." [43] Now, by contrast, he proceeds to lead atomism *ad absurdum*, even if still on epistemological grounds. For he suggests that atomism is due to an erroneous conception of the nature of cognition: the more adequate conception of it is to consider it as a process of abstraction. (The abstract character of sociology is discussed in Sect. 2.)

But Simmel is here engaging in a fallacious argument. Actually, he is *not* distinguishing between two conceptions of cognition, but between two heterogeneous inquiries (about whose connection, furthermore, he is silent). The first inquiry, to which "atomism" is a possible answer, is into the nature of reality; it is ontological. The second inquiry, to which "cognition is abstraction" is a possible answer, is into the nature of cognition; it is epistemological. Thus, by switching from one inquiry (ontological) to another (epistemological), Simmel tries to validate the concept of "society" epistemologically; but as a sociologist, that is, as a scientist, he needs no such validation. For as a scientist, he needs only a *pragmatic* justification: he must merely

xxx Introduction

show that a concept (in this instance, the concept of "society") is useful for his theory or research; the pragmatic justification requires no ontological or epistemological supplement.

To make this clearer, attention may be called to Simmel's discussion of the isolated individual as a sociological phenomenon (Part Two, Ch. 3, Sects. 2-4). There he simply finds it useful so to consider the individual, because he thus discovers matters he would not otherwise have noticed; and he is far from raising such ontological questions as whether the individual is a marginal case or a residuum of sociation or whether, inversely, society is a mere instrument of individuation, etc. It is precisely this kind of question, however, which Simmel asks in the present context, his general development of sociology. He is aware, here, of his "insecure foundations," while in the discussion of the quantitative aspects of the group (which contains the treatment of the isolated individual), he is preoccupied with empirical challenges and thus is sure of his "solid structures." (On the contrast between "insecure foundations" and "solid structures," see below.)

At any rate, in the present context, Simmel fails to distinguish between a philosophical and a pragmatic justification.[44] Is this an oversight? Or does it suggest that Simmel's conception of "sociology" is not that of a science alone, but of a scientific-philosophical enterprise, or of a strictly philosophical enterprise? We shall see, on the analysis of further arguments, that the imputation of an "oversight" is uncalled for since the second hypothesis (to be specified) is the more plausible one.

"Society" itself is presently defined as "a number of individuals connected by interaction." But at the same time, Simmel seems to suggest that it is only the sum total of these interactions, *without* the individuals. For a more explicit statement, we must look elsewhere (*Soziologie*, Ch. 1):

" 'Society' is, first, the complex of societalized individuals, the societally formed human material, as it constitutes the whole historical reality. Secondly, however, 'society' is also the sum of those forms of relationship by virtue of which individuals are transformed, precisely, into 'society' in the first sense. . . . 'Society,' then, in the sense that is of use to sociology, is either the abstract, general concept of all these forms—the genus whose species they are—or it is their sum operating at a particular time." [45]

Thus even here, we do not find an unambiguous statement but must simply conclude that Simmel leans toward the second definition, without clearly deciding in favor of it or suggesting what use the first might have. In his studies (as against his theoretical statements), he appears to be no clearer, but likewise only to *tend* toward the second; yet in regard to his studies, the question of defining "society" is practically irrelevant.

[b] SOCIOLOGY

In Sect. 2, on the abstract character of sociology, Simmel comes back to the problem of establishing a science of sociology in the face of the observation that "man in all aspects of his life and action is determined by the fact that he is a social being." Does this not, he asks (as is maintained by that "exaggerated" notion of "society" which was mentioned earlier by him)—does this not reduce all sciences of man to mere parts of the science of social life? Since Simmel is convinced that the "special social sciences" will continue no matter how sociology may develop, the answer can only be negative. Hence, in order to establish sociology as a science which is yet no utopian "master science," a different route must be taken.

[c] SOCIOLOGY AS A METHOD

Simmel suggests this route by calling attention to the "sociological viewpoint"—in his words, to the recognition of "societal production," that is, the social explanation (or interpretation) of historical phenomena. This explanation historically superseded explanations in terms of production by individuals and by divine interference. To act on the knowledge (or interpretation) that historical phenomena are social products, is to view them in a new light, is to adopt a new method for studying them—in short, is to institute a new method for "the historical disciplines and . . . the human studies in general." This method is "sociology." Sociology yields possibilties of solution or of deeper study which may be derived from fields of knowledge contentually quite different (perhaps) from the field of the particular problem under investigation.

An inspection of the three examples which illustrate the application of this method suggests that it consists in the abstraction of certain elements from historical reality, and in their recombination for specific study. (Note particularly the end of the second example.) In the instances given, these elements are, first, the effect of a mass upon the individual; second, readiness for sacrifice (and other attitudes) found in religious devotion but associated not only with religious groups; and, third, generalized attitudes toward the world (here, individualism as against concentration upon uniformities). Obviously, these elements, the objects of sociological abstraction, are, in some sense, heterogeneous. What they have in common is clarified, though only indirectly, by recalling the historical role of sociology mentioned before: all three examples reflect "societal production." Their common features are further illuminated by Simmel's statements concerning the problem areas of sociology.

[d] "GENERAL" SOCIOLOGY

The first "problem area," resulting in the articulation of "general sociology," is introduced by the proposition that human life may be considered from three (or possibly more) standpoints: objective, individual (subjective), and social. That the last of these, the social standpoint, is not perfectly clear, is no objection, according to Simmel, "for it is a characteristic of the human mind to be capable of erecting solid structures, while their foundations are still insecure." [46] And from the immediately following examples of sociological investigations (fall of the Roman Empire, relation between religion and economics in the great civilizations, etc.), it appears that his methodology is propaedeutic rather than specific (which may be one implication of his remark on "solid structures" vs. "insecure foundations"). To grasp Simmel's position in another frame of reference: he has not been able to objectify his attitude toward sociology, or toward the sociologically relevant world. He himself comes close to making this point in the following passage from *Soziologie* (especially in the parts here italicized):

"If I myself stress the wholly fragmentary, incomplete character of this book, I do not do so in order to protect myself, in a cheap manner, against objections to this character. For when measured by the ideal of objective perfection, the selection of the particular problems and examples contained in this work doubtless presents a haphazard character. Yet if this character should strike one as a defect, this would only go to prove that *I have not been able to clarify the fundamental idea of the present volume.* For according to this idea, nothing more *can* be attempted than to establish the beginning and the direction of an infinitely long road—the pretension of any systematic and definitive completeness would be, at least, a self-illusion. *Perfection can here be obtained by the individual student only in the subjective sense that he communicates everything he has been able to see.*" [47]

The nature of the "sociological problems in the narrower sense of this term," on which Simmel continues the discussion, is another indication of the merely propaedeutic or programmatic character of his sociology as methodology. One of these more narrowly sociological problems belongs to the general question of whether sociology, in the course of investigating historical phenomena, can hope to establish laws.[48] Another problem is that of group power; and a third is constituted by the "value relations between collective and individual conduct, action, and thought"—a phrase which, in the next chapter, turns out to have anticipated a treatise on (chiefly) group characteristics as compared with individual characteristics, the distinction (within the individual) of private and group aspects, and "mass psychology" or "collective behavior" (in contemporary terminology). What, then, in brief, *is* "general sociology?" Simmel answers (but only in the subsequent discussion of "pure or formal sociology"): the study "of the whole of historical life insofar as it is formed societally."

[e] "FORMAL" SOCIOLOGY

The second problem area and kind of sociology, "pure" or "formal" sociology, investigates "the societal forms themselves," which make "society (and societies) out of the mere sum of living men." Examples of such "forms" are

"superiority and subordination, competition, division of labor, formation of parties, representation, inner solidarity coupled with exclusiveness toward the outside."

These and similar forms, Simmel points out, may be exhibited by the most diverse *groups;* and, the same *interest* may be realized in very different forms. He subsumes "groups" and "interests," together, under the category of "content," which is sharply contrasted with that of "(societal) form" or "sociation."

In terms of its subject matter, "formal" sociology

"is not a special science, as . . . [sociology] was in terms of the first problem area. Yet in terms of its clearly specified way of asking questions, . . . [sociology] is a special science even here."

The implication seems to be that "formal" and "general" sociology have different *kinds* of subject matter, and for this reason are special sciences in different senses of the term.

[f] "PHILOSOPHICAL" SOCIOLOGY

The discussion of "philosophical sociology," the third and last kind, begins with a treatment of the philosophical dimensions of science (including the social sciences), but then leads to the surprising conclusion that

"sociology . . . emerges as the epistemology of the special social sciences, as the analysis and systematization of the bases of their forms and norms." [49]

And likewise, it seems problematical to call the inquiry into the metaphysical (rather than epistemological) ramifications of sociological study, "philosophical sociology." For, the discussion refers to a topic which is hardly suggested by this name: it would more accurately be designated as "an inquiry into the nature of reality suggested by the study of social phenomena" or, briefly, as "ontology on the occasion of social phenomena." And the confusion is increased by the fact that only the first three sections of Ch. 4, "an *example of philosophical sociology*," constitute an ontological discussion, while the major part is a study in intellectual history. To a careful reader of the last paragraph in Sect. 3 of that chapter, however, it may appear that Simmel's road to ontology is intellectual history, in the sense of ontological induction from history or in a sense even closer, once more, to Dilthey (or even to Hegel). Does Simmel suggest that there is no philosophy of history other than sociology?

It is important to elucidate the problems raised by these obscurities, surprises, and inconsistencies—the last among the problems here proposed for clarification. All the puzzles that have been noted are interrelated, and can be redefined, if not solved, together.

[g] SIMMEL'S SOCIOLOGY AS THE EXPRESSION OF AN ATTITUDE

But what is the value of Simmel's conception of sociology given in the *Grundfragen,* a work written by him (according to von Wiese and Becker)

"when he was already suffering greatly from the illness which resulted in his death, and . . . [which] must be regarded as an unsuccessful attempt to popularize his theories?" [50]

And worse: the methodological statements in *Soziologie* (published long before that illness) are no clearer, as the few quotations from that work have probably shown; and Simmel admitted some lack of clarity by his insistence, in both works, upon the idea of "insecure foundations." Yet the question is rhetorical: the study of Simmel is worth our effort—provided we realize that Simmel's vagueness derives from an attitude, and that this attitude is of great importance and can be clarified by analysis.

[h] SIMMEL'S PROBLEMS

A clue to an understanding of Simmel's sociology is furnished by the suggestion that Simmel did not succeed in objectifying his attitude.[51] Or, to set this idea into an even broader framework: he confronts the student of *all* of his philosophy with the problem of the nature of attitude, on the one hand, and of validity, on the other, and of their relation. In the course of articulating his attitude, Simmel may have come to find the study of "sociology" fascinating, because it helped his own articulation and clarification.[52] In his pursuit of particular topics within this study, he made numerous finds that are objective or scientific, and are there for the sociologist to ponder or delight in, whether or not he be plagued by problems of attitude or of the philosophical implications of his pursuit. Some pages even in Part One, but especially the subsequent Parts, bear witness to this. But the "foundations" were "insecure"; and Simmel's inquiry was not articulated even to the point of his asking in *what* the insecurity consisted, by *what* he was worried. The problems stated in the foregoing appraisal may thus be interpreted as important and closely interrelated grounds of his worry: the nature and "kinds" of sociology, and the nature of society, of "form," and of "content."

The first of these implies almost all others. It is: what "way of asking questions" *was* sociology for Simmel? It is close to the modern concern with "social structure"; one does justice to a great portion of Simmel's sociology by saying that he attempted to throw light on the structure of society. But his very definitions of "society" indicate what portions of his sociology are *not* caught by this interpretation: he wavered, as we have seen, between the inclusion and the exclusion of the individuals connected by interaction. (And it may also be noted that he failed to distinguish between "society" and "group," or to show that no such distinction is required.) The fact that one of the admittedly central concepts of sociology remains vague, suggests that its clear-cut definition was not central to Simmel nor, therefore, to *his* sociology. Perhaps he was too much engrossed in a way of grasping the world to find the questions whose answers would have clarified the issue.

[i] THE "SOCIALIZATION OF THE SPIRIT" VS. SOCIOLOGY AS A METHOD

An important component of this way of grasping the world within the framework of his sociology, was what he conceived to be "sociology as a method." Our attention, he seems to say, has so insistently and constantly been called to the usefulness of investigating and interpreting historical affairs sociologically, that if we would understand them, we no longer can afford to do without the sociological viewpoint. And it is true that the sociological perspective has penetrated, for the last half century and, in a wider sense, for much longer, not only the social sciences (as Simmel pointed out that it might), but also the humanities. But to emphasize this viewpoint, Simmel noted, is not the same as to establish sociology as a special discipline. He did *not* note, however, that his emphasis itself is part of that modern attitude which is interested (and often in a metaphysically not disinterested manner) in socializing the spirit: in conceiving of mind as a product, or by-product, of society, in locating, tracing, and finding mind in society.[53] But Simmel did *not* want to socialize the spirit: he wished (half-heartedly in his sociology and wholeheartedly elsewhere) to preserve its *autonomy*. He insisted that the realms of the objective and of the individual are coordinate with the social realm; and he may also have wanted to save the spirit by finding "subject matter" for sociology—for otherwise, its subject matter might become the whole world.

[j] "GENERAL" VS. "FORMAL" SOCIOLOGY

But his first attempt at establishing a subject matter failed: it is difficult to distinguish the sociological method from the first "kind of sociology" proper, "general sociology," whose subject matter is "the whole of historical life insofar as it is formed societally." Throughout his discussion of sociology as a method and of sociology's first "problem area" or "subject matter" (resulting in the postulation of "general sociology"), Simmel defines neither—and yet, the reader may well be fascinated by Simmel's attitude (or, as Sorokin put it in a derogatory fashion, by "a talented man").

In comparison with his discussions of the sociological method and of general sociology, his "formal" sociology—which has drawn the greatest attention and has aroused the greatest controversy—is in fact a successful thrust in the direction where his worries must lead him to seek sociological subject matter: the "societal forms themselves." But why did Simmel insist that "general" sociology and "formal" sociology are not special disciplines in the same sense of the term? Assuming that we know what to understand by "history," on the one hand, and by the "sociological viewpoint," on the other, the two can be easily distinguished: "general" sociology is only a way of looking at history (or its subject matter), only a method of handling it (whereby the method interferes with the subject matter of history as much as any method with any subject matter)—whereas "formal" sociology is not a method but a special science with its own subject matter, "the forms of sociation" (and with a method). But for Simmel, this was not so simple, because he thought "general sociology," too, had its subject matter ("historical life insofar . . ."), while "formal sociology" did not: he took method for subject matter in the first instance, and did the reverse in the second.

The reason may be that in his ambivalent attitude toward the socialization of the spirit, he hesitated to throw the whole world, that is, *any* subject matter, open to the sociological approach. If so, he did not here apply his knowledge (and his insistence on it) that sociology, like any other science, proceeds by abstraction. Did Simmel fear sociology might abstract too much, might, as it were, "pre-empt" the spirit? In one of his essays, reflecting upon the sadness of ruins, he suggested that

"the collapse strikes us as nature's revenge of the violation which the spirit, by producing a form in its own image, has perpetrated upon it. . . . The balance between nature and spirit, which the building itself presented, shifts in favor of nature. This shift becomes a cosmic tragedy." [54]

Was he overpowered, too, not by nature,[55] but by the "socialization of the spirit" itself?

[k] THE "SOCIETAL FORMS"

His Kantian heritage probably prevented him from seeing "forms" as subject matter because they are merely "injected" into social life. Perhaps if he had been clearer in regard to the nature of science, he might have been content to say that subject matter is whatever a science studies. But perhaps he was aware of his uncertainty concerning *what* "formal" sociology was designed to study; at any rate, whether aware or not, he actually was not clear in regard to the nature of the "forms." Again, if he came upon them out of his ambivalence, it is understandable that he should not have been; in addition, his own achievements in his sociological studies proper (his "solid structures") may well have made him feel that he could afford a merely cursory treatment of the definition and of the methodological and philosophical status of the "forms." [56] To the student of Simmel, in any event—since "general sociology" turned out to be a program of a method only —the notion of "form" is the most promising methodological or philosophical contribution toward the establishment of sociology as a science.

Despite the relatively numerous discussions of the "forms," [57] the concept has yet to be specified in a satisfactory manner. To do so requires a painstaking collection and juxtaposition of all passages in which Simmel employs the term,[58] and the subsequent formulation of a definition which does justice to all of them, in a way to be determined by the study itself. This is clearly beyond the scope of the present interpretation. But there is one sense which probably all of Simmel's usages of "form" have in common, although it has not been noted in the literature; [59] and unfortunately, it is neither as specific as it might be, nor is it capable of answering many pertinent questions. It is "form" understood as that element which, among the elements relevant to a particular inquiry as well as to the general viewpoint of sociology, is relatively stable—as against "content" which, with the same specifications, is relatively variable.[60]

[l] THE RELATION OF SIMMEL'S PHILOSOPHICAL TO HIS SOCIOLOGICAL CONCERNS

The chief question in regard to Simmel's "philosophical sociology" concerns the reason which led him to designate it as "the epistemology of the social sciences." Reading the pages which lead from his statements on the philosophical dimensions of the social sciences to this designation, one is impressed by a *non sequitur*. Perhaps it may be resolved by suggesting that the sociological grasp of the world tempted Simmel to ennoble, to "spiritualize," sociology by elevating it to the rank of epistemological inquiry.[61] Also, his statement that "individual" and "society" are "the only sociological themes that have thus far been realized," [62] may indicate his wish to reserve sociology for the task of checking both stagnation and the premature articulation of other themes. If so, he gave "philosophical sociology" a second role, in addition to that of social epistemology and ontology, namely, the role of general philosophy of the social sciences.

These arguments may make Simmel's leaps into philosophy less surprising. But there is the further fact that Simmel hardly went beyond the programmatic announcement of his epistemology and ontology into actual inquiries in these fields, neither in his *Soziologie* nor in his *Grundfragen*.[63] The significance of this merely negative fact is greatly increased by the positive fact that he did call the last chapter of *Grundfragen* (Part One, Ch. 4, in this volume) an "example of philosophical sociology," while it is predominantly a study in intellectual history, rather than in epistemology or ontology. This positive fact, along with the propositions of the preceding arguments, makes it plausible to suspect Simmel's philosophical concerns to be no more deeply related to his sociological concerns than was necessary for the production of his programmatic statement—and not deeply enough to enforce it.

§ 5. *The Methodological and Philosophical Importance of Simmel's Sociology*

This whole introduction, practically, has been an attempt to evoke an image of Simmel's significance. The reader's attention is called particularly to the paragraph preceding [a] in Sect. 4 above, the most explicit relevant passage. A succinct concluding statement seems in order.

Irrespective of his "insecure foundations," Simmel has given us penetrating analyses of sociological problems. To repeat, since these are almost entirely matters to delight in, they have not been reviewed here; and the tool for their review is scientific procedure as ordinarily understood, and no more. They not only make up the bulk of Simmel's work in sociology, as well as of this book, but will also be the chief attraction to most readers, and they are, furthermore, his most important contribution to sociology as a science.

But the historian and philosopher of sociology, rather than the sociologist proper, will have reason for wonder: although there is hardly a *logical* connection between Simmel's general statements on sociology (for instance, his threefold subdivision of the field) and his topical statements (for instance, his discussion of the metropolis), nevertheless, since both types of statements come from the same person, there must be some *psychological* connection between them. While no attempt has been made here to trace this connection, the two mental sets which may account for the two respective kinds of statements have been suggested: worry and creativity. Yet the main topic has been an analysis of the "worries": from them, it is submitted, Simmel wrested sociology as the scientific study of social life by means of the heuristic construct of "societal forms." This construct, along with related constructs, especially "interaction," has contributed (for reasons which may be no more scientific than is the origin of "form" itself) to other constructs that are still in the center of contemporary sociological thought, are still (among other things) articulations of the sociological attitude. Among these are "social process," "processes" and "types of interaction," "social structure," "social relations," "social system."

But Simmel (it has been suggested) was most profoundly important on another count. There is a more recent viewpoint than the sociological attitude, although it is closely related to it; perhaps it is a later phase of the "socialization of the spirit." It is embodied in that fumbling branch of sociology itself that goes by the name of "sociology of knowledge." Should this branch grow and exemplify as unquestioned an attitude as sociology does now, then Simmel, because of his very confusion, might fully come into his own: he might emerge, not as the exemplifier of creativity, which to some he must have been as a speaker, but as the incarnation of the scope, the dangers, and the potentialities, not yet foreseeable, of the "socialization of the spirit" itself. If such a time comes, sociologists may have to collaborate with "social ontologists" and with philosophers of history and of science; and a new appraisal of our intellectual efforts and of their functions may be the intent or result (or only the result) of such a collaboration.

Notes

(Capital letters refer to Appendices below. Names refer to authors of works listed in A, B, E; titles without indication of author refer to works by Simmel listed in B, C, or D; numbers are page references. Items preceded by [*] were not available for inspection at the time of writing.)

1. Tagger, 37; Ludwig, 412; Flexner, 108. Cf. also Fechter, 53-54.
2. Simmel, "The Stranger" (Part V, Ch. 3, below).
3. The only biographical sketch: Spykman, xxiii-xxix (source: Simmel's widow). Only-published letters: Weber, 382-383, 384-385, 386-387. Practically nothing of Simmel's possessions was salvaged when his son and family left Nazi Germany. Attempts are being made to gather what scattered remains may turn up.
4. Sources: Acknowledgements; Spykman.
5. For an illuminating description of the generally slow university career in the Germany of the Kaiser: Max Weber, "Science as a Vocation" (1918), in *From Max Weber: Essays in Sociology*, tr., ed., and with intr. by H. H. Gerth and C. Wright Mills, New York: Oxford University Press, 1946, pp. 129-156, esp. 129-134.
6. Hurwicz; the last quotation (198) is taken (though not quite exactly) from Frischeisen-Köhler, 36. Hurwicz is trying to point to "Jewish elements" in Simmel's thought. Simmel's parents, baptized Jews, baptized the child a Protestant; later Simmel left the church without, however, joining a synagogue. He must have taken his Jewishness for granted, although he never wrote about the Jews except, here and there, sociologically. Cf. Fischer, 46: "And if—as has been said repeatedly—it appears strange that a man of non-Germanic blood found the hitherto most profound insights into the Germanic way of art, then I want to say only that all cognition presupposes, or includes, a being-different, a setting-oneself-off, and that, for this very reason the Semitic thinker, at whom people like to look askance, was capable of circumscribing the German spirit in

art and philosophy more easily than others can who live and work in it." Needless to say, this passage illustrates a well-known variety of anti-Semitism.

7. An allusion to this episode in Hurwicz, 197.

8. Spykman, xxv.

9. B.

10. C.

11. "Aus einer Aphorismensammlung," *Der Kunstfreund, Zeitschrift der Vereinigung der Kunstfreunde*, 2: 284-286, June, 1914; "Aus dem nachgelassenen Tagebuche" (first published in *Logos*, 8:121-151, 1919-1920, as "Aus Georg Simmels nachgelassenem Tagebuch," which in turn was a reprint of many of the aphorisms published in the *Kunstfreund*), 1-46; "Bruchstücke und Aphorismen" at the end of Simmel's long essay on love ("Über die Liebe"), 100-123; the fragments at the end of his essay on the actor ("Zur Philosophie des Schauspielers"), 260-265; and the fragments rounding out his study of naturalism ("Zum Problem des Naturalismus"), 297-304; all in Simmel, *Fragmente und Aufsätze*; also "Aus Georg Simmels nachgelassner Mappe 'Metaphysik'."

12. Utitz, 12, 8.

13. See also, e.g., Part I, Ch. 1, Sect. 4a, below.—Cf. Delbos in Mamelet, iv: Simmel "evidently gets the greatest pleasure from pursuing the collaboration between intelligence and things . . ." Or, in a negative version, Lessing, 336, in the pun for which he humorously apologizes: "Quae non sunt simulo. (Was nicht ist wird ersimmelt.)" (Things that don't exist I simmelate.)

14. Diary excerpts in *Fragmente und Aufsätze*, 1-46 (see n. 11 above). The filing-away is suggested by the title of Gertrud Simmel's contribution to the Buber volume (B, no. 23, also cited in n. 11 above): "From Georg Simmel's Posthumous Folder, 'Metaphysics'." —At a party in his home, Simmel noted that his wife didn't fill his tea cup properly and asked her why. Gertrud Simmel, who was tall, answered that she hadn't noticed this from her height. "Now I understand," Simmel replied, "why the Lord God doesn't fill the cups to the brim!"—In conversation with another person, he interrupted himself, wonderingly: "Isn't it something strange that one should be no less than oneself?" ("Ist es nicht etwas Merkwürdiges, kein Geringerer als man selbst zu sein?")—"That Bergson is more important than I, may well be; but what I can't see is that I should

be less important than he." (Fechter, 55.)—"Thinking hurts." ("Denken tut weh.")—The following utterance may be apocryphical: "She has a great past ahead of her" (said of a young lady Simmel had met).

15. From Simmel's diary (cited in preceding n.), 35, 37, 20, 39, 4, 4, respectively.

16. Simmel wrote some newspaper articles on current social questions, e.g., *"Die Bauernbefreiung in Böhmen" (1894), *"Der Militarismus und die Stellung der Frauen" (1894), *"Soziale Medizin" (1897), *"Über die Zurechenbarkeit perverser Verbrecher" (1904), as well as several anonymous pieces. For bibliographical references, see Rosenthal-Oberlaender. See *ibid.*, and B, for relevant items concerning Simmel's interest in, and literary activities in behalf of, Rodin, Bergson, and above all, Stefan George.

17. "Deutschlands innere Wandlung" (a speech delivered in Strasbourg, November, 1914), in: *Der Krieg und die geistigen Entscheidungen*, 12, 13, 20, 21, 27, 28, respectively.—The fourth passage quoted is presumably referred to by Joël, 247, when he writes of Simmel's "love for his people which now [during the war] he felt so deeply that he, the thinker, wanted to keep all reasons out of it." Joël's manner of reference shows more than approval, whereas here, the suggestion is made that Simmel was under the impact of war excitement. The discrepancy presents the general problem of appraising divergent interpretations. Joël knew Simmel personally, for perhaps twenty-five years (*ibid.*, 242), and stood under the impression of his recent death; the present writer did not know Simmel. In the meantime, furthermore, there has been a second world war and an increase in insight into the possible ramifications of such words as were quoted of Simmel. But these considerations only throw light on different valuations in whose terms the difference in interpretation may be understandable. The test of preferability of one to another interpretation is coherence with other aspects of Simmel. Joël, because of his personal friendship with Simmel, probably was more certain of his image than the present writer can be; but it is also possible that in the particular case at issue he was swayed by more ephemeral impressions, deriving from the point in time at which he wrote, than this writer is. (For an interpretation of Simmel's intellectual activity during the war, which is considerably closer to the one here presented than Joël's is, see Utitz, 9.)

18. "Die Krisis der Kultur" (1916), in: *Der Krieg und die geistigen Entscheidungen*, 64, 63, respectively.

19. "Die Idee Europa" (1915? See Rosenthal-Oberlaender, no. 189), *ibid.*, 67-72; *Der Konflikt der modernen Kultur, ein Vortrag.*— As an example of Simmel's moral criticism, see, e.g., his sermon to the wealthy, exhorting them to buy war bonds: "Eine Fastenpredigt: Von dem Opfer der Wohlhabenden."

20. Weber, 387.

21. *Ibid.*, 391.

22. Gertrud Simmel, 221.

23. Including most of what Mamelet understands by "le relativisme de Georg Simmel," and in full cognizance of Troeltsch's critique of Simmel. (See also Kracauer, 331-332, on Simmel's *"Kerngedanke."*) Hence, also, there is no contradiction in Mandelbaum's counting Simmel (as a philosopher of history) among the "counter-*relativists.*"

24. A proposition worked out, though not in the largest perspective, by Mamelet, through an exposition of Simmel's major works up to 1914.

25. Frischeisen-Köhler, 36-37.

26. See, e.g., *Hauptprobleme der Philosophie*, Ch. I. Also, Mamelet, Ch. X.

27. Utitz, 41.

28. *Ibid.*, 19—Beginnings of a "negative determination" may be found in Kracauer, 307-308.

29. Cf. Kurt H. Wolff, "The Sociology of Knowledge: Emphasis on an Empirical Attitude," *Philosophy of Science*, 10:111-114, 1943.

30. See the first 13 entries in D.

31. At one point, Small calls Simmel "one of the keenest thinkers in Europe" (Albion W. Small, *General Sociology*, Chicago: University of Chicago Press, 1905, p. 498); he admittedly used some of Simmel's concepts (*ibid.*, *passim*), as did Park and Burgess, in whose work Simmel is referred to more often than any other author (see index). Characteristic comments: "Simmel has made a brilliant contribution in his analysis of the sociological significance of 'the stranger' " (286); "Georg Simmel has made the one outstanding contribution to a sociology or, perhaps better, a social philosophy of the city in his paper 'The Great City and Cultural Life' " [D, no. 15] (331); "Georg Simmel, referring, in his essay on 'The Stranger,' to the poor and the criminal, bestowed upon them the suggestive title

of 'The Inner Enemies' " (559); "Simmel has made the outstanding contribution to the sociological conception of conflict" (639); "Simmel's observation upon subordination and superordination is almost the only attempt that has been made to deal with the subject from the point of view of sociology" (720).

32. For references to Spykman's and Sorokin's works, see Appendix A. Sorokin wrote: "From a purely methodological standpoint, Simmel's sociological method lacks scientific method. I must express my complete disagreement with Dr. R. Park's or Dr. Spykman's high estimation of the sociological method of Simmel. Besides the above logical deficiency [due to the ambiguous term 'form': *ibid.*, 501-502], Simmel's method entirely lacks either experimental approach, quantitative investigation, or any systematic factual study of the discussed phenomena. In vain one would look in his work for a systematic method like that of the Le Play school, or of the methodological principles of social sciences developed by A. Cournot . . .; or some principles like those of H. Rikkert [*sic*] and W. Windelbandt [*sic*] concerning the classification of sciences . . .; or something like Max Weber's method of the 'ideal typology'; or Galton's, Pearson's, and A. Tchuproff's quantitative methods of investigation; or even a simple, careful and attentive study of the facts he is talking about. All this is lacking. What there is represents only the speculative generalization of a talented man, backed by the 'method of illustration' in the form of two or three facts incidentally taken and often one-sidedly interpreted. Without Simmel's talent the same stuff would appear poor. Simmel's talent saves the situation, but only as far as talent compensates for lack of scientific methodology. Under such conditions, to call the sociologists 'back to Simmel,' as Drs. Park and Spykman do, means to call them back to a pure speculation, metaphysics, and a lack of scientific method. Speculation and metaphysics are excellent things in their proper places, but to mix these with the science of sociology means to spoil each of those sciences." (502, n. 26.) (See von Wiese's critique of Sorokin's critique: *Systematic Sociology On the Basis of the* Beziehungslehre *and* Gebildelehre *of Leopold von Wiese,* adapted and amplified by Howard Becker, New York: Wiley; London: Chapman and Hall, 1932, pp. 44-47.)

33. For Abel reference, see A; for Wiese-Becker (consult index), see preceding n. See E for a list of discussions of Simmel in English.

34. Especially in and through *The American Journal of Sociology*

(published since July, 1895). In the second issue, a group of "advising Editors" of three American and seven foreign sociologists, among them Simmel, was announced. Cf. Ethel Shanas, "The *American Journal of Sociology* through Fifty Years," *American Journal of Sociology*, 50: 523, May, 1945. (On the beginning of the *Journal,* cf. also Bernhard J. Stern, ed., "The Letters of Albion W. Small to Lester F. Ward," *Social Forces,* 12: 163-173 [1933]; 13: 323-340 [1935]; 15: 174-186 [1936], 305-327 [1937]. For European, especially German and Austrian contacts by Ward, Ross, and several other early American sociologists, see also Bernhard J. Stern, ed., "The Ward-Ross Correspondence," *American Sociological Review,* 3: 362-401 [1938]; 11: 593-605, 734-748 [1946]; 12: 703-720 [1947]; 13: 82-94 [1948]; 14: 88-119 [1949].)

35. Talcott Parsons, *The Structure of Social Action, a Study in Social Theory with Special Reference to a Group of Recent European Writers* [Durkheim, Pareto, M. Weber], New York and London: McGraw-Hill, 1937 (reprinted, Glencoe, Ill.: Free Press, 1949).— Max Weber, *The Protestant Ethic and the Spirit of Capitalism,* tr. Talcott Parsons, London: Allen and Unwin; New York: Scribner, 1930; *From Max Weber: Essays in Sociology* (see n. 5 above); *The Theory of Social and Economic Organization,* tr. A. M. Henderson and Talcott Parsons, New York: Oxford University Press, 1947; *On the Methodology of the Social Sciences,* tr. and ed. Edward A. Shils and Henry A. Finch, Glencoe, Ill.: Free Press, 1949. Other translations are in preparation.

36. Cf. the short but suggestive remarks on this point by Robert Schmid in his review of Loomis' translation of Tönnies, *American Sociological Review* 6: 581-582, August, 1941.

37. See F for the detailed sources of the translations contained in this volume, and G for a note on the translation itself.

38. Cf. Utitz's suggestion of an indexed edition of Simmel's works (see passage to which n. 27 above refers).

39. See "Acknowledgements."

40. *Goethe* (5th ed.), vii.

41. Cf. *Über sociale Differenzierung,* 10-11. It should be noted that no attempt is made here to present all of Simmel's views, even upon one topic, in their chronological development. Some of his very relevant writings, above all, "Das Problem der Soziologie" ([Schmollers] *Jahrbuch für Gesetzgebung, Verwaltung und Volks-*

wirtschaft im Deutschen Reich, Vol. XVIII [1894]; for tr., see D, no. 2), are not referred to at all. Furthermore, this attempt, *not* made here, would also have to use many among Simmel's primarily *non*-sociological writings. The most successful and painstaking effort of this sort, with reference to one particular theme, namely, "form," is Steinhoff.—In *Grundfragen,* in formulating the individual as an object of experience, Simmel does not raise the question whether it is the only object of experience, nor does he reveal whether by "object of experience" he uses a synonym of some sort of "given." The two questions: why he does not, and what his givens are, promise well for a study of Simmel, and are related to the questions raised (earlier and below) in regard to such a study.

42. See also Part III, Ch. 4, Sect. 4 below.—The similarity of Simmel's and Dilthey's conceptions is also seen, in the field of sociology, by Simmel's emphasis that Kant's "nature" as the subject's synthesis does not apply to "society," to which the "synthesis" is intrinsic: *Soziologie,* 22.—The quotation is from Hodges, 133, from Dilthey's "Ideen über eine beschreibende und zergliedernde Psychologie" (1894). It is characteristic of Simmel not to refer to Dilthey or to this particular work (with which he was most likely acquainted if only because Dilthey taught at Berlin from 1882 to his death in 1911), much less to analyze similarities and differences of their respective positions. This (systematic) analysis is one of the many tasks that result from a study of Simmel's work and remain yet to be done. (Their conceptions of sociology itself were dissimilar, in spite of Dilthey's approval of Simmel's "sociology." For reference to Dilthey's relevant statement, see A.)

43. *Über sociale Differenzierung,* 12.

44. In this particular case under discussion, Simmel's earlier position (in *Über sociale Differenzierung,* quoted) was more scientific except that, as a scientist, he could not have pronounced judgment (of agreement) on the metaphysical status of atomism. It should be noted that in the chronologically intermediate *Soziologie* (1908), Simmel does not directly tackle the problem, but at one point (13) speaks of "individual existences—the real bearers of conditions." But this, probably, is intended as a scientific statement, which also seems the significance of the passage in *Grundfragen* following upon the propositions discussed in the text above. There, Simmel in effect suggests that even from an empirical standpoint

one must note that "individual" is no more "real" than "society"; that is (one may put it), both are equally heuristic concepts. (For an avowedly epistemological treatment of the question, "how is society possible," see the *"Exkurs"* by this title which is a part of the first chapter of *Soziologie*. For a somewhat unsatisfactory translation of this *"Exkurs,"* see reference in D, no. 13.)

45. *Soziologie,* 8, 9. (For Small's translation, see item referred to in D, no. 12, pp. 301, 303.)

46. This is a favorite observation, but may also stem from another realm of inquiry not otherwise studied by Simmel, namely, ontology, in particular, the ontology of mind. See the following quotation (*Soziologie,* 13): "After all, in intellectual matters it is not too rare—and, when it comes to the most general and the most profound problems, it is, as a matter of fact, the rule—that (what by an unavoidable metaphor is called) the foundation is less secure than the superstructure erected upon it. And thus, scientific practice, too, especially when it works in new areas, cannot do without a certain measure of merely instinctive advance. Only later is it possible to become fully conscious of the motives and norms of that stage and to penetrate it conceptually. Certainly, scientific work must never be satisfied solely by such vague, instinctual procedures. . . . Yet, one would condemn science to sterility if, before new tasks, one made a completely formulated methodology the condition of taking even the first step." (Cf. Bentley, *Relativity in Man and Society,* 158, 297.) This is elaborated in the following footnote (of which only the beginning is quoted here): "If we compare the infinite complexity of socal life with the initial crudeness which the concepts and methods employed to master it intellectually are only now beginning to overcome, we realize that it would be sheer megalomania to expect, at this juncture, radical clarity of questions and correctness of answers. It seems to me more dignified to admit this from the start (since by doing so, at least a decisive first step can be taken) than to pretend definitiveness, and thereby to jeopardize even the pioneering significance of our efforts."

47. *Ibid.* (This is the remainder of the footnote quoted in the preceding n. Italics added.)

48. At this point, Simmel merely poses the question, and thereby, clearly, entertains Comtean and Spencerian ideas (without, however, committing himself). He investigated the question more fully,

though not in an ultimately satisfactory way, and with changing positions, in his studies in the philosophy of history. For discussion, see above all Troeltsch; also Spykman, Book I, Ch. V; Mandelbaum, Collingwood.

49. It will be remembered that shortly before this passage, Simmel gives as examples of "special social sciences," "the study of economics and of institutions, the history of morals and of parties, population theory, and the discussion of occupational differentiation." The intent of Simmel's argument, or its surprising character, would presumably not be changed if, instead of these, the currently more customary disciplines of economics, sociology of institutions, and other social sciences or parts of them were named.

50. Wiese-Becker, 83, n. 5.

51. In interpreting the development of recent philosophy, Heinemann locates Simmel (along with several other thinkers) on the road that led "from life to existence" (not in the sense of contemporary "existentialism"). This is one way of alluding to Simmel's attitude.

52. Quite irrespective of his confession to Troeltsch (Troeltsch, 573, n. 309) that in his last years "sociological questions" "no longer interested him."

53. Among important American exemplifiers of this attitude, Charles Horton Cooley and George Herbert Mead in the social sciences, and John Dewey in philosophy, may be recalled.

54. Simmel, "Die Ruine," in *Philosophische Kultur* (2nd ed.), 128, 125. (The same passage is quoted by Utitz, 15, who adds: "This cosmic tragedy is ultimately also the tragedy of Simmel.")

55. As Wiese-Becker suggest in the passage quoted earlier.

56. Here the closing sentence of Steinhoff's excellent study of "forms" is relevant (259): "That which is lacking in his work, the 'grouping' and the 'systematization' of the relationships analyzed, remains as a task for those who are willing to continue his work."

57. Steinhoff (most important); Knevels, 51-57; also Abel, esp. 19-49; Bouglé, 345-346; Heberle, 250-255, 264-267; Mamelet, 9, 38, 47, 209-210; Salomon, 607-608; Sorokin; Spykman, Book I and "Conclusion"; Wiese-Becker, 705-708; and others.

58. For beginnings of this, see Steinhoff and Knevels.

59. Except, possibly, by Salomon: cf. his section title (604), "A Theory of Social Invariables: Georg Simmel."

60. "Form" as the relatively stable variable in the context of inquiry and viewpoint is not a specifically sociological referent. Among the many questions which the equation leaves unanswered are: (1) (a) What is the ontological status of "form?" (b) Is "form" to be so defined as to make its ontological status irrelevant; and if so, is "form" merely a heuristic, methodological construct? (c) If the latter, what is the empirical referent that is methodologically constructed into "form?" (2) How can sociology be so transformed as to make all these questions unnecessary? (3) What is the relevance to the "socialization of the spirit" of the two respective sociologies implied—one to which the above questions regarding forms are relevant, and the other to which they are not?—It should be noted that all these questions must be asked, also, in regard to the complementary notion of "content" (or the like). Finally, the whole inquiry should likewise extend to an investigation, comparative and synthesizing, of current concerns with "structure" and "function." Cf. discussions in cultural anthropology and social psychology and, more specifically, the works by Sorokin, Bennett-Tumin, and Davis cited at the end of E; and Robert K. Merton, *Social Theory and Social Structure, Toward the Codification of Theory and Research* (Glencoe, Ill.: Free Press, 1949), Parts I and II.

61. This is very similar to Karl Mannheim's fascination by the "sociology of knowledge" and to his attempt at establishing it as epistemology. See, e.g., his *Ideology and Utopia, An Introduction to the Sociology of Knowledge,* (tr. Louis Wirth and Edward Shils, New York: Harcourt, Brace, 1936), esp. 256-275; for criticism, see esp. Virgil G. Hinshaw, Jr., "The Epistemological Relevance of Mannheim's Sociology of Knowledge," *Journal of Philosophy*, 40: 57-72, 1943, and "Epistemological Relativism and the Sociology of Knowledge," *Philosophy of Science*, 15: 4-10, 1948.

62. Part I, last paragraph, below.

63. A further striking similarity between Simmel and Mannheim.

Appendices

[a] LITERATURE ON SIMMEL

On the whole, the literature on Simmel fails to convey the uniqueness of his mind, nor does it—with hardly more than one exception

—possess the creative anxiety, excitement, and thrill which were typical qualities of his own work. Below is a selective, roughly classified list. (Items preceded by [*] were not available for inspection at the time of writing.)

The one certain exception is Gertrud Kanterowicz's short "Vorwort" to Simmel's posthumous *Fragmente und Aufsätze* (edited by her), v-x. But see also Emil Utitz, "Simmel und die Philosophie der Kunst," *Zeitschrift für Aesthetik und allgemeine Kunstwissenschaft,* XIV: 1-41, 1920; Max Frischeisen-Köhler, "Georg Simmel," *Kant-Studien,* 24: 1-51, 1920; Karl Joël, "Georg Simmel, ein Nachruf," *Neue Rundschau* (XXXter Jahrg. d. Freien Bühne), 1919, Band 1, pp. 241-247 (rhapsodic; obituary; the year, incidentally, is erroneously indicated as 1911 in Rosenthal-Oberlaender); and perhaps Albert Mamelet, *Le Relativisme philosophique chez Georg Simmel,* Paris: Alcan, 1914 (pp. ix, 215; preface by Victor Delbos), although this is to a large extent expository.

Sociology: Theodore Abel, *Systematic Sociology in Germany, A Critical Analysis of Some Attempts to Establish Sociology as an Independent Science,* New York: Columbia University Press, 1929, Chapter I, "The Formal Sociology of Georg Simmel," pp. 13-49; Nicholas J. Spykman, *The Social Theory of Georg Simmel,* Chicago: University of Chicago Press, 1925 (pp. xxix, 297; incidentally, Spykman, on p. xxvii, gives Simmel's death date erroneously as Sept. 28— though, on p. xxiii, correctly, as Sept. 26); Pitirim Sorokin, *Contemporary Sociological Theories,* New York and London: Harper, 1928, pp. 489-491, 495-507; Rudolf Heberle, "The Sociology of Georg Simmel: The Forms of Social Interaction," in: Harry Elmer Barnes, ed., *An Introduction to the History of Sociology,* Chicago: University of Chicago Press, 1948, pp. 249-273; C. Bouglé, "Les sciences sociales en Allemagne: G. Simmel," *Revue de Métaphysique et de morale,* 2: 329-355, 1894; Maria Steinhoff, "Die Form als soziologische Grundkategorie bei Georg Simmel," *Kölner Vierteljahrshefte für Soziologie,* 4: 215-259, 1925; Walter Frost, "Die Soziologie Simmels," *Latvijas Universitates Raksti (Acta Universitatis Latviensis),* XII: 219-313, 1925, XIII: 149-225, 1926 (largely expository, to introduce Simmel "abroad"; inferior to the preceding, esp. Steinhoff); Paul Barth, *Die Philosophie der Geschichte als Soziologie* (1897), I (no more published), Leipzig: Reisland, 3rd and 4th ed., 1922, pp. 149-151; Wilhelm Dilthey, "Soziologie" (1904), *Einleitung*

in die Geisteswissenschaften (1883), *Wilhelm Diltheys Gesammelte
Schriften, I. Band,* Leipzig and Berlin: Teubner, 3rd ed., 1933, pp.
420-422 (tr. in H. A. Hodges, *Wilhelm Dilthey, An Introduction,*
New York: Oxford University Press, 1944, pp. 139-141; see also *id.,*
60-61; Dilthey's rejection of all sociology, but not of Simmel's).

 History: R. G. Collingwood, *The Idea of History,* Oxford: Claren-
don Press, 1946, pp. 170-171, 174-175; Maurice Mandelbaum, *The
Problem of Historical Knowledge, An Answer to Relativism,* New
York: Liveright, 1938, pp. 101-119, 166-170; Ernst Troeltsch, *Der
Historismus und seine Probleme,* Tübingen: Mohr (Siebeck), 1922,
pp. 572-596.—*Philosophy:* Traugott Konstantin Oesterreich, *Die
deutsche Philosophie des XIX. Jahrhunderts und der Gegenwart*
("Friedrich Ueberwegs Grundriss der Philosophie, Vierter Teil,"
12th ed.), Berlin: Mittler, 1923, pp. 467-471; Frischeisen-Köhler;
Siegfried Kracauer, "Georg Simmel," *Logos,* 9: 307-338, 1920-21;
Mamelet; Max Adler, *Georg Simmels Bedeutung für die Geistes-
geschichte,* Wien, Leipzig: Anzengruber, 1919 (pp. 44); Wilhelm
Knevels, *Simmels Religionstheorie, ein Beitrag zum religiösen Problem der Gegenwart,* Leipzig: Hinrichs, 1920 (pp. vi, 107; see esp.
Part II); Fritz Heinemann, *Neue Wege der Philosophie,* Leipzig:
Quelle und Meyer, 1929, pp. 230-250; *Herwig Müller, *Georg Simmel
als Deuter und Fortbildner Kants,* Dresden: Dittert, 1935; Thomas
A. Vannatta, *A Study in Polarities in the Writings of George Simmel*
(unpubl. Ph.D. diss.), Columbus: Ohio State University, 1948 (pp.
163, v).—*Art:* Utitz.

 Briefly appraising: Ernst Bernhard, "Georg Simmel als Soziologe
und Sozialphilosoph," *Die Tat,* 5: 1080-1086, January, 1914; *Jonas
Cohn, in: *Deutsches biographisches Jahrbuch,* 1917-1920 (Berlin,
1928), 326-333; Herman Schmalenbach, "Simmel," *Sozialistische
Monatshefte,* Vol. 52, Jahrg. 25: 283-288, March 24, 1919 (obituary);
Aloys Fischer, "Georg Simmel (geb. 1. März 1856 [*sic*], gest. 27. [*sic*]
September 1918)," *Deutscher Wille,* 32. Jahrgang, 2. Oktoberheft,
pp. 43-47 (October, 1918; anti-Semitic); Theodor Lessing, "Georg
Simmel, Betrachtungen und Exkurse" (1912-13), in his: *Philosophie
als Tat,* Göttingen: Otto Hapke, 1914, pp. 303-343 (self-and-Jew-
accusing); Fritz Hoeber, "Georg Simmel, Der Kulturphilosoph
unserer Zeit," *Neue Jahrbücher für das klassische Altertum, Geschichte und deutsche Literatur,* 41: 475-477, 1918 (obituary).

 Anecdotal, impressionistic, journalistic: Emil Ludwig, "Simmel auf dem Katheder," *Die Schaubühne,* Vol. X, Nr. 15: 411-413, April 9, 1914 (on the occasion of Simmel's leaving the University of Berlin, after almost thirty years of teaching, for the University of Strasbourg); Theodor Tagger, "Georg Simmel," *Die Zukunft,* Vol. LXXXXIX, Jahrg. XXIII, Nr. 2, pp. 36-41, October 10, 1914 (on same occasion); Elias Hurwicz, "Simmel als jüdischer Denker," *Neue jüdische Monatshefte,* III, Nrs. 9-12, pp. 196-198, February 10-25, March 10-25, 1919.

Reminiscent: (Abraham Flexner,) *I Remember, the Autobiography of Abraham Flexner,* New York: Simon and Schuster, 1940, p. 108 (Berlin student days); J. Loewenberg, "Problematic Realism," in: George P. Adams and Wm. Pepperell Montague, eds., *Contemporary American Philosophy: Personal Statements,* London: Allen and Unwin; New York: Macmillan, 1930, Volume 2, pp. 80-81 (Simmel's inspiration of the pragmatic element in Loewenberg's philosophy); Paul Fechter, *Menschen und Zeiten, Begegnungen aus fünf Jahrzehnten,* Gütersloh: Bertelsmann, 1948, pp. 52-56; Marianne Weber, *Lebenserinnerungen,* Bremen: Johs. Storm, 1948, pp. 375-409 (more on Gertrud Simmel, Simmel's wife, than on Simmel himself).

[b] THE BIBLIOGRAPHY OF SIMMEL'S WRITINGS

The only bibliography existing to date is Erich Rosenthal and Kurt Oberlaender, "Books, Papers, and Essays by Georg Simmel," *American Journal of Sociology,* 51: 238-247, November, 1945 (252 items, not counting 11 incomplete and doubtful ones; there are also 24 items *on* Simmel). The following items may be added, although the list remains incomplete; e.g., various translations of Simmel's works (among them into Polish and Spanish), discussion speeches, etc., are known to be missing. The items are given in as complete a form as is available. Most of them were communicated by Dr. Else Simmel from an as yet unpublished bibliography compiled by Kurt Gassen (Greifswald) and Michael Landmann (Basel). (Items preceded by [*] were not available for inspection at the time of writing.)

1. *"Humanistische Märchen" (anonymous), *Die neue Zeit,* No. 49, 1891-92; (2) *"Etwas vom Spiritismus," *Vorwärts,* July, 1892; (3) *"Weltpolitik" (anonymous), *Die neue Zeit,* No. 32, 1893-94; (4) *"Frauenstudium an der Berliner Universität," *Vossische Zeitung,* December 21, 1899; (5) *Review of Joël, *Philosophenwege, Die Zeit,*

April 21, 1901; (6) *"Rodins Plastik und die Geistesrichtung der Gegenwart," *Berliner Tageblatt*, September 29, 1902; (7) "De la religion au point de vue de la théorie de la connaissance," *Bibliothèque du Congrès International de Philosophie, II, Morale Générale, La Philosophie de la Paix, Les Sociétés d'Enseignement Populaire*, Paris: Colin, 1903, pp. 319-337; (8) *"Das Abendmahl Leonardo da Vincis," *Der Tag*, 1905? (9) *"Psychologie der Diskretion," *Der Tag*, September 2-4 (?), 1906; (10) *"Die Zukunft unserer Kultur," *Frankfurter Zeitung*, April 14, 1909; (11) *"Brücke und Tür," *Der Tag*, September 15, 1909; (12) *"Beiträge zur Philosophie der Geschichte," *Scientia*, Vol. 6, 1909; (13) *"Nietzsches Moral," *Der Tag*, May 4, 1911; (14) *"Goethe und die Frauen," *St. Petersburger Montagsblatt*, 463, 1912; (15) *"Über Takt, Soziologie der Geselligkeit," *Frankfurter Zeitung*, October 22, 1912; (16) *"Goethe und die Jugend," *Der Tag*, October 4, 1914; (17) *"Rembrandt und die Schönheit," *Vossische Zeitung*, December 25, 1914; (18) *"Die Umwertung der Werte: Ein Wort an die Wohlhabenden," *Frankfurter Zeitung*, March 5, 1915; (19) *"Individualismens Formen" (Danish), *Spectator*, January 28, 1917; (20) "Eine Fastenpredigt: Von dem Opfer der Wohlhabenden," *Frankfurter Zeitung*, March 18, 1917; (21) *"Panta rhei" (anonymous), *Simplicissimus*, August 28, 1917; (22) *"Über Verantwortlichkeit," *Kalender* (?), 1918; (23) "Aus Georg Simmels nachgelassner Mappe 'Metaphysik'" (intr. Gertrud Simmel), in: *Aus unbekannten Schriften, Festgabe für Martin Buber zum 50. Geburtstag*, Berlin: Schneider, 1928, pp. 221-226; (24) *Cultura femenina y otros ensayos* ("Colección Austral," No. 38), Buenos Aires-Mexico: Espasa-Calpe Argentina, 1938 (2nd ed., 1939; 3rd ed., 1941, pp. 153; contains "Cultura femenina," "Filosofia de la coqueteria," "Lo masculino y lo femenino," and "Filosofia de la moda," i.e., the second, third, fourth, and sixth essay of Rosenthal-Oberlaender, no. 252 [the last item in C], tr. by the same translators); (25) a series of pseudonymous articles in *Die Jugend*.

[C] SIMMEL'S MAJOR WORKS

Sociology: Über sociale Differenzierung, sociologische und psychologische Untersuchungen ("Staats- und socialwissenschaftliche Forschungen," Gustav Schmoller, ed., Zehnter Band, Erstes Heft), Leipzig: Duncker und Humblot, 1890, pp. vii, 147 (2nd ed., 1905);

Philosophie des Geldes, Leipzig: Duncker und Humblot, 1900 (2nd ed., 1907; 3rd ed., 1920; 4th ed., München und Leipzig, 1922, pp. xiv, 585; 5th ed., München, 1930); *Soziologie, Untersuchungen über die Formen der Vergesellschaftung,* Leipzig: Duncker und Humblot, 1908 (2nd ed., München und Leipzig, 1922; 3rd ed., 1923, pp. 578); *Grundfragen der Soziologie* ("Sammlung Göschen," No. 101), Berlin und Leipzig: de Gruyter, 1917 (2nd ed., 1920, pp. 103).

Philosophy of History: Die Probleme der Geschichtsphilosophie, Eine erkenntnistheoretische Studie, Leipzig: Duncker und Humblot, 1892 (2nd rev. ed., 1905; 3rd ed., 1907; 4th ed., München und Leipzig, 1922; 5th ed., 1923, pp. ix, 229); *Das Problem der historischen Zeit* ("Philosophische Vorträge veröffentlicht von der Kantgesellschaft," No. 12), Berlin: Reuther und Reichard, 1916, pp. 31; *Vom Wesen des historischen Verstehens* ("Geschichtliche Abende im Zentralinstitut für Erziehung und Unterricht, Fünftes Heft"), Berlin: Mittler, 1918, pp. 31.

Ethics: Einleitung in die Moralwissenschaft, eine Kritik der ethischen Grundbegriffe, Berlin: Hertz (Besser), Vol. I, 1892, pp. viii, 467; Vol. II, 1893, pp. viii, 426 (2nd ed., Stuttgart und Berlin: Cotta, 1904; 3rd ed., 1911).

General Philosophy: Philosophie des Geldes; Kant, Sechzehn Vorlesungen gehalten an der Berliner Universität, Leipzig: Duncker und Humblot, 1904 (2nd ed., 1905; 3rd enl. ed., München und Leipzig, 1913; 4th ed., 1918; 5th ed., 1921; 6th ed., 1924, pp. vi, 266); **Kant und Goethe* ("Die Kultur, Sammlung illustrierter Einzeldarstellungen," Cornelius Gurlitt, ed., Vol. X), Berlin: Marquardt, 1906, pp. 71 (2nd ed., Leipzig: Wolff, 1907; 3rd rev. ed., *Kant und Goethe; zur Geschichte der modernen Weltanschauung,* 1916, pp. 117; 4th ed., 1918; 5th ed., München und Leipzig, 1924); *Die Religion* ("Die Gesellschaft, Sammlung sozialpsychologischer Monographien," Martin Buber, ed., Vol. II), Frankfurt am Main: Rütten und Loening, 1906, pp. 79 (2nd rev. and enl. ed., 1912; 3rd ed. [9.-11. Tausend], 1922); *Schopenhauer und Nietzsche, Ein Vortragszyklus,* Leipzig: Duncker und Humblot, 1907 (2nd ed., München und Leipzig, 1920; 3rd ed. [not contained in Rosenthal-Oberlaender], 1923, pp. vii, 192); *Hauptprobleme der Philosophie* ("Sammlung Göschen," No. 500), Leipzig: Göschen, 1910, pp. 175 (2nd ed., 1911; 3rd ed., 1913; 4th ed., Berlin und Leipzig: de Gruyter, 1917; 5th ed., 1920; 6th ed.,

1927); *Goethe,* Leipzig: Klinkhardt und Biermann, 1913 (4th ed., 1921; 5th ed., 1923, pp. vii, 264).

Philosophy of Art: Rembrandt, Ein kunstphilosophischer Versuch, Leipzig: Wolff, 1916 (2nd ed., 1919, pp. viii, 208).

Philosophy of Contemporary Civilization: Der Krieg und die geistigen Entscheidungen, Reden und Aufsätze, München und Leipzig: Duncker und Humblot, 1917, pp. 72 (2nd ed., Leipzig, 1920); *Der Konflikt der modernen Kultur, ein Vortrag, ibid.,* 1918 (2nd ed., 1921, pp. 30; 3rd ed., 1926).

Metaphysics: Lebensanschauung, vier metaphysische Kapitel, München und Leipzig: Duncker und Humblot, 1918 (2nd ed., 1922, pp. 239).

There also exist several important collections of essays: *Philosophische Kultur, gesammelte Essais* ("Philosophisch-soziologische Bücherei," Vol. XXVII), Leipzig: Kröner, 1911 (2nd enl. ed., 1919, pp. 295); *Mélanges de Philosophie relativiste, Contribution a la culture philosophique,* tr. Alix Guillain ("Bibliothèque de Philosophie contemporaine"), Paris: Alcan, 1912 pp. vi, 268; *Zur Philosophie der Kunst, philosophische und kunstphilosophische Aufsätze* (Gertrud Simmel, ed.), Potsdam: Kiepenheuer, 1922, pp. 175; *Fragmente und Aufsätze aus dem Nachlass und Veröffentlichungen der letzten Jahre* (Gertrud Kantorowicz, ed.), München: Drei Masken Verlag, 1923, pp. x, 304; *Cultura femenina y otros ensayos* (Eugenio Imaz, Jose R. Perez Bances, M. G. Morente, and Fernando Vela, trs.), Madrid: Revista de occidente, 1934.

[d] SIMMEL'S WRITINGS AVAILABLE IN ENGLISH

The following is as complete a list of Simmel's writings available in English as could be obtained (in chronological order of publication):

(1) "Moral Deficiencies as Determining Intellectual Functions," *International Journal of Ethics,* III, No. 4, 490-507, July, 1893. Tr. not indicated. ("This article is part of the second volume of the author's 'Einleitung in die Moralwissenschäft [*sic*],' which is shortly to appear. The reader finds here hardly more than a general outline of the original article. From want of space, it has been considerably shortened without being able to consult the author.")

(2) "The Problem of Sociology," *Annals of the American Acad-*

emy of Political and Social Science, VI, No. 3, 412-423, November, 1895. Tr. not indicated.

(3) "Superiority and Subordination as Subject-Matter of Sociology," *The American Journal of Sociology*, II, No. 2, 167-189, September, 1896; No. 3, 392-415, November, 1896. Tr. Albion W. Small.

(4) "The Persistence of Social Groups," *ibid.*, III, No. 5, 662-698, March, 1898; No. 6, 829-836, May, 1898; IV, No. 1, 35-50, July, 1898. Tr. Albion W. Small.

(5) "A Chapter in the Philosophy of Value," *ibid.*, V, No. 5, 577-603, March, 1900. Tr. not indicated. ("A fragment from a volume entitled *The Philosophy of Money* to be published this year by Duncker and Humblot, Leipzig. Translated for this JOURNAL from the author's manuscript.")

(6) "Tendencies in German Life and Thought Since 1870," *International Monthly*, V, No. 1, 93-111, January, 1902; No. 2, 166-184, February, 1902. Tr. W. D. Briggs.

(7) "The Number of Members as Determining the Sociological Form of the Group," *The American Journal of Sociology*, VIII, No. 1, 1-46, July, 1902; No. 2, 158-196, September, 1902. Tr. Albion W. Small.

(8) "The Sociology of Conflict," *ibid.*, IX, No. 4, 490-525, January, 1904; No. 5, 672-689, March, 1904; No. 6, 798-811, May, 1904. Tr. Albion W. Small.

(9) "Fashion," *International Quarterly*, 10, No. 1, 130-155, October, 1904. Tr. not indicated.

(10) "A Contribution to the Sociology of Religion," *The American Journal of Sociology*, XI, No. 3, 359-376, November, 1905. Tr. W. W. Elwang.

(11) "The Sociology of Secrecy and of Secret Societies," *ibid.*, XI, No. 4, 441-498, January, 1906. Tr. Albion W. Small.

(12) "The Problem of Sociology," *ibid.*, XV, No. 3, 289-320, November, 1909. Tr. Albion W. Small. ("This is a portion of the first chapter in Simmel's *Soziologie*, a brief notice of which appeared in this *Journal*, Vol. XIV, p. 544. The translation is as literal as possible. The notes, unless otherwise indicated, are my own.—Albion W. Small.")

(13) "How is Society Possible?" *ibid.*, XVI, No. 3, 372-391, November, 1910. Tr. Albion W. Small. ("This is a translation of the passage entitled, 'Exkurs über das Problem: Wie ist Gesellschaft

möglich?' in Simmel's *Soziologie* (pp. 27-45). Although I have often argued (e.g., *General Sociology*, pp. 183-85, 504-8, etc.) that the term 'society' is too vague to be made into an instrument of precision, I am glad to assist in getting a hearing for Simmel's efforts to prove the contrary. I have therefore done my best to render his essay literally as far as possible, and in all cases faithfully. A.W.S.")

(14) In: Robert E. Park and Ernest W. Burgess, *Introduction to the Science of Sociology*, Chicago: University of Chicago Press, 1921:

> (a) 322-327: "The Sociological Significance of the 'Stranger'," from: Simmel, *Soziologie*, 1908, pp. 685-691;
>
> (b) 356-361: "Sociology of the Senses: Visual Interaction," from: *id.*, 646-651;
>
> (c) 552-553: "Money and Freedom," from: Simmel, *Philosophie des Geldes*, 1900, pp. 351-352.
> (These three passages were presumably translated by Park and/or Burgess. Numerous other short translations contained in the book were taken from several of Simmel's writings listed above.)

(15) (a) "The Metropolis and Mental Life" [1902-03], *Second-Year Course in the Study of Contemporary Society (Social Science II), Syllabus and Selected Readings* (5th ed. [and subsequent eds.], Chicago: University of Chicago Bookstore, September, 1936, pp. 221-238. Tr. Edward A. Shils.

> (b) *Id.*, Department of Sociology, The University of Wisconsin, n.d., mimeographed, pp. 10. Tr. H. H. Gerth with the assistance of C. Wright Mills. (Used as Part V, Ch. 4, below.)

(16) "The Sociology of Sociability," *The American Journal of Sociology*, LV, No. 3, 254-261, November, 1949. Tr. Everett C. Hughes. (The original, of 1910, is an earlier version of the original rendered as Part I, Ch. 3, below.)

[e] DISCUSSIONS, IN ENGLISH, OF SIMMEL AS A SOCIOLOGIST

The following is, at least, the beginning of an alphabetical list of discussions in English, most of them short, of Simmel as (wholly or in part) a sociologist. (Book reviews are not included.)

(1) Theodore Abel (see A). Next to Spykman's, this is the most comprehensive treatment.

(2) S. P. Altmann, "Simmel's Philosophy of Money," *American Journal of Sociology,* 9: 46-68, 1903.

(3) Harry Elmer Barnes and Howard Becker, *Social Thought from Lore to Science,* Boston: Heath [1938], Vol. II, 889-891.

(4) Arthur F. Bentley, *The Process of Government, A Study of Social Pressures,* Chicago: University of Chicago Press, 1908, pp. 472-476.

(5) ———, *Relativity in Man and Society,* New York: Putnam; London: Knickerbocker, 1926, pp. 163-165, 306-310.

(6) ———, "Simmel, Durkheim, and Ratzenhofer," *American Journal of Sociology,* 32: 250-256, 1926. (Cf. Ch. XX in preceding item.)

(7) Rudolf Heberle (see A).

(8) Floyd Nelson House, *The Development of Sociology,* New York and London: McGraw-Hill, 1936, pp. 386-390.

(9) ———, *The Range of Social Theory, a Survey of the Development, Literature, Tendencies and Fundamental Problems of the Social Sciences,* New York: Holt, 1929. (Consult index.)

(10) Albert Salomon, "German Sociology," 586-614, in: Georges Gurvitch and Wilbert E. Moore, eds., *Twentieth Century Sociology,* New York: Philosophical Library, 1945, pp. 604-609.

(11) Pitirim Sorokin (see A).

(12) Nicholas J. Spykman (see A).

(13) A. Vierkandt, "Simmel, Georg," *Encyclopaedia of the Social Sciences,* 14: 61.

(14) Wiese-Becker (see n. 32 above), esp. 705-708.

Among more recent American sociology texts, the following (in chronological order) refer to Simmel more than bibliographically (consult indices): R. M. MacIver, *Society: A Textbook of Sociology,* New York: Farrar and Rinehart, 1937 (also: MacIver, *Community, a Sociological Study,* London: Macmillan, 1917; MacIver and Charles H. Page, *Society: An Introductory Analysis,* New York: Rinehart, 1949); Kimball Young, *An Introductory Sociology,* New York: American Book, 1939; *Sociology: A Study of Society and Culture, ibid.,* 1942 (see also his *Social Psychology,* New York: Crofts, 1944); John Lewis Gillin and John Philip Gillin, *An Introduction to Sociology,* New York: Macmillan, 1942; E. T. Hiller, *Social Relations and*

Structures, A Study in Principles of Sociology, New York and London: Harper, 1947; Pitirim A. Sorokin, *Society, Culture, and Personality: Their Structure and Dynamics*, New York and London: Harper, 1947; John W. Bennett and Melvin M. Tumin, *Social Life: Structure and Function*, New York: Knopf, 1948; Kingsley Davis, *Human Society*, New York: Macmillan, 1949.

[f] SOURCES OF THE TRANSLATIONS CONTAINED IN THIS VOLUME

(1) Georg Simmel, *Grundfragen der Soziologie (Individuum und Gesellschaft)* ("Sammlung Göschen," No. 101), Berlin und Leipzig: Vereingung wissenschaftlicher Verleger, Walter de Gruyter & Co., 1917, pp. 103. For the translation, the second edition (identical with the first), of 1920, was used. The four chapters of this work have the following original titles: "Das Gebiet der Soziologie," "Das soziale und das individuelle Niveau (Beispiel der Allgemeinen Soziologie)," "Die Geselligkeit (Beispiel der Reinen oder Formalen Soziologie)," and "Individuum und Gesellschaft in Lebensanschauungen des 18. und 19. Jahrhunderts (Beispiel der Philosophischen Soziologie)."

(2) Georg Simmel, *Soziologie, Untersuchungen über die Formen der Vergesellschaftung* (Sociology, Studies of the Forms of Societalization), Leipzig: Verlag von Duncker & Humblot, 1908, pp. 782. For the translation, the third, revised edition of 1923 (pp. 578) was used. The following table of contents is supplemented by translations of headings and by information concerning available translations or their non-existence. Titles of portions contained in the present volume are printed in capital letters.

I. Das Problem der Soziologie (The Problem of Sociology, pp. 1-31). For translation, see D, no. 12.

Exkurs über das Problem: wie ist Gesellschaft möglich? (Note on the Problem: How Is Society Possible? Pp. 21-30). For translation, see D, no. 13.

II. DIE QUANTITATIVE BESTIMMTHEIT DER GRUPPE (The Quantitative Determinateness of the Group, pp. 32-100), tr. as Part II of the present volume. For translation of an earlier and shorter draft, see D, no. 7. (For a summary, see Spykman, Book II, Ch. III.)

III. ÜBER- UND UNTERORDNUNG (Superordination and Subordination, pp. 101-185), tr. as Part III of the present volume.

For translation of an earlier and much shorter draft, see D, no. 3. (Cf. Spykman, Book II, Ch. I.)

EXKURS ÜBER DIE ÜBERSTIMMUNG (Note on Out-Votting, pp. 142-147), tr. as Part III, Ch. 3, Sect. 5. Not previously translated.

IV. Der Streit (Conflict, pp. 186-255). For translation of an earlier and shorter draft, see D, no. 8. (Cf. Spykman, Book II, Ch. II.)

V. DAS GEHEIMNIS UND DIE GEHEIME GESELLSCHAFT (The Secret and the Secret Society, pp. 257-304), tr. as Part IV of the present volume. For translation of an earlier and shorter draft, see D, no. 11.

EXKURS ÜBER DEN SCHMUCK (Note on Adornment, pp. 278-281), tr. as Part IV, Ch. 3, Sect. 5. Not previously translated.

EXKURS ÜBER DEN SCHRIFTLICHEN VERKEHR (Note on Written Communication, pp. 287-288), tr. as Part IV, Ch. 4, Sect. 3. Not previously translated.

VI. Die Kreuzung sozialer Kreise (The Intersection of Social Circles, pp. 305-344). No translation existing. (Cf. Spykman, Book II, Ch. VI.)

VII. Der Arme (The Poor, pp. 345-374). No translation existing.

EXKURS ÜBER DIE NEGATIVITÄT KOLLEKTIVER VERHALTUNGSWEISEN (Note on the Negativity of Collective Modes of Behavior, pp. 359-362), tr. as Part V, Ch. 2. Not previously translated.

VIII. Die Selbsterhaltung der sozialen Gruppe (The Self-Preservation of the Social Group, pp. 375-459). For translation of an earlier and much shorter draft, see D, no. 4. (Cf. Spykman, Book II, Ch. V.)

Exkurs über das Erbamt (Note on Hereditary Office, pp. 391-396). No translation existing.

Exkurs über Sozialpsychologie (Note on Social Psychology, pp. 421-425). No translation existing.

EXKURS ÜBER TREUE UND DANKBARKEIT (Note on Faithfulness and Gratitude, pp. 438-447), tr. as Part V, Ch. 1. Not previously translated.

IX. Der Raum und die räumlichen Ordnungen der Gesellschaft (Space and the Spatial Organization of Society, pp. 460-526). No translation existing. (Cf. Spykman, Book II, Ch. IV.)

Exkurs über die soziale Begrenzung (Note on Social Delimitation, pp. 467-470). No translation existing.

Exkurs über die Soziologie der Sinne (Note on the Sociology of the Senses, pp. 483-493). For a partial translation, see D, no. 14b.

EXKURS ÜBER DEN FREMDEN (Note on the Stranger, pp. 509-512), tr. as Part V, Ch. 3. For an earlier translation, see D, No. 14a, above.

X. Die Erweiterung der Gruppe und die Ausbildung der Individualität (The Enlargement of the Group and the Development of Individuality, pp. 527-573). No translation existing. (Cf. Spykman, Book II, Ch. VII.)

Exkurs über den Adel (Note on Nobility, pp. 545-552). No translation existing.

Exkurs über die Analogie der individualpsychologischen und der soziologischen Verhältnisse (Note on the Analogy of Individual-Psychological and Sociological Conditions, pp. 565-568). No translation existing.

(3) Georg Simmel, "Die Grossstädte und das Geistesleben" (The Large Cities [Metropoles] and Intellectual [Mental] Life), pp. 185-206, in: *Die Grossstadt*. Vorträge und Aufsätze zur Städteausstellung von K. Bücher, F. Ratzel, G. v. Mayr, H. Waentig, G. Simmel, Th. Petermann und D. Schäfer. Gehe-Stiftung zu Dresden, Winter 1902-1903. *Jahrbuch der Gehe-Stiftung zu Dresden*. Band IX. Dresden: v. Zahn & Jaensch, 1903. For the translation used in the present volume, see D, no. 15b; for another translation, see D, no. 15a.

[g] A NOTE ON THE TRANSLATION

With the exception of the last chapter (cf. F, no. 3), all translations were made by the present writer. The attempt at utilizing extant renditions was abandoned, after some experimentation, as impracticable. The key term *"Vergesellschaftung,"* misleadingly rendered as "socialization" by Small (cf. D) and Spykman, and literally as "societalization" by Abel, has consistently been translated as "sociation." A precedent for this is Wiese-Becker; see esp. p. 10, n. 11, and pp. 113-114 and n. 6, on the different referents of their and Stuckenberg's "sociation," a term coined by the latter. (On this coinage, in J. H. W. Stuckenberg, *Introduction to the Study of Sociology*, 1898, pp. 126-127, cf. Barnes, ed., *An Introduction to the History of Sociol-*

ogy, 806.) The other key term, *"Wechselwirkung,"* literally "recipro-cal effect," has been found to have in "interaction" its contextually closest English equivalent, and has thus been translated throughout the volume. The only place where this translation has been found before is Bentley, *Relativity in Man and Society,* 353.

One of the most tangible changes wrought on Simmel's text is its breakup into more manageable portions. The original sentences, paragraphs, and chapters are considerably longer than are those of this translation. Most sentences and paragraphs were broken up, and most headings were added. Only those of the following portions of the book are Simmel's own: Parts I, II, III, IV; all chapters in Parts I and V; Part II, Ch. 4, Sects. 2, 3, 4; Part III, Ch. 3, Sect. 5; Part IV, Ch. 3, Sect. 5, and Ch. 4, Sect. 3.

In their "Preface" to *From Max Weber,* Gerth and Mills give an excellent account of their translation. The interested reader is in-vited to inspect that preface, thinking of Simmel rather than of Weber, in order to have a fairly accurate idea of the English, in its relation to the original German, that he finds in the following pages.

The Sociology of Georg Simmel

Part One

Fundamental Problems
of Sociology

Individual and Society

Chapter 1

The Field
of Sociology

THE FIRST DIFFICULTY
which arises if one wants to make a tenable statement about the
science of sociology is that its claim to *be* a science is not undisputed. Further, there is a chaotic multitude of opinions concerning its contents and aims. There are so many contradictions and
confusions, that one doubts again and again whether one deals
with a scientifically justifiable problem at all here. The lack of
an undisputed and clear definition would not be so bad if it
were made up for by the existence of a certain number of specific
problems which are not, or not exhaustively, treated in other
disciplines and which contain the fact or concept of "society"
as their common element and point of contact. They might be
too different from one another in content, orientation, and
method of solution to be treated as if they amounted to a homogeneous field of inquiry. Yet even then, they could at least find
a preliminary refuge under the heading of "sociology"; at least
superficially, it would be clear where to look for them. In such
a scheme, sociology would resemble technology, a tag quite legitimately attached to an immense range of tasks whose understanding and solution are not too greatly helped by the suggestion
(through the name "technology") that they have some feature
in common.

§ 1. *Society and Knowledge of Society*

Such a tenuous tie among heterogeneous problems might hold
out the promise of their unity at a deeper level. Yet even this
tenuous tie appears impossible because of the problematic char-

acter of the only concept that holds these problems together—
"society." In fact, all existing denials of the possibility of sociology as a science arise on the basis of this problematic character.
It is remarkable that the denials either minimize or exaggerate
this concept. Existence, we hear, is an exclusive attribute of
individuals, their qualities and experiences. "Society," by contrast, is an abstraction. Although indispensable for practical purposes and certainly very useful for a rough and preliminary survey of the phenomena that surround us, it is no real *object*. It
does not exist outside and in addition to the individuals and the
processes among them. After each of these individuals is investigated in his natural and historical characteristics, nothing is left
by way of subject matter for a particular science.

For this sort of critique, "society," obviously, is too slight
a matter to constitute a field of science. For another kind of
critique, however, it is too big: for on the other hand it is said
all that men are and do occurs within society, is determined by
society, and is part of its life; there is no science of man that is
not science of society. The science of society thus ought to replace
the artificially compartmentalized special disciplines, historical,
psychological, and normative. It ought to make it evident that
it is *sociation* which synthesizes all human interests, contents, and
processes into concrete units. But, obviously, this definition,
which wants to give sociology everything, takes as much away
from it as did the first conception that left it nothing. For jurisprudence and philology, political science and literary criticism,
psychology and theology, and all the other disciplines that have
divided up the study of human life among themselves, will certainly continue to exist. Nothing is gained by throwing their sum
total into a pot and sticking a new label on it: "sociology."

The trouble is that the science of society, in contrast to other
sciences that are well established, is in the unfortunate position
of still having to prove its right to exist. Yet this is fortunate, too,
for sociology's struggle for existence is bound to lead to a clarification of its basic concepts (which is good and necessary in itself)
and to the establishment of its specific manner of investigating
reality.

Let us grant for the moment that only individuals "really"
exist. Even then, only a false conception of science could infer

from this "fact" that any knowledge which somehow aims at synthesizing these individuals deals with merely speculative abstractions and unrealities. Quite on the contrary, human thought always and everywhere synthesizes the given into units that serve as subject matters of the sciences. They have no counterpart whatever in immediate reality. Nobody, for instance, hesitates to talk of the development of the Gothic style. Yet nowhere is there such a thing as "Gothic style," whose existence could be shown. Instead, there are particular works of art which along with individual elements, also contain stylistic elements; and the two cannot be clearly separated. The Gothic style as a topic of historical knowledge is an *intellectual* phenomenon. It is abstracted from reality; it is not itself a given reality. Innumerable times, we do not even want to know how individual things behave in all detail: we form new units out of them. When we inquire into the Gothic style, its laws, its development, we do not describe any particular cathedral or palace. Yet the *material* that makes up the unit we are investigating—"Gothic style"—we gain only from a study of the details of cathedrals and palaces. Or, we ask how the "Greeks" and the "Persians" behaved in the battle of Marathon. If it were true that only individuals are "real," historical cognition would reach its goal only if it included the behavior of each individual Greek and each individual Persian. If we knew his whole life history, we could psychologically understand his behavior during the battle. Yet even if we could manage to satisfy such a fantastic claim, we would not have solved our problem at all. For this problem does not concern this or that individual Greek or Persian; it concerns all of them. The notion, "the Greeks" and "the Persians," evidently constitutes a totally different phenomenon, which results from a certain intellectual synthesis, not from the observation of isolated individuals. To be sure, each of these individuals was led to behave as he did by a development which is somehow different from that of every other individual. In reality, none of them behaved precisely like any other. And, in no one individual, is what he shares with others clearly separable from what distinguishes him from others. Both aspects, rather, form the inseparable unity of his personal life. Yet in spite of all this, out of all these individuals we form the more comprehensive units, "the Greeks" and "the Persians."

Even a moment's reflection shows that similar concepts constantly supersede individual existences. If we were to rob our cognition of all such intellectual syntheses because only individuals are "real," we would deprive human knowledge of its least dubious and most legitimate contents. The stubborn assertion that after all there exist nothing but individuals which alone, therefore, are the concrete objects of science, cannot prevent us from speaking of the histories of Catholicism and Social Democracy, of cities, and of political territories, of the feminist movement, of the conditions of craftsmen, and of thousands of other synthetic events and collective phenomena—and, therefore, of society in general. It certainly is an abstract concept. But each of the innumerable articulations and arrangements covered by it is an object that can be investigated and is worth investigation. And none of them consists of individual existences that are observed in all their details.

This whole consideration, however, might be due, simply, to an imperfect grasp of the matter at issue. It might merely be a (perhaps) necessary preliminary that would, potentially or actually, be overcome by a more intimate knowledge of the individuals as the ultimately concrete elements. Yet if we examine "individuals" more closely, we realize that they are by no means such ultimate elements or "atoms" of the human world. For the unit denoted by the concept "individual" (and which, as a matter of fact, perhaps is insoluble, as we shall see later) is not an object of cognition at all, but only of experience. The way in which each of us, in himself and in others, knows of this unit, cannot be compared to any other way of knowing. What we know about man *scientifically* is only single characteristics. They may exist once, or they may stand in a relation of reciprocal influence to one another; but each of them requires its special investigation and derivation, which leads to innumerable influences of the physical, cultural, personal environment—influences that come from everywhere and extend infinitely in time. Only by isolating and grasping them and by reducing them to increasingly simple, covert and remote elements do we approach what is really "ultimate," that is, what is real in the rigorous sense of the word. This "real" alone must form the basis for any higher intellectual synthesis. Color molecules, letters, particles of water indeed "exist";

but the painting, the book, the river are syntheses: they are units that do not exist in objective reality but only in the consciousness which constitutes them. But what is more, even *these* so-called elements are highly synthetic phenomena. It is, therefore, not true that reality can be attributed only to properly ultimate units, and not to phenomena in which these units find their forms. Any form (and a form always is a synthesis) is something added by a synthesizing subject. Thus, a conception that considers only individuals as "real" lets what *should* be considered real get out of hand. It is perfectly arbitrary to stop the reduction, which leads to ultimately real elements, at the individual. For this reduction is interminable. In it, the individual appears as a composite of single qualities, and destinies, forces and historical derivations, which in comparison to the individual himself have the same character of elementary realities as do the individuals in comparison to society.

In other words, the alleged realism that performs this sort of critique of the concept of society, and thus of sociology, actually eliminates all knowable reality. It relegates it into the infinite and looks for it in the realm of the inscrutable. As a matter of fact, cognition must be conceived on the basis of an entirely different structural principle. This principle is the abstraction, from a given complex of phenomena, of a number of heterogeneous objects of cognition that are nevertheless recognized as equally definitive and consistent. The principle may be expressed by the symbol of different *distances* between such a complex of phenomena and the human mind. We obtain different pictures of an object when we see it at a distance of two, or of five, or of ten yards. At each distance, however, the picture is "correct" in its particular way and only in this way. And the different distance also provides different margins for error. For instance, if the minute detail of a painting that we gain at very close range were injected into a perspective gained at a distance of several yards, this perspective would be utterly confused and falsified. And yet on the basis of a superficial conception, one might assert that the detailed view is "truer" than the more distant view. But even this detailed perception involves some distance whose lower limit is, in fact, impossible to determine. All we can say is that a view gained at any distance whatever has its own justification. It cannot be replaced or corrected by any other view emerging at another distance.

In a similar way, when we look at human life from a certain distance, we see each individual in his precise differentiation from all others. But if we increase our distance, the single individual disappears, and there emerges, instead, the picture of a "society" with its own forms and colors—a picture which has its own possibilities of being recognized or missed. It is certainly no less justified than is the other in which the parts, the individuals, are seen in their differentiation. Nor is it by any means a mere preliminary of it. The difference between the two merely consists in the difference between purposes of cognition; and this difference, in turn, corresponds to a difference in distance.

The right to sociological study thus is not in the least endangered by the circumstance that all real happenings only occur in individuals. Yet the independence of sociology from this circumstance can be argued even more radically. For it is not true that the cognition of series of individual occurrences grasps immediate reality. This reality, rather, is given to us as a complex of images, as a surface of contiguous phenomena. We articulate this datum—which is our only truly primary datum—into something like the destinies of individuals. Or we reduce its simple matter-of-factness to single elements that are designed to catch it as if they were its nodal points. Clearly, in either case there occurs a process which *we* inject into reality, an *ex-post-facto* intellectual *transformation* of the immediately given reality. Because of constant habit, we achieve this almost automatically. We almost think it is no transformation at all, but something given in the natural order of things. Actually, this transformation is exactly as subjective—but also, since it yields valid cognition, exactly as objective—as is the synthesis of the given under the category of society. Only the particular purpose of cognition determines whether reality, as it emerges or is experienced in its immediacy, is to be investigated in a personal or in a collective frame of reference. Both frames of reference, equally, are "standpoints." Their relation to one another is not that of reality to abstraction. Rather, since both are interpretations, though different ones, both are detached from "reality," which itself cannot be the immediate subject matter of science. It becomes amenable to cognition only by means of categories such as, for instance, "individual," or "society."

Nor is the concept of society invalidated by the fact that, if we look at it from still another angle, we must admit that human existence is real only in individuals. If the concept "society" is taken in its most general sense, it refers to the psychological interaction among individual human beings. This definition must not be jeopardized by the difficulties offered by certain marginal phenomena. Thus, two people who for a moment look at one another or who collide in front of a ticket window, should not on these grounds be called sociated. Yet even here, where interaction is so superficial and momentary, one could speak, with some justification, of sociation. One has only to remember that interactions of this sort merely need become more frequent and intensive and join other similar ones to deserve properly the name of sociation. It is only a superficial attachment to linguistic usage (a usage quite adequate for daily practice) which makes us want to reserve the term "society" for *permanent* interactions only. More specifically, the interactions we have in mind when we talk about "society" are crystallized as definable, consistent structures such as the state and the family, the guild and the church, social classes and organizations based on common interests.

But in addition to these, there exists an immeasurable number of less conspicuous forms of relationship and kinds of interaction. Taken singly, they may appear negligible. But since in actuality they are inserted into the comprehensive and, as it were, official social formations, they alone produce society as we know it. To confine ourselves to the large social formations resembles the older science of anatomy with its limitation to the major, definitely circumscribed organs such as heart, liver, lungs, and stomach, and with its neglect of the innumerable, popularly unnamed or unknown tissues. Yet without these, the more obvious organs could never constitute a living organism. On the basis of the major social formations—the traditional subject matter of social science—it would be similarly impossible to piece together the real life of society as we encounter it in our experience. Without the interspersed effects of countless minor syntheses, society would break up into a multitude of discontinuous systems. Sociation continuously emerges and ceases and emerges again. Even where its eternal flux and pulsation are not sufficiently strong to form organizations proper, they link individuals together. That people look at one another and are jealous of one another; that they exchange letters or dine together; that irrespective of all tangible interests they strike one another as pleasant or unpleasant; that gratitude for altruistic acts makes for inseparable union; that one asks another man after a certain street, and that people dress and adorn themselves for one another—the whole gamut of relations that play from one person to another and that may be momentary or permanent, conscious or unconscious, ephemeral or of grave consequence (and from which these illustrations are quite casually chosen), all these incessantly tie men together. Here are the interactions among the atoms of society. They account for all the toughness and elasticity, all the color and consistency of social life, that is so striking and yet so mysterious.

The large systems and the super-individual organizations that customarily come to mind when we think of society, are nothing but immediate interactions that occur among men constantly, every minute, but that have become crystallized as permanent fields, as autonomous phenomena. As they crystallize, they attain their own existence and their own laws, and may even confront or oppose spontaneous interaction itself. At the same time, society, as its life is constantly being realized, always signifies that individuals are connected by mutual influence and determination. It is, hence, something functional, something individuals do and suffer. To be true to this fundamental character of it, one should properly speak, not of society, but of sociation. Society merely is the name for a number of individuals, connected by interaction. It is because of their interaction that they are a unit—just as a system of bodily masses is a unit whose reciprocal effects wholly determine their mutual behavior. One may, of course, insist that only these masses are true "realities," and that their mutually stimulated movements and modifications are something intangible, and thus only secondary realities, so to speak, for they have their locus only in the concrete bodies themselves. The so-called unit merely is the synopsis of these materially separated existences: after all, the impulses and formations they receive and produce remain in *them*. In the same sense one may insist that ultimately it is the human individuals that are the true realities. But this adds nothing to our argument. In accordance with it, <u>society</u> certainly is not a "substance," nothing concrete, <u>but an *event*</u>: it is the function of receiving and effecting the fate and development of one individual by the other. Groping for the tangible, we find only individuals; and between them, only a vacuum, as it were. Later, we shall consider the consequences of this conception. At any rate, if it leaves "existence" (more strictly speaking) only to individuals, it must nevertheless accept the process and the dynamics of acting and suffering, by which the individuals modify one another, as something "real" and explorable.

§ 2. *The Abstract Character of Sociology*

Under the guidance of its particular conception, any science extracts only one group or aspect out of the totality or experienced immediacy of phenomena. Sociology does so, too. It acts no less legitimately than does any other science if it analyzes individual existences and recomposes them in the light of its own conception. Sociology asks what happens to men and by what rules they behave, not insofar as they unfold their understandable individual existences in their totalities, but insofar as they form groups and are determined by their group existence because of interaction. It treats the history of marriage without analyzing particular couples; the principle underlying the organization of offices, without describing a "typical day" at a particular office; the laws and consequences of the class struggle, without dealing with the development of a particular strike or of particular wage negotiations. The topics of its researches certainly arise in a process of abstraction. But this feature does not distinguish sociology from such sciences as logic or economic theory. They, too, under the guidance of certain conceptions (such as cognition and economics, respectively), produce, out of reality, interrelated phenomena that do not exist as something experienceable but whose laws and evolution they discover.

Sociology thus is founded upon an abstraction from concrete reality, performed under the guidance of the concept of society. We have already noted the invalidity of the accusation of unreality, which was derived from the assertion of the exclusive reality of individuals. But this realization also protects our discipline from the exaggeration that I have mentioned, earlier, as an equally grave danger for its existence as a science. To repeat: since man in all aspects of his life and action is determined by the fact that he is a social being, all sciences of him are reduced to parts of the science of social life. All subject matters of these sciences are nothing more than particular channels, as it were, in which social life, the only bearer of all energy and of all significance, flows. I have shown that all this conception does is to yield a new common name for all the branches of knowledge that will continue to exist anyway, unperturbed and autonomous, with all their specific contents and nomenclatures, tendencies and methods. Nevertheless, this erroneous exaggeration of the concepts "society" and "sociology" is based upon a fact of great significance and consequence. For, the recognition that man in his whole nature and in all his manifestations is determined by the circumstance of living in interaction with other men, is bound to lead to a new viewpoint that must make itself felt in all so-called human studies.[1]

As recent a period as the eighteenth century explained the great contents of historical life—language, religion, the formation of states, material culture—essentially, as inventions of single individuals. Where the reason and interests of the individual were not adequate explanations, transcendental forces were resorted to. The "genius" of the single inventor, incidentally, served as a link between the two explanatory principles: it suggested that the known and understandable forces of the individual did not suffice to produce the phenomenon in question. Thus, language was either the invention of individuals or a divine gift; religion (as a historical event), the invention of shrewd priests or divine will; moral laws were either inculcated into the mass by heroes or bestowed by God, or were given to man by "nature," a no less mystical hypostasis. These two insuffi-

---

[1] *"Geisteswissenschaften."* Unless otherwise indicated, this term will always be rendered as "human studies," a usage which follows Hodges. (Cf. H. A. Hodges, *Wilhelm Dilthey: An Introduction,* New York: Oxford University Press, 1944, esp. p. 157.)—Tr.

cient alternatives were replaced by the notion of societal production, according to which all these phenomena emerge in interactions among men, or sometimes, indeed, *are* such interactions. They cannot be derived from the individual considered in isolation. In addition to the two earlier possibilities, therefore, we now have a third: the production of phenomena through social life. This production occurs in a twofold manner. In the first place, there is the simultaneity of interacting individuals which in each produces what cannot be explained on the basis of him alone. In the second place, there is the succession of generations. The inheritance and tradition of this succession inseparably fuse with the acquisitions made by the individual himself: social man, in contrast to all subhuman animals, is not only a successor but also an heir.

§ 3. *Sociology as a Method*

The notion of societal production lies, as it were, somewhere between the notions of purely individual and transcendental production. It has provided all human studies with a genetic method, with a new tool for the solution of their problems, whether they concern the state or church organization, language or moral conditions. Sociology thus is not only a science with its own subject matter that is differentiated, by division of labor, from the subject matters of all other sciences. It also has become a *method* of the historical disciplines and of the human studies in general. Yet in order to use it, these sciences by no means need abandon their own particular viewpoints. They need not become mere parts of sociology, as that fantastic exaggeration of its idea, which I mentioned earlier, would make us believe. Rather, sociology adapts itself to each specific discipline—economics, history of culture, ethics, theology, or what not. In this respect, it is essentially like induction. At its time, induction, as a new principle of investigation, penetrated into all kinds of problem areas. It thus contributed new solutions for tasks well established in these areas. The parallel suggests that sociology is no more a special science than induction is (and surely, it is not an all-embracing science). Insofar as it is based on the notions that man must be understood as a social animal and that society is the

f all historical events, sociology contains no subject
is not already treated in one of the extant sciences.
is up a new avenue for all of them. It supplies them
scientific method which, precisely because of its applica-
bility to all problems, is not a science with its own content.[2]

In its very generality, this method is apt to form a common
basis for problem areas that previously, in the absence of their
mutual contact, lacked a certain clarity. The universality of
sociation, which makes for the reciprocal shaping of the individuals, has its correspondence in the singleness of the sociological way of cognition. The sociological approach yields possibilities of solution or of deeper study which may be derived from
fields of knowledge contentually quite different (perhaps) from
the field of the particular problem under investigation. I will
mention three examples, which range from the most specific to
the most general.

(1) The criminologist may learn much concerning the nature
of so-called mass crimes from a sociological investigation of the
psychology of the theatre audience. For here, the stimulus of a
collective-impulsive behavior can still be clearly ascertained.
Furthermore, this behavior occurs in the sphere of art which,
as it were, is abstract and precisely delimited. Thus here—and
this is very important for the problem of guilt in regard to "mass
crimes"—the extent to which the individual can be determined
by a mass in physical proximity with him, and the extent to
which subjective and objective value judgments can be eliminated under the impact of contagion, may be observed under
conditions that are as purely experimental and crucial as scarcely
anywhere else.

(2) The student of religion is often inclined to explain the
life of the religious community and its readiness to sacrifice in
terms of their devotion to an ideal that is common to all members. He may tend to ascribe the conduct of life, inspired as it is
by the hope in a perfect state beyond the lives of the existing individuals, to the strength in content of the religious faith. Yet

---

[2] These last and some later sentences are taken from my larger work, *Soziologie:
Untersuchungen über die Formen der Vergesellschaftung* (1908) [Sociology: Studies
in the Forms of Sociation], which treats some of the thoughts sketched here in
greater detail and, particularly, with more thorough historical documentation.

the members of a Social-Democratic labor union may exhibit the
same traits in their common and mutual behavior. If the student
of religion notes this similarity, he may learn that religious behavior does not exclusively depend on religious contents, but
that it is a generally human form of behavior which is realized
under the stimulus not only of transcendental objects but also
of other motivations. He will also gain insight into something
even more important to him. This is the fact that, even in its
autonomy, religious life contains elements that are not specifically
religious, but social. Certainly, these elements—particular kinds
of reciprocal attitude and behavior—are fused organically with
the religious mood itself. But only when they are isolated by
means of the sociological method, will they show what within
the whole complex of religious behavior may legitimately be
considered purely religious, that is, independent of anything
social.

(3) I will give one last example of the mutual fertilization
of problem areas that is suggested by the common involvement
of human sociation in all of them. The contemporary student
of political or cultural history is often inclined, for instance, to
derive the character of the domestic policy pursued by a given
country from its economic conditions and processes as sufficient
causes. Suppose he explains the strong individualism of early
Italian Renaissance political constitutions as the effect of the
liberation of economic life from guild and church ties. Here it is
an observation of the historian of art that may greatly qualify
his conception. The observation is that already in the beginning
of the epoch under discussion there was an immense spread of
naturalistic and individualistic portrait busts. Thus the general
attention appears to have shifted from what men have in common (and what therefore can easily be relegated into somewhat
more abstract and ideal spheres) to what must be left to the
individual. Attention is focused on the significance of personal
strength; the concrete is preferred to the general law that is
valid "on the whole." And this discovery suggests that the observed economic individualism is the manifestation of a fundamental sociological change which has found its expression in the
fields of art and politics as well. It suggests that none of these
immediately caused the other.

Perhaps, in fact, sociological analyses of this sort are apt quite generally to point the way toward a conception of history which is more profound than historical materialism, and which may even supersede it. Historical changes, at their properly effective level, are possibly changes in sociological forms. It is perhaps the way in which individuals and groups behave toward one another; in which the individual behaves toward his group; in which value accents, accumulations, prerogatives, and similar phenomena shift among the elements of society—perhaps it is *these* things which make for truly epochal events. And if economics seems to determine all the other areas of culture, the truth behind this tempting appearance would seem to be that it itself is determined—determined by sociological shifts which similarly shape all other cultural phenomena. Thus, the form of economics, too, is merely a "superstructure" on top of the conditions and transformations in the purely sociological structure. And this sociological structure is the ultimate historical element which is bound to determine all other contents of life, even if in a certain parallelism with economics.

§ 4. *The Problem Areas of Sociology*

[a] THE SOCIOLOGICAL STUDY OF HISTORICAL LIFE ("GENERAL SOCIOLOGY")

These considerations afford a glimpse, beyond the mere concept of sociological *method,* at the first basic *problem area* of sociology. Although it covers almost all of human existence, it does not therefore lose that character of one-sided abstraction that no science can get rid of. For however socially determined and permeated, as it were, each item in the economic and intellectual, political and juridical, even religious and generally cultural spheres may be, nevertheless, in the actuality of concrete life, this social determination is interwoven with other determinations that stem from other sources. Above all, from the circumstance that things also have a purely objective character. It is always some objective content—technical, dogmatic, intellectual, physiological—which channels the development of the social forces and which, by virtue of its own character, logic, and law, keeps it within certain directions and limits. Any social phenomenon, no matter in what material it realize itself, must submit to the natural laws of this material. Any intellectual achievement is tied, in however various ways, to the laws of thought and to the behavior of objects. Any creation in the fields of art, politics, law, medicine, philosophy, or in any other field of invention, observes a certain order that we can understand in terms of the objective situation of its contents and that is characterized by such relations as intensification, connection, differentiation, combination, etc. No human wish or practice can take arbitrary steps, jump arbitrary distances, perform arbitrary syntheses. They must follow the intrinsic logic of things.

Thus, one could very well construct the history of art, as a perfectly understandable development, by presenting works of art themselves, anonymously, in their temporal sequence and stylistic evolution; or the development of law, as the sequence of particular institutions and laws; or that of science, as the mere series, historical or systematic, of its results; etc. Here, as in the cases of a song that is analyzed in terms of its musical value, or of a physical theory in terms of its truth, or of a machine in terms of its efficiency, we realize that all contents of human life, even though they materialize only under the conditions and in the dynamics of social life, nevertheless permit interpretations ignoring it. Objects embody their own ideas; they have significance, laws, value standards which are independent of both the social and the individual life and which make it possible to define and understand them in their own terms. In comparison with full reality, of course, even this understanding involves abstraction, since no objective content is realized by its own logic alone but only through the cooperation of historical and psychological forces. Cognition cannot grasp reality in its total immediacy. What we call objective content is something conceived under a specific category.

Under one of these categories, the history of mankind appears as the behavior and product of *individuals*. One may look at a work of art only in regard to its artistic significance; one may place it, as if it had fallen from the sky, within a series of artistic products. Yet one may also understand it in terms of the artist's personality and development, his experiences and tendencies. One may interpret it as a pulsation or immediate experience of individual life. Thus viewed, the work of art remains within the bounds of the individual and his continuity. Certain cultural data—above all art and, in general, everything that has the breath of creativity—appear more easily graspable in such a perspective than do other data. Quite generally, to look at the world as something that is carried by the active and receptive, typical or unique subject, is one of the possibilities of translating the unity of all human creation into understandability. The manifestation of the individual strikes us as an active element everywhere. Its laws permit us to form a plane, as it were, on which to project reality in all its fullness.

The purpose of this discussion is to show that there exists *not only* social life as a basis for the life of mankind and as a formula of it. This life may also be derived from the objective significance of its contents, and be interpreted in *these* terms. And it may finally be conceived in the framework of the nature and creativity of the individual. Perhaps there are other interpretive categories that have not yet been clearly developed. At any rate, all these analyses and structuralizations of our immediate life and creativity experience this life as a unity. They lie on the same plane and have the same right to be heard. Therefore—and this is the point—no one of them can claim to be the only or the only adequate manner of cognition. Naturally, neither can such a claim be made by the approach which proceeds in terms of the social form of our existence. It, too, is limited; and it supplements other approaches by which in turn it is supplemented. With this qualification, however, it can, in principle, offer a possibility of cognition in front of the totality of human existence.

The facts of politics, religion, economics, law, culture styles, language, and innumerable others can be analyzed by asking how they may be understood, not as individual achievements or in their objective significance, but as products and developments of society. Nor would the absence of an exhaustive and undisputed definition of the nature of society render the cognitive value of this approach illusory. For it is a characteristic of the human mind to be capable of erecting solid structures, while their foundations are still insecure. Physical and chemical propositions do not suffer from the obscure and problematical character of the concept of matter; juridical propositions, not from the quarrel over the nature of law and of its first principles; psychological ones, not from the highly questionable "nature of the soul." If, therefore, we apply the "sociological method" to the investigation of the fall of the Roman Empire or of the relation between religion and economics in the great civilizations or of the origin of the idea of the German national state or of the predominance of the Baroque style; if, that is, we view these and similar phenomena as the result of indistinguishable contributions made by the interaction of individuals, or as life stages in the lives of superindividual groups; then we are, in point of fact, conducting our investigations according to the sociological method. And these investigations may be designated as sociology.

Yet from these sociological investigations there emerges a further abstraction that may well be characterized as the result of a highly differentiated scientific culture. This abstraction yields a group of sociological problems in the narrower sense of this term. If we study all kinds of life data in terms of their development within and by means of social groups, we must assume that they have common elements in their materialization (even though different elements, under different circumstances). These common elements emerge if, and only if, social life itself emerges as the origin or the subject of these data. The question thus arises whether perhaps it is possible to find, in the most heterogeneous historical developments that share nothing but the fact that they are exhibited by one particular group, a common law, or a rhythm, that is fully derivable from this one fact.

It has been maintained, for instance, that all historical developments pass through three phases. The first is the undifferentiated unity of manifold elements. The second is the differentiated articulation of these elements, that have become alienated from one another. The third is a new unity, the harmonious interpenetration of the elements that have been preserved, however, in their specific characters. More briefly, the road of all completed developments leads from an undifferentiated unity through a differentiated manifoldness to a differentiated unity. Another conception of historical life sees it as a process which progresses from organic commonness to mechanical simultaneousness. Property, work, and interests originally grow out of the solidarity of the individuals, the carriers of the group life; but later are distributed among egoists each of whom seeks only his own benefit and, only because of this motive, enters into relations with others. The first stage is the manifestation of an unconscious will which inheres in the very depth of our nature and becomes evident only as a feeling; the second stage, by contrast, is the product of an arbitrary will and of the calculating intellect. According to a still different conception, it is possible to ascertain a definite relation, in any given epoch, between its intellectual world view and its social conditions: both equally are manifestations, in some sense, of biological development. Finally, there is the notion that human cognition, on the whole, must go through three stages. In the first, or theological stage, natural phenomena are explained by recourse to the arbitrary will of all kinds of entities. In the second, metaphysical stage, the supernatural causes are replaced by laws which, however, are mystical and speculative (as, for instance, "vital force," "ends of nature," etc.). Finally, the third, or positive stage corresponds to modern experimental and exact science. Each particular branch of knowledge develops by passing through these three stages; and the knowledge of this fact removes the enigmatic character of social development, which pervades areas of all kinds.

A further sociological question under this category is the problem concerning conditions of group *power,* as distinguished from individual power. The conditions for the power of individuals are immediately evident: intelligence, energy, an apt alternation between consistency and elasticity, etc.; but to account for the historical power of such extraordinary phenomena as Jesus, on the one hand, and Napoleon, on the other, there must also exist as yet unexplained forces which are by no means clarified by labels like "power of suggestion," "prestige," and so forth. But in the exercise of power by groups, both over their members and over other groups, there operate still other factors. Some of these are the faculty of rigid concentration, as well as of diversion into independent activities by individual group members; conscious faith in leading minds; groping toward expansion; egoism of the individual paralleled by sacrificial devotion to the whole; fanatic dogmatism, as well as thoroughly critical intellectual freedom. All these are effective in the rise (and, negatively, in the decay) not only of political nations but also of countless economic and religious, party-like and family groups. In all investigations of group power, the question, clearly, is not the origin of sociation as such, but the fate of society as something already constituted. And this fate is ascertained inductively.

Another question that arises out of the sociological consideration of conditions and events is that of the *value* relations between collective and individual conduct, action, and thought. Which differences of level, as measured by certain ideal standards, exist between social and individual phenomena? The inner, fundamental structure of society itself here becomes as little the central problem as it did in connection with the preceding question. Again, this structure is already presupposed, and the data are considered on the basis of this presupposition. The question, rather, is: which general principles are revealed in these data if they are considered in this particular perspective? In the next chapter, this problem of levels will be examined as an example of a sociological type that may be called "general sociology."

[b] THE STUDY OF SOCIETAL FORMS ("PURE, OR FORMAL, SOCIOLOGY")

Scientific abstraction cuts through the full concreteness of social phenomena from yet a different angle. It thereby connects all that is "sociological"—"sociological" in a sense that will be discussed presently and that appears to me to be the most decisive sense of the term. In doing this, scientific abstraction produces a consistent manner of cognition. Yet it fully realizes that in actuality, sociological phenomena do not exist in such isolation and recomposition, but that they are factored out of this living reality by means of an added concept. It will be remembered that societal facts are not *only* societal. It is always an objective content (sense-perceived or intellectual, technical or physiological) which is socially embodied, produced, or transmitted, and which only thus produces the totality of social life. Yet this societal formation of contents itself can be investigated by a science. Geometrical abstraction investigates only the spatial forms of bodies, although empirically, these forms are given merely as the forms of some material content. Similarly, if society is conceived as interaction among individuals, the description of the forms of this interaction is the task of the science of society in its strictest and most essential sense.

The first problem area of sociology, it will be remembered, consisted of the whole of historical life insofar as it is formed societally. Its societal character was conceived as an undifferentiated whole. The second problem area now under consideration, consists of the societal forms themselves. These are conceived as constituting society (and societies) out of the mere sum of living men. The study of this second area may be called "pure sociology," which abstracts the mere element of sociation. It isolates it inductively and psychologically from the heterogeneity of its contents and purposes, which, in themselves, are not societal. It thus proceeds like grammar, which isolates the pure forms of language from their contents through which these forms, nevertheless, come to life. In a comparable manner, social groups which are the most diverse imaginable in purpose and general significance, may nevertheless show identical forms of behavior toward one another on the part of their individual members. We find superiority and subordination, competition, division of labor, formation of parties, representation, inner solidarity coupled with exclusiveness toward the outside, and innumerable similar features in the state, in a religious community, in a band of conspirators, in an economic association, in an art school, in the family. However diverse the interests are that give rise to these sociations, the *forms* in which the interests are realized may yet be identical. And on the other hand, a contentually identical interest may take on form in very different sociations. Economic interest is realized both in competition and in the planned organization of producers, in isolation against other groups as well as in fusion with them. The religious contents of life, although they remain identical, sometimes demand an unregulated, sometimes a centralized form of community. The interests upon which the relations between the sexes are based are satisfied by an almost innumerable variety of family forms; etc.

Hence, not only may the form in which the most divergent contents are realized be identical; but, inversely, the content, too, may persist, while its medium—the interactions of the individuals—adopts a variety of forms. We see, then, that the analysis in terms of form and content transforms the facts—which, in their immediacy, present these two categories as the indissoluble unity of social life—in such a way as to justify the sociological problem. This problem demands the identification, the systematic ordering, the psychological explanation, and the historical development of the pure forms of sociation. Obviously, in terms of its subject matter, sociology thus seen is not a special science, as it was in terms of the first problem area. Yet in terms of its clearly specified way of asking questions, it is a special science even here. The discussion of "sociability," in the third chapter of the present sketch, will offer an example that may serve to symbolize the total picture of the investigations in "pure sociology." [3]

[c] THE STUDY OF THE EPISTEMOLOGICAL AND METAPHYSICAL ASPECTS OF SOCIETY ("PHILOSOPHICAL SOCIOLOGY")

The modern scientific attitude toward facts finally suggests a third complex of questions concerning the fact "society." Insofar as these questions are adjacent (as it were) to the upper and lower limits of this fact, they are sociological only in a broad sense of the term; more properly, they are philosophical. Their *content* is constituted by this fact itself. Similarly, nature and art, out of which we develop their *immediate* sciences, also supply us with the subject matters of their philosophies, whose interests and methods lie on a different level. It is the level on which factual details are investigated concerning their significance for the totality of mind, life, and being in general, and concerning their justification in terms of such a totality.

Thus, like every other exact science which aims at the immediate understanding of the given, social science, too, is surrounded by two *philosophical* areas. One of these covers the conditions, fundamental concepts, and presuppositions of concrete research, which cannot be taken care of by research itself since it is based on them. In the other area, this research is carried toward completions, connections, questions, and concepts that have no place in experience and in immediately objective knowledge. The first area is the epistemology, the second, the metaphysics of the particular discipline.

[3] I may be allowed to call attention to the fact that my above-mentioned *Soziologie* tries to present the "forms of sociation" in a completeness which is by no means definitive but is the best I can attain at this time.

The tasks of the special social sciences—the study of economics and of institutions, the history of morals and of parties, population theory, and the discussion of occupational differentiation—could not be carried out at all if they did not presuppose certain concepts, postulates, and methods as axiomatic. If we did not assume a certain drive toward egoistic gain and pleasure, but at the same time the limitability of this drive through coercion, custom, and morals; if we did not claim the right to speak of the moods of a mass as a unit, although many of the members of this mass are only its superficial followers or even dissenters; if we did not declare the development within a particular sphere of culture understandable by recreating it as an evolution with a psychological logic—if we did not proceed in this way, we should be utterly unable to cast innumerable facts into a social picture. In all these and in countless other situations, we operate with methods of thinking that use particular events as raw materials from which we derive social-scientific knowledge. Sociology proceeds like physics, which could never have been developed without grasping external phenomena on the basis of certain assumptions concerning space, matter, movement, and enumerability. Every special social science customarily and quite legitimately accepts without question such a basis of itself. Within its own domain, it could not even come to grips with it; for, in order to do so, obviously it would also have to take all other social sciences into consideration. Sociology thus emerges as the epistemology of the special social sciences, as the analysis and systematization of the bases of their forms and norms.

If these problems go beneath the concrete knowledge of social life, others, as it were, go beyond it. They try, by means of hypothesis and speculation, to supplement the unavoidably fragmentary character of the empirical facts (which always are fragmentary) in the direction of a closed system. They order the chaotic and accidental events into series that follow an idea or approach a goal. They ask where the neutral and natural sequences of events might provide these events or their totality with *significance*. They assert or doubt—and both assertion and doubt, equally, derive from a super-empirical world view—that the play of social-historical phenomena contains a religious significance, or a relation (to be known or at least sensed) to the metaphysical ground of being. More particularly, they ask questions such as these: Is society the purpose of human existence, or is it a means for the individual? Does the ultimate value of social development lie in the unfolding of personality or of association? Do meaning and purpose inhere in social phenomena at all, or exclusively in individuals? Do the typical stages of the development of societies show an analogy with cosmic evolutions so that there might be a general formula or rhythm of development in general (as, for instance, the fluctuation between differentiation and integration), which applies to social and material data alike? Are social movements guided by the principle of the conservation of energy? Are they directed by material or by ideological motives?

Evidently, this type of question cannot be answered by the ascertainment of facts. Rather, it must be answered by interpretations of ascertained facts and by efforts to bring the relative and problematical elements of social reality under an over-all view. Such a view does not compete with empirical claims because it serves needs which are quite different from those answered by empirical propositions.

The investigation of such problems, clearly, is more strictly based on differences in world views, individual and party valuations, and ultimate, undemonstrable convictions than is the investigation within the other two, more strictly fact-determined branches of sociology. For this reason, the discussion of a single problem as an example could not be as objective and could not as validly suggest the whole type of similar problems here, as is possible in the case of the other two branches. It therefore seems to me more advisable to trace, in the last chapter, a line of pertinent theories as they have been developed, in the course of many controversies, during a particular period of general intellectual history.

Chapter 2

The Social and the Individual Level

An Example of General Sociology

THERE WAS A TIME WHEN
the only topic of social investigation was the historical fate or the
practical politics of particular groups. During the last decades,
however, *sociation,* or the life of groups as units, has become such
a topic. Attention thus was attracted by what is common to *all*
groups inasmuch as they are societies. This presently led to the
examination of a closely related problem—of the characteristics
which distinguish social from individual life. At first glance, the
differences seem obvious. For instance, there is the basic im-
mortality of the group, as against the mortality of the individual.
There is the possibility of the group eliminating even its most
important elements without collapsing—an elimination which,
applied to the individual, would annihilate him. But the problem was of a more subtle, perhaps psychological, nature. No matter whether one considers the group that exists irrespective of its
individual members a fiction or a reality, in order to understand
certain facts one must treat it as if it actually did have its own
life, and laws, and other characteristics. And if one is to justify
the sociological standpoint, it is precisely the differences between
these characteristics and those of the individual existence that
one must clarify.

§ 1. *The Determinateness of the Group and the Vacillation of the Individual*

A clue for the ascertainment of these differences lies in the
suggestion that societal actions have incomparably greater pur-

posiveness and to-the-pointness than individual actions. The individual, the argument goes, is torn by conflicting feelings, impulses, and considerations. In his conduct, he is not always certain subjectively, much less correct objectively, in his knowledge of alternatives. Although it often changes its line of action, the social group is, by contrast, nevertheless determined at any one moment to follow, without reservation, the line of that moment. Above all, it always knows whom to consider its enemy and whom its friend. Furthermore, it shows less discrepancy than the individual between will and deed, and between means and ends. Individual actions, therefore, strike us as "free," and mass actions impress us as if they were determined by natural laws.

This whole formulation is highly questionable. Nevertheless, it merely exaggerates a real and highly significant difference between group and individual. The difference results from the fact that the aims of the public spirit, as of any collective, are those that usually strike the individual as if they were his own fundamentally simple and primitive aims. There are two reasons why this fact is so often not realized. One is the power that public aims have gained with the expansion of their range. The other is the highly complex techniques with which especially *modern* public life appeals to the individual intelligence when trying to put these aims into practice. The social group does not vacillate or err in *all* its aims, just as the individual does not in only his most *primitive* ones. The insurance of his existence, the acquisition of new property, the pleasure derived from the maintenance and expansion of his power, and the protection of his possessions are fundamental drives of the individual. In pursuing their satisfaction, he associates with an indefinite number of other individuals. It is because he does not choose these aspirations nor vacillate in their pursuit that the social aspiration, which unites him with others, knows no choice or vacillation either. Furthermore, just as the individual proceeds with clarity, determination, and certainty of aim in his purely egoistic actions, so the mass in regard to all of its aims. The mass does not know the dualism of egoistic and altruistic impulses, a dualism that often renders the individual helpless and makes him embrace a vacuum. Law, the first and essential condition of the life of groups, large and small, has aptly been called the "ethical minimum." As a matter of fact, the norms adequate to secure the continuation of the group (even if only precariously), constitute a bare minimum for the external existence of the individual as a social being. If he observed only them, without tying himself to a large number of additional laws, he would be an ethical abnormality, an utterly impossible being.

§ 2. *Individual vs. Group Member*

This consideration hints at the nature of the difference in level between the mass and the individual. The difference becomes clearly visible, and can be understood, on the basis of only one fact. This fact is the possibility of separating, in the individual himself, the qualities and behaviors by which he "forms" the "mass" and which he contributes to the collective spirit, on the one hand; and, on the other, different qualities which constitute his private property, as it were, and which lift him out of everything he may have in common with others. The first part of his nature can evidently consist only in more primitive elements, that are inferior in terms of finesse and intellectuality. This is so, above all, because it is the existence of these elements alone that we can be relatively sure of in *all* individuals. If the organic world gradually develops from lower to higher forms, the lower and more primitive ones, obviously, are the oldest. But thus, they are also the most widely diffused: the heredity of the species is the more certainly transmitted to the individual, the longer it has been in existence and has become fixed. By contrast, more recently acquired organs—such as the higher and more complex organs are to a much greater extent—always are more variable; and it is impossible to be sure whether all members of a given species already possess them. Thus the length of time during which a given trait has been inherited constitutes the real relation that exists between its primitive character and its diffusion. But we must consider not only biological heredity. There also are intellectual traits that manifest themselves in word and knowledge, in orientation of feeling, and in norms of will and judgment. As traditions, both conscious and unconscious, they permeate the individual; and the more so, the more generally, firmly, and unquestionably they have become parts of the intellectual life of his society—that is, the older they are. To this same extent, however, they are also less complex; they are coarser and closer to the immediate manifestations and necessities of life. As they become more refined and differentiated, they lose the probability of being the property of all. Rather, they become more or less individual, and are only accidentally shared with others.

§ 3. *Esteem of the Old and of the New*

This fundamental relationship is apt to explain a characteristic phenomenon of culture: the fact, namely, that both the old, and at the same time the new and rare, enjoy particular esteem. The esteem of the old needs little comment. Perhaps what has existed always and has been transmitted since time immemorial, owes the respect in which it is held not only to the patina of age, with its mystical-romantic fascination. It is also esteemed, precisely, because of the fact I stress here, namely, that it is also most widely diffused and most deeply rooted in the individual. It resides at or near the layer which is the soil of the individual's instinctive, undemonstrable, and irrefutable valuations. In early medieval litigations, for instance, the decision was generally made on the basis of the older of two contradictory royal charters. This was probably due, not so much to the conviction of the greater justice of the older document, as to the feeling that because of its greater age it had diffused justice more widely and had defined it more firmly than the more recent charter could have done. In other words, the older document enjoyed greater prestige because its longer existence was the real cause for its accord with the majority sentiment of justice. We will probably have to assume quite generally (in spite of all exceptions which certainly must be admitted) that the older is also the simpler, less specialized, and less articulated. We must also assume, then, that it is accessible to the mass at large not only for this reason but also because it *is* the older, that is, that which is more securely transmitted to the individual, externally and internally, and therefore is something apt to be justified and cherished as a matter of course.

Yet the same assumption also accounts for the opposite valuation. Lessing's dictum, "The first thoughts are everybody's thoughts," suggests that the thoughts which emerge in us instinctively, namely, from the most secure (because oldest) layers of our minds, are the most generally diffused. And this explains Lessing's derogatory tone when he speaks of them. For him, obviously, more valuable thoughts—those that exhibit an indissoluble interaction of individuality with newness—begin only beyond the primitive ones. Another example: in India we find that the social hierarchy of occupations depends on their age. The more recent occupations are esteemed more highly—presumably because they are more complex, refined, and difficult, and are therefore accessible only to the individual talent. To recapitulate: the reason for the esteem of the new and rare lies in the discriminatory power of our psychological make-up. Whatever attracts our consciousness, excites our interest, or increases our alertness, must somehow distinguish itself from what in and outside ourselves is matter-of-fact, everyday, and habitual.

§ 4. *The Sociological Significance of Individual Similarity and Dissimilarity*

It is above all the practical significance of men for one another that is determined by both similarities and differences among them. Similarity, as fact or as tendency, is no less important than difference. In the most varied forms, both are the great principles of all external and internal development. In fact, the cultural history of mankind can be conceived as the history of the struggles and conciliatory attempts between the two. For the actions of the individual, his difference from others is of far greater interest than is his similarity with them. It largely is differentiation from others that challenges and determines our activity. We depend on the observation of their differences if we want to use them and adopt the right attitude toward them. Our practical interest concentrates on what gives us advantages and disadvantages in our dealings with them, not on that in which we coincide. Similarity, rather, provides the indispensable condition for any developing action whatever. Darwin reports that in his many contacts with animal breeders he never met one who believed in the common origin of species. The interest in the slight variation that characterized the particular stock which he happened to breed and which constituted a practical value for him, so occupied his consciousness that it left no room for noting the basic similarity of this stock with other races and species. It is understandable that such an interest in the differentiae of his property should extend to all other possessions and relations of the individual. In general, we may say that if something is objectively of equal importance in terms of both similarity with a type and differentiation from it, we will be more conscious of the differentiation. In regard to the similarity, organic purposiveness perhaps proceeds without consciousness, because in practical life it needs all the consciousness there is for the awareness of differences. The interest in differentiation in fact is so great that in practice it produces differences where there is no objective basis for them. We note, for instance, that organizations, whether they be legislative bodies or committees in charge of "social functions," in spite of their outspoken and unifying positions and aims, are apt, in the course of time, to split up into factions; and these factions stand in relations to one another that are similar to those between the original organization as a whole and another organization with a totally different character. It is as if each individual largely felt his own significance only by contrasting himself with others. As a matter of fact, where such a contrast does not exist, he may even artificially create it. He may do so even when the whole solidarity and unity he now scans in his search for a contrast, derive from the existence of a united front that he and others have formed in opposition to another similar united front.

§ 5. *The Individual's Superiority over the Mass*

Countless additional examples from cultural and social history testify to the fact that the new, the rare, and the individual (merely three aspects, evidently, of the same fundamental phenomenon) are rated as the valuationally preferred. This discussion, however, only has the purpose of throwing light on the inverse phenomenon, the fact, that is, that the qualities and behaviors with which the individual forms a mass, because he shares them with others, are rated valuationally inferior. Here we deal with what might be called the sociological tragedy as such. The more refined, highly developed, articulated the qualities of an individual are, the more unlikely are they to make him similar to other individuals and to form a unit with corresponding qualities in others. Rather, they tend to become incomparable; and the elements, in terms of which the individual can count on adapting himself to others and on forming a homogeneous mass with them, are increasingly reduced to lower and primitively more sensuous levels. This explains how it is possible for the "folk" or the "mass" to be spoken of with contempt, without there being any need for the individual to feel himself referred to by this usage, which actually does not refer to any individual. As soon as the individual is considered in his entirety, he appears to possess much higher qualities than those he contributes to the collective unit. This situation has found its classical formulation in Schiller: "Seen singly, everybody is passably intelligent and reasonable; but united into a body, they are blockheads." The fact that individuals, in all their divergencies, leave only the lowest parts of their personalities to form a common denominator, is stressed by Heine: "You have rarely understood me, and rarely did I understand you. Only when we met in the mire did we understand each other at once."

This difference between the individual and the mass level is so profoundly characteristic of social existence and is of such important consequences that it is worthwhile quoting additional observations. They come from authorities of extremely different historical positions who are similar, however, in the sense that these positions gave them exceptional insight into collective phenomena. Solon is supposed to have said that each of his Athenians is a shrewd fox; but that, if assembled on the Pnyx, they amount to a herd of sheep. The Cardinal Retz, when describing the procedure of the Parisian parliament at the time of the *Fronde,* notes in his memoirs that numerous bodies, even if their members include many high-stationed and cultivated individuals, in common discussion and procedure always act as a mob, reverting to the conceptions and passions of the common people. Frederick the Great, in a remark that is very similar to that of Solon, says that his generals are the most reasonable people as long as he talks to them as individuals, but that they are "sheep-heads" when assembled in war council. Evidently something comparable is suggested by the English historian Freeman, who observes that the House of Commons, though an aristocratic body in terms of the ranks of its members, nevertheless, when assembled, behaves like a democratic rabble. The best authority on British trade unions notes that their mass assemblies often result in very stupid and pernicious resolutions, so that most of such meetings have been given up in favor of assemblies of delegates. This is confirmed by observations that are insignificant in their contents but are sociologically relevant, not only because of their frequency, but also because they symbolize historically very important situations and events. I shall give only a few examples. Eating and drinking, the oldest and intellectually most negligible functions, can form a tie, often the only one, among very heterogeneous persons and groups. Stag parties may be attended by highly cultivated individuals who, nevertheless, have the tendency to pass the time by telling off-color jokes. Among younger people, the peak of gaiety and harmony is always attained by means of the most primitive and intellectually least pretentious social games.

The difference between the individual and collective levels accounts for the fact that the necessity to oblige the masses, or even habitually to expose oneself to them, easily corrupts the character. It pulls the individual away from his individuality and down to a level with all and sundry. To consider it a questionable virtue of the journalist, the actor, and the demagogue to "seek the favor of the masses" would not be altogether justified if these masses consisted of the sum of the total personal existences of their members. For there is no reason whatever to despise *them*. But actually, the mass is no such sum. It is a new phenomenon made up, not of the total individualities of its members, but only of those fragments of each of them in which he coincides with all others. These fragments, therefore, can be nothing but the lowest and most primitive. It is *this* mass, and the level that must always remain accessible to each of its members, that these intellectually and morally endangered persons serve—and not each of its members in its entirety.

§ 6. *The Simplicity and Radicalism of the Mass*

Evidently, this level does not permit ways of behavior which presuppose a plurality of alternatives. All mass actions avoid detours. Successfully or not, they attack their aims by the shortest route. They always are dominated by one idea, and by as simple an idea as possible. It is hardly possible for every member of the mass to have the consciousness and conviction of a more varied complex of ideas which, in addition, is identical with that of everybody else. In view of the complex conditions under which we live, any idea that seeks to gain adherents must be radical, and must disregard a great many claims with which it is, or could be, confronted. It thus is understandable that in general, in periods of mass activation, radical parties should be powerful, and mediating parties that insist on the right of both sides, should be weak. It is exceedingly characteristic of the difference between the Greek and the Roman temper that the Greek citizens voted as a unified mass under the immediate impact of the orator, while the Romans voted in pre-established groups (*centuriatim, tributim,* etc.) that in a certain sense functioned as individuals. We thus understand the relative calm and reasonableness characteristic of Roman decisions, and the intransigence and passion that so frequently marked the Greeks. Yet this psychological harmony of the mass also produces certain negative virtues, whose opposite presupposes a plurality of simultaneously conscious alternatives. Thus, the mass neither lies nor simulates. Usually, however, and because of the same psychological constitution, it also lacks consciousness of responsibility.

§ 7. *The Emotionality of the Mass Appeal and of the Mass*

If one arranges psychological manifestations in a genetic and systematic hierarchy, one will certainly place, at its basis, feeling (though naturally not *all* feelings), rather than the intellect. Pleasure and pain, as well as certain instinctive feelings that serve the preservation of individual and species, have developed prior to all operation with concepts, judgments, and conclusions. Thus, the development of the intellect, more than anything else, reveals the lag of the social behind the individual level, whereas the realm of feeling may show the opposite. Carl Maria von Weber's statement about the public at large—"The individual is an ass, and yet the whole is the voice of God"—does not conflict with the appraisals of collective behavior that have been quoted earlier. For it expresses the experience of the musician, who appeals to the *feeling,* not to the intellect.

Whoever wants to affect the masses always succeeds by an appeal to their feelings, very rarely by theoretical discussion, however concise it may be. This is particularly true of masses that are together in physical proximity. They exhibit something one might call collective nervousness—a sensitivity, a passion, an eccentricity that will hardly ever be found in anyone of their members in isolation. The phenomenon has been observed even in animal herds: the softest wing beat, the slightest jump of a single animal often degenerate into a panic of the whole herd. Human crowds, too, are characterized by casual stimuli making for enormous effects, by the avalanche-like growth of the most negligible impulses of love and hate, by an objectively quite understandable excitation in the throes of which the mass blindly storms from thought to deed—by an excitation that carries the individual without meeting any resistance.

These phenomena must probably be traced to mutual influences through effusions of feeling that are hard to ascertain. Yet because they occur between each and all others, they come to cause, in every member of the mass, an excitation that cannot possibly be explained either in terms of him or of the matter at issue. It is one of the most revealing, purely sociological phenomena that the individual feels himself carried by the "mood" of the mass, as if by an external force that is quite indifferent to his own subjective being and wishing, and yet that the mass is exclusively composed of just such individuals. Their interaction pure and simple shows a dynamic, which because of its power appears as something objective. It conceals their own contributions from the interacting individuals. Actually the individual, by being carried away, carries away.

Such an extreme intensification of feeling due to mere physical proximity is shown, for instance, by the Quakers. Although the inwardness and subjectivism of their religion really oppose any sharing of worship, such a sharing nevertheless often emerges in their silent gatherings. The unintended feeling is justified by the suggestion that it serves to bring them closer to the spirit of God. Yet for them, such closeness can only come from inspiration and nervous exaltation. These feelings must therefore be evoked by mere physical proximity, even if it is silent. After describing certain ecstatic traits of a member of the assembly, a late seventeenth-century English Quaker suggests that, by virtue of the members' unification into one body, the ecstasy of an individual often spreads to all others. It thereby moves them deeply and fruitfully, and this irresistible experience, he writes, gains the association many members. Innumerable other cases teach us that a similar intensification of emotionality overpowers individual intellectuality. It is as if numbers in physical proximity multiplied the individual's feeling power. In the theatre or at other gatherings all of us laugh at jokes that, in a smaller company, would merely make us shrug our shoulders. What embarrassingly harmless quips scatter parliamentary records with the annotation "Laughter!" But not only critical but also moral inhibitions are easily suspended in this sociological state of inebriation. This suspension alone explains so-called mass crimes, of which, afterward, the individual participant declares himself innocent. He does so with good subjective conscience, and not even without some objective justification: the overpowering predominance of feeling destroyed the psychological forces that customarily sustain the consistency and stability of the person, and hence, his responsibility. Mass excitement, however, also has its ethically valuable aspect: it may produce a noble enthusiasm and an unlimited readiness to sacrifice. Yet this does not eliminate its distorted character and its irresponsibility. It only stresses our removal from the value standards that individual consciousness has developed, whether practically effective or not.

§ 8. *The Level of Society as the Approximation to the Lowest Common Level of its Members*

On the basis of all we have said so far, we can bring the formation of the social level under the following valuational formula: what is common to all can be the property of only those who possess least. This is symbolized even by the notion of "property" in its material sense. Thus, an English law of 1407 gave the initiative for monetary allotments to the House of Commons; and the constitutional historian of the period explicitly states that the fundamental motive for this act was the idea that it behooves the poorest of the three estates to determine the maximum limit of the financial burden to be carried by the general public. What all give equally can only be based on the quota of the poorest. Here, too, is the purely sociological among the various reasons for the phenomenon that the usurper, who wants to dominate a society that is stratified by estates, usually tries to gain support from the lowest classes. For, in order equally to rise above all, he must level all; and this he can achieve, not by raising the lower strata, but only by lowering the higher to the level of the lower.

It is thus quite misleading to designate the level of a society that considers itself a unit and practically operates as a unit, as an "average" level. The "average" would result from adding up the levels of the individuals and dividing the sum by their number. This procedure would involve a raising of the lowest individuals, which actually is impossible. In reality, the level of a society is very *close* to that of its lowest components, since it must be possible for all to participate in it with identical valuation and effectiveness. The character of collective behavior does not lie near the "middle" but near the lower limits of its participants. And if I am not mistaken, this accounts for the fact that the term "mediocrity" refers, not at all to the actual value average of a collection of individuals or achievements, but to a quality considerably below it.

Here we have room, of course, to cover only short tracts of the road of sociology, rather than all of it. Our treatment, in other words, does not aim at a definitive statement concerning the content of our science, but only at a sketch of the form and method of dealing with this content. I shall therefore limit myself to pointing out two of the many qualifications that must be mentioned in connection with the general conception of the formation of the social level that I have presented. In the first place, this level, as indicated, is practically almost never fixed by the very lowest among the group members. Rather, it only tends toward it, but usually stops somewhat above it, since the higher elements of the collective usually resist this descent, in however varying measures. Their countermovement results in the arrest of the collective action before it arrives at the lowest possible value.

More significant is another limitation of the scheme that must be recognized even if the principle of the scheme is correctly understood. We said that what all have and are can be the exclusive property only of the poorest. Therefore, the creation of the mass, that is, the leveling of heterogeneous persons, can be brought about only by the lowering of the higher elements, which is always possible, rather than by the raising of the lower elements, which is rarely if ever possible. This psychological mechanism, however, must be questioned. For the lowering of the higher elements actually is *not* always possible. Our whole discussion was based on the conception (which naturally was very crude and even problematical) of a psychological structure consisting of several layers. At its bottom we placed the primitive, unintellectual elements, which biologically are more certain than any others and which therefore can be presupposed to exist everywhere. On top of them we placed the rarer, more recent, and more refined elements that eventually are differentiated to the point of complete individuality. This allowed us to conceive of the possibility that even in the case of the highest development of the latter they could consciously or unconsciously be eliminated, and the behavior of the individual could exclusively be determined by the former. Thus, a homogeneous group spirit could result from contributions which had become identical.

Yet this whole process may occur sometimes, or even often, but it does not occur always. For in some individuals, the lower elements are so interfused with the higher ones that the tempting physical analogy, according to which man can always easily descend but can ascend only with difficulty and sometimes not at all, becomes quite inapplicable. This is at once evident in the field of ethics. Here, such traits as the desire for pleasure, cruelty, acquisitiveness, and mendacity are lowest in the psychological hierarchy. To a decent man, even if he should not be free of residues or suppressed fragments of such traits, it is simply impossible to be motivated by them in his actions or even to lower his level casually, and thereby to suspend his higher qualities. Such impossibility, however, is found far beyond the field of ethics. However true it may be that the valet does not understand the hero because he cannot rise to his height, it is equally true that the hero does not understand the valet because he cannot lower himself to his subordinate level.

In general, it is very revealing to distinguish men according to their capacity or incapacity to suppress their most valuable powers and interests in favor of their lower qualities which certainly exist in them in varying degrees. The incapacity to do so, at any rate, is one of the main reasons why at all times certain noble and intellectual personalities have kept aloof from public life. In spite of the possibility of their roles as leaders, they must have felt what a great statesman once formulated in regard to his party when he said: "I am their leader, therefore I must follow them." In spite of Bismarck's dictum that "politics corrupts character," however, this aloofness does not by itself imply that these abstinent individuals are generally more valuable than are more public-minded persons. It rather reveals a certain weakness and lack of confidence in his higher elements, if the individual does not dare descend far enough toward the social level to be prepared for the fight against the social level—which is always a fight *for* it. And evidently, the fact that men of the highest individual caliber so often avoid contact with the social level delays its general rise.

Chapter 3

Sociability

An Example of Pure, or Formal, Sociology

IN THE INTRODUCTORY
chapter, I mentioned the motive which is responsible for the
constitution of "pure sociology" as a specific problem area. This
motive must now be formulated once more before an example
of its application is given. For in its capacity of one among many
principles of investigating it, it not only determines this example;
what is more, the motive itself furnishes the *material* of the application to be described.

§ 1. *Contents (Materials) vs. Forms of Social Life*

The motive derives from two propositions. One is that in
any human society one can distinguish between its content and
its form. The other is that society itself, in general, refers to the
interaction among individuals. This interaction always arises on
the basis of certain drives or for the sake of certain purposes.
Erotic instincts, objective interests, religious impulses, and purposes of defense or attack, of play or gain, of aid or instruction,
and countless others cause man to live with other men, to act
for them, with them, against them, and thus to arrange their conditions reciprocally—in brief, to influence others and to be
influenced by them. The significance of these interactions lies
in their causing the individuals who possess those instincts, interests, etc., to form a unit—precisely, a "society." Everything
present in the individuals (who are the immediate, concrete data
of all historical reality) in the form of drive, interest, purpose,
inclination, psychic state, movement—everything that is present
in them in such a way as to engender or mediate effects upon

others or to receive such effects, I designate as the *content*, as the *material*, as it were, of sociation. In themselves, these materials with which life is filled, the motivations by which it is propelled, are not social. Strictly speaking, neither hunger nor love, neither work nor religiosity, neither technology nor the functions and results of intelligence, are social. They are factors in sociation only when they transform the mere aggregation of isolated individuals into specific forms of being with and for one another—forms that are subsumed under the general concept of interaction. Sociation thus is the form (realized in innumerable, different ways) in which individuals grow together into units that satisfy their interests. These interests, whether they are sensuous or ideal, momentary or lasting, conscious or unconscious, causal or teleological, form the basis of human societies.

§ 2. *The Autonomization of Contents*

These facts have very far-reaching consequences. On the basis of practical conditions and necessities, our intelligence, will, creativity, and feeling work on the materials that we wish to wrest from life. In accord with our purposes, we give these materials certain forms and only in these forms operate and use them as elements of our lives. But it happens that these materials, these forces and interests, in a peculiar manner remove themselves from the service of life that originally produced and employed them. They become autonomous in the sense that they are no longer inseparable from the objects which they formed and thereby made available to our purposes. They come to play freely in themselves and for their own sake; they produce or make use of materials that exclusively serve their own operation or realization.

For instance, originally all cognition appears to have been a means in the struggle for existence. Exact knowledge of the behavior of things is, in fact, of extraordinary utility for the maintenance and promotion of life. Yet cognition is no longer used in the service of this practical achievement: science has become a value in itself. It quite autonomously chooses its objects, shapes them according to its own needs, and is interested in nothing beyond its own perfection. Another example: the interpretation of realities, concrete or abstract, in terms of spatial systems, or of rhythms or sounds, or of significance and organization, certainly had its origins in practical needs. Yet these interpretations have become purposes in themselves, effective on their own strength and in their own right, selective and creative quite independently of their entanglement with practical life, and not because of it. This is the origin of art. Fully established, art is wholly separated from life. It takes from it only what it can use, thus creating itself, as it were, a second time. And yet the forms by means of which it does this and of which it actually consists, were produced by the exigencies and the very dynamics of life.

The same dialectic determines the nature of law. The requirements of social existence compel or legitimate certain types of individual behavior which thus are valid and followed, precisely because they meet these practical requirements. Yet with the emergence of "law," this reason for their diffusion recedes into the background: now they are followed simply because they have become the "law," and quite independently of the life which originally engendered and directed them. The furthest pole of this development is expressed by the idea of *"fiat justitia, pereat mundus"* [justice be done, even if the world perish]. In other words, although lawful behavior has its roots in the purposes of social life, law, properly speaking, has no "purpose," since it is not a means to an ulterior end. On the contrary, it determines, in its own right and not by legitimation through any higher, extrinsic agency, how the contents of life should be shaped.

This complete turnover, from the determination of the forms by the materials of life to the determination of its materials by forms that have become supreme values, is perhaps most extensively at work in the numerous phenomena that we lump together under the category of *play*. Actual forces, needs, impulses of life produce the forms of our behavior that are suitable for play. These forms, however, become independent contents and stimuli within play itself or, rather, *as* play. There are, for instance, the hunt; the gain by ruse; the proving of physical and intellectual strength; competition; and the dependence on chance and on the favor of powers that cannot be influenced.

All these forms are lifted out of the flux of life and freed of their material with its inherent gravity. On their own decision, they choose or create the objects in which they prove or embody themselves in their purity. This is what gives play both its gaiety and the symbolic significance by which it is distinguished from mere joke. Here lies whatever may justify the analogy between art and play. In both art and play, forms that were originally developed by the realities of life, have created spheres that preserve their autonomy in the face of these realities. It is from their origin, which keeps them permeated with life, that they draw their depth and strength. Where they are emptied of life, they become artifice and "empty play," respectively. Yet their significance and their very nature derive from that fundamental change through which the forms engendered by the purposes and materials of life, are separated from them, and themselves become the purpose and the material of their own existence. From the realities of life they take only what they can adapt to their own nature, only what they can absorb in their autonomous existence.

§ 3. *Sociability as the Autonomous Form, or Play-Form, of Sociation*

This process also is at work in the separation of what I have called content and form in societal existence. Here, "society," properly speaking, is that being with one another, for one another, against one another which, through the vehicle of drives or purposes, forms and develops material or individual contents and interests. The forms in which this process results gain their own life. It is freed from all ties with contents. It exists for its own sake and for the sake of the fascination which, in its own liberation from these ties, it diffuses. It is precisely the phenomenon that we call sociability.

Certainly, specific needs and interests make men band together in economic associations, blood brotherhoods, religious societies, hordes of bandits. Yet in addition to their specific contents, all these sociations are also characterized, precisely, by a feeling, among their members, of being sociated and by the satisfaction derived from this. Sociates feel that the formation

of a society as such is a value; they are driven toward this form
of existence. In fact, it sometimes is only this drive itself that
suggests the concrete contents of a particular sociation. What
may be called the art drive, extracts out of the totality of phenomena their mere form, in order to shape it into specific structures that correspond to this drive. In similar fashion, out of the
realities of social life, the "sociability drive" extracts the pure
process of sociation as a cherished value; and thereby it constitutes sociability in the stricter sense of the word. It is no mere
accident of linguistic usage that even the most primitive sociability, if it is of any significance and duration at all, places
so much emphasis on *form,* on "good form." For form is the
mutual determination and interaction of the elements of the
association. It is form by means of which they create a unit. The
actual, life-conditioned motivations of sociation are of no significance to sociability. It is, therefore, understandable that the
pure form, the individuals' suspended, interacting interre-
latedness (we might say), is emphasized the more strongly and
effectively.

Sociability is spared the frictions with reality by its merely
formal relation to it. Yet just because of this, it derives from
reality, even to the mind of the more sensitive person, a significance and a symbolic, playful richness of life that are the
greater, the more perfect it is. A superficial rationalism always
looks for this richness among concrete *contents* only. Since it does
not find it there, it dispenses with sociability as a shallow foolish-
ness. Yet it cannot be without significance that in many, perhaps
in all European languages, "society" simply designates a *sociable*
gathering. Certainly, the political, economic, the purposive society of whatever description, is a "society." But only the "sociable society" is "a society" without qualifying adjectives.[4] It is
this, precisely because it represents the pure form that is raised
above all contents such as characterize those more "concrete"
"societies." It gives us an abstract image in which all contents
are dissolved in the mere play of form.

[4] *"Gesellschaft"* is both "society" and "party" (in the sense of "social, or
sociable, gathering").—Tr.

[a] UNREALITY, TACT, IMPERSONALITY

As a sociological category, I thus designate sociability as the *play-form of sociation*. Its relation to content-determined, concrete sociation is similar to that of the work of art to reality. The great, perhaps the greatest, problem of society finds in it a solution which is possible nowhere else. This problem is the question concerning the proportions of significance and weight that, in the total life of the individual, are properly his, and properly those of his social sphere's. Inasmuch as in the purity of its manifestations, sociability has no objective purpose, no content, no extrinsic results, it entirely depends on the personalities among whom it occurs. Its aim is nothing but the success of the sociable moment and, at most, a memory of it. Hence the conditions and results of the process of sociability are exclusively the persons who find themselves at a social gathering. Its character is determined by such personal qualities as amiability, refinement, cordiality, and many other sources of attraction. But precisely because everything depends on their personalities, the participants are not permitted to stress them too conspicuously. Where specific interests (in cooperation or collision) determine the social form, it is these interests that prevent the individual from presenting his peculiarity and uniqueness in too unlimited and independent a manner. Where there are no such interests, their function must be taken over by other conditions. In sociability, these derive from the mere form of the gathering. Without the reduction of personal poignancy and autonomy brought about by this form, the gathering itself would not be possible. *Tact*, therefore, is here of such a peculiar significance: where no external or immediate egoistic interests direct the self-regulation of the individual in his personal relations with others, it is tact that fulfills this regulatory function. Perhaps its most essential task is to draw the limits, which result from the claims of others, of the individual's impulses, ego-stresses, and intellectual and material desires.

Sociability emerges as a very peculiar sociological structure. The fact is that whatever the participants in the gathering may possess in terms of objective attributes—attributes that are centered outside the particular gathering in question—must not enter it. Wealth, social position, erudition, fame, exceptional capabilities and merits, may not play any part in sociability. At most they may perform the role of mere nuances of that immaterial character with which reality alone, in general, is allowed to enter the social work of art called sociability. But in addition to these objective elements that, as it were, surround the personality, the purely and deeply personal traits of one's life, character, mood, and fate must likewise be eliminated as factors in sociability. It is tactless, because it militates against *inter*action which monopolizes sociability, to display merely personal moods of depression, excitement, despondency—in brief, the light and the darkness of one's most intimate life. This exclusion of the most personal element extends even to certain external features of behavior. Thus, for instance, at an intimately personal and friendly meeting with one or several men, a lady would not appear in as low-cut a dress as she wears without any embarrassment at a larger party. The reason is that at the party she does not feel involved as an individual to the same extent as she does at the more intimate gathering, and that she can therefore afford to abandon herself as if in the impersonal freedom of a mask: although being *only* herself she is yet not *wholly* herself, but only an element in a group that is held together *formally*.

[b] "SOCIABILITY THRESHOLDS"

Man in his totality is a dynamic complex of ideas, forces, and possibilities. According to the motivations and relations of life and its changes, he makes of himself a differentiated and clearly defined phenomenon. As an economic and political man, as a family member, and as the representative of an occupation he is, as it were, an elaboration constructed *ad hoc*. In each of these capacities, the material of his life is determined by a particular idea and is cast into a particular form. Yet, the relative autonomy of his roles feeds on a common source of his energy, which is difficult to label. Sociable man, too, is a peculiar phenomenon; it exists nowhere except in sociable relations. On the one hand, man has here cast off all objective qualifications of his personality. He enters the form of sociability equipped only with the capacities, attractions, and interests with which his pure human-ness provides him. On the other hand, however, sociability also shies away from the entirely subjective and purely inwardly spheres of his personality. Discretion, which is the first condition of sociability in regard to one's behavior toward others, is equally much required in regard to one's dealing with oneself: in both cases, its violation causes the sociological art form of sociability to degenerate into a sociological naturalism. One thus may speak of the individual's upper and lower *"sociability thresholds."* These thresholds are passed both when individuals interact from motives of objective content and purpose and when their entirely personal and subjective aspects make themselves felt. In both cases, sociability ceases to be the central and formative principle of their sociation and becomes, at best, a formalistic, superficially mediating connection.

[c] THE "SOCIABILITY DRIVE" AND THE DEMOCRATIC NATURE OF SOCIABILITY

Perhaps it is possible, however, to find the positive formal motive of sociability which corresponds to its negative determination by limits and thresholds. As the foundation of law, Kant posited the axiom that each individual should possess freedom to the extent which is compatible with the freedom of every other individual. If we apply this principle to the sociability drive (as the source or substance of sociability itself), we might say that each individual ought to have as much satisfaction of this drive as is compatible with its satisfaction on the part of all others. We can also express this thought not in terms of the sociability drive itself but in terms of its results. We then formulate the principle of sociability as the axiom that each individual should *offer* the maximum of sociable values (of joy, relief, liveliness, etc.) that is compatible with the maximum of values he himself *receives*.

Just as Kant's law is thoroughly democratic, this principle, too, shows the democratic structure of all sociability. Yet, this democratic character can be realized only within a given social stratum: sociability among members of very different social strata often is inconsistent and painful. Equality, as we have seen, results from the elimination of both the wholly personal and the wholly objective, that is, from the elimination of the very material of sociation from which sociation is freed when it takes on the form of sociability. Yet the democracy of sociability even among social equals is only something *played*. Sociability, if one will, creates an ideal sociological world in which the pleasure of the individual is closely tied up with the pleasure of the others. In principle, nobody can find satisfaction here if it has to be at the cost of diametrically opposed feelings which the other may have. This possibility, to be sure, is excluded by many social forms other than sociability. In all of these, however, it is excluded through some superimposed ethical imperative. In sociability alone is it excluded by the intrinsic principle of the social form itself.

[d] THE ARTIFICIAL WORLD OF SOCIABILITY

Yet, this world of sociability—the only world in which a democracy of the equally privileged is possible without frictions—is an *artificial* world. It is composed of individuals who have no other desire than to create wholly pure interaction with others which is not disbalanced by a stress of anything material. We may have the erroneous notion that we enter sociability purely "as men," as what we really are, without all the burdens, conflicts, all the too-much and too-little which in actual life disturb the purity of our images. We may get this notion because modern life is overburdened with objective contents and exigencies. And forgetting these daily encumbrances at a social gathering, we fancy ourselves to return to our natural-personal existence. But under this impression we also forget that sociable man is constituted by this personal aspect, not in its specific character and in its naturalistic completeness, but only in a certain reservedness and stylization. In earlier periods of history, sociable man did not have to be wrested from so many objective and contentual claims. His form, therefore, emerged more fully and distinctly in contrast with his *personal* existence: behavior at a social gathering was much stiffer, more ceremonial, and more severely regulated super-individually than it is today. This reduction of the personal character which homogeneous interaction with others imposes on the individual may even make him lean over backward, if we may say so: a characteristically sociable behavior trait is the courtesy with which the strong and extraordinary individual not only makes himself the equal of the weaker, but even acts as if the weaker were the more valuable and superior.

If sociation itself is interaction, its purest and most stylized expression occurs among equals—as symmetry and balance are the most plausible forms of artistic stylization. Inasmuch as it is abstracted from sociation through art or play, sociability thus calls for the purest, most transparent, and most casually appealing kind of interaction, *that among equals*. Because of its very nature, it must create human beings who give up so much of their objective contents and who so modify their external and internal significance as to become sociable equals. Each of them must gain for himself sociability values only if the others with whom he interacts also gain them. Sociability is the game in which one "does as if" all were equal, and at the same time, as if one honored each of them in particular. And to "do as if" is no more a lie than play or art are lies because of their deviation from reality. The game becomes a lie only when sociable action and speech are made into mere instruments of the intentions and events of practical reality—just as a painting becomes a lie when it tries, in a panoramic effect, to simulate reality. What is perfectly correct and in order if practised within the autonomous life of sociability with its self-contained play of forms, becomes a deceptive lie when it is guided by non-sociable purposes or is designed to disguise such purposes. The actual entanglement of sociability with the events of real life surely makes such a deception often very tempting.

[e] SOCIAL GAMES

The connection between sociability and play explains why sociability should cover all phenomena that already by themselves may be considered sociological play-forms. This refers above all to games proper, which in the sociability of all times have played a conspicuous role. The expression *"social* game" is significant in the deeper sense to which I have already called attention. All the forms of interaction or sociation among men—the wish to outdo, exchange, the formation of parties, the desire to wrest something from the other, the hazards of accidental meetings and separations, the change between enmity and co-operation, the overpowering by ruse and revenge—in the seriousness of reality, all of these are imbued with purposive contents. In the game, they lead their own lives; they are propelled exclusively by their own attraction. For even where the game involves a monetary stake, it is not the money (after all, it could be acquired in many ways other than gambling) that is the specific characteristic of the game. To the person who really enjoys it, its attraction rather lies in the dynamics and hazards of the sociologically significant forms of activity themselves. The more profound, double sense of "social game" is that not only the game is played in a society (as its external medium) but that, with its help, people actually "play" "society."

[f] COQUETRY

In the sociology of sex, we find a play-form: the play-form of eroticism is coquetry. In sociability, it finds its most facile, playful, and widely diffused realization.[5] Generally speaking, the erotic question between the sexes is that of offer and refusal. Its objects are, of course, infinitely varied and graduated, and by no means mere either-ors, much less exclusively physiological. The nature of feminine coquetry is to play up, alternately, allusive promises and allusive withdrawals—to attract the male but always to stop short of a decision, and to reject him but never to deprive him of all hope. The coquettish woman enormously enhances her attractiveness if she shows her consent as an almost immediate possibility but is ultimately not serious about it. Her behavior swings back and forth between "yes" and "no" without stopping at either. She playfully exhibits the pure and simple form of erotic decisions and manages to embody their polar opposites in a perfectly consistent behavior: its decisive, well-understood content, that would commit her to one of the two opposites, does not even enter.

This freedom from all gravity of immutable contents and permanent realities gives coquetry the character of suspension,

[5] I have treated coquetry extensively in my book, *Philosophische Kultur* [Philosophic Culture].

distance, ideality, that has led one to speak, with a certain right, of its "art," not only of its "artifices." Yet in order for coquetry to grow on the soil of sociability, as we know from experience it does, it must meet with a specific behavior on the part of the male. As long as he rejects its attractions or, inversely, is its mere victim that without any will of his own is dragged along by its vacillations between a half "yes" and a half "no," coquetry has not yet assumed for him the form that is commensurate with sociability. For it lacks the free interaction and equivalence of elements that are the fundamental traits of sociability. It does not attain these until he asks for no more than this freely suspended play which only dimly reflects the erotically definitive as a remote symbol; until he is no longer attracted by the lust for the erotic element or by the fear of it which is all he can see in the coquettish allusions and preliminaries. Coquetry that unfolds its charms precisely at the height of sociable civilization has left far behind the reality of erotic desire, consent, or refusal; it is embodied in the interaction of the mere silhouettes, as it were, of their serious imports. Where they themselves enter or are constantly present in the background, the whole process becomes a private affair between two individuals: it takes place on the plane of reality. But under the sociological sign of sociability from which the center of the personality's concrete and complete life is barred, coquetry is the flirtatious, perhaps ironical play, in which eroticism has freed the bare outline of its interactions from their materials and contents and personal features. As sociability plays with the forms of society, so coquetry plays with those of eroticism, and this affinity of their natures predestines coquetry as an element of sociability.

[g] CONVERSATION

Outside sociability, the sociological forms of interaction are significant in terms of their contents. Sociability abstracts these forms and supplies them—which circle around themselves, as it were—with shadowy bodies. The extent to which it attains this aim—becomes evident, finally, in *conversation,* the most general vehicle for all that men have in common. The decisive point here can be introduced by stressing the very trivial experience that people talk seriously because of some content they want to communicate or come to an understanding about, while at a social gathering they talk for the sake of talking. There, talk becomes its own purpose; but not in the naturalistic sense that would make it mere chatter, but as the *art* of conversation that has its own, artistic laws. In purely sociable conversation, the topic is merely the indispensable medium through which the lively exchange of speech itself unfolds its attractions. All the forms in which this exchange is realized—quarrel, appeal to norms recognized by both parties, pacification by compromise and by discovery of common convictions, grateful acceptance of the new, and covering up of anything on which no understanding can be hoped for—all these forms usually are in the service of the countless contents and purposes of human life. But here, they derive their significance from themselves, from the fascinating play of relations which they create among the participants, joining and loosening, winning and succumbing, giving and taking. The double sense of *"sich unterhalten"* [6] becomes understandable. For conversation to remain satisfied with mere form it cannot allow any content to become significant in its own right. As soon as the discussion becomes objective, as soon as it makes the ascertainment of a truth its *purpose* (it may very well be its *content*), it ceases to be sociable and thus becomes untrue to its own nature—as much as if it degenerated into a serious quarrel. The *form* of the ascertainment of a truth or of a quarrel may exist, but the seriousness of their contents may as little become the focus of sociable conversation as a perspectivistic painting may contain a piece of the actual, three-dimensional reality of its object.

This does not imply that the content of sociable conversation is indifferent. On the contrary, it must be interesting, fascinating, even important. But it may not become the purpose of the conversation, which must never be after an objective result. The objective result leads an ideal existence, as it were, outside of it. Therefore, of two externally similar conversations, only that is

---

[6] This double sense is not obvious in English. *"Unterhalten"* literally is "to hold under," "to sustain." Customarily, however, *"sich unterhalten"* is "to entertain or enjoy oneself," as well as "to converse." This is the double sense Simmel emphasizes.—Tr.

(properly speaking) sociable, in which the topic, in spite of all its value and attraction, finds its right, place, and purpose only in the functional play of the conversation itself that sets its own norms and has its own peculiar significance. The ability to change topics easily and quickly is therefore part of the nature of social conversation. For since the topic is merely a means, it exhibits all the fortuitousness and exchangeability that characterize all means as compared with fixed ends. As has already been mentioned, sociability presents perhaps the only case in which talk is its own legitimate purpose. Talk presupposes two parties; it is two-way. In fact, among all sociological phenomena whatever, with the possible exception of looking at one another, talk is the purest and most sublimated form of two-way-ness. It thus is the fulfillment of a relation that wants to be nothing but relation—in which, that is, what usually is the mere form of interaction becomes its self-sufficient content. Hence even the telling of stories, jokes, and anecdotes, though often only a pastime if not a testimonial of intellectual poverty, can show all the subtle tact that reflects the elements of sociability. It keeps the conversation away from individual intimacy and from all purely personal elements that cannot be adapted to sociable requirements. And yet, objectivity is cultivated not for the sake of any particular content but only in the interest of sociability itself. The telling and reception of stories, etc., is not an end in itself but only a means for the liveliness, harmony, and common consciousness of the "party." It not only provides a content in which all can participate alike; it also is a particular individual's gift to the group—but a gift behind which its giver becomes invisible: the subtlest and best-told stories are those from which the narrator's personality has completely vanished. The perfect anecdote attains a happy equilibrium of sociable ethics, as it were, with its complete absorption of both subjective-individual and objective-contentual elements in the service of pure sociable form.

[h] SOCIABILITY AS THE PLAY-FORM OF ETHICAL PROBLEMS
AND OF THEIR SOLUTION

Thus sociability also emerges as the play-form of the ethical forces in concrete society. In particular, there are two problems that must be solved by these forces. One is the fact that the individual has to function as part of a collective for which he lives; but that, in turn, he derives his own values and improvements from this collective. The other is the fact that the life of the individual is a roundabout route for the purposes of the whole; but that the life of the whole, in turn, has this same function for the purposes of the individual. Sociability transfers the serious, often tragic character of these problems into the symbolic play of its shadowy realm which knows no frictions, since shadows, being what they are, cannot collide. Another ethical task of sociation is to make the joining and breaking-up of sociated individuals the exact reflection of the relations among these individuals, although these relations are spontaneously determined by life in its totality. In sociability, this freedom to form relations and this adequacy of their expression are relieved of any concrete contentual determinants. The ways in which groups form and split up and in which conversations, called forth by mere impulse and occasion, begin, deepen, loosen, and terminate at a social gathering give a miniature picture of the societal ideal that might be called the freedom to be tied down. If all convergence and divergence are strictly commensurate with inner realities, at a "party" they exist in the absence of these realities. There is left nothing but a phenomenon whose play obeys the laws of its own form and whose charm is contained in itself. It shows *aesthetically* that same commensurateness which those inner realities require as *ethical* commensurateness.

[i] HISTORICAL ILLUSTRATIONS

Our general conception of sociability is well illustrated by certain historical developments. In the early German Middle Ages, there existed brotherhoods of knights. They consisted of patrician families that entertained friendly relations with one another. The originally religious and practical purposes of these groups seem to have been lost fairly early. By the fourteenth century, *knightly* interests and ways of behavior alone were left as their contentual characteristics. Soon afterward, however, even they disappeared, and there remained nothing but purely sociable aristocratic associations. Here then, evidently, is a case where sociability developed as the residuum of a society that had been determined by its content. It is a residuum which, since all content was lost, could consist only of the form and forms of reciprocal behavior.

The fact that the autonomy of such forms is bound to exhibit the nature of play or, more deeply, of art, becomes even more striking in the courtly society of the *Ancien Régime*. Here, the disappearance of any concrete content of life—which royalty, so to speak, had sucked out of French aristocracy—resulted in the emergence of certain freely suspended forms. The consciousness of the nobility became crystallized in them. Their forces, characteristics, and relations were purely sociable. They were by no means symbols or functions of any real significances or intensities of persons and institutions. The etiquette of courtly society had become a value in itself. It no longer referred to any content; it had developed its own, intrinsic laws, which were comparable to the laws of art. The laws of art are valid only in terms of art: by no means have they the purpose of imitating the reality of the models, of things outside of art itself.

[j] THE "SUPERFICIAL" CHARACTER OF SOCIABILITY

In the *Ancien Régime,* sociability attained perhaps its most sovereign expression. At the same time, however, this expression came close to being its own caricature. Certainly, it is the nature of sociability to free concrete interactions from any reality and to erect its airy realm according to the form-laws of these relations, which come to move in themselves and to recognize no purpose extraneous to them. Yet the deep spring which feeds this realm and its play does not lie in these forms, but exclusively in the vitality of concrete individuals, with all their feelings and attractions, convictions and impulses. Sociability is a *symbol* of life as life emerges in the flux of a facile and happy play; yet it also is a symbol of *life*. It does not change the image of life beyond the point required by its own distance to it. In like manner, if it is not to strike one as hollow and false, even the freest and most fantastic art, however far it is from any copying of reality, nevertheless feeds on a deep and loyal relation to this reality. Art, too, is *above* life, but it is also above *life*. If sociability entirely cuts its ties with the reality of life out of which it makes its own fabric (of however different a style), it ceases to be a play and becomes a desultory playing-around with empty forms, a lifeless schematism which is even proud of its lifelessness.

Our discussion shows that people both rightly and wrongly lament the *superficiality* of sociable intercourse. To account for this, we must remember and appreciate one of the most impressive characteristics of intellectual life. This is the fact that if certain elements are taken out of the totality of existence and united into a whole that lives by its own laws and not by those of the totality, it shows, if it is completely severed from the life of that totality, a hollow and rootless nature, in spite of all intrinsic perfection. And yet, and often only by an imponderable change, this same whole, in its very distance from immediate reality, may more completely, consistently, and realistically reveal the deepest nature of this reality than could any attempt at grasping it more directly. Applying this consideration to the phenomenon of sociability, we understand that we may have two different reactions to it. Accordingly, the independent and self-regulated life, which the superficial aspects of social interaction attain in sociability, will strike us as a formula-like and irrelevant lifelessness, or as a symbolic play whose aesthetic charms embody the finest and subtlest dynamics of broad, rich social existence.

In regard to art, in regard to all the symbolism of religious and church life, and to a large extent even in regard to the formulations of science, we depend on a certain faith, or feeling, which assures us that the intrinsic norms of fragments or the combinations of superficial elements do possess a connection with the depth and wholeness of reality. Although it can often not be formulated, it nevertheless is this connection which makes of fragments embodiments and representations of the immediately real and fundamental life. It accounts for the redeeming and relieving effect that some of the realms, constructed of mere forms of life, have on us: although in them we are unburdened of life, we nevertheless *have* it. Thus, the view of the sea frees us internally, not in spite, but because of the fact that the swelling and ebbing and the play and counterplay of the waves stylize life into the simplest expression of its dynamics. This expression is quite free from all experienceable reality and from all the gravity of individual fate, whose ultimate significance seems yet to flow into this picture of the sea. Art similarly seems to reveal the mystery of life, the fact, that is, that we cannot be relieved of life by merely looking away from it, but only by shaping and experiencing the sense and the forces of its deepest reality in the unreal and seemingly quite autonomous play of its forms.

To so many serious persons who are constantly exposed to the pressures of life, sociability could not offer any liberating, relieving, or serene aspects if it really were nothing but an escape from life or a merely momentary suspension of life's seriousness. Perhaps it often *is* no more than a negative conventionalism, an essentially lifeless exchange of formulas. Perhaps it frequently was this in the *Ancien Régime* when the numb fear of a threatening reality forced men merely to look away and to sever all relations with it. Yet it is precisely the more serious person who derives from sociability a feeling of liberation and relief. He can do so because he enjoys here, as if in an art play, a concentration and exchange of effects that present all the tasks and all the seriousness of life in a sublimation and, at the same time, dilution, in which the content-laden forces of reality reverberate only dimly, since their gravity has evaporated into mere attractiveness.

Chapter 4

Individual and Society in Eighteenth- and Nineteenth-Century Views of Life

An Example of Philosophical Sociology

§ 1. *Individual Life as the Basis of the Conflict between Individual and Society*

THE REALLY PRACTICAL problem of society is the relation between its forces and forms and the individual's own life. The question is not whether society exists only in the individuals or also outside of them. For even if we attribute "life," properly speaking, only to individuals, and identify the life of society with that of its individual members, we must still admit the existence of conflict between the two. One reason for this conflict is the fact that, in the individuals themselves, social elements fuse into the particular phenomenon called "society." "Society" develops its own vehicles and organs by whose claims and commands the individual is confronted as by an alien party. A second reason results from another aspect of the inherency of society in the individual. For man has the capacity to decompose himself into parts and to feel any one of these as his proper self. Yet each part may collide with any other and may struggle for the dominion over the individual's actions. This capacity places man, insofar as he feels himself to be a social being, into an often contradictory relation with those among his impulses and interests that are *not* preempted by his social character. In other words, the conflict between society and individual

58

is continued in the individual himself as the conflict among his component parts. Thus, it seems to me, the basic struggle between society and individual inheres in the general form of individual life. It does not derive from any single, "anti-social," individual interest.

Society strives to be a whole, an organic unit of which the individuals must be mere members. Society asks of the individual that he employ all his strength in the service of the special function which he has to exercise as a member of it; that he so modify himself as to become the most suitable vehicle for this function. Yet the drive toward unity and wholeness that is characteristic of the individual himself rebels against this role. The individual strives to be rounded out in himself, not merely to help to round out society. He strives to develop his full capacities, irrespective of the shifts among them that the interest of society may ask of him. This conflict between the whole, which imposes the one-sidedness of partial function upon its elements, and the part, which itself strives to be a whole, is insoluble. No house can be built of houses, but only of specially formed stones; no tree can grow from trees, but only from differentiated cells.

§ 2. *Individual Egoism vs. Individual Self-Perfection as an Objective Value*

The formulation presented seems to me to describe the contrast between the two parties much more comprehensively than does its customary reduction to the egoism-altruism dichotomy. On the one hand, the individual's striving for wholeness appears as egoism, which is contrasted with the altruism of his ordering himself into society as a selectivity formed social member of it. Yet on the other hand, the very quest of society is an egoism that does violence to the individual for the benefit and utility of the many, and that often makes for an extremely one-sided individual specialization, and even atrophy. Finally, the individual's urge toward self-perfection is not necessarily an expression of egoism. It may also be an objective ideal whose goal is by no means success in terms of happiness and narrowly personal interests but a super-personal value realized in the personality.

What has just been suggested—and what will be elaborated

presently—appears to me to exemplify a very significant stage in the development of cultural-philosophical consciousness. It also throws new light on the ethics of the individual and, indirectly, on the ethics of society. It is popularly held that all intentions which do not break through the orbit of the individual existence and interest are of an egoistic nature, and that egoism is overcome only when concern shifts toward the welfare of the Thou or of society. Yet it is already some time that a deeper reflection on the values of life has ascertained a third alternative, most impressively perhaps in the figures of Goethe and Nietzsche (though not in any abstract formula). It is the possibility that the perfection of the individual as such constitutes an objective value, quite irrespective of its significance for any other individuals, or in merely accidental connection with it. This value, moreover, may exist in utter disregard for the happiness or unhappiness of this individual himself, or may even be in conflict with them. What a person represents in terms of strength, nobility of character, achievement, or harmony of life, is very often quite unrelated to what he or others "get out" of these qualities. All that can be said about them is that the world is enriched by the existence in it of a valuable human being who is perfect in himself. Certainly, his value often consists in his practical devotion to other individuals or groups; but to limit it to this would be to proceed by an arbitrary moralistic dogma. For, beauty and perfection of life, the working upon oneself, the passionate efforts to obtain ideal goods, do not always result in happiness. These efforts and aims are inspired by certain *world* values, and may have no other effect than to create and maintain a particular attitude in the individual consciousness.

Countless times, the individual craves situations, events, insights, achievements, in whose particular existence or general nature he simply sees ultimately satisfactory aims. Occasionally the content of such cravings may be the improvement or well-being of others. But not necessarily: the aim is striven after for the sake of its own realization; and, therefore, to sacrifice others or even oneself may not be too high a price. *"Fiat justitia, pereat mundus";* the fulfillment of divine will merely because it is divine; the fanaticism of the artist, completion of whose work makes him forget any other consideration, altruistic or egoistic;

the political idealist's enthusiasm for a constitutional reform that renders him entirely indifferent to the question of how the citizens would fare under it—these are examples of purely objective valuations that permeate even the most trivial contents. The acting individual feels himself to be only the object or executor—who at bottom is accidental—of the task his cause puts to him. The passion for this cause is as little concerned with the I, Thou, or society as the value of the state of the world can be measured in terms of the world's pleasure or suffering (although it can, of course, be partly so measured). Yet, evidently, the claims made by individuals or groups, insofar as they, too, are agents of ultimate values, do not necessarily coincide with the individual's striving after such objective values. Particularly if he tries to realize a value either in himself or in an accomplishment that is unappreciated socially, the super-egoistic nature of his procedure is not rewarded by society. Society claims the individual for itself. It wants to make of him a form that it can incorporate into its own structure. And this societal claim is often so incompatible with the claim imposed on the individual by his striving after an objective value, as only a purely egoistic claim can be incompatible with a purely social one.

§ 3. *The Social vs. the Human*

The stage reached by the interpretation presented certainly goes beyond the customary contrast between egoism and altruism, as I have already pointed out. But even this interpretation cannot resolve the basic contrast between individual and society. And a related contrast that deals with the same content but springs from another ultimate world view is suggested by the modern analysis of certain sociological concepts.

Society—and its representative in the individual, social-ethical conscience—very often imposes a specialization upon him. I have already called attention to the fact that this specialization not only leaves undeveloped, or destroys, his harmonious wholeness. What is more, it often foists contents on the individual that are wholly inimical to the qualities usually called general-human. Nietzsche seems to have been the first to feel, with fundamental distinctness, the difference between the interest of humanity, of mankind, and the interest of society. Society is but one of the forms in which mankind shapes the contents of its life, but it is neither essential to all forms nor is it the only one in which human development is realized. All purely objective realms in which we are involved in whatever way—logical cognition or metaphysical imagination, the beauty of life or its image in the sovereignty of art, the realms of religion or of nature—none of these, to the extent to which they become our intimate possessions, has intrinsically and essentially anything whatever to do with "society." The human values that are measured by our greater or smaller stakes in these ideal realms have a merely accidental relation to social values, however often they intersect with them.

On the other hand, purely personal qualities—strength, beauty, depth of thought, greatness of conviction, kindness, nobility of character, courage, purity of heart—have their autonomous significance which likewise is entirely independent of their social entanglements. They are values of human existence. As such they are profoundly different from social values, which always rest upon the individual's *effects*. At the same time, they certainly are elements, both as effects and causes, of the social process. But this is only one side of their significance—the other is the intrinsic fact of their existence in the personality. For Nietzsche, this, strictly speaking, *immediate* existence of man is the criterion by which the level of mankind must be gauged at any given moment. For him, all social institutions, all giving and receiving by which the individual becomes a social being, are mere preconditions or consequences of his own nature. It is by virtue of this intrinsic nature that he constitutes a stage in the development of mankind.

Yet utilitarian-social valuation does not entirely depend on this intrinsic nature. It also depends on other individuals' responses to it. Thus, the individual's value does not wholly reside in himself: part of it he receives as the reflection of processes and creations in which his own nature has fused with beings and circumstances outside of him. It is on the basis of this relation between him and others that ethics (above all, Kantian ethics) has shifted the ground on which to appraise man, from his deeds to his attitude. Our value lies in our good will—a certain quality of the ultimate springs of our action that must be left undefined. It lies behind all appearance of our actions which, along with the effects they may have, are its mere consequences. They sometimes express it correctly, sometimes distort it—since they are mere "phenomena," they have but an accidental relationship to this fundamental value, good will itself.

Kant's position was expanded, or conceived more profoundly, by Nietzsche. He translated the Kantian contrast between attitude and success of external action (which already had freed the value of the individual from its social dependence) into the contrast between the existence and the effect of man in general. For Nietzsche, it is the qualitative *being* of the personality which marks the stage that the development of mankind has reached; it is the highest exemplars of a given time that carry humanity beyond its past. Thus Nietzsche overcame the limitations of merely social existence, as well as the valuation of man in terms of his sheer effects. It thus is not only quantitatively that mankind is more than society. Mankind is not simply the sum of all societies: it is an entirely different synthesis of the same elements that in other syntheses result in societies. Mankind and societies are two different vantage points, as it were, from which the individual can be viewed. They measure him by different standards, and their claims on him may be in violent conflict. What ties us to mankind and what we may contribute to the development of mankind—religious and scientific contributions, inter-family and international interests, the aesthetic perfection of personality, and purely objective production that aims at no "utility"— all this, of course, may on occasion also help develop the historical society of which we are members. But, essentially, it is rooted in claims that go far beyond any given society and that serve the elevation and objective enrichment of the type "man" itself. They may even be in pointed conflict with the more specific claims of the group that for any given man represents "his society."

In many other respects, however, society promotes a leveling of its members. It creates an average and makes it extremely difficult for its members to go beyond this average merely through the individual excellence in the quantity or quality of life. Society requires the individual to differentiate himself from the humanly general, but forbids him to stand out from the socially general. The individual is thus doubly oppressed by the standards of society: he may not transcend them either in a more general or in a more individual direction. In recent historical periods, these conflicts into which he falls with his political group, with his family, with his economic association, with his party, with his religious community, etc., have eventually become sublimated into the abstract need, as it were, for individual freedom. This is the general category that came to cover what was common in the various complaints and self-assertions of the individual against society.

§ 4. *The Eighteenth Century*

[a] THE FREEDOM OF THE INDIVIDUAL

The need for freedom in general, for the severance of the ties between society as such and individual as such, found its most highly developed consciousness and its strongest effects in the eighteenth century. This fundamental quest can be observed, in its economic form, in the Physiocrats' praise of free competition of individual interests as the natural order of things; in its sentimental elaboration, in Rousseau's notion of the rape of man by historical society as the origin of all corruption and evil; in its political aspect, in the French Revolution's intensification of the idea of individual liberty to the point of prohibiting workers from associating even for the protection of their own interests; in its philosophical sublimation, in Kant's and Fichte's conceptions of the ego as the bearer of the cognizable world and of its absolute autonomy as the moral value as such. The inadequacy of the socially accepted forms of life of the eighteenth century, in contrast with its material and intellectual productions, struck the consciousness of the individual as an unbearable limitation of his energies. Examples of these restrictive forms of life are the privileges of the higher estates, the despotic control of commerce and life in general, the still potent survivals of the guilds, the intolerant coercion by the church, the feudal obligations of the peasantry, the political tutelage dominating the life of the state, and the weakness of municipal constitutions. The oppressiveness of these and similar institutions which had lost their inner justifications, resulted in the ideal of the mere liberty of the individual. It was believed that the removal of these ties, which pressed the forces of the personality into unnatural grooves, would result in the unfolding of all the inner and outer values (that were there potentially, but whose free action was paralyzed politically, economically, and religiously), and would lead society out of the epoch of historical unreason into that of natural reason. Since nature did not know any of these ties, the ideal of freedom appeared as that of the "natural" state. If nature is conceived as the original existence of our species, as well as of each individual, as the starting point of the cultural process (irrespective of the ambiguity of "original," which may stand for "first in time" or for "essential and basic"), the eighteenth century tried to reconnect, in a gigantic synthesis, the end or peak of this process with its starting point. The freedom of the individual was too empty and weak to carry his existence; since historical forces no longer filled and supported it, it could now be filled and supported by the idea that it was merely necessary to gain this freedom as purely and completely as possible to recapture the original basis of the existence of our species and of our personality, a basis which was as certain and fruitful as nature itself.

[b] THE ANTINOMY BETWEEN FREEDOM AND EQUALITY

Yet this need for the freedom of the individual who feels himself restricted and deformed by historical society results in a self-contradiction once it is put into practice. For evidently, it can be put into practice permanently only if society exclusively consists of individuals who externally as well as internally are equally strong and equally privileged. Yet this condition exists nowhere. On the contrary, the power-giving and rank-determining forces of men are, in principle, unequal, both qualitatively and quantitatively. Therefore, complete freedom necessarily leads to the exploitation of this inequality by the more privileged, to the exploitation of the stupid by the clever, of the weak by the strong, of the timid by the grasping. The elimination of all external impediments must result in the expression of different inner potentialities in correspondingly different external positions. Institutionalized freedom is made illusory by personal relations. Furthermore, since in all power relations an advantage once gained facilitates the gaining of additional advantages (the "accumulation of capital" is merely a specific instance of this general proposition), power inequality is bound to expand in quick progression, and the freedom of the privileged always and necessarily develops at the expense of the freedom of the oppressed.

For this reason it was quite legitimate to raise the paradoxical question whether the socialization of all means of production is not the only condition of free competition. For, only by forcibly taking from the individual the possibility of fully exploiting his superiority over the weaker, can an equal measure of freedom reign throughout society. Therefore, if it is this ideal that is aimed at, "socialism" does not refer to the suspension of freedom. Rather, socialism suspends only that which, at any given degree of freedom, becomes the means for suppressing the freedom of some in favor of others. This means is private property. It is more than the expression of individual differences; it multiplies them; it intensifies them to the point, to put it radically, where at one pole of the society a maximum of freedom has developed, and at the other, a minimum. Full freedom of each can obtain only if there is full equality with everybody else. But as long as the economic set-up permits the exploitation of personal superiorities, this equality is unattainable both in strictly personal and in economic matters. Only when this exploitation is eliminated; when, that is, the private ownership of the means of production is suspended, is economic equality possible. Only then is there no longer a barrier to freedom—a barrier which is inseparable from inequality. It is precisely this possibility of exploiting personal superiorities which conclusively shows the deep antinomy between freedom and equality: the antinomy can be resolved only if both are dragged down to the negative level of property-lessness and powerlessness.

In the eighteenth century, only Goethe seems to have seen this antinomy with full clarity. Equality, he said, demands submission to a general norm; freedom "strives toward the unconditional." "Legislators or revolutionaries," he pointed out, "who promise at the same time equality and freedom are fantasts or charlatans." Perhaps it was an instinctive intuition of this condition which made for the addition, to freedom and equality, of a third requirement: fraternity. For the rejection of coercion as a means of resolving the contradiction between freedom and equality leaves as this means only emphatic altruism. Equality, after being destroyed by freedom, can be re-established only through the ethical renunciation to utilize natural gifts. Except for this notion, however, the typical individualism of the eighteenth century is completely blind to the intrinsic difficulty of freedom. The intellectual limitations and the restrictions by estates, guilds, and the church, against which it fought, had created innumerable inequalities whose injustices were deeply felt but were seen to derive from merely external-historical origins. The removal of these institutions, which was bound to eliminate the inequalities caused by *them,* was therefore thought to eliminate *all* inequalities. Freedom and equality thus appeared as self-evidently harmonious aspects of the same human ideal.

[c] "NATURAL MAN"

This ideal was carried by still another and deeper historical current, the peculiar contemporaneous conception of nature. In its theoretical interests, the eighteenth century was decisively oriented toward the natural sciences. Continuing the work of the seventeenth, it established the modern concept of natural law as the highest ideal of cognition. This concept, however, eliminates individuality, properly speaking. There no longer exist the incomparability and indissolubility of the single existence, but only the general law. Any phenomenon, be it an individual or a nebula in the Milky Way, is merely one of its instances. In spite of the utter unrepeatability of its form, the individual is a mere crosspoint and a resolvable pattern of fundamentally general laws. This, at least, was the understanding of "nature" of the time—only poets understood it differently. For this reason, man in general, man as such, is the central interest of the period; not historically given, particular, differentiated man. Concrete man is reduced to general man: he is the essence of each individual person, just as the universal laws of matter in general are embodied in any fragment of matter, however specifically it be formed. This argument gives one the right to see freedom and equality together from the beginning. For, the general-human man, the natural-law man, exists as the essential core in each empirical man, who is individualized by virtue of particular qualities, social position, and contingencies. Therefore, all that is needed to make appear what is common to all men, or man's essence, or man as such, is to *free* the individual from all these historical influences and distortions which merely hide his deepest nature.

Thus, the crucial point of this conception of individuality—which is one of the great conceptions of intellectual history—is this: if man is freed from all that he is not purely himself, if man has found himself, there emerges as the proper substance of his being, man-as-such or humanity. This humanity lives in all individuals. It is their constant, fundamental nature which only empirically and historically is disguised, made smaller, distorted. Freedom is the expression without restrictions or residues and in all domains of existence, of this essence of man, of this central ego, of this unconditioned self, which alone reigns over man's existence. In terms of the pure concept of mankind, all men are essentially alike. Compared with this general element, all *differentiated* individuality is something external and accidental. It is the significance of this general element that makes the literature of the revolutionary period continuously speak of the "people," the "tyrant," "freedom" in general. It is for this reason that the "natural religion" contains providence "as such," justice "as such," divine education "as such," but does not recognize the right of any specific elaborations or manifestations of these ideas. It is for this reason that "natural law" is based on the fiction of isolated and similar individuals. Commonness in the sense of collective unity has disappeared—whether this unity be economic or of the church or of the estate or of the state itself. (The only function of which the state has not been deprived is the negative function of protection, of the prevention of disturbances.) Only the free, self-contained individual is left. Historical-social units have yielded to the conviction of the generality of human nature, which subsists as the essential, inalienable, and always traceable characteristic of each individual, and which must only be found and pointed out in him to make him perfect. This generality of human nature attenuates and makes bearable the isolation of the individual. At the same time, it makes freedom possible as an ethical concept, for it appears to eradicate the very development of inequality (which nevertheless is the inevitable consequence of freedom). In this sense it was possible for Frederick the Great to speak of the prince as "the first judge, the first financier, the first minister of society," but in the same breath, as "a *man* like the least among his subjects." Thus, eighteenth-century individualism made the sociological antinomy between freedom and inequality, with which I began my discussion, into an ethical paradox, too: the antinomy was conceived as the innermost spring of man's nature, and yet as imposing the renunciation of the self. And it also makes it into a religious paradox that is expressed in the axiom, "He who loses his soul shall find it."

[d] INDIVIDUALISM IN KANT

It is in the philosophy of Kant that this conception of individuality attains its highest intellectual sublimation. All cognition, Kant taught, results from the fact that the intrinsically heterogeneous variety of sense impressions is formed into units. This unification is possible because the mind, in which it occurs, itself is a unit, an *ego*. The fact that instead of fleeting sensations we have a consciousness of *objects* is the expression of the unification which the ego brings about in these sensations. The object is the counterpart of the subject. Thus the ego—not the accidental, psychological, individual ego, but the fundamental, creative, unchangeable ego—becomes the vehicle and producer of objectivity. Cognition is objectively true and necessary in the measure in which it is formed by this pure ego, the ultimate legislator of the cognizing mind. From this unshakable assumption of *one* truth, of *one objective* world, it follows that in all men the ego which forms or could form this world, must always be identical. Kantian idealism thus makes the knowable world the product of the ego. At the same time, it insists on the oneness and perpetual identity of true cognition. This idealism is the expression of an individualism which sees in all that is human an unconditionally identical core. It is forced to hold that, just as the cognized world is the same for all men, so the deepest productive element in all men is homogeneous, even if it is not always equally developed or manifest.

Thus, for Kant, the identity of the egos results in the identity of their worlds. It is in this notion that he also discovers the root of freedom. The world can be given only as the representation of the idealistic ego, which embodies the absolute independence of the person from all extrinsic conditions and determinations. Inasmuch as the ego creates all conscious contents of existence— and among them, the empirical ego itself—it cannot in turn be created by any of them. In Kantian philosophy, the ego has wrested its absolute sovereignty from all possible entanglements with nature, Thou, society. It stands so much on itself alone that even its world, *the* world, can stand on it. It is no use for the powers of history to interfere with this ego since there is nothing above or even beside it: by definition, it can go no other road than that prescribed to it by its own nature. Kant and his epoch make abstract man, the individuality that is freed from all ties and specificities and is therefore always identical, the ultimate substance of personality and, thereby, the ultimate *value* of personality. However unholy man may be, Kant says, humanity in him is holy. And Schiller: "The idealist thinks so highly of mankind that he runs the risk of despising single men."

[e] THE DUAL ROLE OF "NATURE"

Even for Rousseau, who certainly was sensitive to individual differences, these differences, nevertheless, are superficial. He argues that the more completely man returns to his own heart and grasps his inner absoluteness instead of mere external relations, the more forcefully flows in him, that is, in each individual equally, the fountain of goodness and happiness. When man thus really is himself, he possesses a sustained strength that is abundant for more than his own maintenance. He can make it flow over to others, as it were; it is sufficient to absorb others in himself and to identify himself with them. We are ethically the more valuable, charitable, and good, the more each of us is purely himself; the more, that is, one allows that innermost core to become sovereign in himself in which all men are identical in spite of all social ties and accidental guises. Inasmuch as he is more than sheer empirical individuality, the true individual has in this "more" the possibility to give of himself and thus to overcome his empirical egoism.

We realize how the peculiar eighteenth-century conception of nature establishes a close relation to ethics; and in all of the eighteenth century, the double role of nature finds its strongest expression in Rousseau. I already called attention to the significance of nature for the problem of individuality: nature not only is what really alone exists—the substance of all historical oscillations and shifts—but also, at the same time, it is what ought to be, the ideal with whose growing realization all men must be concerned. To say that what truly exists is, at the same time, an aim that must yet be reached, sounds contradictory. Yet actually, these two propositions are the two sides of a consistent psychological position which is taken in regard to more than one value complex. We can simply not express it otherwise than in this logically contradictory dualism. And it is precisely in its specific stand on the problem of the ego that the dual significance of the "natural" becomes most readily plausible. We feel in ourselves an ultimate reality which forms the essence of our nature, but which is yet only very imperfectly represented by our empirical reality. But it is by no means merely a fantasy-like ideal which hovers above this empirical reality; for, in some shape it already exists, traced in ideal lines, as it were, into our existence; and yet it contains the *norm* for this existence, and only requires to be fully worked out and elaborated in the material of our existence. That the ego which we already are, nevertheless is something yet to be achieved because we are it not yet purely and absolutely but only in the disguise and distortion of our historical-social destinies—this argument became an extremely powerful feeling in the eighteenth century. The ego's setting-of-norms for the ego is ethically justified because the ideal ego is real in a higher sense of the word: it is the generally human ego. When it is attained, the true equality of all that is man is also attained. This thought was expressed most exhaustively by Schiller: "Every individual man carries a pure and ideal man in himself, as disposition and destination. It is the great task of his life, in all his changes, to coincide with the unchangeable unity of this ideal man. This pure man makes himself manifest, more or less distinctly, in every individual."

[f] KANT'S "CATEGORICAL IMPERATIVE": INDIVIDUALITY AS THE
SYNTHESIS OF FREEDOM AND EQUALITY

The formula of the "categorical imperative," in which Kant
epitomized man's moral task, is the most profound elaboration
of this concept of individuality. It bases man's whole moral value
upon freedom. As long as we are mere parts of the mechanism
of the world, including the social world, we have as little "value"
as the passing cloud or the withering stone. Only when we cease
being a mere product and crosspoint of external forces and become a being that develops out of his own ego, can we be *responsible*. Only then can we acquire the possibility of both guilt and
moral value. Within the natural-social cosmos, "being-for-oneself" or "personality" do not exist. Only when we are rooted
in absolute freedom (the metaphysical counterpart of *laissez-
faire*) do we gain both personality and the dignity of the moral.
And what this morality is, is expressed by the categorical imperative as follows: "Act in such a way that the principle governing
your will could at the same time be valid as the principle of a
general legislation." With the categorical imperative, the ideal
of equality has become the meaning of every Ought. Self-flatter-
ing arrogance has been made impossible: the individual can no
longer feel himself entitled to indulge in special actions and en-
joyments because he fancies that he is "different from the others."
Moral trial "without regard to person," equality before the
moral law, is perfected in the requirement that it must be possible to think consistently of one's own action as of everybody's necessary manner of acting. Equality supplies freedom,
which is the mainspring of all ethics, with its content. The absolutely self-dependent and self-responsible personality is precisely the personality whose action is ethically justified by the
identical claim to this action on the part of all others. Not merely,
only the man who is free is moral, but also, only the man who is
moral is free, because only *his* action possesses the character of
the general law that is real exclusively in the uninfluenced and
self-based ego. Thus, the eighteenth-century conception of individuality, with its emphasis on personal freedom that does not
exclude, but includes, equality, because the "true person" is

the same in every accidental man, has found its abstract perfection in Kant.

§ 5. *The Nineteenth Century*

In the nineteenth century, this conception splits up into two ideals. Crudely and without regard for many necessary qualifications, these ideals may be identified as the tendencies toward equality without freedom, and toward freedom without equality.

[a] SOCIALISM

The former is characteristic of socialism. Although it does not, of course, exhaustively define socialism, it is yet more profoundly a part of it than is admitted by the majority of its adherents. In energetically rejecting mechanical equalization, the socialists are mistaken about the central role that the idea of equality will always play in the formation of socialist ideals. Socialization of the means of production may, as I have already stressed, bring out many individual differences which in the present social system are atrophied because of their disappearance into class levels, and because of imperfect education, overwork, indigence, and worry. Nevertheless, the elimination of undeserved advantages and disadvantages due to birth, fluctuation of the stock market, accumulation of capital, differential evaluation of identical quantities of work, etc., would certainly lead to a very considerable leveling of economic conditions as compared with the present state of affairs. And according to the close dependence which precisely in socialist theory exists between the economic and the general cultural situation, the relative economic equilibration is bound to be paralleled by a comprehensive personal equilibration. Yet the crucial point is that the various measures of leveling (which differ with different socialist programs) only concern the oscillations in the *theory* of the ideal of equality—an ideal which is one of the great character traits of human nature. There will always be a type of person whose notions regarding social values are contained in the idea of the equality of all, however nebulous and unthinkable in the concrete this idea may be. And there will also be a type to whom individual differences and distances constitute an ultimate, irreducible, and self-justified value of the social form of existence. One of the leading socialists asserts that all socialist measures, including those which superficially strike one as coercive, actually aim at the development and security of the free personality. Thus, the institution of maximum hours of work is merely a prohibition to give up personal freedom for more than a particular number of hours. It is thus basically the same as the prohibition to sell oneself permanently into personal servitude. But this sort of argument shows our particular socialist to think in terms of eighteenth-century individualism with its schematic conception of freedom.

Perhaps no empirical man is guided exclusively by any one of these two tendencies, freedom and equality. Perhaps, too, the exclusive realization of either of them is entirely impossible. Yet this does not prevent them from socially manifesting themselves as fundamental types of character differences. Once one of them exists, the individual who is dominated by it, will not be swayed by rational argument. For in spite of any retrospective rationalizations to the contrary, such a tendency does not originate in its appraisal as a means for the attainment of an ultimate end, such as general happiness or personal perfection or the rationalization of life. It rather itself is the ultimate ground on which all intentions, decisions, and deductions are built. It expresses the existence of man, the substance of his essence. His relation to his fellowmen is something very important, grave, and basic to him. Hence his decision as to whether he is, or wants, or ought to be, like or unlike them (individually, as well as in principle) is bound to come from the very depth of his being. It seems to me that socialism recruits most of its adherents, at any rate its most fanatic adherents, from individuals who tend in the manner suggested toward this quite general ideal of equality.

The relation between the relative equality of a socialized system, and freedom is very complex. It is characterized by the typical ambiguity which class differentiation commonly inflicts upon general influences or modifications that concern the whole of a given society. For, since the development and the life conditions of the various parts of a society are extremely different, any general modification must result in extremely different, even diametrically opposed consequences for these various parts. The same measure of general equalization that would give a great deal of freedom to the laborer who is constantly exposed to the threat of hunger and the hardships of wage work, would entail at least an equal limitation of freedom for the entrepreneur, the *rentier*, the artist, the scholar, and other leaders of the present order. A formally corresponding sociological ambiguity characterizes the woman question. The freedom to engage in economic production is sought after by the women of the higher classes in an effort to secure their solid independence and a satisfactory demonstration of their ability. Yet, for the woman factory worker, this same freedom constitutes a terrible obstacle to the fulfillment of her duties and to her happiness as wife and mother. As it hits two different classes, the elimination of domestic and family restrictions results in totally different values. To recapitulate, in the socialist movement, the synthesis of freedom and equality has been modified by the emphasis upon equality. And only because the class, whose interests are represented by socialism, would feel equality *as* freedom (at least during the initial period of socialist equalization), can socialism overlook the antagonism between the two ideals.

One might suggest that the loss of freedom which socialism would impose on certain layers of the society, will be only transitional, will last only as long as the aftereffects of present conditions still allow for sensitivity to individual differences. In fact, in view of the difficulties of reconciling freedom and equality, touched upon above, socialism has been forced to resort to an *adjustment* to equality which, as an overall satisfaction, is supposed to reduce the desires for freedom that go beyond it. Yet this resort to such a panacea of adjustment is a questionable device, if only because it can be used with equal readiness by any contrary position. For, one could assert no less plausibly that the drives toward freedom which are based on social *differences* could adjust to any degree of reduction in the absolute quantity of these differences. But the fact is that the nature of our sensitivity depends on *differences in stimulus*. Therefore, after a brief period of adjustment, the individual differences would base their utterly inevitable passions of greed and envy, of domination and feeling of oppression, on the slight differences in social position that have remained because they cannot be removed in even the most socialized situation. By virtue of this psychological structure of man, the exercise of freedom at the expense of others would find a fertile field of expansion, even if the extreme degree of equality attainable were actually attained.

One might, however, understand equality only in the sense of equal justice. One might hold, that is, that the social institutions should give each individual a certain quantity of freedom, not on the basis of some mechanical and constant criterion, but in exact proportion to his qualitative importance. Yet even this conception could not be acted upon in practice. The reason is a largely neglected fact which, nevertheless, is of the greatest significance for an understanding of the relation between individual and society. Any social order requires a hierarchy of superordinations and subordinations, even if only for technical reasons. Therefore, equality in the sense of justice can only be the exact correspondence of personal qualification with position in this hierarchy. Yet, this harmonious correspondence is in principle impossible for the very simple reason that there always are more persons qualified for superior positions than there are superior positions. Among the million subjects of a prince, there surely is a large number who would make equally good or better princes. A good many factory workers could as well be entrepreneurs or at least foremen. A large portion of the common soldiers have full officer qualifications, even if only latently. Here lies the observational truth of the proverb, "If God gives somebody an office, he also gives him the mind necessary for it." [7] Many people presumably have the qualifications required for the filling of higher positions, but they demonstrate, develop, and make them manifest only once they occupy these positions. Let us only remember the often grotesque accidents by which men in all spheres attain their positions. Is it not an incomprehensible miracle that there should not be an incomparably greater amount of incompetence than there actually is? No—precisely because we must assume that competence is actually very widely diffused.

This incommensurability between the quantity of superior competence and its possible use can perhaps be explained on the basis of the difference (discussed earlier) between the character of man as group member and as individual. The group as such

[7] *"Wem Gott ein Amt gibt, dem gibt er auch den Verstand dazu."*—Tr.

is on a low level and is in need of leadership because its members generally contribute to it only those aspects of their personalities that are common to all. These aspects always are the coarser, more primitive, and more "subordinate" aspects. Hence, whenever men associate in groups, it serves the purpose of the group to organize in the form of subordination to a few. But this does not prevent any single member from individually possessing higher and finer qualities. But these are, precisely, individual qualities. They diverge in different directions, all of them irrelevant to any common group possession. They do not therefore raise the low level of the qualities in which all securely meet. It follows that the group as a whole needs a leader—that there are bound to be many subordinates and only few superordinates. It further follows that each individual group member is more highly qualified or more often capable of occupying a leading position than he is able to make use of in his capacity as a group member. The axiom, "Many are called but few are chosen," also applies to social structures. The antinomy is met by *a priori* limiting the number of persons who are considered "qualified" to occupy leading positions. Both the principle of estates and the contemporary social order implement this limitation by building classes one on top of the other in the form of a pyramid which contains increasingly fewer members as it approaches its top. The equal right of all to occupy all positions obviously makes it impossible to satisfy any justified claim whatever. Therefore, an estate or class arrangement of the social order intrinsically exerts a limiting selection. This selection is far from being determined by considering the individuals but on the contrary, shapes them.

It is questionable whether a socialist order could eventually do without such *a priori* super-subordination. Socialism postulates that any accidental chance be eliminated from the determination of positions to be occupied, and that individual qualification alone decide the attainment of positions. On the other hand, it also postulates that any talent develop "freely," that is, that it find the position commensurate with it. From this and from what has been pointed out before, it follows that in socialism there would be more superordinates than subordinates, more persons who command than execute commands. If freedom in the social sense refers to the adequate expression of any measure of indi-

vidual strength and importance in the configuration of leading
and following within the group, then freedom is here excluded
from the start. We have seen that the conflict between man's
individual wholeness and his nature as a group member, makes
the harmonious proportion between personal qualification and
social position impossible; and thus makes impossible the synthesis, on the basis of justice, between freedom and equality.
And this conflict cannot be eliminted even by a socialist order,
because it may be called a *logical* presupposition of society itself.

[b] THE NEW INDIVIDUALISM: THE INCOMPARABILITY OF THE INDIVIDUAL

I must limit myself to presenting these fragments in the field
of the much-discussed relation of socialism to individual freedom. I shall now sketch the peculiar form of individualism that
dissolved the eighteenth-century synthesis which based equality
upon freedom, and freedom upon equality. In place of the
equality which (it will be recalled) expressed the deepest nature
of man and which, at the same time, had yet to be realized, it puts
inequality. Just as equality in the eighteenth century, so now
inequality in the nineteenth, only needs freedom to emerge from
its mere latency and potentiality and to dominate all of human
life. Freedom remains the general denominator even if its correlate is the opposite of what it had been. It seems that, as soon
as the ego had become sufficiently strengthened by the feeling of
equality and generality, it fell back into the search for inequality.
Yet this new inequality was posited from within. First, there had
been the thorough liberation of the individual from the rusty
chains of guild, birth right, and church. Now, the individual that
had thus become independent also wished to distinguish himself
from other individuals. The important point no longer was the
fact that he was a free individual as such, but that he was this
specific, irreplaceable, given individual.

In this development, the modern tendency toward differentiation attains an intensification that leads it away from the form
it had just reached in the preceding century. But in stressing this
contrast, one must not overlook the fact that the fundamental
direction, which actually pervades all of the modern period,
remains identical. This direction may be expressed by stating

that the individual seeks his *self* as if he did not yet have it, and yet, at the same time, is certain that his only fixed point is this self. In the light of the unbelievable expansion of theoretical and practical horizons, it is understandable that the individual should ever more urgently seek such a fixed point, but that he should be no longer capable of finding it in anything external to himself. The double need for unquestionable clarity and for enigmatic unfathomableness—a need whose two components have been diverging ever further in the course of the development of modern man—is satisfied, as if it were one homogeneous need, in the idea of the ego and in the feeling of personality. Yet even socialism receives psychological help from both a conceptually demonstrated rationalism and from very obscure, possibly atavistic-communistic instincts. Thus, in the end, all relations to others are merely stations on the road on which the ego arrives at itself. His relations may be such stations in two respects. Either the ego may ultimately come to feel that it is like the others because, living as it does on nothing but its own forces, it may still need this encouraging and supporting consciousness. Or, on the contrary, it may be strong enough to bear the loneliness of its own quality, and may hold that the only reason for a multitude of individuals to exist at all is the possibility of each component individual to measure his own incomparability and the individuality of his own world by those of the others.

Historically, then, the tendency toward individualization, as I have already suggested, leads from one ideal to a very different ideal. The first is the ideal of fundamentally equal, even if wholly free and self-responsible personalities. The other is that of the individuality which, precisely in its innermost nature, is incomparable and which is called upon to play an irreplaceable role. Intimations of the later ideal are already found in the eighteenth century, in Lessing, Herder, and Lavater. Lavater's Christ cult has been ascribed to his desire to individualize even God, and the intensification of this cult, to his quest for ever new images of Christ. Yet it is in a work of art that this form of individualism finds its first full elaboration—in Goethe's *Wilhelm Meister*. *Wilhelm Meister's Apprenticeship*, for the first time, shows a world which is based exclusively on the individual peculiarities of its protagonists and which is organized and developed only on this basis, quite irrespective of the fact that these protagonists are designed as types. For, however often they may be repeated in reality, it still is the essential significance of each of them that, in his ultimate ground, he is different from the other with whom fate has thrown him together. The *accent* of life and development does not lie on similarity but on absolute peculiarity. In *Wilhelm Meister's Travels,* the interest shifts from the individual to mankind—not in the sense of eighteenth-century abstract man-in-general, but of the collective, of the concrete totality of the living species. It is most remarkable to note how this individualism with its emphasis on individual incomparability and uniqueness, comes to the fore even on the basis of this interest in mankind. The individualistic requirement of specificity does not make for the valuation of total personality within society, but for the personality's objective achievement for the benefit of society. "Your general culture and all its institutions," Goethe says in the *Travels,* "are fooleries. Any man's task is to do *something* extraordinarily well, as no other man in his immediate environment can." This is the absolute opposite of the ideal of free and equal personalities that Fichte had compressed into this one sentence: "A rational being must simply be an individual— but precisely, *not* this or that particular individual." The older ideal had resulted in the imperative that the individual differentially characterized ego develop itself, through the moral process, into the pure, absolute ego, which was the philosophical crystalization of eighteenth-century "general man." In pointed antithesis to this position, Frederick Schlegel formulated the new individualism thus: "It is precisely individuality that is the original and eternal aspect of man; personality is less important. To see one's noblest calling in the cultivation and development of this individuality would be divine egoism."

The new individualism found its philosophical expression in Schleiermacher. For Schleiermacher, the moral task consists in each individual's *specific* representation of mankind. Each individual is a "compendium" of mankind; what is more, he is a synthesis of the forces that constitute the universe. Yet out of this material that is common to all, each individual creates an entirely unique form. And here, too, as in the earlier conception of individualism, reality also is the blueprint of what *ought* to be.

Not only as something already existing is man incomparable, placed into a framework which can be filled out only by him. There also is another aspect: the realization of this incomparability, the filling-out of this framework, is man's *moral* task. Each individual is *called* or destined to realize his own, incomparable image. The great world-historical idea that not only the equality of men but also their differentiation represents a moral challenge, becomes the core of a new world view in Schleiermacher. The idea that the absolute only lives in the form of the individual, and that individuality is not a restriction of the infinite but its expression and mirror, makes the principle of the social division of labor part of the metaphysical ground of reality itself. To be sure, a differentiation that thus penetrates the last depths of the individual nature, easily exhibits a mystical-fatalistic character. ("This is the way thou hast to be; thou canst not escape thyself. *Sibyls and prophets have always said this.*") For this reason, it remained foreign to the bright rationalism of the Enlightenment and, on the other hand, recommended itself to Romanticism, with which Schleiermacher was very closely connected.

The new individualism might be called qualitative, in contrast with the quantitative individualism of the eighteenth century. Or it might be labeled the individualism of uniqueness [*Einzigkeit*] as against that of singleness [*Einzelheit*]. At any rate, Romanticism perhaps was the broadest channel through which it reached the consciousness of the nineteenth century. Goethe had created its artistic, and Schleiermacher its metaphysical basis: Romanticism supplied its sentimental, experiential foundation. After Herder (in whom therefore one of the mainsprings of qualitative individualism must be sought), the Romanticists were the first to absorb and to emphasize the particularity and uniqueness of historical realities. They deeply felt the important claim and the fascinating beauty of the Middle Ages, which had been neglected, and of the Orient, which had been despised by the activistic culture of a liberal Europe. In this sense, Novalis wanted his "one spirit" to transform itself into infinitely many alien spirits; the "one spirit inheres, as it were, in all objects it contemplates, and it feels the infinite, simultaneous sensations of a harmonious plurality." Above all, the Romanticists experienced the inner rhythm of the incomparability, of the specific claim, of the sharp qualitative differentiation of the single element, which the new individualism also sees in the *social* element, among the components of *society*. Here, too, Lavater is an interesting predecessor. Occasionally, his physiognomy so stubbornly pursues the special characteristics of man's visible and inner traits that he cannot find his way back to man's total individuality, but remains arrested in his interest in the completely individual and single. The Romantic mind, too, feels its way through an endless series of contrasts. At the instant it is being lived and experienced, each of them appears as something absolute, completed, self-contained, but at the next moment it is left behind. The Romanticist enjoys the very essence of each of these contrasts only in its difference from every other. "He who is glued to only one point," Frederick Schlegel says, "is nothing but a rational oyster." In the protean succession of its contrasts of mood and task and conviction and sentiment, the life of the Romanticist reflects the social scene in which each individual finds the sense of his existence—individual no less than social—only in contrast with others, in the personal uniqueness of his nature and his activities.

In its purely societal version, this conception of the task of the individual evidently points toward the constitution of a more comprehensive whole that is composed of the differentiated elements. The more specific the achievements (but also the needs) of the individuals, the more urgent becomes their reciprocal supplementation. In the same measure, the total organism which has grown out of the individuals engaged in the division of labor and which includes and mediates their interrelated effects and countereffects, shifts, so to speak, into a location high above them. The specificity of the individual thus requires a powerful political constitution which allocates his place to him, but in this fashion also becomes his master. It is for this reason that this individualism, which restricts freedom to a purely inward sense of the term, easily acquires an anti-liberal tendency. It thus is the complete antithesis of eighteenth-century individualism which, in full consistency with its notion of atomized and basically undifferentiated individuals, could not even conceive the idea of a collective as an organism that unifies heterogeneous elements. The eighteenth-century collective holds its elements together exclusively by means of the *law* that is above all of them. The function of this law is to restrict the freedom of the individual to the point where this freedom can coexist with that of every other individual. The godfathers of this law were, on the one hand, the laws of a mechanically construed nature and, on the other, law in the Roman-legal sense. By virtue of these two origins, the social scene in its concreteness entirely escapes eighteenth-century individualism. For, the social scene cannot be put together through the mere addition of isolated and equal individuals. It only arises from individual interactions within a division of labor. And it rises above these interactions as a unit which cannot be found in the individual, not even as some sort of proportionate quantity.

In terms of intellectual history, the doctrine of freedom and equality is the foundation of free competition; while the doctrine of differentiated personality is the basis of the division of labor. Eighteenth-century liberalism put the individual on his own feet: in the nineteenth, he was allowed to go as far as they would carry him. According to the new theory, the natural order of things saw to it that the unlimited competition of all resulted in the harmony of all interests, that the unrestricted striving after individual advantages resulted in the optimum welfare of the whole. This is the metaphysics with which the nature-optimism of the eighteenth century socially justified free competition. The metaphysical foundation of the division of labor was discovered with the individualism of difference, with the deepening of individuality to the point of the individual's incomparability, to which he is "called" both in his nature and in his achievement. The two great principles which operate, inseparably, in nineteenth-century economic theory and practice—competition and division of labor—thus appear to be the economic projections of the philosophical aspects of social individualism. Or inversely, these philosophical aspects appear to be the sublimations of the concrete economic forms of production of the period. Or, finally and more correctly, and thus suggesting the very possibility of this mutual interdependence: they both derive from one of the profound transformations of history which we cannot know in their essential nature and motivation but only in the manifestations they engender, as it were, when fusing with particular, contentually determined spheres of life.

To be sure, unlimited competition and individual specialization through divison of labor have affected individual culture in a way that shows them not to be its most suitable promoters. Perhaps, however, beyond the economic form of cooperation between the two great sociological themes, individual and society (the only sociological themes that have thus far been realized), there yet exists a higher form that might be the latent ideal of our culture. I should prefer to believe, however, that the ideas of free personality as such and of unique personality as such, are not the last words of individualism. I should like to think that the efforts of mankind will produce ever more numerous and varied forms for the human personality to affirm itself and to demonstrate the value of its existence. In fortunate periods, these varied forms may order themselves into harmonious wholes. In doing so, their contradictions and conflicts will cease to be mere obstacles to mankind's efforts: they will also stimulate new demonstrations of the strength of these efforts and lead them to new creations.

Quantitative Aspects
of the Group

Chapter 1

On the Significance
of Numbers for Social Life

THE PRESENT STUDIES BEGIN
by examining forms of social life, combinations and interactions
among individuals. But they do so in one respect only: the bearing which the mere *number* of sociated individuals has upon
these forms of social life. It will immediately be conceded on
the basis of everyday experiences, that a group upon reaching
a certain size must develop forms and organs which serve its
maintenance and promotion, but which a smaller group does
not need. On the other hand, it will also be admitted that smaller
groups have qualities, including types of interaction among their
members, which inevitably disappear when the groups grow
larger. This quantitative determination of the group, as it may
be called, has a twofold function. Negatively speaking, certain
developments, which are necessary or at least possible as far as
the contents or conditions of life are concerned, can be realized
only below or above a particular number of elements. Positively,
certain other developments are imposed upon the group by certain purely quantitative modifications. Yet not even these developments emerge automatically, for they also depend on other
than numerical characteristics. The decisive point, however, is
that they are not the result of these characteristics alone, for they
emerge only under certain numerical conditions.

§ 1. *Small Groups*

[a] SOCIALISM

It can be shown, for instance, that, up to this day at least,
socialistic or nearly socialistic societies have been possible only in

very small groups and have always failed in larger ones. The principle of socialism—justice in the distribution of production and reward—can easily be realized in a small group and, what is surely quite as important, can be safeguarded there by its members. The contribution of each to the whole and the group's reward to him are visible at close range; comparison and compensation are easy. In the large group they are difficult, especially because of the inevitable differentation of its members, of their functions, and claims. A very large number of people can constitute a unit only if there is a complex division of labor. The reason is not only the obvious one of economic technique; there also is the fact that only the division of labor produces the sort of interpenetration and interdependence which (through innumerable intermediaries) connects each with everybody, and without which a far-flung group would break apart on every occasion. Therefore, the closer the group unity that is desired, the more articulate must be the specialization of its members, and the more unconditionally must this specialization bind the individual to the whole and the whole to him. The socialism of a large group thus would require the sharpest differentiation among the component personalities, and this differentiation would necessarily have to extend beyond their occupations, and include their feelings and wishes as well. But this would make comparisons among individual achievements and among individual rewards, and adjustments between them, extremely difficult. And yet it is on them that rests the possibility of approximate socialism in small, and therefore undifferentiated, groups.

In an advanced civilization, these groups are limited to numerical insignificance even logically, as it were, by their dependence on goods which they cannot supply under their own conditions of production. To my knowledge, there is only a single approximately socialistic organization [1] in existence in Europe

[1] The reliability of the historical materials used in these essays is conditioned, as far as their content is concerned, by two circumstances. Because of the particular function that these materials have here, they had to be culled from so many and heterogenous areas of historico-social life that the limited labor power of a single person could in general only draw on secondary sources for their collection; they could rarely be verified by direct firsthand investigation. On the other hand, the fact that these materials were collected over a long period of years will make it understandable that not every single item could be checked against the latest research before the publication of the book. If the communication of social facts

today. It is the *Familistère de Guise,* a large factory of cast-iron products. It was founded in 1880 by a disciple of Fourier on the principle of complete welfare for each worker and his family, of the guarantee of a minimum existence, of free care and education for the children, and of the collective attainment of subsistence. During the 1890's, the enterprise employed approximately two thousand people and appeared to be viable. But evidently it did or does so only because it is surrounded by a society that lives under very different life conditions, out of which the *Familistère* can fill the inevitable gaps of its own production. For, human needs cannot be rationalized in the way production can be. They seem to have a contingency or incalculability about them, which is the reason why their satisfaction can be achieved only at the cost of producing innumerable irrational and unusable goods. A group, therefore, which does not carry on such a production and relies instead on a complete systematization and perfect rationality of its activities, will always necessarily be a small group. For it can obtain only from a surrounding larger group that which at an advanced stage of civilization it needs for a satisfactory living standard.

[b] RELIGIOUS SECTS

There also are group formations of a religious sort, whose sociological structure makes it impossible for them to support a large membership. Such are, for instance, the sects of the Waldenses, Mennonites, and Herrnhuter. Where dogma forbids oath, military service, and occupancy of offices; where very per-

were one of the purposes of this volume, even though only secondary, the latitude given to undemonstrated statements and errors that has just been implied would be inadmissible. But in the present attempt at eliciting from social life the possibility of a new scientific abstraction, the essential aim can only be the achievement of this abstraction by means of any examples whatever, and thus the proof that it makes sense. If, for the sake of methodological clarification I should express the matter in a somewhat exaggerated fashion, I would say that the only importance of the examples is that they are *possible,* and less that they are *real.* For, their truth is not (or only in a few cases) designed to demonstrate the truth of a general proposition. Rather, even where some expression might not indicate it, they are only the object of an analysis; and the object itself is irrelevant. It is the correct and fruitful manner of performing this analysis, not the truth about the reality of its object, which is either achieved here or not. The investigation could be carried out even on the basis of fictitious examples, whose importance for the interpretation of reality could be left to the reader's accidental knowledge of fact.

sonal affairs, such as occupation, daily schedule, and even marriage, are regulated by the community; where a specific dress separates the faithful from the others and symbolizes their belonging together; where the subjective experience of immediate rapport with Christ constitutes the real cohesion of the community—in such situations, extension to large groups would evidently break the tie of solidarity which consists to a large degree precisely in the position of being singled out of larger groups and being in contrast with them. At least in this sociological respect, the claim of these sects that they represent original Christianity is not without justification. For, original Christianity, a yet undifferentiated unit of dogma and way of life, was possible only in such small communities within surrounding larger ones; and the larger groups not only served to supplement their external needs but also to form a contrast by which the sects became aware of their own specific nature. The diffusion of Christianity to society at large was therefore bound to change completely its sociological character, no less than its spiritual content.

[c] ARISTOCRACIES

It is, furthermore, the very idea of *aristocracies* that they can be only relatively small. This obvious fact, however, does not merely follow from the dominance of aristocracy over the masses. There also seems to be an *absolute* (though greatly varying) limitation in number. In other words, there is not only a certain proportion which would allow the ruling aristocracy to grow indefinitely in some prorated fashion as the mass of the ruled grows. There also is an *absolute* limit beyond which the aristocratic form of the group can no longer be maintained. The point at which it breaks down is determined in part by external, in part by psychological circumstances. If it is to be effective as a whole, the aristocratic group must be "surveyable" by every single member of it. Each element must still be personally acquainted with every other. Relations by blood and marriage must be ramified and traceable throughout the whole group. Thus the tendency of extreme numerical limitation, characteristic of historical aristocracies from Sparta to Venice, is not only due to the egoistic disinclination to share a ruling position but also to the instinct that the vital conditions of an aristocracy can be maintained only if the number of its members is small, relatively and absolutely. The unconditional right of primogeniture, which is of an aristocratic nature, is the means for preventing expansion. Both the old Theban law against increase in the number of landed estates and the Corinthian law requiring constancy in the number of families, were based on it. It is very characteristic that at one point, when Plato speaks of the Ruling Few, he also directly designates them as the Not-Many.

Where an aristocracy yields to democratic and centrifugal tendencies which usually accompany the transition to very large communities, it becomes entangled in deadly conflicts with its own life principle. A case in point is the nobility of Poland before the division. Under more favorable conditions, the conflict is resolved by transformation into a pervasive democratic form. The ancient free Germanic peasant community with the wholly personal equality of its members, for instance, was thoroughly aristocratic, but in its continuation in urban communities became the fountainhead of democracy. If this solution is shunned, there is nothing left but to draw at a certain point a hard line against expansion, and to stem the quantitatively closed group against whatever outside elements may want to enter it, no matter how much they may be entitled to do so. The aristocratic nature often becomes conscious of itself only in this situation, in this increased solidarity in the face of the tendency to expand. Thus, the old constitution of the *gens* seems to have been transformed several times into a real aristocracy only because a new population pressed upon it—a population alien and too numerous to be absorbed even gradually. Confronted with this increase of the total group, the associations of *gentes,* which in their whole nature were quantitatively limited, could maintain themselves only as aristocracies. In a very similar way, the protective guild *Richerzeche* of Cologne originally consisted of all free burghers. In the measure, however, in which the population of the city increased, it became a closed aristocratic association.

Yet the tendency of political aristocracies not to become "many" under any circumstances, usually leads to their decrease and extinction, rather than to their continuation. The reason is not only physiological. In general, small and very exclusive groups also distinguish themselves from large ones by the fact that the very fate that strengthens and renews the latter may destroy the former. A lost war can ruin a small city-state, but regenerate a large state. The explanation is not so simple as it might seem: there is also the difference in the ratio of potential to actual energies. Small, centripetally organized groups usually call on and use all their energies, while in large groups, forces remain much oftener potential, absolutely as well as relatively. The need of the collectivity here does not claim continuously the total personality of every member but can afford not to exploit some of the energies, which in an emergency may be drawn upon and actualized. Therefore, where circumstances exclude dangers that require an unused quantity of social energy, certain measures of numerical limitation, even beyond endogamy, may be highly appropriate. The polyandry of the Tibetan mountains is socially beneficial, as even the missionaries recognize. For, the soil is so infertile that a rapid population increase would result in the direst need; and polyandry is an excellent preventive against this. We hear that the members of Bushman families occasionally have to separate because of the sterility of the soil; in view of this, the rule which limits family size to a level compatible with subsistence opportunities, appears entirely in line with the very interest of family unity and all its social significance, while the external life conditions of the group, and their consequences for the internal group structure, obviate the dangers that otherwise inhere in numerical limitation.

Where the small group, especially the political group, to a great extent preempts the personalities of its members, the very character of its unity forces the members to take decisive stands in regard to persons, objective tasks, and other groups. On the other hand, the large group with its many different elements requires such a stand much less, or cannot even afford it. The histories of the Greek and Italian cities and of the Swiss cantons show that small contiguous communities either federate or live in a state of mutual, more or less latent hostility. Warfare and its rules are much more bitter, and particularly much more radical, between them than they are between great states: the lack of group organs, reserves, and relatively undefined and transitional elements, makes modification and adaptation difficult. Thus their fundamental sociological structure, in conjunction with their external conditions, makes them face the question of life or death much more often than larger societies.

§ 2. *Large Groups: the Mass*

Aside from these traits of small groups I will mention, with the same inevitably arbitrary selection from among innumerable features, the following which characterize the sociological structure of large groups. I begin by suggesting that large groups, in comparison with smaller ones, seem to show less radicalism and decisiveness. Yet this statement must be qualified. For, precisely where large masses are activated by political, social, or religious movements, they are ruthlessly radical, and extreme parties overwhelm moderate ones. The reason is that large masses can always be animated and guided only by *simple* ideas: what is common to many must be accessible even to the lowest and most primitive among them. Even nobler and more differentiated personalities in relatively large numbers never meet on complex and highly developed ideas and impulses but only on those that are relatively simple and generally human. Yet the realities in which the ideas of the mass are designed to function are always very complex and made up of a large number of divergent elements. Simple ideas, therefore, must always have the effect of being very one-sided, ruthless, and radical.

This is even more true where the mass is in physical proximity. Here innumerable suggestions swing back and forth, resulting in an extraordinary nervous excitation which often overwhelms the individuals, makes every impulse swell like an avalanche, and subjects the mass to whichever among its members happens to be the most passionate. The rule according to which the voting of the Roman people took place in fixed groups (*tributim et centuriatim descriptis ordinibus, classibus, aetatibus* [by urban and recruiting districts, by estates, military classes, age-groups], etc.), has been interpreted as a means essential for keeping democracy under control—the Greek democracies voted in masses, under the immediate impact of the orator. The fusion of masses under one feeling, in which all specificity and reserve of the personality are suspended, is fundamentally radical and hostile to mediation and consideration. It would lead to nothing but impasses and destructions if it did not usually end before in inner exhaustions and repercussions that are the consequences of the one-sided exaggeration. Furthermore, the masses, as the term is used here, have little to lose but, on the contrary, believe that they have everything to gain; most inhibitions of radicalism, therefore, are usually suspended. Finally, groups, more frequently than individuals, forget that their power has limits at all. More precisely, they ignore these limits; and they do so the more easily, the less known to one another are their members—and mutual lack of knowledge is typical of a larger group that has come together by accident.

§ 3. *Group Size, Radicalism, and Cohesiveness*

This sort of radicalism is distinguished by its emotionality and is indeed characteristic of large groups. But it is an exception, for in general, small parties are more radical than large ones, whereby, of course, the ideas that form the basis of the party itself put the limits on its radicalism. Radicalism here is sociological in its very nature. It is necessitated by the unreserved devotion of the individual to the rationale of the group, by the sharp delimitation of the group against other nearby groups (a sharpness of demarcation required by the need for the self-preservation of the group), and by the impossibility of taking care of widely varying tendencies and ideas within a narrow social framework. Of all this, the radicalism of *content* is largely independent.

It has been noted, for instance, that the conservative-reactionary elements in present-day Germany are forced by their very numerical strength to moderate their extreme aspirations. These groups draw upon so many and heterogeneous social strata that they cannot pursue any one of their tendencies to the end without giving offense to some portion of their constituency. In the same way, the Social-Democratic party has been forced by the fact of its large membership to dilute its qualitative radicalism, to give some room to deviations from its dogma, and to allow certain compromises with its intransigence—if not expressly, at least here and there in its actions. It is the unconditional solidarity of elements on which the sociological possibility of radicalism is based. This solidarity decreases in the measure in which numerical increase involves the admission of heterogeneous individual elements. For this reason, professional coalitions of workers, whose purpose is the improvement of labor conditions, know very well that they decrease in inner cohesion as they increase in volume. In this case, on the other hand, the numerical extension has the great significance of freeing the coalition, through each additional member who joins it, of a competitor who might otherwise have undersold it and thus have threatened its existence.

For, evidently, there emerge very specific conditions for the life of a group which develops within a larger one under the idea that it includes *all* elements which fall under its assumptions—of a group which thus realizes its very function. In these cases the axiom applies, "Who is not for me is against me." And the person who ideally, as it were, belongs to the group but remains outside it, by his mere indifference, his non-affiliation, positively harms the group. This non-membership may take the form of competition, as in the case of workers' coalitions; or it may show the outsider the limits of the power which the group yields; or it may damage the group because it cannot even be constituted unless *all* potential candidates join as members, as is the case in certain industrial cartels. Where, therefore, a group is confronted with the question of completeness (which by no means applies to all groups), with the question, that is, whether all elements to which the group's principles apply actually are members of it, there the consequences of this *completeness* must be carefully distinguished from those of its *size*. To be sure, the complete group is also larger. But what is important is not size as such but the problem (which nevertheless depends upon size) whether this size fills a prescribed framework. This problem can become so important that (as in the case of workers' coalitions) the disadvantages for cohesion and unity, which follow from mere numerical increase, are directly antagonistic to the advantages of nearing completeness.

§ 4. *Paradoxes in Group Structure*

More generally, the characteristics of the large group can, to a considerable extent, be explained as surrogates for the personal and immediate cohesion typical of the small group. The large group creates organs which channel and mediate the interactions of its members and thus operate as the vehicles of a societal unity which no longer results from the direct relations among its elements. Offices and representations, laws and symbols of group life, organizations and general social concepts are organs of this sort. Their formations and functions are dealt with in many passages of the present volume. At this point, therefore, only their connection with the quantitative aspect of the group needs discussion. Typically, all of them develop fully and purely only in large groups. They are the abstract form of group cohesion whose concrete form can no longer exist after the group has reached a certain size. Their utility, which ramifies into a thousand social characteristics, ultimately depends on numerical premises. They are the embodiment of the group forces and thus have a super-personal and objective character with which they confront the individual. But this character springs from the very *multitude* of the individual members and their effects, whatever they may be. For, it is this large number which paralyzes the individual element and which causes the general element to emerge at such a distance from it that it seems as if it could exist by itself, without any individuals, to whom in fact it often enough is antagonistic.

Here we find a parallel in the phenomenon of the *concept*. A concept isolates that which is common to singular and heterogeneous items. It stands the more highly above each of them, the more of them it comprises. It is, therefore, the most general concepts, that is, those which comprehend the largest number of items—such as the abstractions of metaphysics—that gain, as it were, a separate existence, the norms and developments of which are often alien or even hostile to those of more tangible, single items. In a similar manner, the large group gains its unity, which finds expression in the group organs and in political notions and in ideals, only at the price of a great distance between all of these structures and the individual. In the social life of a small group, by contrast, the individual's views and needs are directly effective, are objects of immediate consideration. This situation accounts for the frequent difficulties characteristic of organizations which are composed of a number of smaller units. Matters at issue here can be appraised correctly and treated with interest and care only at close range; but, on the other hand, a just and regular arrangement of all details can be secured only from the distance which is reserved for the central organ alone. Such a discrepancy is revealed again and again by charitable organizations, labor unions, school administrations, etc. In all these instances, it is hard to reconcile personal relations, which are the very life principle of small groups, with the distance and coolness of objective and abstract norms without which the large group cannot exist.[2]

§ 5. *Numerical Aspects of Prominent Group Members*

The structural differences among groups, that are produced by mere numerical differences, become even more evident in the roles played by certain prominent and effective members. It is obvious that a given number of such members has a different significance in a large group than in a small one. As the group changes quantitatively, the effectiveness of these members also changes. But it must be noted that this effectiveness is modified even if the number of outstanding members rises or falls in exact proportion to that of the whole group. The role of one million-

---

[2] Here emerges a typical difficulty of the human condition. Our theoretical and practical attitudes toward all kinds of phenomena constantly causes us to stay, simultaneously, within and without them. The person, for instance, who argues against smoking must himself both smoke and not smoke: if he does not, he does not know the attraction he condemns; but if he does, he is not considered entitled to make a judgment which he belies. Another example: in order to have an opinion about women "in general," one must have known intimate relations with them and, at the same time, be free and distant from such relations, because they would change one's judgment. Only where we are close, are on the inside, are equals, do we know and understand; only where distance precludes immediate contacts in every sense of the word do we have the objectivity and detachment which are as necessary as knowledge and understanding. This dualism of nearness and distance is necessary for our behavior to be consistently correct. It inheres, so to speak, in the fundamental forms and problems of our life. Just so, the fact that the same affair can be correctly treated only within a small group *and* only within a large one, is a formal, sociological contradiction; it is merely a special case of this generally human contradiction.

aire who lives in a city of ten thousand middle-class people, and the general physiognomy which that city receives from his presence, are totally different from the significance which fifty millionaires or, rather, each of them, have for a city of 500,000 population—in spite of the fact that the numerical relation between the millionaire and his fellow citizens, which alone (it would seem) should determine that significance, has remained unchanged. If, in a parliamentary party of twenty, there are four who criticize the political program or want to secede, their significance in terms of party tendencies and procedures is different from what it would be if the party were fifty strong and had ten rebels within it: although the numerical ratio has not changed, the importance of the ten in the larger party will in general be greater. To give a final example: it has been noted that a military tyranny (other things being equal) is the more tenable, the larger the territory over which it extends. If its army includes one per cent of the population, it is easier for an army of 100,000 to keep a population of ten million under control than it is for a hundred soldiers to hold a city of 100,000 in check, or for one soldier, a village of a hundred. The strange thing is that the *absolute* numbers of the total group and of its prominent elements so remarkably determine the relations within the group—in spite of the fact that their numerical ratio remains the same. These examples can easily be multiplied. They show that the relation of sociological elements depends not only on their relative but also on their absolute quantities. Suppose we have a party within a larger society. The relation between the two changes not only when the society remains stationary while the party increases or decreases in membership, but also when they both change in the same sense and to the same extent. This fact reveals the sociological significance of the magnitude or smallness of the total group even for the numerical relations of its elements. And yet, at a first glance, only these numerical relations seem to have to do with the significance of numbers for the relations within the group.

§ 6. *Custom, Law, Morality*

The formal difference in the individual's group behavior, as it is determined by the quantity of his group, is not only of factual but also of normative and moral significance. This is perhaps most clearly evident in the difference between custom and law. Among Aryan peoples, the earliest ties of the individual to a super-individual order of life seem to be rooted in a very general instinct or concept of the normative, the decent, the Ought in general. The Hindu *dharma,* the Greek *themis,* the Latin *fas,* all express this undifferentiated "normative as such." The more special regulations, religious, moral, conventional, legal, are still enfolded in it, are not yet ramified and separated out: the general notion of the normative is their original unity, not a unity abstracted from them in retrospect. In contrast with the opinion according to which morality, custom, and law have developed as supplementations out of this germinal state, it seems to me that this germinal state is perpetuated in what we call custom. And custom, I think, represents a stage of non-differentiation that in different directions sends forth two forms, law and morality.

Morality here concerns us only insofar as it results from the behavior of the individual toward other individuals or groups, that is, insofar as it has essentially the same contents as custom and law. Morality develops in the individual through a second subject that confronts him in himself. By means of the same split through which the ego says to itself "I am"—confronting itself, as a knowing subject, with itself as a known object—it also says to itself "I ought to." The relation of two subjects that appears as an imperative is repeated within the individual himself by virtue of the fundamental capacity of our mind to place itself in contrast to itself, and to view and treat itself as if it were somebody else. (I do not here answer the question whether this phenomenon represents a transference of the empirically prior inter-individual relation to the elements within the individual, or whether it is a purely spontaneous process originating in these elements.)

On the other hand we find this. Once the normative forms have received particular contents, these contents are emancipated from their original sociological vehicles, and attain an inner and autonomous necessity that deserves the designation of "ideal." At this stage, these contents, which actually are behaviors or states of individuals, are in themselves valuable; they *ought* to be. Their social nature or significance is no longer alone in giving them their imperative character: at this stage, it rather derives from their objectively ideal significance and value. It is true that morality becomes personalized. It is furthermore true that the three general norms of custom, law, and morality itself develop into objective and super-social phenomena. But neither fact prevents our emphasizing here that their contents are socially purposeful, and that those three forms themselves make sure that their contents are actually realized through the individual.

We deal here with *forms* of the intrinsic and extrinsic relation of the individual to his social group. For, the same contents of this relation has historically been clothed in different motivations or forms. What at one time or place was a custom, elsewhere or later has been a law of the state or has been left to private morality. What was under the coercion of law, has become mere good custom. What was the matter of individual conscience, later has often enough been legally enforced by the state, etc. The poles of this continuum are law and morality, and between them stands custom, out of which both have developed. In the legal code and in the executive, law has specialized organs through which its contents are precisely defined and externally enforced. For this reason, law is best limited to the indispensable presuppositions of group life: what the group *can* unconditionally require of the individual is only what it *must* require unconditionally. By contrast, the free morality of the individual knows no other law than that which he autonomously gives himself, and no other executive power than his own conscience. In practice, therefore, its jurisdiction has accidental and fluid borderlines that change from case to case,[3] although in principle it extends to the totality of action.

[3] The fact that law and morality derive (as it were) together from one shift in societal development, is reflected in their teleological functions which are more closely interrelated than appears on first sight. When strict individual conduct, which is characteristic of a life pervasively regulated by custom, yields to a general legal norm with its much greater distance from all individual matters, the freedom

A group secures the suitable behavior of its members through custom, when legal coercion is not permissible and individual morality not reliable. Custom thus operates as a supplement of these other two orders, whereas at a time when these more differentiated kinds of norms did not yet exist, or existed only in a germinal form, it was the only regulation of life. This indicates the sociological locus of custom. Custom lies between the largest group, as a member of which the individual is rather subject to law, and absolute individuality, which is the sole vehicle of free morality. In other words, it belongs to smaller groups, intermediate between these two extremes. In fact, almost all custom is custom of estate or class. Its manifestations, as external behavior, fashion, or honor, always characterize only a section of the society, while the whole of this society is dominated by the same law.[4] It is the smaller group, composed of those whom the violation of good custom somehow concerns or who witness it, which reacts to this violation, whereas a breach of the legal order provokes the whole society. Since the only executive organs of custom are public opinion and certain individual reactions di-

that the individual has thus gained must nevertheless, in the interest of society, not be left to itself. Legal imperatives are supplemented by moral imperatives, and fill the gaps that the disappearance of ubiquitous custom has left in the norms. In comparison with custom, moral and legal norms lie much higher above the individual and, at the same time, much more deeply within him. For, whatever personal and metaphysical values may be constituted by conscience and autonomous morality, their *social* value, which alone is in question here, lies in their extraordinary prophylactic efficiency. Law and custom seize the will externally and in its realization; they anticipate and threaten; and, in order to be effective without fear, they usually, though not always, must become part of personal morality. It is personal morality which is at the root of action. It so transforms the innermost aspect of the individual that he automatically does the right deed without the help of the relatively external forces of law and custom. Yet society is not interested in his purely moral perfection. Individual morality is important to society and is bred by it only insofar as it guarantees as much as possible that the individual act in a socially efficient manner. In individual morality, society creates an organ which is not only more deeply effective than law and custom, but which also saves society the expenditures and labors involved in these institutions. In its tendency to obtain its prerequisites as cheaply as possible, society also makes use of "good conscience." For through his conscience the individual rewards himself for his good deeds; while if he had no conscience, society would probably have to guarantee him this reward somehow by means of law or custom.

4 Cf. the discussion of the sociological form of honor in the chapters on the self-preservation of the group and on the intersection of groups. [Neither of these is contained in the present volume.]

rectly related to public opinion, a large group itself cannot administer custom. The everyday experience in which business custom permits and enjoins other things than aristocratic custom, in which the custom of a religious group involves other things than that of a literary society, etc., suggests that the content of custom consists of the specific conditions necessary for a particular group. For in order to guarantee these conditions, the group can use neither the coercive power of the state law nor any reliable autonomous morality of the individual.

The only aspect which these groups share with primitive groups, with which social history begins for us, is numerical smallness. Life forms that originally were sufficient for the totality have come to characterize its subdivisions, as the totality itself has increased. For it is these totalities which now contain the possibilities of personal relation, the approximately equal level among their members, and the common interests and ideals, by virtue of which social regulations can be left to such precarious and elastic a norm as custom. But when the members increase in number and thereby inevitably become more independent, these conditions no longer obtain for the whole group. The peculiar cohesive power of custom is not enough for the State and too much for the individual, while its *content* is too much for the State and too little for the individual. The State requires surer guarantees; the individual requires greater freedom. Only in those aspects in which the individual is still a member of smaller groups is he still governed, socially, by custom.

The fact that the large group both requires and permits the rigorous and objective norm which is crystallized in law, is somehow related to the greater freedom, mobility, and individualization of its members. This process involves the need for a clearer determination and severer surveillance of socially necessary inhibitions. But on the other hand, the increased restriction is more bearable for the individual because, outside of it, he has a sphere of freedom which is all the greater. The process becomes the more evident, the more law, or a norm approaching it, is an agency of inhibition and forbiddance. Among Brazilian aborigines, a man is in general not allowed to marry the daughter of his sister or his brother. This tabu is the more severe the larger the tribe; while, in smaller, more isolated hordes brother and sister frequently live together. The prohibitive character of the norm—which is more characteristic of law than of custom—is more indicated in the larger group, because this group compensates the individual more richly and positively than the small group does. There is still another aspect which shows that the enlargement of the group favors the transition of its norms to the form of law. Numerous unifications of smaller groups into larger ones occurred originally (or are maintained even permanently) only for the sake of law enforcement; and their unity is founded exclusively in a pervasive legal order. The county of the New England states was originally only "an aggregation of towns for judicial purposes."

There are apparent exceptions to this dependence of custom and law on quantitative differences of groups. The original units of the Germanic tribes, which resulted in the great Frankish, English, and Swedish realms, were often able to preserve for long periods their own jurisdictions that became state matters only relatively late. Inversely, in modern international relations there are many customs that have not yet become fixed as laws. Again, within a particular state, certain modes of conduct are regulated by law which in relation to the outside, that is, within the ultimate group, must be left to the looser form of custom.

It is simple to account for these apparent exceptions. Obviously, the size of the group requires the law form only to the extent to which its elements form a unity. Where only tenuous common characteristics, rather than a firm centralization, permit the designation of the group as a group, the relative character of this designation becomes clearly evident. "Social unity" is a concept of degree. Variations in unity may be accompanied by changing the forms of group regulations, or by changing group size. Accordingly, a given form of regulation required by a certain group size may be the same as that required by a group of a different size, or it may be different from that required by a group of the same size. The significance of numerical conditions is thus not impaired when we find that a large group, because of its special tasks, may do, or even must do, without the legalization of its norms—something which in general is characteristic only of smaller groups. The cumbersome state forms of Germanic antiquity simply did not yet possess the cohesion of their members which, if it occurs in the large group, is both cause and effect of its legal constitution. By a similar argument we can explain why, in the collective as well as in the individual relations among modern states, certain norms are constituted by mere custom. The reason is the lack of a unity above the parties which would be the vehicle of a legal order. In both smaller and looser groups, this unity is replaced by the immediate interaction among their members; and the regulation which corresponds to this intimate interaction is custom. In other words, the seeming exceptions actually confirm the connection between custom and law, on the one hand, and the quantitative aspects of the group, on the other.

Chapter 2

The Quantitative Determination of Group Divisions and of Certain Groups

§ 1. *Introduction*

OBVIOUSLY, THE NOTIONS "large" and "small" groups are extremely crude scientific designations, indeterminate and vague. They are useful, really, only as a suggestion that the sociological form of the group depends upon its quantitative aspects. But they are quite insufficient to show the real connection between the two in any more precise manner. Yet it is perhaps not always impossible to determine this relation more exactly. To be sure, during the foreseeable future in the development of our knowledge, it would be a wholly fantastic enterprise if we wanted to express the formations and relations so far discussed in exact numerical values. Nevertheless, within modest limits, namely in regard to characteristic sociations among small numbers of persons, certain traits can be indicated even at this stage of our knowledge. As transitions from complete numerical determinateness, I shall discuss some cases in which the quantitative determination of the group is already of some sociological significance but is not yet fixed in every detail.

§ 2. *Numerically Equal Subdivisions*

The number operates as a classificatory principle within the group. That is, parts of the group which are formed through enumeration function as relative units. At this point, I merely emphasize this general principle; later I shall discuss the significance of particular individual numbers. The division of a unified group, and more especially, its division not only from top to bottom, in terms of ruling and being ruled, but among its coordinated members, is one of the most extraordinary advances made by mankind. It is the anatomical structure which forms the basis of the higher organic and social processes. The classification may derive from ancestry, or from associations based on voluntary pledges, or from identity of occupation, or from grouping by local districts. All these principles of classification are combined with the quantitative principle: the mass of existing men or families is divided by a certain number and thus yields numerically equal subdivisions. To each of them, the whole has approximately the same relation as each subdivision has to its component individuals. This principle is, however, so mechanical that in order to operate it must be combined with a more concrete one: numerical equal subdivisions are composed either of persons who are somehow related—relatives, friends, neighbors—or of equals or unequals who supplement one another. Yet the numerical identity constitutes the formal principle of classification, even though it never decides *alone*. But it always plays its role, which may be very important, or may be almost negligible.

Nomadic tribes, for instance, often lack all stable content life; they hardly have any possibility of organization except by number; and the significance of number for a group on the march determines military organization to this day. Quite naturally, the principle of division according to numerically equal cadres is often applied to the distribution of a conquered territory or to the colonization of a newly discovered country when (in the beginning at least) objective criteria of organization are lacking. It governs, for instance, the oldest constitution of Iceland. By its very pure application, Kleisthenes' reform achieved one of the greatest social-historical innovations: when he instituted the Council of 500 members, fifty from each of the ten phyles, he had every *demos* receive a number of councilorships proportionate to the number of its inhabitants. The rational idea of constituting a representative body out of the total group, on a wholly numerical basis, transcends the stage of development characterized by the "century" [group of one hundred] (which will be discussed later). For the first time in history, the purely numerical division is used for establishing governmental units as symbols of the population.

§ 3. *The Number as a Symbol of Group Division*

Thus far we have discussed cases where different subdivisions are numerically equal. Numbers can also be used, however, to characterize a group, more particularly, a leading group of persons, within a larger totality. Thus, guild masters were often designated by their number: in Frankfort, the wool weavers' heads were called the "Six," and the bakers' the "Eight"; in medieval Barcelona, the senate was known as the "Hundred"; etc. It is very remarkable how the most outstanding persons are called after the least characteristic feature, number, which is completely indifferent to all quality. The basis of this, it seems to me, lies in the fact that "six" (or any other such number) does not refer to six individual and isolated elements but to their synthesis. "Six" is not "1 plus 1 plus 1," etc., but a new concept emerging from the synthesis of these elements: it is *not,* so to speak, proportionately present in each of them. In this book, I often designate the living, functional interaction of elements as their unity, which is above their mere sum, and in sociological contrast with it. And we do find here that when an administrative body or a committee, etc., is called by its mere number, in reality the idea expressed by this sum is the functional interactive togetherness of the group; and the numerical designation is possible because a number does refer to a unit consisting of other units. In the case mentioned, the "Six" are *not* dispersed over a homogeneous group but reflect a particular differentiation of it, by virtue of which six of its members are singled out and grow together into a leading unit. It is exactly the characterless and impersonal nature of numerical designation which is characteristic here: more forcefully than any other less formal concept could do it, it indicates the fact that it refers not to individuals as persons but to a purely social structure. The structure of the group requires a certain quota of its members for leadership. The purely numerical concept implies the purely objective character of the formation, which is indifferent to any personal features the member may have, and only requires that he be one of the "Six." Really, there is perhaps no more effective way of expressing an individual's high social status, along with the complete irrelevance of whatever he may be as a person outside his group function.

This sort of group unit which is revealed by the numerical distinction of certain group elements receives particular emphasis in an apparently contradictory case. The above-mentioned Barcelona senate, the "Hundred," actually came to have more than 100 members (up to 200), without for that reason changing its name. A similar phenomenon occurs when the number operates not as a distinguishing, but as a classifying principle: where populations are divided by hundreds (see below), the exact preservation of this number for each subdivision is probably never strictly enforced. This is explicitly reported in regard to the old Germanic Hundreds. The number, in other words, becomes the immediate synonym of the social subdivision (which only originally included, or was supposed to include, exactly such a number of individuals). This seemingly trifling fact shows the enormous importance which the numerical character has for the structure of the group. The number becomes independent even of its arithmetic content: all it indicates is that the relation of the members to the whole is numerical; the number, which has become stable, represents this relation. To consist of a hundred elements remains, as it were, the idea of the subdivision, while empirical conditions reflect this idea only imperfectly. It has been said of the Germanic Hundreds that they were supposed to express only an indeterminate number somewhere between the single individual and the whole society; and, in fact, this very clearly describes the sociological phenomenon discussed here. The life of the group requires some medium between the One and the All, an agent of certain functions that neither the individual nor the totality can carry out, and the group designated for this task is called after its numerical determination. It is not its functions which give it its name, for they are numerous and changing; what is stable is only the articulation of some part of the totality into a unit. The size of this part varies from case to case; the ever-recurring designation by number shows that the numerical relation itself is felt to be essential.

We are here confronted in the social field with a process whose psychological form is also seen elsewhere. Thus, the various types of Russian coins are supposed to derive from an old system of weights in which each higher denomination contained ten times the amount of the next lower. In actuality, however, both the absolute and the relative metallic contents of the coins changed, while their respective values, once they had been brought into the numerical order described, remained the same. In other words, the actual metallic-value relations among the coins shift. But the function, which the coins fulfill by virtue of their constant nominal-value relations, derives from the historically earliest weight proportions which have given the nominal-value relations permanent names and symbols. There are still more cases in which the number comes to represent the thing that it counts. In all of them the essential feature is, once more, that the relation between whole and part is designated by the earliest numerical concept that covers all later changes. The tax on miners in sixteenth-century Spain was called the *quinto* because it amounted to one-fifth the value of the mined metal; and it kept this name although value proportions changed considerably. The word "tithe," among the old Israelites and in many other places, came to refer to any sort of tribute whatever— as "Hundred" came to stand for "subdivision" in general. Psychologically, the quantitative relation, which is the principle of taxation as much as of social division, leaves its particular contents behind. This is seen most decisively in the fact that the original numerical characterization comes to designate any modifications of the subdivision to which it originally referred.

§ 4. *Group Organization on Numerical Principles and Its Effect upon the Individual*

Numerical characterization as a form of organization marks an important step in the development of society. Historically, numerical division replaces the principle of the sib. It seems that in many places groups originally consisted of subgroups which were tied to one another by kinship and each of which formed a unit in economic, political, penal, and other respects. The fact that this intrinsically well-founded organization was replaced by divisions of ten or a hundred men each, who were united for the performance of particular tasks, looks, at first glance, like a strange, superficial process, like a schematization lacking all inner life. And indeed, we would search the inherent, cohesive principles of these groups in vain to find a justification why the older order with its organic roots was replaced by a mechanic and formalistic one. The reason for this change rather lies in the *whole* group which is composed of such subdivisions and whose requirements are autonomous and not the same as the life principles of its parts. In the measure in which the whole unit gains in content and strength, its parts lose their own significance—at least in the beginning, and at the stage preceding the highest development, as we shall see presently. The parts transfer their own significance to the larger group. They are the more useful, the less they embody their own ideas and the more, as colorless parts, they receive some position and significance from their contributions to the whole. This is not true in certain highest types of development: there are social structures which precisely when they have attained a very large size and a perfect organization, can grant the individual the greatest freedom to live his life according to his own particular norms and in the most individualized form. And on the other hand, there are groups which reach their greatest strength only when their members have attained the most intense and differentiated individualization. The transition from sib to Hundred, however, seems to characterize that intermediate stage where the members' intrinsic lack of significance and character marks an advance of the whole. For only in divisions by Hundreds are the individual members easily surveyed and guided according to simple norms and without resistance to the central power, a resistance which arises only too easily when each subgroup has a strong feeling of inner solidarity.

Where the organization or action of the group is numerically defined—from the old Hundred to modern majority rule—the individual is violated. This is a point at which the profound inner discrepancy between the properly democratic and the liberal-individualistic idea of society appears with striking evidence. That personalities are transformed into "round numbers" operating without regard for the peculiarities of the individuals who constitute these numbers; that votes are counted rather than weighed; that institutions, commands, prohibitions, services, and privileges are defined in terms of certain numbers of persons, at least in principle—this is either despotic or democratic. Whether it is one or the other, it involves a diminution of the specific and full content of the individual personality and its substitution by the formal fact that the personality is, simply, *one*. By occupying a place in an organization which is determined by number only, its character as a group member has completely superseded its individual and differentiated character. Whether the division into numerically equal subgroups be as crude and practically as often modified as it was in the Germanic, Peruvian, Chinese Hundreds, or as refined, efficient, and exact as it is in the modern army—it always shows the autonomy of the group in the clearest and most pitiless manner. In the first case, this group autonomy is a newly emerging tendency which still fights and compromises with other tendencies; in the second case, it is an absolute victory. The super-individual character of the group, the fact that its form no longer depends upon any contents of the component individuals, is nowhere seen in a more absolute and emphatic manner than in the reduction of the principles of organization to purely arithmetic relations. The measure to which these numerical principles are approximated in practice—a matter which greatly varies from group to group—also is the measure to which the group idea in its most abstract form absorbs the individualities of its members.

§ 5. *The Social Gathering ("Party")*

The sociological importance of quantitative aspects may also be observed in a social type which is characteristic of modern society, namely, the social gathering, or "party." The number of persons at a "party" greatly varies, of course, according to circumstances. But there is still the question of how many persons must be invited before a "party" results. Evidently, this question is not answered by qualitative relations between host and guests. On the other hand, the group of two or three persons whom we meet quite formally and without any real contact, never constitutes a "party." But we do have one when we invite, say, fifteen of our closest friends. The number always remains decisive, although its specific magnitude depends, of course, on the kind and intimacy of the relations among the people. Three circumstances—the host's relations to each of the guests, the relations among the guests, and the way in which each participant interprets these relations—form the basis upon which the number of members decides whether there occurs a "party" or a mere togetherness of a friendly or of an objective-utilitarian sort. A numerical modification, therefore, here produces a distinctly felt transformation into a specific sociological category, however little our psychological means enable us to determine the measure of this modification. But we can approximately describe at least the qualitative and sociological consequences of this quantitative occurrence.

In the first place, a "party" requires a very specific external setup. If one invites one or two persons out of some thirty friends, one does not have to "put oneself to any trouble." But if one invites all thirty at the same time, entirely new requirements come up at once—in regard to food, drink, dress, forms of behavior; in short, there is a greatly increased consumption of things attractive and enjoyable to the senses. This is a very clear example of how seriously the mere formation of a mass lowers the level of the personality. A gathering of only a few persons permits considerable mutual adaptation. Common traits, which make up the content of sociability among these few individuals, may include such comprehensive or refined aspects of their personalities that the gathering attains a character of spiritual refinement, of highly differentiated and developed psychic energies. But the more persons come together, the less is it probable that they converge in the more valuable and intimate sides of their natures, and the lower, therefore, lies the point that is common to their impulses and interests.[5]

[5] Hence the complaint about the banality of social contact in the large betrays a complete lack of sociological understanding. It is unavoidable in principle, that the level at which a larger group in physical proximity can meet at all, should be relatively low. For, all higher and finer differentiations are of an individual nature and therefore are unsuitable for contents that could be shared. It is true that they may have a sociating effect, namely, where a unity is striven for by means of a

In the same degree in which the sheer number of individuals curtails the play of their higher and specific psychologies, an attempt must be made to compensate for this lack by an intensification of external and sensuous attractions. Large numbers of persons that are assembled for some celebration have always been closely associated with a display of sensuous pleasure and luxury. At the end of the Middle Ages, for instance, the luxury exhibited at weddings by the mere number of attendants that accompanied the bridal pair increased to such a point that the sumptuary laws sometimes prescribed the exact maximum number of persons that were allowed to form the escort. In an analogous manner, food and drink have always been the common denominators of large groups for which any other shared mood or interest are hard to attain. A "party," therefore, merely because of its emphasis on number, which excludes a common interaction of more refined and intellectual moods, must all the more strongly make use of these sensuous joys, that are shared by all with incomparably greater certainty.

There is a second characteristic of the "party" that is based on its numerical difference from the meeting of only a few individuals. It is the fact that a complete harmony of mood, which is so characteristic of the small group, is here neither sought, nor could it be attained if it were. On the contrary—and this is a further difference—there easily occurs the formation of subgroups. The nature of a friendly gathering among few persons strenuously militates against its splitting up into two moods, even only into two conversations. In fact, the moment there is a dualism instead of an undisputed single center, we have a "party." The dualism consists in this. On the one hand, there is a general but very loose core, which has only an external or even only a spatial basis. This is the reason why "parties" whose members come from the same social stratum resemble one another as wholes the more closely the larger they are, irrespective of any variation or change in personnel. On the other hand, there is a continuous alteration between involvement and

division of labor. This, however, is possible at a "party" only to a very slight extent, and if it were to occur in a more considerable measure, it would destroy the very nature of the "party." It is therefore a sociologically quite correct instinct which often makes us consider the stressing of personal characteristics at a "party," as a slight tactlessness—even where these characteristics are interesting and pleasing.

release which, according to the nature of the individual, affects him as the most unbearable superficiality, or as a playful rhythm of great aesthetic charm.

The formal-sociological type under discussion is embodied very clearly by the modern ball. Here the momentary, peculiar intimacy of the couple is transformed into a new phenomenon by its constant change among all the couples. The physical nearness between total strangers is made possible by two factors. On the one hand, all participants in the ball are guests of a host who, however loose their relations may be to him, nevertheless guarantees a certain reciprocal security and legitimation. On the other hand, relations are impersonal and as it were anonymous, because of the magnitude of the group and the associated formalism of behavior. These characteristics of the large "party," which the ball presents in a sublimated if not caricatured form, depend on a certain minimum number of participants. In fact, occasionally one can make the interesting observation that an intimate circle of a few persons attains the character of a "party" if only one more person is added to it.

§ 6. *The Extended Family*

There is one case (which, however, concerns a much less complex human group) where the number that produces a particular sociological structure appears rather definitely fixed. In many different places, the extended patriarchal family always numbers from twenty to thirty members, in spite of very different economic conditions. These conditions, therefore, cannot, or not exclusively, determine the recurrence of the number. It is rather probable that the kind of intrinsic interactions that is characteristic of this particular family structure, produces the required proportions of narrowness and latitude only within these numerical limits.

The patriarchal family is everywhere characterized by great intimacy and solidarity with its center in the *pater familias,* and by the guardianship over the affairs of each member that is exerted by the father, both in the interest of the whole and in his own. This determines the upper limit: given the psychological development that corresponds with this form of the family, the kind of dependence and control characteristic of it seems to fail if it is extended over a larger number of individuals. The lower limit is given by the fact that autonomous groups must develop certain collective psychological features if they are to be self-sufficient and to maintain themselves; and this is possible only above a certain number. These features are readiness for offense and defense, confidence of each member to find at all times what support and supplementation he may need, and above all, a religious mood whose elevation and sublimation rise above the individual (or elevate the individual above himself) only if there is a mixture of many contributions and an extinction of the separate, individual religiosity. The number mentioned may have indicated the approximate range, as found by experience, above and below which the group could not go if it was to develop these traits of the extended patriarchal family. Before this range was found, increasing individualization seems to have restricted such intimacy to ever smaller numbers of persons, while on the other hand, the factors which appealed to an increased *size* of the family required, in fact, an ever larger group. The needs from above and from below that were satisfied precisely by this numerical structure have since become differentiated. Part of them demands a smaller, part a larger group, so that later we no longer find a structure which meets them in the same unified manner as the patriarchal family did.

§ 7. *Quantity and Quality*

Aside from such singular cases, all questions of which the numerical requirements of a "party" was an example, have the tone of sophistry. How many soldiers make an army? How many participants are needed to form a political party? How many people make a crowd? All seem to repeat the classical riddle: How many grains of wheat make a heap? Since one, two, three, or four grains do not, while a thousand certainly do, there must be a limit after which the addition of a single grain transforms the existing single grains into a "heap." But if the attempt at such an enumeration is made, it appears that nobody can indicate this limit. The logical ground of the difficulty lies in this. We are dealing with a quantitative series each of whose individual members is relatively insignificant. For this reason, the series appears to be continuous and ascending without break. Yet at the same time, this same series is supposed to permit, at a certain point, the application of a qualitatively new concept which is completely different from the concept previously employed. This, obviously, is an inconsistent demand: the continuous, by its very definition, cannot evolve, purely out of itself, a sudden break and transmutation. Yet the sociological difficulty shows a complication beyond the problem faced by the ancient Sophists. For, "heap" of grains either refers to a pile, and then the designation is logically justified as soon as one other layer is added to the undermost layer. Or "heap" refers to "quantity in general," and then it is quite unjustifiable to demand of this concept, which by definition is vague and undetermined, that it apply only to strictly determined and unequivocally defined realities.

In sociological cases, however, increasing quantity results in entirely new phenomena which, in a smaller number, seem to be absent even in a slighter proportion. A political party has a qualitatively different significance from a small clique. A few people who stand together from curiosity show traits different from those of a "crowd"; etc. The uncertainty of all these concepts results from the impossibility of ascertaining any particular quantity. It may perhaps be removed in this manner. Evidently the uncertainty only applies to certain intermediate magnitudes. Very small numbers unquestionably do not result in political parties, crowds, etc., while very large ones do so most assuredly. But the numerically small structures also have characteristic sociological qualities—as, for instance, the gathering which is not yet a "party," the troop of soldiers which does not yet make up an army, the conniving rogues who do not yet constitute a "gang." These qualities contrast with other qualities which are unquestionably the traits of the large group. The character of the numerically intermediate structure, therefore, can be explained as a mixture of both: so that each of the features of both the small and the large group appears, in the intermediate group, as a fragmentary trait, now emerging, now disappearing or becoming latent.

Thus, the intermediate structures objectively share the essential character of the smaller and of the larger structures—partially or alternately. This explains the subjective uncertainty regarding the decision to which of the two they belong. The point, thus, is not that a highly specific sociological constellation suddenly emerges (like a crystal in a solution) in a structure which has no sociological quality whatever, and that there is no way of ascertaining the moment of this transformation. Rather, there are two different formations each of which has certain traits and can be arranged on many qualitative continua. Under certain quantitative conditions, these two formations fuse into a social structure which they divide between themselves in varying degrees. The question, therefore, in which of the two formations the social structure belongs, does not suffer from any epistemological difficulties characteristic of continuous series, but is an objectively false question.[6]

[6] More exactly, however, the situation is probably this. To each particular number of elements, according to the purpose and significance of their grouping, there corresponds a sociological form, organization, firmness, stability, relation of whole to parts, etc., which changes with each added or subtracted element, although the change may be immeasurably small and not ascertainable. We do not have a particular term for each of these innumerable sociological states, even where we notice its character. We, therefore, are often forced to think of it as composed of two states, of which the one strikes us as more important, and the other as less. But we have as little to do with sums, properly speaking, as we do in the case of the so-called mixed feelings of friendship and love, hate and contempt, or pleasure and pain. Rather (we shall have to come back to this), we usually deal here with uniform feelings, for which we merely have no directly applicable concept. Therefore, instead of describing them, we circumscribe them by means of a synthesis and mutual delimitation of two other concepts.

Here as elsewhere, the intrinsic unity of being is inconceivable to us. We are forced to dissolve it into a duality of elements, neither of which quite covers it and from whose interweaving we make it result. But to do this is only a conceptual analysis which is possible in retrospect and which does not retrace the real genetic process, the real being of the unit. Therefore, where the available designations of social units—"gathering" and "society," "troop" and "army," "clique" and "party," "pair" and "band," "personal following" and "school," "small group" and "mass demonstration"—cannot be applied with certainty, because the number of people under consideration seems too slight for one and too large for another, we are nevertheless dealing with a specific sociological form. It is exactly as unified as is the more clearly defined case, and it corresponds to an equally precise numerical condition. Only the lack of specific concepts for the designation of these innumerable nuances compels us to denote their qualities as mixtures of forms correlated with numerically inferior and numerically superior structures.

Chapter 3

The Isolated Individual
and the Dyad

§ 1. *Introduction*

OUR STATEMENTS UP TO
this point concerned social formations which depend on the
number of their component elements. But our insight was incapable of formulating this dependence in a way which would
have allowed us to derive sociological consequences from certain
specific numbers. This is not impossible, however, if we content ourselves with sufficiently simple structures. If we begin
with the lower limit of the numerical series, there appear
arithmetically definite magnitudes as the unequivocal presuppositions of characteristic sociological formations.

§ 2. *The Isolated Individual*

The numerically simplest structures which can still be designated as social interactions occur between two elements. Nevertheless, there is an externally even simpler phenomenon that
belongs among sociological categories, however paradoxical and
in fact contradictory this may seem—namely, the isolated individual. As a matter of fact, however, the processes that shape
elements in the *dual* are often simpler than those required for
the sociological characterization of the *singular*. For this, two
phenomena are above all relevant here: isolation and freedom.
The mere fact that an individual does not interact with others
is, of course, not a sociological fact, but neither does it express
the whole idea of isolation. For, isolation, insofar as it is important to the individual, refers by no means only to the absence

of society. On the contrary, the idea involves the somehow imagined, but then rejected, existence of society. Isolation attains its unequivocal, positive significance only as society's effect at a distance—whether as lingering-on of past relations, as anticipation of future contacts, as nostalgia, or as an intentional turning away from society. The isolated man does not suggest a being that has been the only inhabitant of the globe from the beginning. For his condition, too, is determined by sociation, even though negatively. The whole joy and the whole bitterness of isolation are only different reactions to socially experienced influences. Isolation is interaction between two parties, one of which leaves, after exerting certain influences. The isolated individual is isolated only in reality, however; for ideally, in the mind of the other party, he continues to live and act.

A well-known psychological fact is very relevant here. The feeling of isolation is rarely as decisive and intense when one actually finds oneself physically alone, as when one is a stranger, without relations, among many physically close persons, at a "party," on a train, or in the traffic of a large city. The question whether a group favors or even permits such loneliness in its midst is an essential trait of the group structure itself. Close and intimate communities often allow no such intercellular vacuums. When we speak of anti-socal phenomena like wretched persons, criminals, prostitutes, suicides, etc., we may refer to them as a social deficit that is produced in a certain proportion to social conditions. In a similar way, a given quantity and quality of social life creates a certain number of temporarily or chronically lonely existences, although they cannot as easily be ascertained by statistics as can these others.

§ 3. *Isolation*

Isolation thus is a relation which is lodged within an individual but which exists between him and a certain group or group life in general. But it is sociologically significant in still another way: it may also be an interruption or periodic occurrence in a given relationship between two or more persons. As such, it is especially important in those relations whose very nature is the denial of isolation. This applies, above all, to monogamous marriage. The structure of a particular marriage, of course, may not even involve the finest and most intimate nuances of the mates. But where it does, there is an essential difference between the case in which they have preserved the joy of individual isolation in spite of the perfect happiness of their life in common, and the case in which the relation is never interrupted by devotion to solitude. The second case may have various reasons. Habituation to the life in common may have deprived isolation of its attractiveness; or insufficient certainty of love may make interruption by solitude feared as unfaithfulness or, what is worse, as a danger to faithfulness. At any rate, it is clear that isolation is not limited to the individual and is not the mere negation of association. It also has a positive sociological significance. As a conscious feeling on the part of the individual, it represents a very specific relation to society. And furthermore, its occurrence changes the nature of both large and very intimate groups, whereby it may be the cause as well as the effect of this change.

§ 4. *Freedom*

Here, too, belongs one of the many sociological aspects of freedom. At first glance, freedom, like isolation, seems to be the mere negation of sociation. For, while every sociation involves a tie, the free man does not form a unit with others, but is a unit by himself. It may be that there is a kind of freedom which is actually nothing but the lack of relations, or the absence of restrictions by others. A Christian or Hindu hermit, a lonely settler in the old Germanic or, more recently, in the American forests, may enjoy freedom in the sense that his existence is completely filled by non-social contents; and something similar may be said of a collectivity (a house community or a state, for instance) that exists, like an island, with no neighbors and with no relations to other collectivities. But, for an individual who does have relations to other individuals, freedom has a much more positive significance. For him, freedom itself is a specific relation to the environment. It is a correlative phenomenon which loses its very meaning in the absence of a counterpart. In regard to this counterpart, freedom has two aspects that are of the greatest importance for the structure of society.

(1) For social man, freedom is neither a state that exists always and can be taken for granted, nor a possession of a material substance, so to speak, that has been acquired once and all. One reason why freedom is none of these things we shall see in a moment. It should be noted that every important claim which engages the strength of the individual in a certain direction has the tendency to go on indefinitely, to appear completely autonomous. Almost all relations—of the state, the party, the family, of friendship or love—quite naturally, as it were, seem to be on an inclined plane: if they were left to themselves, they would extend their claims over the whole of man. They are, often uncannily, surrounded by an ideal halo from which the individual must explicitly mark off some reserve of forces, devotions, and interests that he has taken away from these relations. But it is not only through the extensity of claims that the egoism of every sociation threatens the freedom of the individuals engaged in it. It does so also through the relentlessness of the claim itself, which is one-tracked and monopolistic. Usually, each claim presses its rights in complete and pitiless indifference to other interests and duties, no matter whether they be in harmony or in utter incompatibility with it. It thus limits the individual's freedom as much as does the large number of the claims on him. In the face of this nature of our relations, freedom emerges as a continuous process of liberation, as a fight, not only for our independence, but also for the right, at every moment and of our own free will, to remain *dependent*. This fight must be renewed after every victory. Thus, the absence of relations, as a negative social behavior, is almost never a secure possession but an incessant release from ties which actually limit the autonomy of the individual or which ideally strive to do so. Freedom is not solipsistic existence but sociological action. It is not a condition limited to the single individual but a relationship, even though it is a relationship from the standpoint of the individual.

(2) Freedom is something quite different from rejection of relations or immunity of the individual sphere from adjacent spheres—not only in the function described, but also in its contents. This is suggested by the simple recognition of the fact that man does not only want to be free, but wants to use his freedom for some purpose. In large part, however, this use is

nothing but the domination and exploitation of other men. To the social individual, that is, the individual who lives in constant interaction with others, freedom is very often without any content and purpose if it does not permit, or even consist in, the extension of his will over others. Our idiom correctly characterizes certain brusque and violent acts as "taking liberties with somebody." In related fashion, many languages use their word for "freedom" in the sense of "right" or "privilege." The purely negative character of freedom, as a relation of the individual to himself, is thus supplemented in two directions by a very positive character. To a great extent, freedom consists in a process of liberation; it rises above a bond, contrasts with a bond; it finds its meaning, consciousness, and value only as a reaction to it. But it no less consists in a power relation to others, in the possibility of making oneself count within a given relationship, in the obligation or submission of others, in which alone it finds its value and application. The significance of freedom as something limited to the subject himself, thus, appears as the watershed between its two social functions, as it were; and they are based on the simple fact that the individual is tied by others and ties others. The subjective significance of freedom hence approximates zero, but it reveals its real significance in this twofold sociological relation, even where freedom is conceived as an individual quality.

§ 5. *The Dyad*

We see that such phenomena as isolation and freedom actually exist as forms of sociological relations, although they often do so only by means of complex and indirect connections. In view of this fact, the simplest sociological formation, methodologically speaking, remains that which operates between two elements. It contains the scheme, germ, and material of innumerable more complex forms. Its sociological significance, however, by no means rests on its extensions and multiplications only. It itself is a sociation. Not only are many general forms of sociation realized in it in a very pure and characteristic fashion; what is more, the limitation to two members is a condition under which alone several forms of relationship exist. Their typically sociological nature is suggested by two facts. One is that the greatest variation of individualities and unifying motives does not alter the identity of these forms. The other is that occasionally these forms exist as much between two groups—families, states, and organizations of various kinds—as between two individuals.

Everyday experiences show the specific character that a relationship attains by the fact that only two elements participate in it. A common fate or enterprise, an agreement or secret between two persons, ties each of them in a very different manner than if even only three have a part in it. This is perhaps most characteristic of the secret. General experience seems to indicate that this minimum of two, with which the secret ceases to be the property of the one individual, is at the same time the maximum at which its preservation is relatively secure. A secret religious-political society which was formed in the beginning of the nineteenth century in France and Italy, had different degrees among its members. The real secrets of the society were known only to the higher degrees; but a discussion of these secrets could take place only between any two members of the high degrees. The limit of two was felt to be so decisive that, where it could not be preserved in regard to knowledge, it was kept at least in regard to the verbalization of this knowledge. More generally speaking, the difference between the dyad [7] and larger groups consists in the fact that the dyad has a different relation to each of its two elements than have larger groups to *their* members. Although, for the outsider, the group consisting of two may function as an autonomous, super-individual unit, it usually does not do so for its participants. Rather, each of the two feels himself confronted only by the other, not by a collectivity above him. The social structure here rests immediately on the one and on the other of the two, and the secession of either would destroy the whole. The dyad, therefore, does not attain that super-personal life which the individual feels to be independent of himself. As soon, however, as there is a sociation of three, a group continues to exist even in case one of the members drops out.

This dependence of the dyad upon its two individual members causes the thought of its existence to be accompanied by

[7] Never Simmel's term, but shorter and more convenient than his, which here, for instance, is *"Zweierverbindung"* ("union of two").—Tr.

the thought of its termination much more closely and impressively than in any other group, where every member knows that even after his retirement or death, the group can continue to exist. Both the lives of the individual and that of the sociation are somehow colored by the imagination of their respective deaths. And "imagination" does not refer here only to theoretical, conscious thought, but to a part or a modification of existence itself. Death stands before us, not like a fate that will strike at a certain moment but, prior to that moment, exists only as an idea or prophecy, as fear or hope, and without interfering with the reality of this life. Rather, the fact that we shall die is a quality inherent in life from the beginning. In all our living reality, there is something which merely finds its last phase or revelation in our death: we are, from birth on, beings that will die. We are this, of course, in different ways. The manner in which we conceive this nature of ours and its final effect, and in which we react to this conception, varies greatly. So does the way in which this element of our existence is interwoven with its other elements. But the same observations can be made in regard to groups. Ideally, any large group can be immortal. This fact gives each of its members, no matter what may be his personal reaction to death, a very specific sociological feeling.[8] A dyad, however, depends on each of its two elements alone—in its death, though not in its life: for its life, it needs *both,* but for its death, only one. This fact is bound to influence the inner attitude of the individual toward the dyad, even though not always consciously nor in the same way. It makes the dyad into a group that feels itself both endangered and irreplaceable, and thus into the real locus not only of authentic sociological tragedy, but also of sentimentalism and elegiac problems.

This feeling tone appears wherever the end of the union has become an organic part of its structure. Not long ago, there came news from a city in northern France regarding a strange "Association of the Broken Dish." Years ago, some industrialists met for dinner. During the meal, a dish fell on the floor and broke. One of the diners noted that the number of pieces was identical with that of those present. One of them considered this

8 Cf. the more detailed discussion of this point in the chapter on the persistence of groups. [Not contained in this volume.]

an omen, and, in consequence of it, they founded a society of friends who owed one another service and help. Each of them took a part of the dish home with him. If one of them dies, his piece is sent to the president, who glues the fragments he receives together. The last survivor will fit the last piece, whereupon the reconstituted dish is to be interred. The "Society of the Broken Dish" will thus dissolve and disappear. The feeling within that society, as well as in regard to it, would no doubt be different if new members were admitted and the life of the group thereby perpetuated indefinitely. The fact that from the beginning it is defined as one that will die gives it a peculiar stamp—which the dyad, because of the numerical condition of its structure, has always.

§ 6. *Characteristics of the Dyad*

[a] TRIVIALITY

It is for the same structural reason that in reality dyads alone are susceptible to the peculiar coloration or discoloration which we call triviality. For only where there is a claim on the irreplaceable individuality of appearance or performance, does its failure to materialize produce a feeling of triviality. We have hardly paid sufficient attention to the way in which relationships of like content take on a different color, according to whether their members think that there are many, or only very few, similar ones. And it is by no means only erotic relations which attain a special, significant timbre, beyond their describable content and value, through the notion that an experience like theirs has never existed before. Quite generally in fact, there is perhaps hardly any object of external possession whose value—not only its economic value—is not co-determined, consciously or no, by its rarity or frequency. And so, perhaps no relation is independent, in its inner significance for the participants, of the factor of "how many other times, too"; and this factor may even refer to the repetition of the same contents, situations, excitations within the relationship. "Triviality" connotes a certain measure of frequency, of the consciousness that a content of life is repeated, while the value of this content depends on its very opposite—a certain measure of rarity. In regard to the life of a super-individual societal unit and the relation of the individual to such a unit, this question seems not to emerge. Here, where the content of the relation transcends individuality, individuality in the sense of uniqueness or rarity seems to play no role, and its non-existence, therefore, seems not to have the effect of triviality. But in dyadic relations—love, marriage, friendship —and in larger groupings (often, for instance, "social parties") which do *not* result in higher units, the tone of triviality frequently becomes desperate and fatal. This phenomenon indicates the sociological character of the dyad: the dyad is inseparable from the immediacy of interaction; for neither of its two elements is it the super-individual unit which elsewhere confronts the individual, while at the same time it makes him participate in it.

[b] INTIMACY

In the dyad, the sociological process remains, in principle, within personal interdependence and does not result in a structure that grows beyond its elements. This also is the basis of "intimacy." The "intimate" character of certain relations seems to me to derive from the individual's inclination to consider that which distinguishes him from others, that which is individual in a qualitative sense, as the core, value, and chief matter of his existence. The inclination is by no means always justifiable; in many people, the very opposite—that which is typical, which they share with many—is the essence and the substantial value of their personality. The same phenomenon can be noted in regard to groups. They, too, easily make their specific content, that is shared only by the members, not by outsiders, their center and real fulfillment. Here we have the form of intimacy.

In probably each relation, there is a mixture of ingredients that its participants contribute to it alone and to no other, and of other ingredients that are not characteristic of it exclusively, but in the same or similar fashion are shared by its members with other persons as well. The peculiar color of intimacy exists if the ingredients of the first type, or more briefly, if the "internal" side of the relation, is felt to be essential; if its whole affective structure is based on what each of the two participants gives or shows only to the one other person and to nobody else.

In other words, intimacy is not based on the *content* of the relationship. Two relationships may have an identical mixture of the two types of ingredients, of individual-exclusive and expansive contents. But only that is intimate in which the former function as the vehicle or the axis of the relation itself. Inversely, certain external situations or moods may move us to make very personal statements and confessions, usually reserved for our closest friends only, to relatively strange people. But in such cases we nevertheless feel that this "intimate" *content* does not yet make the relation an intimate one. For in its basic significance, the whole relation to these people is based only on its general, un-individual ingredients. That "intimate" content, although we have perhaps never revealed it before and thus limit it entirely to this particular relationship, does nevertheless not become the basis of its form, and thus leaves it outside the sphere of intimacy.

It is this nature of intimacy which so often makes it a danger to close unions between two persons, most commonly perhaps to marriage. The spouses share the indifferent "intimacies" of the day, the amiable and the unpleasant features of every hour, and the weaknesses that remain carefully hidden from all others. This easily causes them to place the accent and the substance of their relationship upon these wholly individual but objectively irrelevant matters. It leads them to consider what they share with others and what perhaps is the most important part of their personalities—objective, intellectual, generally interesting, generous features—as lying outside the marital relation; and thus they gradually eliminate it from their marriage.

It is obvious that the intimacy of the dyad is closely tied up with its sociological specialty, not to form a unit transcending the two members. For, in spite of the fact that the two individuals would be its only participants, this unit would nevertheless constitute a third element which might interpose itself between them. The larger the group is, the more easily does it form an objective unit up and above its members, and the less intimate does it become: the two characteristics are intrinsically connected. The condition of intimacy consists in the fact that the participants in a given relationship see only one another, and do not see, at the same time, an objective, super-individual structure which they feel exists and operates on its own. Yet in all its purity, this condition is met only rarely even in groups of as few as three. Likewise, the third element in a relation between two individuals—the unit which has grown out of the interaction among the two—interferes with the most intimate nature of the dyad; and this is highly characteristic of its subtler structure. Indeed, it is so fundamental that even marriages occasionally succumb to it, namely, when the first child is born. The point deserves some further elaboration.

§ 7. *Monogamous Marriage*

The fact that male and female strive after their mutual union is the foremost example or primordial image of a dualism which stamps our life-contents generally. It always presses toward reconciliation, and both success and failure of the reconciliation reveal this basic dualism only the more clearly. The union of man and woman is possible, precisely because they are opposites. As something essentially unattainable, it stands in the way of the most passionate craving for convergence and fusion. The fact that, in any real and absolute sense, the "I" can *not* seize the "not-I," is felt nowhere more deeply than here, where their mutual supplementation and fusion seem to be the very reason for the opposites to exist at all. Passion seeks to tear down the borders of the ego and to absorb "I" and "thou" in one another. But it is not they which become a unit: rather, a *new* unit emerges, the child. The parents' nearness, which they can never attain to the extreme extent they desire but which always must remain a distance; and, on the other hand, their distance, which nevertheless to an infinite degree approaches their becoming-one—this is the peculiar dualistic condition in the form of which what *has* become, the child, stands between his creators. Their varying moods now let one of these two elements play its role, now the other. Therefore, cold, intrinsically alienated spouses do not wish a child: it might unify them; and this unifying function would contrast the more effectively, but the less desirably, with the parents' overwhelming estrangement. Yet sometimes ecisely the very passionate and intimate husband and o do not wish a child: it would separate them; the metaphysical oneness into which they want to fuse alone with one another would be taken out of their hands and would confront them as a distinct, third element, a physical unit, that mediates between them. But to those who seek immediate unity, mediation must appear as separation. Although a bridge connects two banks, it also makes the distance between them measurable; and where mediation is superfluous, it is worse than superfluous.

Nevertheless, monogamous marriage does not seem to have the essential sociological character of the dyad, namely, absence of a super-personal unit. For, the common experience of bad marriages between excellent persons and of good marriages between dubious ones, suggests that marriage, however much it depends on each of the spouses, may yet have a character not coinciding with either of them. Each of the two, for instance, may suffer from confusions, difficulties, and shortcomings, but manages to localize them in himself or herself, as it were, while contributing only the best and purest elements to the marital relation, which thus is kept free from personal defects. If this is the case, the defect may still be considered the personal affair of the spouse. And yet we have the feeling that marriage is something super-personal, something which is valuable and sacred in itself, and which lies beyond whatever un-sacredness each of its elements may possess. It is a relationship within which either of the two feels and behaves only with respect to the other. His or her characteristics, without (of course) ceasing to be such, nevertheless receive a coloration, status, and significance that are different from what they would be if they were completely absorbed by the ego. For the consciousness of each of them, their relationship may thus become crystallized as an entity outside of them, an entity which is more and better (or worse, for that matter) than he or she is, toward which he has obligations and from which he receives good or fateful gifts, as if from some objective being.

This rise of the group unit from its structure, which consists of the mere "I" and "thou," is facilitated, in the case of marriage, by two circumstances. First, there is its incomparable closeness. The fact that two fundamentally different beings, man and woman, form such a close union; that the egoism of each is so thoroughly suspended, not only in favor of the other, but also in favor of the general relationship, including the interests and the honor of the family and, above all, the children—this is really a miraculous fact. It is grounded in bases of the ego which rationalistically are inexplicable and which lie beyond its consciousness. It is also expressed in the distinction between the unit and its elements. That each of them feels the relation to be something with its own life-forces, merely indicates that it is incommensurable with the personal, self-contained ego, as we usually conceive it.

The second point is that this idea is further corroborated by the super-individual character of marriage forms, which are socially regulated and historically transmitted. It is impossible to decide whether the immeasurable differences in the nature and value of individual marriages are larger or smaller than are those among individuals. But no matter how great either of the differences may be, no couple has by itself invented the form of marriage. Its various forms are valid, rather, within given culture areas, as relatively fixed forms. In their formal nature, they are not subject to the arbitrary shadings and fates of individuals. If we look at the history of marriage, we are struck, for instance, by the important, always traditional role that is played by third persons during courtship, in negotiations regarding dowry, and in the wedding ceremonies proper. They are not always relatives: they include the priest who seals the marital union. This un-individualized initiation of marriage forcefully symbolizes its sociologically incomparable structure: in regard to its content and interest, as well as to its formal organization, this most personal relation of all is taken over and directed by entirely super-personal, historical-social authority. This inclusion of traditional elements profoundly contrasts marriage with friendship and similar relations, in which individual freedom is permitted much more play. Marriage, essentially, allows only acceptance or rejection, but not modification. It thus evidently favors the feeling of an objective form, of a super-personal unit. Although each of the two spouses is confronted by only the other, at least partially he also feels as he does when confronted by a collectivity; as the mere bearer of a super-individual structure whose nature and norms are independent of him, although he is an organic part of it.

Modern culture seems more and more to individualize the

character of the given marriage, but at the same time to leave untouched, even in some respects to emphasize, its super-individuality, which is the core of its sociological form. At first glance, it may appear as if the great number of marriage forms found in half-cultures and past high-cultures (some of them based on the choice by the parties to the contract, some on their specific social positions), reflected an individualization that is at the service of the individual marriage. Actually, the reverse is true. Each of these types is profoundly un-individual and socially pre-determined; and being more minutely articulated, it is much narrower and tighter than is a very general and pervasive marriage form, whose more abstract character is bound to leave greater play to personal differentiation.

Here we encounter a very general sociological uniformity. If the *general* is socially defined; if, that is, *all* relevant situations are stamped by a pervasive social form, a much greater freedom of individual behavior and creativity prevails than is true when social norms are crystallized in a variety of specific forms, while seemingly paying attention to individual conditions and needs. In the latter case, there is much more interference with what is properly individual: the freedom of differentiation is greater when the lack of freedom concerns very general and pervasive features.[9] The uniform character of the modern marriage form thus certainly leaves more room for individual articulations than do a larger number of socially pre-determined forms. On the other hand, it is true that its generality, which suffers no exception, greatly increases the character of objectivity and autonomous validity that it has in comparison with individual modifications in which we are interested here.[10]

[9] These correlations are treated in detail in the last chapter. ["The Enlargement of the Group and the Development of Individuality"; not contained in this volume.]

[10] The peculiar combination of subjective and objective, personal and super-personal or general elements in marriage is involved in the very process that forms its basis—physiological pairing. It alone is common to all historically known forms of marriage, while perhaps no other characteristic can be found without exceptions. On the one hand, sexual intercourse is the most intimate and personal process, but on the other hand, it is absolutely general, absorbing the very personality in the service of the species and in the universal organic claim of nature. The psychological secret of this act lies in its double character of being both wholly personal and wholly impersonal. It explains why it is precisely this act that could become the basis of the marital relation which, at a higher sociological stage, re-

Something sociologically similar can be seen in the dyad of business partners. Although the formation and operation of the business rests, exclusively perhaps, on the cooperation of these two personalities, nevertheless the subject matter of the cooperation, the business or firm, is an objective structure. Each of the two has rights and duties toward it that in many respects are not different from those of any third party. And yet this fact here has another sociological significance than in the case of marriage. Because of the objective character of the economic system, business is intrinsically separate from the person of the owner, whether he be one or two, or more persons. The interaction among the participants has its purpose outside itself, while in marriage it has it within it. In business, the relationship serves as the means for obtaining certain objective results; in marriage, all objective elements are really nothing but means for the subjective relation. It is all the more remarkable that the psychological objectivity and autonomy of the group structure, which is not so essential to other dyads, does exist in marriage, along with immediate subjectivity.

peats the same duality. But it is in the very relation between marriage and sex behavior that we find a most peculiar formal complication. For, however impossible it is to give a positive definition of marriage in view of the historical heterogeneity of marriage types, it can certainly be said which relation between man and woman is *not* marriage—the purely sexual relation. Whatever marriage is, it is always and everywhere more than sexual intercourse. However divergent the directions may be in which marriage transcends sexual intercourse, the fact that it transcends it at all makes marriage what it is. Here is, sociologically speaking, an almost unique phenomenon: the very point that all marriage forms have in common is the one which they *have to* transcend in order to result in marriage. Elsewhere there seem to be only very distant analogies. Thus all artists, no matter how heterogeneous their stylistic and imaginative tendencies may be, must know natural phenomena very minutely, not in order to stay within them, but in order to fulfill their specific artistic task by going beyond them. In a similar way, all historical and individual variations of gastronomic culture must satisfy relevant physiological needs, but again not to stop there, but to transcend this merely general need satisfaction by means of the most diverse stimuli. But among sociological formations, marriage seems to be the only one, or at least the purest, of this type. Here all cases of a given social form really contain only one common element; but this element is not sufficient to realize the form. This form emerges, rather, only when something else, something inevitably individual, which is different from case to case, is added to the general.

§ 8. *Delegation of Duties and Responsibilities to the Group*

Yet there is one constellation of very great sociological importance which is absent in all dyads, while, in principle at least, it characterizes all larger groups: the delegation of duties and responsibilities to the impersonal group structure. In fact, this delegation frequently, though unfavorably, characterizes social life in general. It may occur in two directions. Any collectivity which is more than a mere aggregation of certain individuals has indefinite boundaries and powers. This indefiniteness easily tempts one to expect from it all kinds of performances which really are the business of the individual members. They are turned over to society. With the same psychological tendency we very often turn them over to our own future, whose nebulous possibilities have room for everything or, as if by spontaneously growing forces, take care of everything which at the moment we do not like to take on ourselves. In these cases, the transparent, but for this very reason clearly limited, power of the individual is always distinguished from the somewhat mystical power of the collectivity. One therefore easily expects of the collectivity not only what one cannot achieve, but also what one does not care to achieve—and this with the feeling of the perfect legitimacy of the transfer. One of the best students of the United States explains many imperfections and obstacles of the American state machinery in terms of the belief in the power of public opinion. The individual, he tells us, is confident that the collectivity will after all find and do what is right, and thus he easily loses his initiative in matters of public interest. And this may result in the positive phenomenon which the same author describes as follows: "The longer public opinion has ruled, the more absolute is the authority of the majority likely to become, the less likely are energetic minorities to arise, the more are politicians likely to occupy themselves, not in forming opinion, but in discovering and hastening to obey it."

But group membership is, for the individual, quite as dangerous in terms of omission as of commission. Here the reference is not only to heightened impulsiveness and elimination of moral restraint which are shown by the individual in a crowd and which lead to mass crimes where even legal responsibility becomes a matter of dispute. In addition, the group interest (true or ostensible) entitles, or even obliges, the individual to commit acts for which, *as* an individual, he does not care to be responsible. Economic groups make shamelessly egoistical demands, officialdoms admit of crying abuses, both political and scientific associations practice outrageous acts of suppressing individual rights. If the individual had to answer for all these acts personally, he would find them impossible—at the very least, they would make him blush. But as a group member, he is anonymous. He feels himself protected if not concealed (so to speak) by the group, whose interests, at least formally, he believes himself to represent. He therefore commits these acts with the best of conscience. There are few cases in which the distance between the social unit and its elements is as great as it is here, where this distance is obvious and effective to a degree that almost degenerates into caricature.

This lowering of the practical personality values often entailed by group membership, had to be indicated because its absence *characterizes* the dyad. Since in this case each element has only one other individual, rather than more, who might form a higher unit with him, the dependence of the whole on him is perfectly clear, and thus his co-responsibility for all collective actions. He can, of course (and it happens often enough), pass responsibilities on to his partner. But this partner can reject them much more immediately and decisively than it is frequently possible for an anonymous whole: the whole lacks energy derived from personal interest, or requisite and legitimate representation. Neither of the two members can hide what he has done behind the group, nor hold the group responsible for what he has failed to do. Here the forces with which the group surpasses the individual—indefinitely and partially, to be sure, but yet quite perceptibly—cannot compensate for individual inadequacies, as they can in larger groups. There are many respects in which two united individuals accomplish more than two isolated individuals. Nevertheless, the decisive characteristic of the dyad is that each of the two must actually accomplish something, and that in case of failure only the other remains—not a super-individual force, as prevails in a group even of three.

The significance of this characteristic, however, is by no means only negative (referring, that is, to what it excludes). On the contrary, it also makes for a close and highly specific coloration of the dyadic relationship. Precisely the fact that each of the two knows that he can depend only upon the other and on nobody else, gives the dyad a special consecration—as is seen in marriage and friendship, but also in more external associations, including political ones, that consist of two groups. In respect to its sociological destiny and in regard to any other destiny that depends on it, the dyadic element is much more frequently confronted with All or Nothing than is the member of the larger group.

§ 9. *The Expansion of the Dyad*

[a] THE TRIAD VS. THE DYAD

This peculiar closeness between two is most clearly revealed if the dyad is contrasted with the triad.[11] For among three elements, each one operates as an intermediary between the other two, exhibiting the twofold function of such an organ, which is to unite and to separate. Where three elements, A, B, C, constitute a group, there is, in addition to the direct relationship between A and B, for instance, their indirect one, which is derived from their common relation to C. The fact that two elements are each connected not only by a straight line—the shortest—but also by a broken line, as it were, is an enrichment from a formal-sociological standpoint. Points that cannot be contacted by the straight line are connected by the third element, which offers a different side to each of the other two, and yet fuses these different sides in the unity of its own personality. Discords between two parties which they themselves cannot remedy, are accommodated by the third or by absorption in a comprehensive whole.

Yet the indirect relation does not only strengthen the direct one. It may also disturb it. No matter how close a triad may be, there is always the occasion on which two of the three members regard the third as an intruder. The reason may be the mere fact that he shares in certain moods which can unfold in all their

[11] Again not Simmel's term, but again more convenient than "*Verbindung zu dreien*" (association of three) and the like.—Tr.

intensity and tenderness only when two can meet without distraction: the sensitive union of two is always irritated by the spectator. It may also be noted how extraordinarily difficult and rare it is for three people to attain a really uniform mood—when visiting a museum, for instance, or looking at a landscape—and how much more easily such a mood emerges between two. A and B may stress and harmoniously feel their m, because the n which A does not share with B, and the x which B does not share with A, are at once spontaneously conceded to be individual prerogatives located, as it were, on another plane. If, however, C joins the company, who shares n with A and x with B, the result is that (even under this scheme, which is the one most favorable to the unity of the whole) harmony of feeling is made completely impossible. Two may actually be *one* party, or may stand entirely beyond any question of party. But it is usual for just such finely tuned combinations of three at once to result in three parties of two persons each, and thus to destroy the unequivocal character of the relations between each two of them.

The sociological structure of the dyad is characterized by two phenomena that are absent from it. One is the intensification of relation by a third element, or by a social framework that transcends both members of the dyad. The other is any disturbance and distraction of pure and immediate reciprocity. In some cases it is precisely this absence which makes the dyadic relationship more intensive and strong. For, many otherwise undeveloped, unifying forces that derive from more remote psychical reservoirs come to life in the feeling of exclusive dependence upon one another and of hopelessness that cohesion might come from anywhere but immediate interaction. Likewise, they carefully avoid many disturbances and dangers into which confidence in a third party and in the triad itself might lead the two. This intimacy, which is the tendency of relations between two persons, is the reason why the dyad constitutes the chief seat of jealousy.

[b] TWO TYPES OF INDIVIDUALITY AND THEIR CONNECTION WITH
DYADIC AND OTHER RELATIONSHIPS

Dyads, wholes composed of only two participants, presuppose a greater individualization of their members than larger groups do (other things being equal). This observation is merely another aspect of the same fundamental sociological constellation. The essential point is that within a dyad, there can be no majority which could outvote the individual. This majority, however, is made possible by the mere addition of a third member. But relations which permit the individual to be overruled by a majority devalue individuality. What is more, if the relations in question are of a voluntary character, persons of a very decided individuality do not care to enter them.

At this juncture, it is important to distinguish a *decided* individuality from a *strong* individuality, two concepts that are very often confused. Certain extremely individualized persons and collectivities do not have the strength to preserve their individualization in the face of suppressive or leveling forces. The *strong* personality, on the other hand, usually intensifies its formation precisely through opposition, through the fight for its particular character and against all temptation to blend and intermix. The *decided,* merely qualitative individuality avoids groups in which it might find itself confronted by a majority. It is rather pre-destined, almost, for dyadic relationships, because its differentiation and its vulnerability make it dependent on supplementation by another personality. The first type—the more intensive individuality—prefers, on the other hand, to confront a plurality against whose quantitative superiority it can test its own, dynamic superiority. This preference is justified even for almost technical reasons: Napoleon's Consulate of Three was decidedly more convenient for him than a group of two, for he had to win over only one colleague (which is very easy for the strongest among three) in order to dominate, in a perfectly legal form, the other, that is, actually, both other colleagues.

In general, it may be said that the dyad does two things in comparison with groups of more members. On the one hand, it favors a relatively greater individuality of the members. On the other hand, it presupposes that the group form does not lower individual particularity to an average level. Now, women are the less individualized sex; variation of individual women from the general class type is less great than is true, in general, of men. This explains the very widespread opinion that, ordinarily, women are less susceptible to friendship than men. For, friendship is a relation entirely based on the individualities of its elements, more so perhaps even than marriage: because of its traditional forms, its social rules, its real interests, marriage contains many super-individual elements that are independent of the specific characters of the personalities involved. The fundamental differentiation on which marriage is based, as over against friendship, is in itself not an individual, but a species, differentiation. It is therefore understandable that real and lasting friendships are rare at the stage of low personality development; and that, on the other hand, the modern, highly differentiated woman shows a strikingly increased capacity for friendship and an inclination toward it, both with men and with women. Individual differentiation here has overwhelmed species differentiation. We thus see a correlation emerge between the most pointed individualization and a relationship which, at this stage at least, is absolutely limited to the dyad. This, of course, does not preclude the possibility that the same person can, at the same time, be engaged in more than one relation of friendship.

[c] DYADS, TRIADS, AND LARGER GROUPS

Dyads thus have very specific features. This is shown not only by the fact that the addition of a third person completely changes them, but also, and even more so, by the common observation that the further expansion to four or more by no means correspondingly modifies the group any further. For instance, a marriage with one child has a character which is completely different from that of a childless marriage, but it is not significantly different from a marriage with two or more children. To be sure, the difference resulting from the advent of the second child is again much more considerable than is that which results from the third. But this really follows from the norm mentioned: in many respects, the marriage with one child is a relation consisting of two elements—on the one hand, the parental unit, and on the other, the child. The.second child is not only a fourth member of a relation but, sociologically speaking, also a third, with the peculiar effects of the third member. For, as soon as infancy has passed, it is much more often the parents who form a functional unit within the family than it is the totality of the children.

In an analogous way, in regard to marriage forms, the decisive difference is between monogamy and bigamy, whereas the third or twentieth wife is relatively unimportant for the marriage structure. The transition to a second wife is more consequential, at least in one sense, than is that to an even larger number. For it is precisely the duality of wives that can give rise to the sharpest conflicts and deepest disturbances in the husband's life, while they do not arise in the case of a greater plurality. The reason is that a larger number than two entails a de-classing and de-individualizing of the wives, a decisive reduction of the relationship to its sensuous basis (since a more intellectual relationship also is always more individualized). In general, therefore, the husband's deeper disturbances that characteristically and exclusively flow from a double relationship cannot come up.

This same fundamental idea can also be seen in Voltaire's statement about the political usefulness of religious anarchy. It says that, within a state, two rivaling sects inevitably produce unrests and difficulties which can never result from two hundred. The significance that the dualism of one element has in a group of several members is, of course, no less specific and decisive when this group serves the maintenance, rather than the disturbance, of the total collectivity of which it is a part. Thus it has been suggested that the collegiate relationship of the two Roman Consuls was perhaps a more effective obstacle to monarchical aspirations than the Athenian system of nine highest officials. It is the same dualistic tension which works now in a conservative, now in a destructive manner, depending on the other circumstances that characterize the total group. The decisive point is that this total group completely changes its sociological character as soon as the function in question is exerted, rather than by two, either by one person or by more than two. Important colleges are often composed of two members, like the Roman Consuls: there are the two kings of the Spartans, whose continuous frictions are explicitly stressed as assuring the continuation of the state; the two highest war chiefs of the Iroquois; the two civic heads of medieval Augsburg, where the aspiration toward a single mayoralty stood under a severe penalty. The peculiar tensions between the dualistic elements of a larger structure guarantee the *status quo* function of the dyad: in the examples given, the fusion into unity could easily have resulted in the predominance of an individual, and the expansion into a plurality, in an oligarchical clique.

This discussion has already shown the general significance of dualism and the comparable insignificance of its numerical increase. In concluding this analysis, I will mention two particular but sociologically highly significant facts. France's political position in Europe was at once changed profoundly as soon as the country entered into a closer relationship with Russia. A third or fourth ally would not have produced any significant modification once this decisive modification had occurred. In general, the contents of human life differ very considerably according to whether the first step is the most difficult and decisive step and all later ones are of a comparatively secondary importance, or whether the first step itself proves nothing, while only later and more outspoken steps realize the turn of events that was merely foreshadowed in the beginning. The numerical aspects of sociation provide numerous illustrations of either case, as will become increasingly clear later on. For a state whose isolation entails the loss of political prestige, the existence of any one alliance whatever is decisive. By contrast, certain economic or military advantages perhaps develop only in a *number* of alliances of which none may be absent if their success is to be guaranteed. Obviously, between these two types there is the intermediate one wherein the particular character and success of the relationship is directly correlated with the number of elements, as is usually true in the aggregation of large masses. The second type is suggested by the experience that relations of command and assistance radically change their character if, instead of one servant, assistant, or other subordinate, there are two. Aside from the question of cost, housewives sometimes prefer to get along with one servant because of the special difficulties that are involved if there are several. Because of a natural need for attachment, one servant tries to approach and enter the employer's personal sphere and interest. But the same need for attachment may lead him to take a stand against the employer by joining a second servant, for each of the two has support in the other. Feelings of specific social status, with their latent or more conscious opposition against the master, become effective only where there are two servants, because they emerge as a feature which they have in common.

In short, the sociological situation between the superordinate and the subordinate is completely changed as soon as a third element is added. Party formation is suggested instead of solidarity; that which separates servant and master is stressed instead of what binds them, because now common features are sought in the comrade and, of course, are found in their common contrast to the superordinate of them both. But this transformation of a numerical into a qualitative difference is no less fundamental if viewed from the master's standpoint. It is easier to keep two rather than one at a desired distance; in their jealousy and competition the master has a tool for keeping them down and making them obedient, while there is no equivalent tool in the case of *one* servant. This is expressed, in formally the same sense, in an old proverb: "He who has one child is his slave; he who has more is their master." It is seen in all these cases that the triad is a structure completely different from the dyad but not, on the other hand, specifically distinguished from groups of four or more members.

Before discussing particular types of triads, we must emphasize the variety of group characteristics that results from the subdivision of the group into two or into three chief parties. Periods of excitement generally place the whole of public life under the slogan, "Who is not for me is against me." The consequence of this is a division of elements into two parties. All interests, convictions, and impulses which put us into a positive or negative relation with others at all, are distinguished from one another by the question of how aptly this alternative applies to them. They may be arranged along a continuum. At the one pole is the radical exclusion of all mediation and impartiality; at the other, tolerance of the opponent's standpoint as legitimate as one's own. Between these extremes lies a whole range of standpoints that concur more or less with one's own position. A point on the continuum is occupied by every decision concerning immediate or remote groups that we have contact with; by every decision defining our positions within these groups; by every decision involving intimate or superficial cooperation, benevolence, or toleration, our increased prestige, or a danger to us. Every decision traces an ideal line around us. This line may definitely include or exclude everybody else; or it may have gaps where the question of inclusion and exclusion does not even arise; or it may permit mere contact, or only a partial inclusion and a partial exclusion. Whether the question of for-or-against-me is raised, and if so how emphatically, is determined not only by the logical rigor of the content of this question, nor only by the passion with which this content is insisted upon, but also by my relation to my social circle. The closer and more solidary this relation is; the more difficult it is for the individual to live with others that are not in complete harmony with him; and the more some ideal claim unites their totality, the more uncompromising is the question for each of them. The radicalism with which Jesus formulated this very decision derives from an infinitely strong feeling of the fundamental unity among all those who had received his message. In regard to it, there can be not only acceptance or rejection but what is more, only acceptance or outright fight against it. This fact is the strongest expression of the unconditional unity of all who belong to Jesus and of the unconditional exclusion of all who do not. For, the fight against the message, the being-against-me, is still an important relation, an inner, though perverted, unity; and this is stronger than any indifferent standing-by or half-hearted fence straddling.

[d] THE FORMAL RADICALISM OF THE MASS

Thus, this fundamental sociological feeling leads to a split of the whole complex of elements into two parties. On the other hand, however, there are cases that show no such passionate feeling which forces everybody into a positive relation, of acceptance or fight, to the new idea or challenge. In these cases, every group that is part of the whole is rather essentially content with its existence as a part-group, and does not seriously request inclusion into the totality. If this is the situation, there is opportunity for a plurality of party formations, for tolerance, for mediating parties, for a whole range of subtly graded modifications. Epochs in which large masses are in movement facilitate party dualism, exclude indifference, and reduce the influence of middle parties. This fact becomes understandable on the basis of the radicalism which appeared to us as the character of mass movements. The simplicity of the ideas by which these movements are guided, imposes the alternative between absolute "yes" and "no." [12]

The radicalism of mass movements does not prevent, however, a complete shift from one extreme to the other. In fact, it is not difficult to understand that such a shift occurs, and for relatively slight reasons. Suppose a stimulus X corresponding to the mood *a* is exerted upon a mass of people who are present in the same place. In this mass there is a number of individuals, perhaps one only, whose temperament and natural passion tend toward *a*. This individual is vividly stimulated by X, which reinforces his own leanings. Understandably enough, this person takes leadership in the mass, which is in some measure already disposed toward *a*, and which follows the mood of the leader whose temperament exaggerates the stimulus. By contrast, the individuals whose natures predispose them toward *b*, the opposite of *a*, keep quiet in the face of X. If now there appears a Y which justifies *b*, the adherents of *a* must be silent, and the movement repeats, with the same exaggeration, in the direction of *b*. This exaggeration derives from two facts. One is that in every mass there are individuals whose temper leans toward the extreme development of whatever mood is stimulated. The other is that these individuals, because at the moment

12 Throughout history, democratic tendencies, insofar as they direct the great mass movements, tend toward *simple* measures, laws, and principles. All complex practices that reject many-sided concerns and pay attention to heterogeneous standpoints, are antipathetic to democracy. Aristocracy, inversely, usually abhors general and coercive principles and tries to do justice to the peculiarities of individual elements, personal, local, and objective.

they are strongest and most emphatic, pull the mass in the direction of their own mood, whereas the individuals who are disposed in the opposite direction remain passive, because the trend of the moment gives them and the whole no opportunity toward their own direction. To put the matter in axiomatic form: it is the contentually variable, formal radicalism of the mass which is the reason why no middle line results from the members of the mass with their dispositions toward different directions. It is the reason why, on the contrary, the momentary predominance of one direction usually silences, at once and completely, the representatives of all others, instead of allowing them to co-determine the mass action in proportion to their relative strengths.

This also explains why once a given direction has been formulated, there is no obstacle in the way of its reaching its extreme. In the face of fundamental practical problems, there are as a rule only two *simple* positions, however many mixed and mediating ones there may be. In a similar way, every lively movement within a group—from the family through the whole variety of organizations based on common interests, including political groups—generally results in the differentiation into a clear-cut dualism. If the rate of speed at which interests develop and general stages of development follow one another is great, we always find that decisions and differentiations are more definitive than they are in slower periods: mediation requires time and leisure. In quiet and stagnant epochs, vital questions are not stirred up but remain concealed under the regular interests of the day. Such epochs easily lead to imperceptible transitions and allow an indifferentism of the individual which a more vivid current would force into the opposition between the chief parties. The typical difference in sociological constellation, thus, always remains that of two, as over against three, chief parties. A number of parties can share in different degrees in the function of the third, which is to mediate between two extremes. The existence of these degrees is, as it were, only an expansion or refinement in the technical execution of the principle of mediation; the principle itself changes the configuration radically, and always emerges and operates when a third party is added.

Chapter 4

The Triad

§ 1. *The Sociological Significance of the Third Element*

WHAT HAS BEEN SAID INDI-
cates to a great extent the role of the third element, as well
as the configurations that operate among *three* social elements.
The dyad represents both the first social synthesis and unification, and the first separation and antithesis. The appearance of
the third party indicates transition, conciliation, and abandonment of absolute contrast (although, on occasion, it introduces
contrast). The triad as such seems to me to result in three kinds
of typical group formations. All of them are impossible if there
are only two elements; and, on the other hand, if there are more
than three, they are either equally impossible or only expand
in quantity but do not change their formal type.

§ 2. *The Non-Partisan and the Mediator*

It is sociologically very significant that isolated elements are
unified by their common relation to a phenomenon which lies
outside of them. This applies as much to the alliance between
states for the purpose of defense against a common enemy as to
the "invisible church" which unifies all faithful in their equal
relation to the one God. The *group-forming*, mediating function
of a third element will be discussed in a later context. In the
cases under examination now, the third element is at such a
distance from the other two that there exist no properly sociological interactions which concern all three elements alike.
Rather, there are configurations of two. In the center of sociological attention, there is either the relation between the two

joining elements, the relation between them as a unit and the center of interest that confronts them. At the moment, however, we are concerned with three elements which are so closely related or so closely approach one another that they form a group, permanent or momentary.

In the most significant of all dyads, monogamous marriage, the child or children, as the third element, often has the function of holding the whole together. Among many "nature peoples," only childbirth makes marriage perfect or insoluble. And certainly one of the reasons why developing culture makes marriages deeper and closer is that children become independent relatively late and therefore need longer care. Perfection of marriage through childbirth rests, of course, on the value which the child has for the husband, and on his inclination, sanctioned by law and custom, to expel a childless wife. But the actual result of the third element, the child, is that it alone really closes the circle by tying the parents to one another. This can occur in two forms. The existence of the third element may directly start or strengthen the union of the two, as for instance, when the birth of a child increases the spouses' mutual love, or at least the husband's for his wife. Or the relation of each of the spouses to the child may produce a new and *indirect* bond between them. In general, the common preoccupations of a married couple with the child reveal that their union passes through the child, as it were; the union often consists of sympathies which could not exist without such a point of mediation. This emergence of the inner socialization of three elements, which the two elements by themselves do not desire, is the reason for a phenomenon mentioned earlier, namely, the tendency of unhappily married couples not to wish children. They instinctively feel that the child would close a circle within which they would be nearer one another, not only externally but also in their deeper psychological layers, than they are inclined to be.

When the third element functions as a non-partisan, we have a different variety of mediation. The non-partisan either produces the concord of two colliding parties, whereby he withdraws after making the effort of creating direct contact between the unconnected or quarreling elements; or he functions as an arbiter who balances, as it were, their contradictory claims against one another and eliminates what is incompatible in them. Differences between labor and management, especially in England, have developed both forms of unification. There are boards of conciliation where the parties negotiate their conflicts under the presidency of a non-partisan. The mediator, of course, can achieve reconciliation in this form only if each party believes that the proportion between the reasons for the hostility, in short, the objective situation justifies the reconciliation and makes peace advantageous. The very great opportunity that non-partisan mediation has to produce this belief lies not only in the obvious elimination of misunderstandings or in appeals to good will, etc. It may also be analyzed as follows. The non-partisan shows each party the claims and arguments of the other; they thus lose the tone of subjective passion which usually provokes the same tone on the part of the adversary. What is so often regrettable here appears as something wholesome, namely, that the feeling which accompanies a psychological content when one individual has it, usually weakens greatly when it is transferred to a second. This fact explains why recommendations and testimonies that have to pass several mediating persons before reaching the deciding individual, are so often ineffective, even if their objective content arrives at its destination without any change. In the course of these transfers, affective imponderables get lost; and these not only supplement insufficient objective qualifications, but, in practice, they alone cause sufficient ones to be acted upon.

Here we have a phenomenon which is very significant for the development of purely psychological influences. A third mediating social element deprives conflicting claims of their affective qualities because it neutrally formulates and presents these claims to the two parties involved. Thus this circle that is fatal to all reconciliation is avoided: the vehemence of the one no longer provokes that of the other, which in turn intensifies that of the first, and so forth, until the whole relationship breaks down. Furthermore, because of the non-partisan, each party to the conflict not only listens to more objective matters but is also forced to put the issue in more objective terms than it would if it confronted the other without mediation. For now it is important for each to win over even the mediator. This, however, can be hoped for only on purely objective grounds, because the mediator is not the arbitrator, but only guides the process of coming to terms; because, in other words, he must always keep out of any decision—whereas the arbitrator ends up by taking sides. Within the realm of sociological techniques, there is nothing that serves the reconciliation of conflicting parties so effectively as does objectivity, that is, the attempt at limiting all complaints and requests to their objective contents. Philosophically speaking, the conflict is reduced to the objective spirit of each partial standpoint, so that the personalities involved appear as the mere vehicles of objective conditions. In case of conflict, the personal form in which objective contents become subjectively alive must pay for its warmth, color, and depth of feeling with the sharpness of the antagonism that it engenders. The diminution of this personal tone is the condition under which the understanding and reconciliation of the adversaries can be attained, particularly because it is only under this condition that each of the two parties actually realizes what the other *must* insist upon. To put it psychologically, antagonism of the will is reduced to intellectual antagonism. Reason is everywhere the principle of understanding; on its basis can come together what on that of feeling and ultimate decision of the will is irreconcilably in conflict. It is the function of the mediator to bring this reduction about, to represent it, as it were, in himself; or to form a transformation point where, no matter in what form the conflict enters from one side, it is transmitted to the other only in an objective form; a point where all is retained which would merely intensify the conflict in the absence of mediation.

It is important for the analysis of social life to realize clearly that the constellation thus characterized constantly emerges in all groups of more than two elements. To be sure, the mediator may not be specifically chosen, nor be known or designated as such. But the triad here serves merely as a type or scheme; ultimately all cases of mediation can be reduced to this form. From the conversation among three persons that lasts only an hour, to the permanent family of three, there is no triad in which a dissent between any two elements does not occur from time to time—a dissent of a more harmless or more pointed, more momentary or more lasting, more theoretical or more practical nature—and in which the third member does not play a mediating role. This happens innumerable times in a very rudimentary and inarticulate manner, mixed with other actions and interactions, from which the purely mediating function cannot be isolated. Such mediations do not even have to be performed by means of words. A gesture, a way of listening, the mood that radiates from a particular person, are enough to change the difference between two individuals so that they can seek understanding, are enough to make them feel their essential commonness which is concealed under their acutely differing opinions, and to bring this divergence into the shape in which it can be ironed out the most easily. The situation does not have to involve a real conflict or fight. It is rather the thousand insignificant differences of opinion, the allusions to an antagonism of personalities, the emergence of quite momentary contrasts of interest or feeling, which continuously color the fluctuating forms of all living together; and this social life is constantly determined in its course by the presence of the third person, who almost inevitably exercises the function of mediation. This function makes the round among the three elements, since the ebb and flow of social life realizes the form of conflict in every possible combination of two members.

The non-partisanship that is required for mediation has one of two presuppositions. The third element is non-partisan either if he stands above the contrasting interests and opinions and is actually not concerned with them, or if he is equally concerned with both. The first case is the simpler of the two and involves fewest complications. In conflicts between English laborers and entrepreneurs, for instance, the non-partisan called in could be neither a laborer nor an entrepreneur. It is notable how decisively the separation of objective from personal elements in the conflict (mentioned earlier) is realized here. The idea is that the non-partisan is not attached by personal interest to the objective aspects of either party position. Rather, both come to be weighed by him as by a pure, impersonal intellect; without touching the subjective sphere. But the mediator must be subjectively interested in the persons or groups themselves who exemplify the contents of the quarrel which to him are merely theoretical, since otherwise he would not take over his function. It is, therefore, as if subjective interest set in motion a purely objective mechanism. It is the fusion of personal distance from the objective significance of the quarrel with personal interest in its subjective significance which characterizes the non-partisan position. This position is the more perfect, the more distinctly each of these two elements is developed and the more harmoniously, in its very differentiation, each cooperates with the other.

The situation becomes more complicated when the non-partisan owes his position, not to his neutrality, but to his equal participation in the interests in conflict. This case is frequent when a given individual belongs to two different interest groups, one local, and the other objective, especially occupational. In earlier times, bishops could sometimes intervene between the secular ruler of their diocese and the pope. The administrator who is thoroughly familiar with the special interests of his district, will be the most suitable mediator in the case of a collision between these special interests and the general interests of the state which employs him. The measure of the combination between impartiality and interest which is favorable to the mediation between two locally separate groups, is often found in persons that come from one of these groups but live with the other. The difficulty of positions of this kind in which the mediator may find himself, usually derives from the fact that his equal interests in both parties, that is, his inner equilibrium, cannot be definitely ascertained and is, in fact, doubted often enough by both parties.

Yet an even more difficult and, indeed, often tragic situation occurs when the third is tied to the two parties, not by specific interests, but by his total personality; and this situation is extreme when the whole matter of the conflict cannot be clearly objectified, and its objective aspect is really only a pretext or opportunity for deeper personal irreconcilabilities to manifest themselves. In such a case, the third, whom love or duty, fate or habit have made equally intimate with both, can be crushed by the conflict—much more so than if he himself took sides. The danger is increased because the balance of his interests, which does not lean in either direction, usually does not lead to successful mediation, since reduction to a merely objective contrast fails. This is the type instanced by a great many family conflicts. The mediator, whose equal distance to both conflicting parties assures his impartiality, can accommodate both with relative ease. But the person who is impartial because he is equally close to the two, will find this much more difficult and will personally get into the most painful dualism of feelings. Where the mediator is *chosen,* therefore, the equally uninterested will be preferred (other things being equal) to the equally interested. Medieval Italian cities, for instance, often obtained their judges from the outside in order to be sure that they were not prejudiced by inner party frictions.

This suggests the second form of accommodation by means of an impartial third element, namely, arbitration. As long as the third properly operates as a mediator, the final termination of the conflict lies exclusively in the hands of the parties themselves. But when they choose an arbitrator, they relinquish this final decision. They project, as it were, their will to conciliation, and this will becomes personified in the arbitrator. He thus gains a special impressiveness and power over the antagonistic forces. The voluntary appeal to an arbitrator, to whom they submit from the beginning, presupposes a greater subjective confidence in the objectivity of judgment than does any other form of decision. For, even in the state tribunal, it is only the action of the complainant that results from confidence in just decision, since the complainant considers the decision that is favorable to him the just decision. The defendant, on the other hand, must enter the suit whether or not he believes in the impartiality of the judge. But arbitration results only when both parties to the conflict have this belief. This is the principle which sharply differentiates mediation from arbitration; and the more official the act of conciliation, the more punctiliously is this differentiation observed.

This statement applies to a whole range of conflicts; from those between capitalist and worker, which I mentioned earlier, to those of great politics, where the "good services" of a government in adjusting a conflict between two others are quite different from the arbitration occasionally requested of it. The trivialities of daily life, where the typical triad constantly places one into a clear or latent, full or partial difference from two others, offer many intermediary grades between these two forms. In the inexhaustibly varying relations, the parties' appeal to the third person, to his voluntarily or even forcibly seized initiative to conciliate, often gives him a position whose mediating and arbitrating elements it is impossible to separate. If one wants to understand the real web of human society with its indescribable dynamics and fullness, the most important thing is to sharpen one's eyes for such beginnings and transitions, for forms of relationship which are merely hinted at and are again submerged, for their embryonic and fragmentary articulations. Illustrations which exemplify in its purity any one of the concepts denoting these forms, certainly are indispensable sociological tools. But their relation to actual social life is like that of the approximately exact space forms, that are used to illustrate geometrical propositions, to the immeasurable complexity of the actual formations of matter.

After all that has been said, it is clear that from an over-all viewpoint, the existence of the impartial third element serves the perpetuation of the group. As the representative of the intellect, he confronts the two conflicting parties, which for the moment are guided more by will and feeling. He thus, so to speak, complements them in the production of that psychological unity which resides in group life. On the one hand, the nonpartisan tempers the passion of the others. On the other hand, he can carry and direct the very movement of the whole group if the antagonism of the other two tends to paralyze their forces. Nevertheless, this success can change into its opposite. We thus understand why the most intellectually disposed elements of a group lean particularly toward impartiality: the cool intellect usually finds lights and shadows in either quarter; its objective justice does not easily side unconditionally with either. This is the reason why sometimes the most intelligent individuals do not have much influence on the decisions in conflicts, although it would be very desirable that such decisions come from *them*. Once the group has to choose between "yes" and "no," *they*, above all others, ought to throw their weight into the balance, for then the scale will be the more likely to sink in favor of the right side. If, therefore, impartiality does not serve practical mediation directly, in its combination with intellectuality it makes sure that the decision is not left to the more stupid, or at least more prejudiced, group forces. And in fact, ever since Solon, we often find disapproval of impartial behavior. In the social sense, this disapproval is something very healthy: it is based on a much deeper instinct for the welfare of the whole than on mere suspicion of cowardice—an attack which is frequently launched against impartiality, though often quite unjustifiably.

Whether impartiality consists in the equal distance or in the equal closeness that connects the non-partisan and the two conflicting parties, it is obvious that it may be mixed with a great many other relations between him and each of the two others and their group as a whole. For instance, if he constitutes a group with the other two but is remote from their conflicts, he may be drawn into them in the very name of independence from the parties which already exist. This may greatly serve the unity and equilibrium of the group, although the equilibrium may be highly unstable. It was this sociological form in which the third estate's participation in state matters occurred in England. Ever since Henry III, state matters were inextricably dependent on the cooperation of the great barons who, along with the prelates, had to grant the monies; and their combination had power, often superior power, over the king. Nevertheless, instead of the fruitful collaboration between estates and crown, there were incessant splits, abuses, power shifts, and clashes. Both parties came to feel that these could be ended only by resort to a third element which, until then, had been kept out of state matters; lower vassals, freemen, counties, and cities. Their representatives were invited to councils; and this was the beginning of the House of Commons. The third element thus exerted a double function. First, it helped to make an actuality of government as the image of the state in its comprehensiveness. Secondly, it did so as an agency which confronted hitherto existing government parties objectively, as it were, and thus contributed to the more harmonious employment of their reciprocally exhausted forces for the over-all purpose of the state.

§ 3. *The* Tertius Gaudens [13]

In the combinations thus far considered, the impartiality of
the third element either served or harmed the group as a whole.
Both the mediator and the arbitrator wish to save the group
unity from the danger of splitting up. But, evidently, the non-
partisan may also use his relatively superior position for purely
egoistic interests. While in the cases discussed, he behaved as
a means to the ends of the group, he may also, inversely, make
the interaction that takes place between the parties and between himself and them, a means for his own purposes. In the
social life of well consolidated groups, this may happen merely
as one event among others. But often the relation between the
parties and the non-partisan emerges as a new relationship:
elements that have never before formed an interactional unit
may come into conflict; a third non-partisan element, which
before was equally unconnected with either, may spontaneously
seize upon the chances that this quarrel gives him; and thus an
entirely unstable interaction may result which can have an animation and wealth of forms, for each of the elements engaged
in it, which are out of all proportion to its brief life.

I will only mention two forms of the *tertius gaudens* in
which the interaction within the triad does not emerge very
distinctly; and here we are interested in its more typical formations. In these two, the essential characteristic is rather a certain
passivity, either of the two engaged in the conflict or of the
tertius [third element, party, or person]. The advantage of the
tertius may result from the fact that the remaining two hold
each other in check, and he can make a gain which one of the
two would otherwise deny him. The discord here only effectuates
a paralyzation of forces which, if they only could, would strike
against him. The situation thus really suspends interaction
among the three elements, instead of fomenting it, although it
is certainly, nonetheless, of the most distinct consequences for
all of them. The case in which this situation is brought about
on purpose will be discussed in connection with the next type
of configuration among three elements. Meanwhile, the second

[13] Literally, "the third who enjoys," that is, the third party which in some
fashion or another draws advantage from the quarrel of two others.—Tr.

form appears when the *tertius* gains an advantage only because action by one of the two conflicting parties brings it about for its own purposes—the *tertius* does not need to take the initiative. A case in point are the benefits and promotions which a party bestows upon him, only in order to offend its adversary. Thus, the English laws for the protection of labor originally derived, in part at least, from the mere rancor of the Tories against liberal manufacturers. Various charitable actions that result from competition for popularity also belong here. Strangely enough, it is a particularly petty and mean attitude that befriends a third element for the sake of annoying a second: indifference to the moral autonomy of altruism cannot appear more sharply than in this exploitation of altruism. And it is doubly significant that the purpose of annoying one's adversary can be achieved by favoring either one's friend or one's enemy.

The formations that are more essential here emerge whenever the *tertius* makes his own indirect or direct gain by turning toward one of the two conflicting parties—but not intellectually and objectively, like the arbitrator, but practically, supporting or granting. This general type has two main variants: either two parties are hostile toward one another and therefore compete for the favor of a third element; or they compete for the favor of the third element and therefore are hostile toward one another. This difference is important particularly for the further development of the threefold constellation. For where an already existing hostility urges each party to seek the favor of a third, the outcome of this competition—the fact that the third party joins one of the two, rather than the other—marks the real beginning of the fight. Inversely, two elements may curry favor with a third independently of one another. If so, this very fact may be the reason for their hostility, for their becoming parties. The eventual granting of the favor is thus the object, not the means of the conflict and, therefore, usually ends the quarrel. The decision is made, and further hostilities become practically pointless.

In both cases, the advantage of impartiality, which was the *tertius'* original attitude toward the two, consists in his possibility of making his decision depend on certain conditions. Where he is denied this possibility, for whatever reason, he cannot fully exploit the situation. This applies to one of the most common cases of the second type, namely, the competition between two persons of the same sex for the favor of one of the opposite sex. Here the decision of the third element does not depend on his or her will in the same sense as does that of a buyer who is confronted with two competing offers, or that of a ruler who grants privileges to one of two competing suppliants. The decision, rather, comes from already existing feelings which cannot be determined by any will, and which therefore do not even permit the will to be brought into a situation of choice. In these cases, therefore, we only exceptionally find offers intended to be decided by choice; and, although we genuinely have a situation of *tertius gaudens,* its thorough exploitation is, in general, not possible.

On the largest scale, the *tertius gaudens* is represented by the buying public in an economy with free competition. The fight among the producers for the buyer makes the buyer almost completely independent of the individual supplier. He is, however, completely dependent on their totality; and their coalition would, in fact, at once invert the relationship. But as it is, the buyer can base his purchase almost wholly on his appraisal of quality and price of the merchandise. His position even has the added advantage that the producers must try to anticipate the conditions described: they must guess the consumer's unverbalized or unconscious wishes, and they must suggest wishes that do not exist at all, and train him for them. These situations of *tertius gaudens* may be arranged along a continuum. At the one end, perhaps, there is the above-mentioned case of the woman between two suitors. Here the decision depends on the two men's natures, rather than on any of their activities. The chooser, therefore, usually makes no conditions and thus does not fully exploit the situation. At the other end, there is the situation which gives the *tertius gaudens* his extreme advantage. It is found in modern market economy with its complete exclusion of the personal element: here the advantage of the chooser reaches a point where the parties even relieve him of the maximum intensification of his own bargaining condition.

Let us come back to the other formation. In its beginning, a dispute is not related whatever to a third element. But then it forces its parties to compete for help from such a third element. Ordinarily an example is provided by the history of every federation, whether it be between states or between members of a family. The very simple, typical course of the process, however, gains a particular sociological interest through the following modification. The power the *tertius* must expend in order to attain his advantageous position does not have to be great in comparison with the power of each of the two parties, since the quantity of his power is determined exclusively by the strength which each of them has relative to the other. For evidently, the only important thing is that his superadded power give one of them superiority. If, therefore, the power quanta are approximately equal, a minimum accretion is often sufficient definitely to decide in one direction. This explains the frequent influence of small parliamentary parties: they can never gain it through their own significance but only because the great parties keep one another in approximate balance. Wherever majorities decide, that is, where everything depends on one single vote, as it often does, it is possible for entirely insignificant parties to make the severest conditions for their support. Something similar may occur in the relations of small to large states which find themselves in conflict. What alone is important is that the forces of two antagonistic elements paralyze one another and thus actually give unlimited power to the intrinsically extremely weak position of a third element not yet engaged in the issue. Of course, intrinsically strong third elements profit no less from such a situation.

Yet within certain formations, as for instance within a highly developed system of political parties, it is more difficult to realize this advantage. For it is precisely the great parties that are often definitely committed, objectively as well as in their relations toward one another. They do not, therefore, have the freedom of decision that would give them all the advantages of the *tertius gaudens*. It was only because of very special favorable constellations that during the last decades the Center Party has escaped this limitation in the German parliaments. Its power position is very much strengthened by the fact that its principles commit it to only a very small portion of the parliamentary decisions; in regard to all others, it can freely decide now in one, now in another direction. It can pronounce for or against protective tariffs, for or against legislation favorable to labor, for or against military demands, without being handicapped by its party program. In all such cases, therefore, it places itself as *tertius gaudens* between the parties, each of which may try to win its favor. No Agrarian will seek the assistance of the Social Democrats in fighting for a wheat tariff, because he knows that their party principles oblige them to be against it; and, in his fight against the tariff, no Liberal will seek their assistance and pay for it, because he knows that their party line makes them agree with him, anyway. But both can go to the Center Party whose non-commitment on this question enables it to make its own price. On the other hand, an already strong element often attains the situation of *tertius gaudens* because it does not have to put its whole power into effect. For, the advantages of *tertius gaudens* accrue to it not only from outright fight, but from the mere tension and latent antagonism between the other two: the advantages derive from the mere possibility of deciding in favor of one or the other, even if the matter does not come to an open contest.

This very situation was characteristic of English politics at the beginning of the modern period, after the medieval phase, to the extent at least, that England no longer sought immediate possessions and dominions on the continent but always had a potential power between the continental realms. Already in the sixteenth century it was said that France and Spain were the scales of the European balance, but England was the "tongue or the holder of the balance." The Roman bishops, beginning with the whole development up to Leo the Great, elaborated this formal principle with great emphasis by forcing conflicting parties within the church to give them the role of the decisive power. Ever since very early times, bishops in dogmatic or other conflict with other bishops have sought the assistance of their Roman colleague who, on principle, always took the party of the petitioner. Thus, nothing was left for others to do but likewise to turn to the Roman bishop, in order not to antagonize him from the start. He came, therefore, to acquire the prerogative and tradition of a decisive tribunal. Here, what might be called the sociological logic of the situation of three, of which two are in conflict, is developed in great purity and intensity in the direction of the *tertius gaudens.*

Thus the advantage accruing to the *tertius* derives from the fact that he has an equal, equally independent, and for this very reason decisive, relation to two others. The advantage, however, does not exclusively depend on the hostility of the two. A certain general differentiation, mutual strangeness, or qualitative dualism may be sufficient. This, in fact, is the basic formula of the type, and the hostility of the elements is merely a specific case of it, even if it is the most common. The following favorite position of the *tertius,* for instance, is very characteristic, and it results from mere dualism. If B is obligated to a particular duty toward A, and if he delegates this duty to C and D among whom it is to be distributed, then A is greatly tempted to impose on each of them, if possible, a little more than half; from both together, therefore, he profits more than he would have earlier, when the duty was in the hand of only one person. In 1751, the government had to issue an explicit decree in regard to the breaking up of peasant holdings in Bohemia. The law was to the effect that if a holding was divided by the manorial lord, each of its parts could not be burdened with more than its por-tion, in correspondence with its size, of the socage that adhered to the whole.

More generally, if a duty is turned over to two, the most important idea is that each of them now has to do less than the one did who formerly had been burdened with it alone: in comparison with *this* notion, the more *exact* definition of the quantum recedes, and can therefore easily be changed. In other words, the merely numerical fact of the party's two-ness, instead of oneness, here engenders, so to speak, the situation of *tertius gaudens.* In the following case, however, it arises on the basis of a duality characterized by qualitative differences. This explains the judicial power of the English king, which was unheard of for the Germanic Middle Ages. William the Conqueror wished to respect the laws of the Anglo-Saxon population as he found them. But his Normans, too, brought their native laws with them. These two law complexes did not fit one another; they did not result in a unitary right of the people as over against the king: consistent with his own interest,the king could force himself between the two laws and thus could practically annul them. The discord of these nations resulted (and in similar cases results) not only from their actual conflicts but also from their actual differences that made a common legal enforcement difficult. In this discord lay the support of absolutism; and, for this reason, the power of absolutism declined steadily as soon as the two nationalities fused into one.

The favorable position of the *tertius* disappears quite generally the moment the two others become a unit—the moment, that is, the group in question changes from a combination of three elements back into that of two. It is instructive, not only in regard to this particular problem but in regard to group life in general, to observe that this result may be brought about without any personal conciliation or fusion of interests. The object of the antagonism can be withdrawn from the conflict of subjective claims by being fixed objectively. This, it seems to me, is shown with particular clarity in the following case. Modern industry leads to ever new interrelations among the most heterogeneous trades. It constantly creates new tasks that historically do not belong to any existing trade. It has thus brought about, especially in England, frequent conflicts over the respective competencies among the different categories of labor. In the large enterprises, shipbuilders and carpenters, plumbers and blacksmiths, boilermakers and metaldrillers, masons and bricklayers are very often in conflict over the question concerning to whom a certain job belongs. Every trade stops working as soon as it believes that another trade interferes with its own tasks. The insoluble contradiction here consists in the presupposition that subjective rights to certain objects are specifically delimited, while they are continuously in flux in their very nature. Often such conflicts among workmen gravely undermine their position toward the entrepreneur. He has a moral advantage as soon as his workers strike because of their own discords, and thereby do him immeasurable harm. Furthermore, he has it in his arbitrary power to subdue any trade by threatening to employ another trade for the work in question. The economic interest that everyone of them has in not losing the job, is based on the fear that the competing worker might do it more cheaply and might, thereby, contribute to lowering the standard wage paid for it. It was therefore proposed, as the only possible solution, that the trade unions should fix the standard wage for every particular work in consultation with the federated entrepreneurs, and then leave it up to the workers which category of laborers they wanted to employ for a job in question. The excluded category thus no longer has to fear any harm to its *basic* economic interest. This objectification of the matter of dispute deprives the entrepreneur of the advantage that he gains by lowering the wages and playing up the two parties against one another. Although he has retained the choice among the different labor groups, he can no longer make any profitable use of it. The earlier mixture of personal and objective elements has become differentiated. In regard to the first, the entrepreneur remains in the formal situation of *tertius gaudens;* but the objective fixation of the second has taken from this situation the chance of exploitation.

Many among the various kinds of conflicts mentioned here and in connection with the next form of triad, must have operated to produce or increase the power position of the church ever since the Middle Ages, when it began to have it among secular powers. In view of the incessant unrests and quarrels in the political districts, large and small, the church, the only stable element, an element already revered or feared by every party, must have gained an incomparable prerogative. Many times, it is quite generally the mere stability of the *tertius* in the changing stages of the conflict—the fact that the *tertius* is not touched by its contents—around which oscillate the ups and downs of the two parties; and this gives the stable third element its superiority and its possibility of gain. Other things being equal, it may be said that the more violently and, especially, the longer the positions of the conflicting parties oscillate, all the more superior, respected, and of greater opportunity will the position of the *tertius* be rendered by firm endurance, as a purely formal fact. There is probably no more gigantic example of this widely observed relationship than the Catholic Church itself.

For the general characterization of the *tertius gaudens,* which applies to all of its particular manifestations alike, a further point must be noted. This is, that among the causes of his prerogative, there is the mere difference of psychological energies which he invests in the relationship, as compared with the others. Earlier, in regard to the non-partisan in general, I mentioned that he represents intellectuality, while the parties in conflict represent feeling and will. If the non-partisan is in the position of *tertius gaudens,* that is, of egoistic exploiter of the situation, this intellectuality gives him a dominating place. It is enthroned, as it were, at an ideal height. The *tertius* fully enjoys that external advantage which every complication bestows upon the party whose feelings are not involved. Certainly, he may scorn the practical exploitation of his less biased grasp of the conjuncture, of his strength, which is not committed one way or another but can always be used for different purposes. But even if he does, his situation gives him at least the feeling of a slight ironical superiority over the parties which stake so much for the sake of what to him is so indifferent.

§ 4.   Divide et Impera

The previously discussed combinations of three elements were characterized by an existing or emerging conflict between two, from which the third drew his advantage. One particular variety of this combination must now be considered separately, although in reality it is not always clearly delimited against other types. The distinguishing nuance consists in the fact that the third element intentionally produces the conflict in order to gain a dominating position. Here too, however, we must preface the treatment of this constellation by pointing out that the number three is merely the minimum number of elements that are necessary for this formation, and that it may thus serve as the simplest schema. Its outline is that initially two elements are united or mutually dependent in regard to a third, and that this third element knows how to put the forces combined against *him* into action against *one another.* The outcome is that the two either keep each other balanced so that he, who is not interfered with by either, can pursue his advantages; or that they so weaken one another that neither of them can stand up against his superiority.

I shall now characterize some steps in the scale on which the relevant phenomena may be arranged. The simplest case is found where a superior prevents the unification of elements which do not yet positively strive after unification but *might* do so. Here, above all, belong the legal prohibitions against political organizations, as well as against leagues of organizations each of which, individually, is permitted. Usually there is no specifically defined fear or demonstrable danger that such organizations might present to the ruling powers. Rather, the form of association as such is feared, because there is the *possibility* that it might be combined with a dangerous content. Pliny, in his correspondence with Trajan, states explicitly that the Christians are dangerous because they form an association; otherwise they are completely harmless. On the one hand, there is the experience that revolutionary tendencies, or tendencies that are at all directed toward changing what *is*, must adopt the form of unifying as many interested parties as possible. But this experience changes into the logically false but psychologically well understandable inverse notion according to which all associations have tendencies directed against the existing powers. Their prohibition thus is founded upon a possibility of the second power, as it were. In the first place, the *a priori* prohibited associations are merely *possible* and very often do not exist even as wishes of the elements separated by the prohibition. In the second place, the dangers for the sake of which the prohibition occurred would only be *possibilities,* even if the associations actually existed. In this elimination of anticipated associations, the "divide and rule," therefore, appears as the subtlest imaginable prophylactic on the part of the one element against all possibilities that might result from the fusion of the others.

This preventive form may exist even where the plurality that confronts one element consists of the various power components of one identical phenomenon. The Anglo-Norman kings saw to it that the manors of the feudal lords were in as widely scattered locations as possible; some of the most powerful vassals had their seats in from seventeen to twenty-one different shires each. Because of this principle of local distribution, the dominions of the crown vassals could not consolidate themselves into great sovereign courts as they could on the continent. Regarding the earlier land distributions among the sons of rulers, we hear that the individual pieces were parceled out as widely as possible in order to preclude their complete separation from the ruler. In this manner, the unified state wishes to preserve its dominion by splitting up all territorial subdivisions: if they were contiguous, they could more easily remove themselves from its influence.

Where there actually exists a desire for unification, the prophylactic prevention of the unification has an even more pointed effect. A relevant case (which, to be sure, is complicated by other motives as well) is the fact that generally, in wage and other controversial matters, employers categorically refuse to negotiate with intermediary persons who do not belong to their own employees. This refusal has two functions. It prevents the workers from strengthening their position by associating with a personality who has nothing to fear or to hope from the employer. In the second place, it is an obstacle to the unified action of workers in different trades toward a common goal, for instance, the general establishment of a uniform wage scale. By rejecting the middle person who might negotiate on behalf of several workers' groups alike, the employer precludes the threatening unification of the workers. In view of the existing tendencies toward such a unification, this refusal is considered very important for his position. For this reason, employers' associations sometimes impose this isolation of the labor force, in the case of conflicts and negotiations, as a statutory duty upon each of their members. It was an extraordinary progress in the history of English trade unions, especially in the third quarter of the nineteenth century, when the institution of an impersonal agency made the employer's exploitation of this *"divide"* impossible. For in this manner, the arbitrations by non-partisans who were resorted to in conflict situations, began to attain a finality which was recognized beyond the individual case by both parties to the matter at issue. Thus a general rule frequently regulated the negotiations between employer and employee, although they still negotiated individually. But this is, obviously, an intermediate step in the direction of collective contracts governing a whole trade and all interests within it; and this stage of collective contracts eliminates in principle the practice of "divide and rule."

In a similar fashion, the attempts of constitutional monarchs at splitting up parliaments in order to prevent the rise of inconvenient majorities, go beyond mere prophylactic measures. I mention only one example which is of major interest because of its radicalism. Under George III, the English court had the practice of declaring the party principle and its operation as actually inadmissible, and incompatible with the welfare of the state. It did so on the thesis that only the individual and his individual capabilities could render political services. By designating laws and general directives as the specific functions of parties, the court requested "men, not measures." It thus played up the practical significance of individuality against the actions by pluralities; it tried to dissolve the plurality into its atoms, allegedly its only real and effective elements, by somewhat derogatorily identifying it with abstract generality itself.

The separation of the elements attains a more active, rather than a merely prohibitive form when the third person creates jealousy between them. The reference here is not yet to cases where he makes them destroy one another. On the contrary, here we are thinking of tendencies which often are conservative: the third wants to maintain his already existing prerogative by preventing a threatening coalition of the other two from arising, or at least from developing beyond mere beginnings. This technique seems to have been used with particular finesse in a case that is reported of ancient Peru. It was the general custom of the Incas to divide a newly conquered tribe in two approximately equal halves and to place a supervisor over each of them, but to give these two supervisors slightly different ranks. This was indeed the most suitable means for provoking rivalry between the two heads, which prevented any united action against the ruler on the part of the subjected territory. By contrast, both identical ranks and greatly different ranks would have made unification much easier. If the two heads had had the same rank, an equal distribution of leadership in case of action would have been more likely than any other arrangement; and, since there would have been need for subordination, peers would have most probably submitted to such a technical necessity. If the two heads had had very different ranks, the leadership of the one would have found no opposition. The *slight* difference in rank least of all allows an organic and satisfactory arrangement in the unification feared, since the one would doubtless have claimed unconditional prerogative because of his superiority, which, on the other hand, was not significant enough to suggest the same claim to the other.

The principle of the unequal distribution of values (of whatever description) in order to make the ensuing jealousy a means for "divide and rule," is a widely popular technique. But it should be noted that there are certain sociological circumstances that offer basic protection against it. Thus, the attempt was made to agitate Australian aborigines against one another by means of unequally distributed gifts. But this always failed in the face of the communism of the hordes, which distributed all gifts among all members, no matter to which they had gone. In addition to jealousy, it is particularly distrust which is used as a psychological means to the same end. Distrust, in contrast to jealousy, is apt to prevent especially larger groups from forming conspiratory associations. In the most effective manner, this principle was employed by the government of Venice which, on a gigantic scale, invited the citizens to denounce all in any way suspect fellow citizens. Nobody knew whether his nearest acquaintance was in the service of the state inquisition. Revolutionary plans, which presuppose the mutual confidence of large numbers of persons, were thus cut at the root, so that in the later history of Venice, open revolts were practically absent.

The grossest form of "divide and rule," the unleashing of positive battle between two parties, may have its intention in the relationship of the third element either to the two or to objects lying outside them. The second of these two alternatives occurs where one of three job applicants manages to turn the two others against one another so that they reciprocally destroy their chances by gossip and calumny which each circulates about the other. In all these cases, the art of the third element is shown by the distance he knows how to keep between himself and the action which he starts. The more invisible the threads are by which he directs the fight, the better he knows how to build a fire in such a way that it goes on burning without his further interference and even surveillance—not only the more pointed and undistracted is the fight between the two until their mutual ruin is reached, but the more likely is it that the prize of the fight be-tween *them,* as well as other objects that are valuable to him, seem almost automatically to fall into his lap. In this technique, too, the Venetians were masters. In order to take possession of estates owned by noblemen on the mainland, they used the means of awarding high titles to younger or inferior members of the nobility. The indignation of their elders and superiors always presented occasions for brawls and breaches of the peace between the two parties, whereupon the government of Venice, in all legal formality, confiscated the estates of the guilty parties.

It is very plausible that in all such cases, the union of the discordant elements against the common suppressor would be a most expedient step to take. The failure of this union quite dis-tinctly shows the general condition of "divide and rule": the fact that hostilities by no means have their sufficient ground in the clash of real interests. Once there is a need for hostility at all, once there is an antagonism which is merely groping for its ob-ject, it is easy to substitute for the adversary against whom hos-tility would make sense and have a purpose, a totally different one. "Divide and rule" requires of its artist that he create a general state of excitation and desire to fight by means of instiga-tions, calumnies, flatteries, the excitement of expectations, etc. Once this is done, it is possible to succeed in slipping in an ad-versary that is not properly indicated. The form of the fight itself can thus be completely separated from its content and the rea-sonableness of this content. The third element, against whom the hostility of the two ought to be directed, can make himself invisible between them, so to speak, so that the clash of the two is not against him but against one another.

Where the purpose of the third party is directed, not toward an object, but toward the immediate domination of the other two elements, two sociological considerations are essential. (1) Certain elements are formed in such a way that they can be fought successfully only by similar elements. The wish to subdue them finds no immediate point of attack. It is, therefore, neces-sary to divide them within themselves, as it were, and to continue a fight among the parts which they can wage with homogeneous weapons until they are sufficiently weakened to fall to the third element. It has been said of England that she could gain India only by means of India. Already Xerxes had recognized that Greeks were best to fight Greece. It is precisely those whose similarity of interests makes them depend upon one another who best know their mutual weaknesses and vulnerable points. The principle of *similia similibus,* of eliminating a condition by producing a similar one, therefore applies here on the largest scale. Mutual promotion and unification is best gained if there is a certain measure of qualitative difference, because this difference produces a supplementation, a growing together, and an organically differentiated life. Mutual destruction, on the other hand, seems to succeed best if there is qualitative homogeneity, except, of course, in those cases where one party has such a quantitative superiority of power that the relation of its particular characteristics to those of the other becomes altogether irrelevant. The whole category of hostilities that has its extreme development in the fight between brothers, draws its radically destructive character from the fact that experience and knowledge, as well as the instincts flowing from their common root, give each of them the most deadly weapons precisely against this specific adversary. The basis of the relations among like elements is their common knowledge of external conditions and their empathy with the inner situation. Evidently, this is also the means for the deepest hurts, which neglect no possibility of attack. Since in its very nature this means is reciprocal, it leads to the most radical annihilation. For this reason, the fight of like against like, the splitting up of the adversary into two qualitatively homogeneous parties, is one of the most pervasive realizations of "divide and rule."

(2) Where it is not possible for the suppressor to have his victims alone do his business, where, that is, he himself must take a hand in the fight, the schema is very simple: he supports one of them long enough for the other to be suppressed, whereupon the first is an easy prey for him. The most expedient manner is to support the one who is the stronger to begin with. This may take on the more negative form that, within a complex of elements intended for suppression, the more powerful is merely spared. When subjugating Greece, Rome was remarkably considerate in her treatment of Athens and Sparta. This procedure is bound to produce resentment and jealousy in the one camp,

and haughtiness and blind confidence in the other—a split which makes the prey easily available for the suppressor. It is a technique employed by many rulers: he protects the stronger of two, both of whom are actually interested in his own downfall, until he has ruined the weaker; then he changes fronts and advances against the one now left in isolation, and subjugates him. This technique is no less popular in the founding of world empires than in the brawls of street urchins. It is employed by governments in the manipulation of political parties as it is in competitive struggles in which three elements confront one another— perhaps a very powerful financier or industrialist and two less important competitors whose powers, though different from one another, are yet both a nuisance to him. In this case, the first, in order to prevent the two others from joining up, will make a price agreement or production arrangement with the stronger of the two, who draws considerable advantages from it, while the weaker is destroyed by the arrangement. Once he is, the second can be shaken off, for until then he was the ally of the first, but now he has no more backing and is being ruined by means of underselling or other methods.

Chapter 5

The Importance of Specific Numbers for Relations among Groups

§ 1. *Group Subdivision*

I NOW PROCEED TO DISCUSS
a totally different type of sociological formations that depend
upon the numerical determination of their elements. In the
case of the dyads and triads, the point at issue was the inner
group life with all its differentiations, syntheses and antitheses,
as it develops at those minimum or maximum numbers of
members. The concern was not with the group as a whole in
its relation to other groups or to a larger group of which it is
a part, but rather with the immanent mutual relationship
among its elements. But we may also ask the inverse question
regarding the significance of numerical determination for the
relations of the group with the outside. Here its most essential function is its possibility of dividing a group into subgroups. The teleological import of this subdivision, as has already
been indicated earlier, is the easier surveillance and manipula-
bility of the total group. It is often its earliest organization or,
more correctly, its mechanization. In a purely formal respect,
it supplies the possibility of preserving the form, character, and
arrangement of the subdivisions, irrespective of the quantitative
development of the total group itself. For, the components with
which the administration of the whole counts remain, in a qualitative sense, sociologically the same: the increase of the whole
merely changes their multiplier. This, for instance, is the immense utility of the numerical division of armies. The increase
of an army is a matter of relatively easy technique: it proceeds

by the ever repeated formation of new cadres which themselves, however, are numerically, and hence organizationally, rigidly fixed.

§ 2. *The Decimal Principle*

Evidently, this advantage is connected with numerical determination in general, but not with any particular numbers. Yet one class of numbers, which has already been mentioned earlier, has attained a particular historical importance for social divisions: ten and its derivations. In this unification of ten members for purposes of solidary work and responsibility, which we find in many of the oldest cultures, no doubt the number of fingers was decisive. Where arithmetical skill is completely lacking, the fingers provide a first principle of orientation for determining a plurality of units and showing their divisions and compositions. This general significance of the principle of five and ten has been noted often enough. Its *social* significance is due to a very special circumstance. The fingers are relatively independent of one another and have relative autonomy in their movements. But, on the other hand, they are inseparable (in France one says of two friends: *"Ils sont unis comme deux doigts de la main"*) and receive their very sense only from their togetherness. They thus offer a highly pertinent model for social groups of individuals: the unity and peculiar co-efficacy among small subgroups of larger collectivities could not be symbolized more impressively.

Even quite recently, the Czech secret society "Omladina" was constituted on the principle of the number five: its leadership belonged to several "hands," each of which consisted of a thumb (the highest leader) and four fingers.[14] How strongly a

14 Looked at from a different and more general angle, the division by numbers of fingers belongs in the typical tendency to use phenomena of a given, impressive, natural rhythm for this sociological purpose, at least as far as name and symbol are concerned. A secret political society under Louis Philippe called itself "The Seasons." Six members under the leadership of a seventh, who was called Sunday, formed a week; four weeks, a month; three months, a season; and four seasons, the highest unit that stood under a supreme commander. In spite of all the playfulness of these designations, the feeling that the group initiated a unit of different elements that was indicated by nature, probably somehow played its role. And the mystical coloration toward which secret societies tend in general was likely to favor this symbolization with which—so one could well believe—one could inject a cosmically formative force into a merely willed structure.

unit of ten within a larger group was felt to belong together, is also shown (perhaps) by the custom, which can be traced back to early antiquity, of decimating army subdivisions in the case of rebellions, desertions, etc. It was ten that were considered a unit which, for the purposes of punishment, could be represented by the individual; or perhaps there also was the vague experience that among each ten men there usually is, on the average, one ringleader. The division of a group into ten numerically equal parts evidently leads to a totally different result than the division into individuals each representing ten others, and the two types of division have no objective or practical connection with one another. Nevertheless, it seems to me that psychologically, the first derives from the second. When the Jews returned from the Second Exile—42,360 Jews with their slaves—they were distributed in such a way that one tenth, drawn out by lot, took residence in Jerusalem, and the remaining nine tenths in the country. For the capital, these were decidedly too few, and indeed one had at once to think of measures to increase the population of Jerusalem. It appears that here the power of the decimal principle as the ground of social division made people blind to practical exigencies.

The Hundred is derived from the same principle. Above all, it is essentially a means of division, and historically the most important one. I already mentioned that it has become the conceptual representative of division itself, so that its name remains attached to the subgroup even when this subgroup contains considerably fewer or more members. The Hundred—most decisively perhaps in the large role that it plays in the administration of Anglo-Saxon England—appears, so to speak, as the idea of the part-group in general; and its external incompleteness does not alter its inner significance. It is very characteristic that in ancient Peru the Hundreds voluntarily continued to pay their tribute to the Incas by exerting all their strength, long after they had sunk to a fourth of their original number. The sociological basis here is that these territorial groups were conceived as units irrespective of their members. Since it seems, however, that the obligation to pay taxes referred, not to the group, but to its one hundred elements, the taking over of this obligation by the re-

maining twenty-five shows all the more distinctly how unconditional, naturally solidary a unit the Hundred was felt to be.

It is inevitable that the division into Hundreds breaks
through various organic relations—of kin, neighborhood, and
sympathy—among elements and their aggregates. The decimal
division is always a mechanical-technical principle: a teleological, not a natural-spontaneous principle. Occasionally, in fact,
it is combined with a more organic division. The medieval army
of the German empire was constituted according to tribes; but
at the same time we hear that the division by Thousands cut
through and superseded the other order which was more natural
and more determined by a *terminus a quo.*[15] Nevertheless, the
strong centripetality, which is revealed by the organization of
the group into Hundreds, suggests that its significance lies not
only in its classificatory purpose. In fact, classification is merely
a superficial feature; by means of it the larger, inclusive group
is served. Aside from this, the number hundred itself is found
to bestow a particular significance and dignity upon the group
so composed. The nobility in Locri Epizephyrii traced its origin
to noble women of the so-called "hundred houses" who participated in the founding of the colony. Likewise, the original set-
tlements through which Rome was founded are said to have
consisted of a hundred Latin *gentes,* a hundred Sabellic *gentes,*
and a hundred *gentes* that were composed of various elements.
One hundred members apparently give the group a certain style,
an exactly delimited, rigorous contour in comparison with which
a slightly smaller or larger number appears relatively vague and
less complete in itself. The Hundred has an inner unity and
systematic character which makes it particularly suitable for
the formation of genealogical myths. It represents a peculiar synthesis of mystical symmetry and rational sense. By comparison,
all other numbers of group elements are felt to be accidental, not
equally held together by their inner coherence, not equally
unchangeable in their very structure. The especially adequate
relation to the categories of our mind, the ease with which one
hundred can be surveyed and controlled and made so suitable
as a classificatory principle, appear to be the reflection of an

[15] "Limit from which; starting-point." Here: "from the standpoint of the component individuals (rather than from that of the administration)."—Tr.

objective characteristic of the group which the group derives from precisely this numerical determination.

§ 3. *The Outside Regulation of Groups according to Their Maximum and Minimum Sizes*

This characteristic is totally different from those so far discussed. In the combinations of two and three, the number determined the inner life of the group. But it did so not in its capacity of mere quantum. The dyad and the triad showed their characteristics not because they had these respective sizes as total groups: what we observed, rather, were the determinations of every single element by its interaction with one as over against two other elements. It is quite different in regard to all derivations of the number of fingers. Here, the ground of the synthesis lies in the greater convenience with which the group can be surveyed, organized, and directed. In brief, it does not properly lie in the group itself but in the subject which theoretically or practically has to deal with it. We come, now, to a third significance of the numbers of members. We now discover that, objectively and as a whole, that is, regardless of differences among the individual positions of its elements, the group shows certain characteristics only below or only above a certain size. In quite general terms, this was already discussed in connection with the difference between large and small groups. But now the question is whether certain characteristics of the total group might not derive from *specific* numbers of members. Even here, of course, the interactions among individuals constitute the real and decisive process of group life. But now it is not these interactions in their details but their fusion into an image of the whole which is the topic of inquiry.

All facts that suggest *this* significance of group quantity belong to one type, namely, to the legal prescriptions regarding the minimum or maximum membership of associations which claim certain functions or rights and carry out certain duties. It is easy to find the reason for this. There are particular qualities which associations develop on the basis of the number of members and which are justified by legal prescriptions regarding these numbers. These qualities and prescriptions, of course, would always be the same and would always be attached to the same numbers, if there were no psychological differences among men. But the effect of a group does not follow its quantity as exactly as does the energy effect of a moved homogeneous mass of matter. The vast individual differences among the members make all exact determinations and pre-determinations completely illusory. They explain why the same measure of strength or thoughtlessness, of concentration or decentralization, of self-sufficiency or need for leadership, are at one moment shown by a group of a certain size, at another by a much smaller group, but, at still another moment, only by a much larger one. On the other hand, the laws that are determined by these characteristics of associations cannot, for technical reasons, be concerned with such oscillations and paralyzations by the accidental human material. They must indicate particular numbers of members which they consider average and with which they connect the groups' rights and duties. They do so on the assumption that a certain common spirit, mood, strength, or tendency among a certain number of persons emerges if, and only if, this number attains a certain limit. According to whether this result is desired or feared, a minimum number is requested, or a maximum number is allowed.

I will first give a few examples of the second alternative. In the early Greek period, there were legal provisions according to which ship crews could not consist of more than five men, in order to prevent them from engaging in piracy. In 1436, the Rhenish cities, fearing the rise of associations among apprentices, prescribed that no more than three apprentices should go about in the same dress. In fact, political prohibitions are most common in this category generally. In 1305, Philip the Fair forbade all meetings of more than five persons, regardless of their rank or the form of the meetings. Under the *Ancien Régime,* twenty noblemen were not allowed without special concession from the King to assemble even for a conference. Napoleon III prohibited all organizations of more than twenty persons that were not specifically authorized. In England, the Conventicle Act under Charles II made all religious home assemblies of more than five persons subject to punishment. English Reaction at the beginning of the nineteenth century prohibited all meetings of more than fifty persons that were not announced long in advance. Under conditions of siege, often not more than three or five persons may stand together in the street. A few years ago, the Berlin Supreme Court of judicature defined a *Versammlung* in the legal sense, that is, an assembly requiring notification of the police, as a meeting of eight persons and more. In the purely economic sphere, we find the same idea, for instance, in the English law of 1708 (established under the influence of the Bank of England), according to which legal financial associations were not permitted to have more than six members.

In all these cases, we may assume, the government is convinced that only within groups of the sizes indicated is found the courage or rashness, the spirit of enterprise, or the capacity for being pushed into certain actions, which it does not wish to emerge. This motive is most distinct in legislation that has to do with moral considerations. If the number of participants in a drinking bout or in a parade or procession, etc., is limited, it is because of the experience that, in a larger mass, sensuous impulses gain more easily the upper hand, contagion by bad example spreads more rapidly, the individual feeling of responsibility is paralyzed.

The opposite direction, on the same basis, is shown in those regulations which require a minimum of participants for groups to attain a certain legal effect. In England, any economic association can obtain the right to incorporate as soon as it has seven members. Everywhere, the law requires a certain (though greatly varying) minimum number of judges for finding a legally valid verdict so that, for instance, in some places certain judicial colleges are simply called the Seven. In regard to the first example, it is assumed that only this particular number of members results in adequate guarantees and an effective solidarity, without which the privileges of corporations are a danger to the national economy. In the second example, only the prescribed minimum number seems to ensure that individual errors and extreme opinions balance one another and, thus, allow a collective opinion to emerge which finds what is objectively correct. This minimum requirement is especially evident in connection with religious phenomena. The regular meetings of the Buddhist monks of a certain territory, which took place for the purpose of renewed religious indoctrination and a kind of confession, required the presence of at least four monks. Only this number completed (as it were) the synod; and, as a member of this synod, each monk had a somewhat different significance from what he had as an individual monk—which he was only as long as no more than three came together. There must always be at least ten Jews for praying in common. According to the Lockean constitution of North Carolina, any church or religious group was allowed to form if it consisted of at least seven members. The strength, concentration, and stability of a common religious mood is expected, in all these cases, only of a certain number of members, who mutually support and strengthen one another. In sum: where the law fixes a minimum, confidence in large numbers and distrust of isolated individual energies are at work; where, inversely, a maximum is prescribed, distrust of large numbers is in operation, but not of their individual components.

But whether a prohibition concerns a maximum, or a permission a minimum, the legislators must know that the results feared or wished are connected only in an uncertain and average way with the sizes established. And yet, the arbitrary character of the determination is as inevitable and as justified as it is in the fixing of a certain age at which a man comes to have the privileges and duties of majority. To be sure, the real capacity to be of "legal age" develops in some individuals earlier, in some later, and in none suddenly at the minute fixed by law. But practice can attain the fixed standards it needs only by splitting up, at a certain point, a continuous series into two segments created for legal purposes. The profoundly different ways of treating these segments cannot be justified on the grounds of their objective natures. For this reason, it is extremely instructive to note that in all regulations of which examples were given above, the specific qualities of the persons involved are not taken into consideration, although it is these qualities which determine the single case. But they are nothing tangible—the only tangible element left is number. And it is essential to observe the ubiquitous, deep feeling that the number would be decisive in case individual differences did not cancel its effects—but that, for this very reason, these effects are sure to be contained in the eventual total phenomenon.

Part Three

Superordination and Subordination

Chapter 1

Introduction

§ 1. *Domination, a Form of Interaction*

NOBODY, IN GENERAL,
wishes that his influence completely determine the other individual. He rather wants this influence, this determination of the other, to act back upon *him*. Even the abstract will-to-dominate, therefore, is a case of interaction. This will draws its satisfaction from the fact that the acting or suffering of the other, his positive or negative condition, offers itself to the dominator as the product of *his* will. The significance of this solipsistic exercise of domination (so to speak) consists, for the superordinate himself, exclusively in the consciousness of his efficacy. Sociologically speaking, it is only a rudimentary form. By virtue of it alone, sociation occurs as little as it does between a sculptor and his statue, although the statue, too, acts back on the artist through his consciousness of his own creative power. The practical function of this desire for domination, even in this sublimated form, is not so much the exploitation of the other as the mere consciousness of this possibility. For the rest, it does not represent the extreme case of egoistic inconsiderateness. Certainly, the desire for domination is designed to break the *internal* resistance of the subjugated (whereas egoism usually aims only at the victory over his *external* resistance). But still, even the desire for domination has some interest in the other person, who constitutes a value for it. Only when egoism does not even amount to a desire for domination; only when the other is absolutely indifferent and a mere means for purposes which lie beyond him, is the last shadow of any sociating process removed.

The definition of later Roman jurists shows, in a relative way, that the elimination of *all* independent significance of one of the two interacting parties annuls the very notion of society. This definition was to the effect that the *societas leonina* [1] must not be conceived of as a social contract. A comparable statement has been made regarding the lowest-paid workers in modern giant enterprises which preclude all effective competition among rivaling entrepreneurs for the services of these laborers. It has been said that the difference in the strategic positions of workers and employers is so overwhelming that the work contract ceases to be a "contract" in the ordinary sense of the word, because the former are unconditionally at the mercy of the latter. It thus appears that the moral maxim never to use a man as a mere means is actually the formula of every sociation. Where the significance of the one party sinks so low that its effect no longer enters the relationship with the other, there is as little ground for speaking of sociation as there is in the case of the carpenter and his bench.

Within a relationship of subordination, the exclusion of all spontaneity whatever is actually rarer than is suggested by such widely used popular expressions as "coercion," "having no choice," "absolute necessity," etc. Even in the most oppressive and cruel cases of subordination, there is still a considerable measure of personal freedom. We merely do not become aware of it, because its manifestation would entail sacrifices which we usually never think of taking upon ourselves. Actually, the "absolute" coercion which even the most cruel tyrant imposes upon us is always distinctly relative. Its condition is our desire to escape from the threatened punishment or from other consequences of our disobedience. More precise analysis shows that the super-subordination relationship destroys the subordinate's freedom only in the case of direct physical violation. In every other case, this relationship only demands a price for the realization of freedom—a price, to be sure, which we are not willing to pay. It can narrow down more and more the sphere of external conditions under which freedom is clearly realized, but, except for physical force, never to the point of the complete disappearance of freedom. The moral side of this analysis does not concern us here, but only its sociological aspect. This aspect consists in

[1] "Sociation with a lion," that is, a partnership in which all the advantage is on one side.—Tr.

the fact that interaction, that is, action which is mutually determined, action which stems exclusively from personal origins, prevails even where it often is not noted. It exists even in those cases of superordination and subordination—and therefore makes even those cases *societal* forms—where according to popular notions the "coercion" by one party deprives the other of every spontaneity, and thus of every real "effect," or contribution to the process of interaction.

§ 2. *Authority and Prestige*

Relationships of superordination and subordination play an immense role in social life. It is therefore of the utmost importance for its analysis to clarify the spontaneity and co-efficiency of the subordinate subject and thus to correct their widespread minimization by superficial notions about them. For instance, what is called "authority" presupposes, in a much higher degree than is usually recognized, a freedom on the part of the person subjected to authority. Even where authority seems to "crush" him, it is based not *only* on coercion or compulsion to yield to it.

The peculiar structure of "authority" is significant for social life in the most varied ways; it shows itself in beginnings as well as in exaggerations, in acute as well as in lasting forms. It seems to come about in two different ways. A person of superior significance or strength may acquire, in his more immediate or remote milieu, an overwhelming weight of his opinions, a faith, or a confidence which have the character of objectivity. He thus enjoys a prerogative and an axiomatic trustworthiness in his decisions which excel, at least by a fraction, the value of mere subjective personality, which is always variable, relative, and subject to criticism. By acting "authoritatively," the quantity of his significance is transformed into a new quality; it assumes for his environment the physical state—metaphorically speaking—of objectivity.

But the same result, authority, may be attained in the opposite direction. A super-individual power—state, church, school, family or military organizations—clothes a person with a reputation, a dignity, a power of ultimate decision, which would never flow from his individuality. It is the nature of an authoritative person to make decisions with a certainty and automatic recognition which logically pertain only to impersonal, objective axioms and deductions. In the case under discussion, authority descends upon a person from above, as it were, whereas in the case treated before, it arises from the qualities of the person himself, through a *generatio aequivoca*.[2] But evidently, at this point of transition and change-over [from the personal to the authoritative situation], the more or less voluntary faith of the party subjected to authortiy comes into play. This transformation of the value of personality into a super-personal value gives the personality something which is beyond its demonstrable and rational share, however slight this addition may be. The believer in authority himself achieves the transformation. He (the subordinate element) participates in a sociological event which requires his spontaneous cooperation. As a matter of fact, the very feeling of the "oppressiveness" of authority suggests that the autonomy of the subordinate party is actually presupposed and never wholly eliminated.

Another nuance of superiority, which is designated as "prestige," must be distinguished from "authority." Prestige lacks the element of super-subjective significance; it lacks the identity of the personality with an objective power or norm. Leadership by means of prestige is determined entirely by the strength of the individual. This individual force always remains conscious of itself. Moreover, whereas the average type of leadership always shows a certain mixture of personal and superadded-objective factors, prestige leadership stems from pure personality, even as authority stems from the objectivity of norms and forces. Superiority through prestige consists in the ability to "push" individuals and masses and to make unconditional followers of them. Authority does not have this ability to the same extent. The higher, cooler, and normative character of authority is more apt to leave room for criticism, even on the part of its followers. In spite of this, however, prestige strikes us as the more voluntary homage to the superior person. Actually, perhaps, the recognition of authority implies a more profound freedom of the subject than does the enchantment that emanates from the prestige of a prince, a priest, a military or spiritual leader. But the matter

2 "Equivocal birth" or "spontaneous generation."—Tr.

is different in regard to the *feeling* on the part of those led. In the face of authority, we are often defenseless, whereas the *élan* with which we follow a given prestige always contains a consciousness of spontaneity. Here, precisely because devotion is only to the wholly personal, this devotion seems to flow only from the ground of personality with its inalienable freedom. Certainly, man is mistaken innumerable times regarding the measure of freedom which he must invest in a certain action. One reason for this is the vagueness and uncertainty of the explicit conception by means of which we account for this inner process. But in whatever way we interpret freedom, we can say that some measure of it, even though it may not be the measure we suppose, is present wherever there is the feeling and the conviction of freedom.[3]

§ 3. *Leader and Led*

The seemingly wholly passive element is in reality even more active in relationships such as obtain between a speaker and his audience or between a teacher and his class. Speaker and teacher appear to be nothing but leaders; nothing but, momentarily, superordinate. Yet whoever finds himself in such or a similar situation feels the determining and controlling re-action on the part of what seems to be a purely receptive and guided mass. This applies not only to situations where the two parties confront one another physically. All leaders are also led; in innumerable cases, the master is the slave of his slaves. Said one of the greatest German party leaders referring to his followers: "I am their leader, therefore I must follow them."

In the grossest fashion, this is shown by the journalist. The journalist gives content and direction to the opinions of a mute multitude. But he is nevertheless forced to listen, combine, and

---

[3] Here—and analogously in many other cases—the point is not to define the concept of prestige but only to ascertain the existence of a certain variety of human interactions, quite irrespective of their designation. The presentation, however, often begins appropriately with the concept which linguistic usage makes relatively most suitable for the discovery of the relationship, because it suggests it. This sounds like a merely definitory procedure. Actually, however, the attempt is never to find the content of a concept, but to describe, rather, an actual content, which only occasionally has the chance of being covered, more or less, by an already existing concept.

guess what the tendencies of this multitude are, what it desires to hear and to have confirmed, and whither it wants to be led. While apparently it is only the public which is exposed to *his* suggestions, actually he is as much under the sway of the *public's* suggestion. Thus, a highly complex interaction (whose two, mutually spontaneous forces, to be sure, appear under very different forms) is hidden here beneath the semblance of the pure superiority of the one element and a purely passive being-led of the other.

The content and significance of certain personal relations consist in the fact that the exclusive function of one of the two elements is service for the other. But the perfect measure of this devotion of the first element often depends on the condition that the other element surrenders to the first, even though on a different level of the relationship. Thus, Bismarck remarked concerning his relation to William I: "A certain measure of devotion is determined by law; a greater measure, by political conviction; beyond this, a personal feeling of *reciprocity* is required.—My devotion had its principal ground in my loyalty to royalist convictions. But in the special form in which this royalism existed, it is after all possible only under the impact of a certain reciprocity—the reciprocity between master and servant." The most characteristic case of this type is shown, perhaps, by hypnotic suggestion. An outstanding hypnotist pointed out that in every hypnosis the hypnotized has an effect upon the hypnotist; and that, although this effect cannot be easily determined, the result of the hypnosis could not be reached without it. Thus here, too, appearance shows an absolute influence, on the one side, and an absolute being-influenced, on the other; but it conceals an interaction, an exchange of influences, which transforms the pure one-sidedness of superordination and subordination into a *sociological* form.

§ 4. *Interaction in the Idea of "Law"*

I shall cite some cases of superordination and subordination in the field of law. It is easy to reveal the interaction which actually exists in what seems a purely unilateral situation. If the absolute despot accompanies his orders by the threat of punishment or the promise of reward, this implies that he himself wishes to be bound by the decrees he issues. The subordinate is expected to have the right to request something of him; and by establishing the punishment, no matter how horrible, the despot commits himself not to impose a more severe one. Whether or not afterward he actually abides by the punishment established or the reward promised is a different question: the *significance* of the relation is that, although the superordinate wholly determines the subordinate, the subordinate nevertheless is assured of a claim on which he can insist or which he can waive. Thus even this extreme form of the relationship still contains some sort of spontaneity on his part.

The motive of interaction within an apparently one-sided and passive subordination appears in a peculiar modification in a medieval theory of the state. According to this theory, the state came into existence because men mutually obligated one another to submit to a common chief. Thus, the ruler—including, apparently, the unconditional ruler—is appointed on the basis of a mutual contract among his subjects. Whereas contemporaneous theories of domination saw its reciprocal character in the contract between ruler and ruled, the theory under discussion located this mutual nature of domination in its very basis, the people: the obligation to the prince is conceived to be the mere articulation, expression, or technique of a reciprocal relation among the individuals of whom his people is composed. In Hobbes, in fact, the ruler has no means of breaking the contract with his subjects because he has not made one; and the corollary to this is that the subject, even if he rebels against his ruler, does not thereby break a contract concluded with *him*, but only the contract he has entered with all other members of the society, to the effect of letting themselves be governed by this ruler.

It is the *absence* of this reciprocity which accounts for the observation that the tyranny of a group over its own members is worse than that of a prince over his subjects. The group—and by no means the political group alone—conceives of its members, not as confronting it, but as being included by it as its own links. This often results in a peculiar inconsiderateness toward the members, which is very different from a ruler's personal cruelty. Wherever there is, formally, confrontation (even if, contentually, it comes *close* to submission), there is interaction; and, in principle, interaction always contains some limitation of *each* party to the process (although there may be individual exceptions to this rule). Where superordination shows an extreme inconsiderateness, as in the case of the group that simply *disposes* of its members, there no longer is any confrontation with its form of interaction, which involves spontaneity, and hence limitation, of both superordinate and subordinate elements.

This is very clearly expressed in the original conception of Roman law. In its purity, the term "law" implies a submission which does not involve any spontaneity or counter-effect on the part of the person subordinate to the law. And the fact that the subordinate has actually cooperated in making it—and more, that *he* has given himself the law which binds him—is irrelevant. For in doing so, he has merely decomposed himself into the subject and object of lawmaking; and the law which the subject applies to the object does not change its significance only by the fact that both subject and object are accidentally lodged in the same physical person. Nevertheless, in their conception of law, the Romans directly allude to the idea of interaction. For originally, *"lex"* means "contract," even though in the sense that the conditions of the contract are fixed by its proponent, and the other party can merely accept or reject it in its totality. In the beginning, the *lex publica populi romani* implied that the King proposed this legislation, and the people were its acceptors. Hence the very concept which most of all seems to exclude interaction is, nevertheless, designed to refer to it by its linguistic expression. In a certain sense this is revealed in the prerogative of the Roman king that he alone was allowed to speak to the people. Such a prerogative, to be sure, expressed the jealously guarded exclusiveness of his rulership, even as in ancient Greece the right of everybody to speak to the people indicated complete democracy. Nevertheless, this prerogative implies that the significance of speaking to the people, and, hence, of the people themselves, was recognized. Although the people merely *received* this one-sided action, they were nonetheless a *contractor* (whose party to the contract, of course, was only a single person, the king).

The purpose of these preliminary remarks was to show the

properly sociological, social-formative character of superordination and subordination even where it appears as if a social relationship were replaced by a purely mechanical one—where, that is, the position of the subordinate seems to be that of a means or an object for the superordinate, without any spontaneity. It has been possible, at least in many cases, to show the sociologically decisive *reciprocal effectiveness*, which was concealed under the one-sided character of influence and being-influenced.

Chapter 2

Subordination under an Individual

§ 1. *Three Kinds of Subordination*

THE KINDS OF SUPERORDI-
nation may be divided according to a three-fold scheme. This is
superficial, but convenient for our discussion. Superordination
may be exerted by an individual, by a group, or by an objective
force—social or ideal. I shall now discuss some of the sociological
implications of these possibilities.

§ 2. *Kinds of Subordination under an Individual*

The subordination of a group under a single person results,
above all, in a very decisive unification of the group. This unification is almost equally evident in both of two characteristic
forms of this subordination. First, the group forms an actual
inner unit together with its head; the ruler leads the group forces
in their own direction, promoting and fusing them; superordination, therefore, here really means only that the will of the
group has found a unitary expression or body. Secondly, the
group feels itself in opposition to its head and forms a party
against him.

In regard to the first form, every sociological consideration
immediately shows the immeasurable advantage which one-man
rule has for the fusion and energy-saving guidance of the group
forces. I will cite only two instances of common subordination to
one element. These cases are very heterogeneous as far as their
contents are concerned, but nevertheless show how irreplaceable
this subordination is for the unity of the whole. The sociolog

of religion must make a basic distinction between two types of religious organization. There may be the unification of group members which lets the common god grow, as it were, out of this togetherness itself, as the symbol and the sanctification of their belonging together. This is true in many primitive religions. On the other hand, only the conception of the god itself may bring the members together into a unit—members who before had no, or only slight, relations with one another. How well Christianity exemplifies this second type need not be described, nor is it necessary to emphasize how particular Christian sects find their specific and especially strong cohesion in the absolutely subjective and mystical relation to the person of Jesus, a relation which each member possesses as an individual, and thus quite independently of every other member and of the total group. But even of the Jews it has been asserted that they feel the contractual relation to Jehovah which they hold in common, that is, which directly concerns every one of them, as the real power and significance of membership in the Jewish nation.

By contrast, in other religions which originated at the same time as Judaism, it was kinship that connected each member with every other, and only later, all of them with the divine principle. On the basis of its widely ramified personal dependencies and "services," medieval feudalism had frequent occasion to exemplify this same formal structure. It is perhaps most characteristically shown in the associations of the "ministers" (unfree court servants and house servants) who stood in a close, purely personal relation to the prince. Their associations had no objective basis whatever, such as the village communities under bondage had by virtue of the nearby manor. The "ministers" were employed in highly varied services and had their residences in different localities, but nevertheless formed tightly closed associations which nobody could enter or leave without their authorization. They developed their own family and property laws; they had freedom of contract and of social intercourse among one another, and they imposed the expiation of breach of peace within their group. But they had no other basis for this close unit than the identity of the ruler whom they served, who represented them to the outside, and who was their legal agent in matters involving the law of the land. Here, as in the case of religion mentioned before, the subordination under an individual power is not the consequence or expression of an already existing organic or interest group (as it is in many, especially political, cases). On the contrary, the superordination of one ruler is the *cause* of a commonness which in the absence of it could not be attained and which is not predetermined by any other relation among its members.

It should be noted that not only the equal, but often precisely the unequal, relation of the subordinates to the dominating head gives solidity to the social form characterized by subordination under one individual. The varying distance or closeness to the leader creates a differentiation which is not less firm and articulate because the internal aspect of these relations to him often is jealousy, repulsion, or haughtiness. The social level of the individual Indian caste is determined by its relation to the Brahman. The decisive questions are: Would the Brahman accept a gift from one of their members? Would he accept a glass of water from his hand without reluctance? Or with difficulty? Or would he reject it with abhorrence? That the peculiar firmness of caste stratification depends on such questions is characteristic of the form under discussion for the reason that the mere fact of a highest point determines, as a purely ideal factor, the structural position of every element, and thus the structure of the whole. That this highest layer should be occupied by a great many individuals is quite irrelevant, since the sociological form of the effect is here exactly like that of an individual: the relation to the "Brahman" is decisive. In other words, the formal characteristic of subordination under an individual *may* prevail even where there is a plurality of superordinate individuals. The *specific* sociological significance of such a plurality will be shown later, in connection with other phenomena.

§ 3. *Unification of a Group in Opposition to the Ruler*

The unificatory consequence of subordination under one ruling power operates even when the group is in opposition to this power. The political group, the factory, the school class, the church congregation—all indicate how the culmination of an organization in a head helps to effect the unity of the whole in the case of either harmony or discord. Discord, in fact, perhaps even more stringently than harmony, forces the group to "pull itself together." In general, common enmity is one of the most powerful means for motivating a number of individuals or groups to cling together. This common enmity is intensified if the common adversary is at the same time the common ruler. In a latent, certainly not in an overt and effective, form, this combination probably occurs everywhere: in some measure, in some respect, the ruler is almost always an adversary. Man has an intimate dual relation to the principle of subordination. On the one hand, he wants to be dominated. The majority of men not only *cannot* exist without leadership; they also *feel* that they cannot: they *seek* the higher power which relieves them of responsibility; they seek a restrictive, regulatory rigor which protects them not only against the outside world but also against themselves. But no less do they need opposition to the leading power, which only through this opposition, through move and countermove, as it were, attains the right place in the life pattern of those who obey it.

One might even say that obedience and opposition are merely two sides or links of one human attitude which fundamentally is quite consistent. They are two sides that are oriented in different directions and only *seem* to be autonomous impulses. The simplest illustration here is from the field of politics. No matter of how many divergent and conflicting parties a nation may be composed, it nevertheless has a common interest in keeping the powers of the crown within limits or in restricting them—in spite of all the practical irreplaceability of the crown and even in spite of all sentimental attachment to it. For hundreds of years following the Magna Charta, there was a lively awareness in England that certain fundamental rights had to be preserved and increased for *all* classes; that nobility could not maintain its freedoms without the freedoms of the weaker classes being maintained at the same time; and that only the law which applied to nobility, burgher, and peasant alike represented a limitation of the personal reign. It has often been remarked that as long as this ultimate goal of the struggle—the restrictions upon monarchy—is endangered, nobility always has people and clergy on its side. And even where one-man rule does not engender this sort of unification, at least it creates a common arena for the fight of its subordinates—between those who are *for* the ruler and those who are *against* him. There is hardly a sociological structure, subject to a supreme head, in which this pro and con does not occasion a vitality of inter- actions and ramifications among the elements that in terms of an eventual unification is greatly superior to many peaceful but indifferent aggregates—in spite of all repulsions, frictions, and costs of the fight.

§ 4. *Dissociating Effects of Subordination under an Individual*

The present discussion is not concerned with constructing dogmatically one-sided series but with presenting basic proc- esses whose infinitely varying extents and combinations often cause their superficial manifestations to contradict one another. It must therefore be emphasized that the common submission to a ruling power by no means always leads to unification but, if the submission occurs under certain conditions, to the very opposite of it. For instance, English legislation directed a num- ber of measures and exclusions concerning military service, the right to vote, ownership, and government positions, against non- Conformists, that is, against Presbyterians, Catholics, and Jews alike. The member of the state church thus used his prerogative to give equal expression to his hatred of all these groups. But this did not fuse the oppressed into a community of any sort; on the contrary, the hatred of the Conformist was even surpassed by the Presbyterian's hatred of the Catholic, and of the Catholic's of the Presbyterian.

Here we seem to deal with a psychological "threshold phe- nomenon." There is a measure of enmity between social ele- ments which becomes ineffectual if they experience a common pressure: it then yields to external, if not internal, unification. But if the original aversion surpasses a certain limit, a common oppression has the opposite effect. This has two reasons. The first is that once there is a dominating resentment in a certain direction, any irritation, no matter from what source it may come, only intensifies the *general* irritation and, contrary to all rational expectation, flows into the already existing river bed and thereby enlarges it. The second, even more important reason is that common suffering, though pressing the suffering elements closer together, reveals all the more strikingly their inner distance and irreconcilability, precisely by virtue of this enforced intimacy. Where unification, however it be created, cannot overcome a given antagonism, it does not preserve this antagonism at its former stage, but intensifies it. In all fields, contrast becomes sharper and more conscious in the measure in which the parties concerned come closer together.

Another, more obvious kind of repulsion among the subjects of a common ruler is created by means of jealousy. It constitutes the negative counterpart of the phenomenon mentioned before, namely, that common hatred is all the more powerful a bond if the object of the common hatred is at the same time the common ruler. We now add that a love shared by a number of elements makes them, by means of jealousy, all the more decisively into mutual enemies if the common loved one is also the common ruler. A student of Turkish conditions reports that the children of different mothers in a harem are always hostile to one another. The reason for this is the jealousy with which their mothers observe the father's manifestations of love for his children who are not their own. Jealousy takes on a particular nuance as soon as it refers to the power which is superordinate to both parties. Under this condition, the woman winning the love of the disputed person triumphs over the rival in a special sense, and has a special success of her power. The subtlety of the fascination consists in the fact that she becomes master over the rival inasmuch as she becomes master over the rival's master. By means of the reciprocity within which the commonness of the master allows this fascination to develop, it must lead to the highest intensification of jealousy.

§ 5. *The "Higher Tribunal"*

I leave these dissociating consequences of subordination under an individual power in order to return to its unifying functions. I will only note how much more easily discords between parties are removed if the parties stand under the same higher power than if each of them is entirely independent. How many conflicts which were the ruin of both the Greek and Italian city states would not have had this destructive consequence if a central power, if some ultimate tribunal, had ruled over them in common! Where there is no such power, the conflict among the elements has the fatal tendency to be fought out only in face-to-face battle between the power quanta. In the most general terms, we have to do here with the concept of "higher tribunal." [4] In varying forms, its operation extends through almost all of human collective life. The question whether or not a given society has a "higher tribunal" concerns a formal sociological characteristic of first-rank importance. The "higher tribunal" does not have to be a ruler in the ordinary or superficial sense of the word. For instance, above the obligations and controversies which are based on interests, instincts, and feelings, there is always a "higher tribunal," namely the realm of the *intellectual,* with its particular contents or representatives. This tribunal may make one-sided or inadequate decisions, and they may or may not be obeyed. But just as above the contradictory contents of our conceptions, logic remains the higher tribunal even where we think non-logically, so in the same fashion, in a group that is composed of many elements, the most intelligent individual remains the higher tribunal in spite of the fact that in particular cases it is rather the person of strong will or warm feeling that may succeed in pacifying conflicts among the members. Nevertheless, the specific character of the "higher tribunal" to which one appeals for decisions or whose interference one accepts because it is felt to be legitimate, is typically on the side of intellectuality alone.

Another mode of unifying divergent parties, which is particularly favored if there exists a dominating "tribunal," is the following. Where it seems impossible to unify elements who are either in conflict or remain indifferent and alien toward one another—where they cannot be unified on the basis of the qualities they have—the unification can sometimes be brought about by so transforming the elements that they become adapted to a new situation which permits harmony, or by causing them

[4] *"Höhere Instanz":* higher tribunal or court, but not necessarily in the technical, legal sense.—Tr.

to acquire new qualities which make their unification possible. The removal of ill-humor, the stimulation of mutual interest, the creation of thoroughly common features, can often be achieved (whether among children at play or among religious or political parties) by adding to the existing dissociative or indifferent intentions or delimitations of the elements some new trait which serves as a point of contact and, thus, reveals that even what was hitherto divergent can in fact be reconciled. Furthermore, features that cannot be directly unified often show the possibility of an indirect reconciliation if they can be developed further or can be augmented by a new element, and thus are placed upon a new and common basis. For instance, the homogeneity of the Gallic Provinces was decisively promoted when all of them in common became Latinized by Rome. Obviously, it is precisely this mode of unification which needs the "higher tribunal." Only a power which stands above the parties and in some manner dominates them can, more or less easily, give each of them interests and regulations which place them on a common basis. If left to themselves, they would perhaps never have found them; or their obstinacy, pride, and perseverance in the conflict would have prevented them from developing common interests. The Christian religion is praised for making its adherents "peaceful." The sociological reason for this is very probably the feeling that all beings alike are subordinate to the divine principle. The faithful Christian is convinced that above him and above each of his adversaries, whether Christian or not, there exists this "highest tribunal"— and this frees him from the temptation to measure his strength by violence. It is precisely because he stands immeasurably high above each individual Christian that the Christian God can be a bond among very large circles, all of which, by definition, are included in his "peace." At any given moment, each of them, along with every other, has a "higher tribunal" in God.

§ 6. *Domination and Leveling*

Unification through common subordination occurs in two different forms: by means of leveling and by means of gradation. Insofar as a number of people are equally subject to one

198 Subordination under an Individual

individual, they are themselves equal. The correlation between despotism and equalization has long been recognized. This correlation occurs not only in the sense that the despot himself tries to level his subjects (a point which will be discussed presently), but also in the reverse sense that strongly developed leveling easily leads to despotism. This is not true, however, of every kind of "leveling." In calling the Sicilian cities "filled with motley masses," Alcibiades wished to characterize them as an easy prey for the conqueror. And, in fact, a homogeneous citizenry offers a more successful resistance to tyranny than a citizenry composed of highly divergent and hence unconnected elements. The leveling most welcome to despotism, therefore, is that of differences in rank, not in character. A society homogeneous in character and tendency, but organized in several rank orders, resists despotism strongly, while a society in which numerous kinds of characters exist side by side with organically inarticulate equality, resists it only slightly.

The ruler's chief motive in equalizing hierarchical differences derives from the fact that relations of strong superordination and subordination among his subjects actually and psychologically compete with his own superordination. Besides, too great an oppression of certain classes by others is as dangerous to despotism as is the too great power of these oppressing classes. For, a revolt of the suppressed against the oppressive class, which is intermediate between them and the despot, can easily be directed against the highest power itself, as if the movement rolled on merely by following its own inertia—unless the despot himself leads the movement, or at least supports it. Oriental despots, therefore, have tried to prevent the formation of aristocracies—as, for instance, the Turkish Sultan, who thus preserved his radical, entirely un-mediated eminence over the totality of his subjects. Every power in the state, of whatever description, derived from him and returned to him with the death of its owner; and thus there never developed an aristocracy of any significance. The absolute sublimity of the sovereign and the leveling of the subjects were realized as correlated phenomena.

This tendency is also reflected in the fact that despots only love servants of average talent, as has been noted particularly of Napoleon I. In a similar fashion, when it was suggested to an outstanding German official that he transfer to another branch of the government, the ruling prince is supposed to have asked his minister: "Is the man indispensable to us?" "Entirely so, Your Highness." "Then we shall let him go. I cannot use indispensable servants." Yet, despotism does not seek particularly *inferior* servants; and, in this, it shows its inner relation to leveling. Tacitus says in regard to the tendency of Tiberius to employ mediocre officials: *"ex optimis periculum sibi, a pessimis dedecus publicum metuebat."* [5] Quite characteristically, where one-man rule does not have the character of despotism, this tendency to employ inferior servants is at once much weaker, if indeed it does not yield to its opposite. Thus, Bismarck said of William I that the emperor not only accepted a respected and powerful servant, but even felt himself elevated by this fact.

Where the ruler does not categorically prevent the development of intermediate powers (as in the Sultan's case), he often tries to create a relative leveling: he favors the efforts of the lower classes which are directed toward legal equality with these intermediate powers. Medieval and recent history offers many examples of this. Ever since Norman times, English royalty has vigorously practiced the correlation between its own omnipotence and the legal equality of its subjects. By forcing every lower vassal to swear feudal duty directly to himself, William the Conqueror broke the bond which, in England as on the Continent, had existed between the directly enfeoffed aristocracy and the lower vassals. This measure prevented the great crown fiefs from developing into sovereignties, and, on the other hand, it laid down the bases of a uniform legislation for all classes. The English kings of the eleventh and twelfth centuries based their extraordinary power upon the regularity with which free property, without any exceptions, was subject to military, court, police, and tax duty. The Roman Empire shows the same form. The Republic had become incapable of existence because the legal and actual superiority of the city of Rome over Italy and the Provinces could no longer be maintained. Only the Empire

[5] "From the best, he feared danger to himself; from the worst, public shame."
—Tr.

resurrected the balance; it did so by making the Romans as powerless as were the peoples whom they had subjugated. In this fashion, an impartial legislation for all citizens, a legal leveling, was made possible; and its correlate was the absolute exaltation and uniqueness of the ruler.

It need hardly be mentioned that "leveling" must always be understood here as a wholly relative tendency with very limited possibilities of realization. A basic science of the forms of society must present concepts and concept complexes in a purity and abstract completeness which are never shown by the historical realizations of their contents. Yet sociological understanding aims at grasping the fundamental concept of sociation in its particular significances and formations; it aims at analyzing phenomenal complexes into their minute factors to the point of approaching inductive regularities. It can do so only through the auxiliary construction of so-to-speak absolute lines and figures which in actual social life are found only as beginnings and fragments, as partial realizations that are constantly interrupted and modified. In every single social-historical configuration, there operates a number of reciprocities among the elements, which can probably never be wholly enumerated. We can no more dissolve its form, as it is given, into its component factors, and then recombine these factors, than we can create out of the ideal figures of our geometry the absolutely identical shape of any piece of matter whatever—in spite of the fact that in principle both must be possible by means of differentiating and combining scientific constructs. Sociological cognition so transforms historical phenomena that their unity is decomposed into a number of concepts and syntheses which are defined in a purely one-sided manner and which run, as it were, in a straight line. As a rule, one of these catches the main characteristic of the historical phenomenon under analysis. By bending and limiting each other mutually, all of them together project its image with increasing exactness upon the new plane of abstraction. The Sultan's reign over subjects who have no rights; that of the English king over a people that already a hundred and fifty years after William the Conqueror courageously rose against King John; that of the Roman Emperor who, properly speaking, was only the overseer of the more or

less autonomous communities which made up the Empire: all
these one-man rules are as profoundly different from one another as are the corresponding "levelings" of their subjects.
And yet, the motive of this correlation operates alike in all of
them; the immense differences among the immediate material
phenomena leaves room for the ideal line, so to speak, with
which this correlation is traced into them. In its purity and
regularity, however, this correlation is a scientific, abstract
construct.

The same tendency of domination by means of leveling is
sometimes disguised by phenomena which on the surface look
like the very opposite of those thus far considered. Philip the
Good of Burgundy behaved very typically when he aimed at
suppressing the freedom of the Dutch cities but, at the same
time, bestowed very comprehensive privileges upon many individual corporations. These legal differences were created
exclusively by the arbitrary pleasure of the ruler. They thus
marked all the more distinctly the common, unalterable subordination of his subjects. In the particular case mentioned,
this is excellently shown by the fact that, although the privileges
were very extensive in terms of their content, they were of only
a short duration: the legal advantage was thus never separated
from the source from which it came. The privilege, seemingly
the very opposite of leveling, thus reveals itself as the intensification of leveling, which adopts it as the correlate of absolute
subjugation.

Rule-by-one has innumerable times been reproached for
the contradiction which is supposed to lie in the purely quantitative disproportion between the one-ness of the ruler and
the many-ness of the ruled. It has been accused of the undig-
nified and unjust character of the ratio of what the two parties
to the relationship invest in it. As a matter of fact, the resolu-
tion of this contradiction reveals a very peculiar, basic sociological constellation, which has important consequences. The
point is that the structure of a society in which only one person
rules while the great mass lets itself be ruled, makes normative
sense only by virtue of a specific circumstance: that the mass,
the ruled element, injects only *parts* of all the personalities
which compose it into the mutual relationship, whereas the

202 Subordination under an Individual

ruler contributes *all* of *his* personality. The ruler and the
individual subject do not enter the relationship with the same
quanta of their personalities. The "mass" is formed through
a process by which a great many individuals unite *parts* of their
personalities—specific impulses, interests, forces—while what
each personality really is, remains outside this common level.
It does not enter the "mass"; it does not enter that which is
actually ruled by the one individual.

It need not be emphasized that this new ratio which balances
the full personality quantum of the ruler with the many partial
quanta of the ruled gains its quantitative form only as a symbolic makeshift expression. Personality itself is completely outside any arithmetic concept. Therefore, when we speak of the
"whole" personality, of its "unity," of a "part" of it, we intend
to convey something qualitative and intimate, something which
can be experienced only through intuition. We have no direct
expression for it, so that these other expressions, taken as they
are from a totally different order of things, are quite inadequate—but, of course, they are nonetheless indispensable. The
whole rulership relation between the one and the many—and
evidently not only in the case of political domination—is based
on this decomposition of personality.

The application of this decomposition within the field of
superordination and subordination is merely a special case of
its significance for all interaction whatever. Even in regard to
such a close union as marriage, it must be pointed out that one
is never "wholly" married. Even in the best case, one is married
only with part of one's personality, however great this part be—
even as one is never wholly a citizen of a city, wholly an economic man, wholly a church member.

This division within the individual—which is the basis for
the subjugation of the many by the one—was already recognized
by Grotius. Grotius countered the objection that the power of
the ruler cannot be acquired by purchase since it concerns free
men, by distinguishing between private and public subjection.
In contrast to *subjectio privata, subjectio publica* does not
eliminate *sui juris esse*.[6] When a people is sold, the object of
the sale are not the individuals but only *jus eos regendi, qua*

---

[6] The autonomy (of the individual).—Tr.

populus sunt [the right of ruling them, *insofar as they are a people*]. It is one of the highest tasks of political art—of church politics, family politics, politics in general—to learn to recognize and, as it were, chemically prepare, those sides of man with which he forms the more or less leveled "mass" and above which the ruler can tower at a height that is alike for all members of the mass. These he needs to distinguish from those other sides that must be left to the freedom of the individual—although it is only the conjunction of *both* which make up the *whole* personality of the subject.

Groups are characteristically different according to the proportion between the members' total personalities and those parts of their personalities with which they fuse in the "mass." The measure of their governability depends on this difference in quanta. More precisely, a group can be dominated by one individual the more easily and radically, the smaller the portion of the total personality that the member contributes to that mass which is the object of subordination. Where, on the other hand, the social unit covers so much of the component personalities; where they are so closely interwoven with the group as was true of the inhabitants of the Greek city states or of the burghers of medieval cities, government-by-one becomes something contradictory and impracticable.

But this essentially simple, basic relationship is complicated by two factors. One is the magnitude or smallness of the subordinate group, and the other is the differentiation of the individual personality. Other things being equal, the larger the group, the smaller is the range of ideas and interests, sentiments and other characteristics in which its members coincide and form a "mass." Therefore, insofar as the domination of the members extends to their common features, the individual member bears it the more easily, the larger his group. Thus, in *this* respect, the essential nature of one-man rule is shown very clearly: the more there are of those over whom the one rules, the slighter is that portion of every individual which he dominates. But secondly, it is extremely important whether the individuals have, or do not have, a psychological structure sufficiently differentiated to separate, in their practice and in their feelings, the elements which lie within and without the sphere of domination. This differentiation must coincide with the art of the ruler, noted earlier, with which he himself distinguishes those elements within each of his subordinates that are accessible to domination from those which are not. It is only when the two coincide that the contradiction between domination and freedom, the disproportionate preponderance of the one over the many, is resolved—at least approximately. If this is the case, individuality can freely develop even in despotically ruled groups. The formation of modern individuality began, in fact, in the despotisms of the Italian Renaissance. Here as in other cases, for instance, under Napoleon I, the ruler was interested in granting the greatest freedom to all those sides of the personality in regard to which the individual does not belong to the "mass," which are, that is, removed from the area of political domination.

In very small groups, the closeness of fusion and the all-pervasive inner and outer solidarities among the members, again and again cut across these two types of personality aspects, and let them grow together, as it were, in a wrong way. It is understandable that, in this case, government can very easily become an unbearable tyranny. Thus, the relation between parents and children becomes frequently most unsatisfactory because of this smallness of the group, often accompanied by the clumsiness of the persons involved. Parents often make the grave mistake of imposing, in a very authoritarian fashion, a life schema upon their children which is supposed to be valid for everybody—even in those matters in which the children are irreconcilably individual. The same error is committed by the priest who, beyond the sphere within which he *can* unify his congregants, also wishes to dominate those spheres of their private lives in which, from the standpoint of the religious community, they are certainly differentiated as individuals. In all these cases, those parts of the character which are suited for "mass" formation and whose subjugation, therefore, is easily borne as something legitimate, are not properly isolated.

The leveling of the mass thus results from the separation and combination of those elements within each of its component individuals which can be subjected to the ruler. This leveling is of the greatest significance for the sociology of domination [*Herrschaft*]. In conjunction with what has been said earlier, it explains why it is often easier to dominate a larger than a smaller group. This is true particularly if the group is made up of highly differentiated individuals: each new one of them further reduces the range of features common to all. If the group is composed of such personalities (other things being equal), the leveling plane of many is lower than that of few, and thus their governability is greater. Here lies the sociological basis of Hamilton's remark, in the *Federalist*, that it is a great popular error to wish to increase the guaranties "against the government of a few" by augmenting the number of members of the parliament. Above a certain number, he continues, popular representation may appear to be more democratic, but actually is more oligarchical: "The machine may be enlarged, but the fewer will be the springs by which its motions are directed." And a hundred years later, but in the same vein, one of the foremost students of Anglo-American party life pointed out that the higher a party leader rises in power and influence, the most strictly is he bound to perceive "by how few persons the world is governed."

Here, also, lies the deeper sociological significance of the close relation which exists between the *law* of a political unit and its ruler. The law which is valid for all is based on the points in which all coincide; these points lie beyond the purely individual life contents or forms of the members or, viewed differently, beyond the totality of the individual. Such super-individual elements of having and being, such interests and qualities, attain an objective, synthesizing form in law—in the same way in which they find their *subjective* form, or their correlate, in the ruler of the political unit. If this peculiar analysis and synthesis within the individual is the general basis of rule-by-one, it also explains that sometimes an astonishingly slight measure of excellence is sufficient to win dominance over a collectivity. It explains why the collectivity should subordinate itself with an ease which a qualitative comparison between the *total* personalities of the ruler and his subjects could not logically justify. Yet where the differentiation of individuals, which is necessary for the domination of a mass, is lacking, the requirements for the quality of the ruler go beyond this modest measure. Aristotle said that in his time legitimate monarchies could no longer arise; for now, he wrote, there are so many equally excellent personalities in every state that no one of them can claim such an advantage above all others. Evidently, the Greek citizen was so closely connected in his interests and feelings with the political whole, and had contributed his total personality to the general life in such a measure, that a factoring-out of his exclusively "political" parts was no longer possible. He could not have withheld from them an essential part of his personality, as his private possession. If this is the situation, monarchy indeed presupposes for its inner legitimation that the ruler be superior to the total personality of every subject. On the other hand, this is a requirement of which there can be no question where the object of his domination is only the sum of factored-out, "mass-combined" parts of the subordinates.

§ 7. *Domination and Downward Gradation*

In addition to this type of domination by one individual, whose correlate is the fundamental leveling of his subjects, there is a second type, in which the group takes on the form of a pyramid. The subordinates face the ruler in gradations of power. Layers whose volume becomes ever smaller and whose significance becomes ever greater lead from the lowest mass to the top of the pyramid. This group form can develop in two ways. It may originate in the full autocratic power of the ruler, who loses the content of this power and lets it glide downward, while its form and title continue to exist. In this process, the layers closest to him naturally retain more of his power than do the more remote ones. This gradual downward penetration of power must result in a continuity and gradation of superordinates and subordinates, unless other events and conditions interfere with this process and deform it. This, presumably, is the way in which social forms frequently originate in oriental states. The power of the highest echelons withers, either because it is internally untenable and does not preserve the proportion between submission and individual freedom which was emphasized above, or because the personalities involved are too indolent and too ignorant of the technique of government to maintain their power.

The pyramidal form of society has a very different character when it originates in the *intention* of the ruler, so that it indicates no weakening of his power but, on the contrary, its extension and consolidation. Here, therefore, the power quantum of domination is not distributed among the lower layers; rather, these layers are being organized with respect to one another in degrees of power and position. The total quantum of subordination remains, as it were, the same as in the case of leveling; it only adopts another form, that of inequality among the individuals who must bear it. Nevertheless, in appearance, the elements here approach the ruler in the measure of their relative ranks. This can result in a great solidity of the total structure: the forces which support its weight flow more securely and in a more concentrated form toward its apex than they do if they are all on one level. The superior significance of the prince and, more generally, of the individual who rates highest in any given group, transcends him and is transferred to the others in the measure in which they are close to him; and this is no diminution of his superiority, but a heightening of it.

During the early English period of the Normans, the King had no permanent, obligatory council whatever. But in more important cases, in consequence of the very dignity and significance of his regime, he did seek the advice of a *consilium baronum*. That is, the dignity which seems to have attained its highest degree by being concentrated in his personality, needed radiation and enlargement nevertheless, as if it did not find enough room in a single person, although it was only the King's own dignity. He called others in to cooperate with him; these others, who helped him carry his power and significance and thus actually shared them somehow, reflected them back upon *him* in a fashion which, thus, was all the more concentrated and effective. Even earlier we find that the attendant of the Anglo-Saxon king has an especially high wergild and a particularly high importance as the king's cojuror; and that his groom and the man in whose house he takes a drink are elevated above the mass by special legal protection. These measures do not simply belong to the prerogative of the king;

instead, the graded descent of the prerogative, which, viewed from below, is an ascent, at the same time greatly supports this prerogative itself. By being shared, the king's superiority becomes more, not less. Furthermore, in a system of such fine gradations, the ruler has at his disposal rewards and distinctions in the form of rank promotions, which cost him nothing but which bind the promoted individuals all the more closely to him. This tendency seems to have directly determined the great number of social echelons created by the Roman Empire—an almost continuous scale, from the slaves and the *humiliores,* through the ordinary freemen, to the senators.

In this respect, aristocracy is formally identical with royalty: it, too, uses a many-leveled organization of its subjects. As late as the middle of the eighteenth century, for instance, there were numerous gradations of rights among the citizens of Geneva, according to whether they were *citoyens, bourgeois, habitants, natifs,* or *sujets.* Inasmuch as the largest possible number of people have still some others below them, all but the lowest are interested in the maintenance of the existing order. In such cases, however, there often is less a gradation of real power than a predominantly *ideal* ranking by titles and positions. Yet the extent to which even this can develop very considerable consequences is perhaps most strikingly shown by the subtle gradations among the dozens of classes in the Indian caste system. Even if such a pyramid built up of honors and social advantages culminates in the ruler, it does not always coincide, by any means, with the formally identical structure of graded, real power positions, which may coexist along with it.

The structure of a power pyramid always suffers from the basic difficulty that the irrational and fluctuating qualities of the persons are never entirely congruent with the delimitations of the various positions which are pre-designed in it with almost logical exactness. This formal difficulty is characteristic of all rank orders that are pre-shaped according to a given scheme. It is a problem not only of organizations headed by a personal ruler, but also of socialist proposals with their confidence that certain institutions will actually bring the individuals who deserve leading and superordinate positions into these positions. In both cases, there is this basic incommensurability between the schematism of the positions and the intrinsically variable nature of man, which never precisely fits conceptually fixed forms.

But there is a further difficulty, namely, that of *recognizing* the personality suited for a given position. The main reason for this is that, whether or not somebody deserves a certain power position is, innumerable times, revealed only once he occupies it. Every employment of a person for exercising a new power or function always involves a risk, always remains an experiment, which may succeed or fail, even when the employment follows the most thorough examination and the most indisputable antecedents. This risk is woven into the deepest, most precious aspects of human nature. Our very relationship to the world and to life forces us to make decisions *beforehand;* to bring about, that is, through our decision, those circumstances which should properly *have been* brought about and known in order to enable us to make the decision reasonably and securely. In the development of social power scales, this general, *a priori* difficulty of all human action emerges, evidently, with particular force when these scales do not grow, so to speak, organically out of the individual's own forces and the natural conditions of the society, but are spontaneously constructed by a ruling personality. To be sure, historically this case probably never exists in absolute purity—at most, it finds a parallel in the socialist utopias mentioned above. But it shows its characteristics and complications even where, in reality, it can be observed only in rudimentary and mixed forms.

§ 8. *Domination and Upward Gradation*

The other way in which a graduated scale of power extending to the highest rung can develop runs in the opposite direction. Some elements of a collectivity which in the beginning is composed of relatively equal members, gain greater significance; and out of the totality of these, some other, particularly powerful individuals, again become differentiated, and so forth; until the development terminates in one or a few supreme heads. Here the pyramid of superordination and subordinations is built from below. This process needs no examples since it occurs everywhere, even though with a variety of rhythms. It is perhaps most purely exemplified in the fields of economics and politics, but is also very notable in the area of intellectual culture, in school classes, in the development of attitudes toward life, in aesthetic respects, and in the initial growth of military organization.

§ 9. *Mixture of Downward and Upward Gradation*

The two ways in which a graduated superordination and subordination of groups can develop may, in actuality, be mixed. The classical example of this is the medieval feudal state. As long as the full citizen, whether Greek, Roman, or old-Germanic, was not subordinated to an individual, he enjoyed full equality with all other citizens; and, on the other hand, he closed himself thoroughly against all who stood below him. This characteristic social form passed through numerous historical links, until it found, in feudalism, its equally characteristic opposite. Feudalism fills the chasm between freedom and unfreedom by a rank order of statuses. "Service," *servitium,* tied all members of the realm to one another and to the king. The king gave of his property in the same way in which his great subjects, in their turn, enfeoffed the vassals, *their* subordinates, with land, so that a graded order of positions, possessions, and obligations developed. But this same result was reached by the social process which started from the opposite end. The intermediate layers developed not only through power distribution from the top but also through accumulation from below. Originally free but small land owners gave their land to more powerful lords in order to receive it back as feudal tenures. At the same time, these landlords more and more increased their power, against which the weakened royalty could not stand up, and in those of their representatives that had advanced highest toward the top, themselves attained royal power.

The form of such a pyramid gives every one of its elements a twofold position between the lowest and the highest layers. Everybody is superordinate and everybody is subordinate; he is dependent on the top and, at the same time, is independent insofar as others are dependent upon *him.* This sociological ambiguity of feudalism very strongly accentuated its dual genesis and was accentuated by it—the genesis through giving from above and through accumulation from below. The ambiguity, perhaps, accounts for the contradictory consequences of feudalism. According to whether consciousness and practice emphasized the independence or the dependence of the intermediate layers, feudalism tended to hollow out the power of the supreme ruler, as it did in Germany, or bestowed an all-pervasive power upon the crown, as in England.

Gradation belongs among those forms of group life and organization which are based upon a quantitative viewpoint. It is therefore more or less mechanical, and historically precedes properly organic groupings, which are based on qualitative differences among individuals. Nevertheless, the quantitative foundation is not simply replaced by the qualitative principle, but continues to exist side by side and in synthesis with it. Here must be noted, above all, the division of the group into subgroups. The social role of subgroups is rooted in their numerical equality or (at least) in their numerical determination, as, for instance, in the case of division by Hundred. Here, further, belongs the allocation of social position merely according to property owned. Finally, here belongs group formation by means of fixed degrees, as it is shown, above all, in feudalism, in ecclesiastical hierarchy, in bureaucracy, and in the army. Already the first example of this form, feudalism, suggests its peculiar objectivity and axiomatic character. It is through this that feudalism, as it developed since the beginnings of the Germanic Middle Ages, broke through the old orders of free and unfree, noble and plebeian, which were based on differences in the individual's relation to the group. Above these old orders, there arose a *generally* valid principle, "service," that is, the objective necessity of everybody serving, in some fashion, a superior individual; and the only difference admitted was the question of who the superior was and under what conditions he was served. The resultant, essentially quantitative gradation of positions was often quite independent of the earlier group positions of the individuals.

It is, of course, not necessary that this organization ascend to a head which is highest in the absolute sense of the word.

Its formal nature is revealed, actually, by every group, no matter how the group as a whole be characterized. Already Roman slavery was most minutely graduated in this sense, from the *villicus* and *procurator,* who independently directed whole branches of production in the great slave industries, through all kinds of classifications, down to the foreman of ten workers. Such a form of organization has a great sensory visibility, as it were. Since every member of it is both superordinated and subordinated, and thus is fixed in two directions, the organization gives him a definite, sociological determination of his life feeling, and this feeling, as closeness and solidity of cohesion, is bound to project itself upon the whole group. For this reason, despotic or reactionary movements, for fear of unifications among their subjects, sometimes persecute *hierarchically* organized unifications with particular zeal. The decree issued in 1831 by the reactionary English Ministry goes into peculiar details which can be understood only if the specific socializing power of super-subordination is appreciated. The decree prohibited all associations "composed of separate bodies, with various divisions and subdivisions, under leaders with a gradation of rank and authority, and distinguished by certain badges, and subject to the general control and direction of a superior council."

It should be noted that this form must be sharply distinguished from another, in which superordination and subordination are simultaneous. In this case, an individual is superordinate on one scale or in one respect, but is subordinate in another. This arrangement has more of an individual and qualitative character. It is usually a combination which derives from the particular disposition or fate of the individual. Superordination and subordination on one and the same scale, on the other hand, is much more objectively pre-formed and, for this reason, is a more unambiguous and definite sociological position. The fact that this form, too, is of great cohesive value for the social scale itself, as I noted a moment ago, is related to the circumstance that it makes the individual's rise in the scale a "given" aim for his endeavor. In Freemasonry, for instance, this motivation, as a purely formal one, has been used for preserving the "degrees." Already the "apprentice" learns all essentials of the objective knowledge (here, ritual knowledge) of the "journeyman" and "master" degrees. But it is pointed out that these stages give the order a certain elasticity and animation through the stimulus of novelty, and that they promote the endeavor of the novice.

§ 10. *Strength and Perseverance of Domination by One*

All sociological structures discussed thus far are equally determined by the superordination of one person, no matter how different the contents of the groups concerned. But evidently, such structures can also emerge in case of subordination under a number of individuals, as I have already indicated. If these superordinate individuals are coordinated with one another, the question whether the superordinate position of *one* is, incidentally, occupied by a plurality of persons, is not decisive, and is therefore sociologically irrelevant. It should be emphasized, however, that domination by one is the primary type and form of the relationship of subordination in general. This fundamental position of it within the whole complex of super-subordination makes it understandable that, within its sphere, it may legitimately give room to other kinds of orders, oligarchical and republican, and not only in the political sense of these terms. It makes it understandable that the sphere dominated by the monarch may very well include secondary structures of these other types, while, where the latter are the supreme and most comprehensive structures, monarchy can find only a small or illegitimate niche.

Monarchy has such a sensuous appeal, is so impressive, that it lives forth even in those constitutions that originated as a reaction to it and were designed as instruments of its abolition. It has been said of the American President, as well as of the Athenian Archon and the Roman Consul, that, with certain limitations, they are after all only the heirs of the royal powers of which the kings were deprived through the various revolutions. Some Americans themselves tell us that their freedom consists only in the alternation of government by the two great parties, each of which exerts a tyranny in an entirely monarchical manner. The attempt, furthermore, has been made to show that the democracy of the French revolution is nothing but royalty turned upside down, and equipped with the same qualities. Rousseau's *"volonté générale,"* to which, he teaches, everybody must submit without resistance, has entirely the character of the absolute monarch. And Proudhon notes that a parliament which is the result of universal suffrage is not distinguishable from him. The popular representative, he argues, is infallible, inviolable, irresponsible—and the monarch, essentially, is no more than this. The monarchical principle, he continues, is as lively and complete in a parliament as in a legitimate king. As a matter of fact, in the relations to a parliament, the phenomenon of flattery is not absent, although this, above all others, seems to be specifically reserved for relations to a single individual.

It is quite characteristic that a formal relationship among group elements continues to prevail even after a change of their whole sociological tendency seems to make this impossible. It is the peculiar strength of domination by one person to survive its own death, as it were—by transferring its own color to structures whose very significance is the negation of such domination. This is one of the most striking cases which illustrate the autonomous life of sociological forms. By virtue of it, they not only can absorb materially different contents, but can also inject into changed *forms* the very spirit that is the opposite of these forms. The formal significance of domination by one is so great that it is *explicitly* preserved where its content is negated, and precisely *because* it is negated. The dogedom of Venice lost more and more of its power until eventually, for all practical purposes, it possessed none whatever. In spite of this, it was preserved most anxiously in order to make developments impossible which might have brought a real ruler upon the throne. The process here is not for the opposition to destroy domination by one, in an effort to consolidate itself in this same form, but to preserve it, in order to prevent its real consolidation. The two, actually contradictory processes attest alike to the formal strength of this form of domination.

As a matter of fact, the contrasts which monarchy forces together are contained in one and the same phenomenon. Monarchy is interested in the monarchic institution even where this institution lies outside the immediate influence sphere of the monarch. The experience that all realizations of a certain social form, however divergent, support one another and, as it were, mutually guarantee the form they realize, seems to apply to very different conditions of domination, most decisively to aristocracy and monarchy. For this reason, a monarchy sometimes has to pay heavily if, for certain political reasons, it weakens the monarchic principle in another country. Mazarin's regime met with almost rebellious resistance from both people and parliament. This resistance has been explained in terms of the fact that French politics had supported rebellions in neighboring countries against their governments. In this way, the explanation continues, the monarchic principle received a blow which acted back on the originator, who had thought he could safeguard his interest by means of those rebellions. Inversely, when Cromwell refused the title of king, the Royalists were saddened. For, however unbearable the thought must have been to them of seeing the murderer of the king on the throne, they would, nevertheless, have greeted the mere fact that once more there was a king as preparing the way for the Restoration.

But the effect of monarchic sentiment goes beyond such utilitarian justifications of expanding the monarchy on the grounds of anticipated consequences. In regard to certain phenomena, the monarchic sentiment even has an effect which is to the personal disadvantage of those who harbor it. When, under the regime of Louis XIV, the Portuguese rebellion against Spain broke out, a rebellion which must have been entirely desirable to the King of France, he nevertheless remarked: "However bad a prince may be, the rebellion of his subjects is always infinitely criminal." And Bismarck tells us that William I felt an "instinctive, monarchic disinclination" toward Bennigsen and his earlier activity in Hanover. For, irrespective of what Bennigsen and his party (Bismarck notes) had done for the Prussianization of Hanover, this behavior of a subject toward his original (Guelphic) dynasty was contrary to William's sentiments as a ruler. The inner strength of monarchy is great enough to include in its pervasive sympathy even its enemy and, on the other hand, very deeply to oppose its friend, as if he were an adversary, once he puts himself in opposition to any king whatever, although, personally, this opposition may be very useful to a particular monarch.

§ 11. *Subordination of the Group to a Member or to an Outsider*

Finally, features of a kind not yet touched upon at all emerge, if between superordinates and subordinates there exists, in some respect, equality or inequality, closeness or distance, which becomes problematical. An essential trait of the sociological form of a group is its preference for subordination to a stranger or to somebody from its own midst; its conception of the expediency and dignity of the one or the other kind of subordination. In Germany, medieval feudal barons had originally the right to nominate whatever judges and leaders from the outside they chose to call to their manors. Eventually, however, the concession was often made to the manor that officials had to be taken from among the bondsmen. In exactly the opposite sense, it was considered a particularly important assurance which the Count of Flanders made to his "beloved jurors and burghers of Ghent" in 1228, an assurance to the effect that the judge and executive officer to be appointed by him, as well as their subalterns, could *not* be chosen from Ghent and could not be married to local women.

The difference between these two cases, of course, has utilitarian reasons: the stranger is more impartial; the member is more understanding. The first reason evidently was decisive for the request of the Ghent citizens; for the same reason, as has already been mentioned, Italian cities often chose their judges from other cities and thus secured themselves against the influence of family connections and inner factions upon the legal system. It was the same motive which moved such clever rulers as Louis XI and Mathias Corvinus to take, if possible, their highest officials from abroad, or from the lower classes. As late as in the nineteenth century, Bentham suggested another utilitarian consideration of the fact that foreigners are often the best state officials: they are watched with more suspicion than anybody else.

The preference for more closely related or similar individ-

uals strikes one as less paradoxical. But it may lead to a peculiarly mechanical conception of the axiom of *similia similibus*.
This is reported of an ancient Libyan tribe, and recently of the
Ashanti, where the king rules over the men, and the queen—
who is his sister—over the women. I have already emphasized
the cohesion of the group as the result of its subordination to
one of its members. It is exactly this cohesion which is confirmed
by the phenomenon of the central power that seeks to break
through the autonomous jurisdiction of subgroups. The idea
that one's local community is one's legitimate judge was still
widely diffused in fourteenth-century England. But Richard II
decreed that nobody could be a judge of assize or of "gaol de-
livery" in his own county. In this case, the correlate of group
cohesion was the freedom of religion. Likewise, during the decay
of Anglo-Saxon royalty, the decision by associates or peers was
highly esteemed as a defense against the arbitrariness of royal
and princely constables. And the severely burdened feudal
peasant jealously held on to this arrangement as to his last possession which gave content and value to the idea of freedom
as an individual right.

Thus, certainly, rational grounds of objective expediency
determine the choice of subordination under the fellow member
or under the stranger. Yet the motives of this choice are not
exhausted under the category of expediency. There are also
other motives, more instinctive and emotional, as well as more
abstract and indirect. These, in fact, are bound to exist because
rational grounds alone may be as much in favor of the one as
of the other of the two choices. The greater understanding of
the fellow member and the greater objectivity of the outsider
may often balance one another, and, therefore, another criterion
is needed for deciding between the two. We here encounter the
phychological antinomy that, on the one hand, we are attracted
by what is like us, and, on the other, by what is unlike us. This
antinomy is extremely important for sociological formation in
general. The question regarding the cases and spheres in which
the one or the other becomes effective, and the question regarding the tendency toward which the whole personality leans,
seem to belong to the individual's absolutely primary characteristics which inhere in his very nature. The contrasting ele-

ment complements us; the similar element strengthens us. Contrast excites and stimulates; similarity reassures. Both, though by very different means, give us the feeling that our particular existence is legitimate. But where we feel that the one is appropriate in regard to a particular phenomenon, the other repels us. Contrast then appears hostile, while similarity bores us. Contrast presents us with too high a challenge; similarity, with too low a task. It is difficult in regard to either to find a tenable position: there, because we have no points of contact and comparison; here, because we feel that what is similar to us, or, what is worse, that we ourselves, are superfluous.

Essentially, the inner variety of our connections with an individual (but also with a group) is based upon the fact that these connections present us with a number of aspects with which we have to establish a relationship. In us, these traits correspond partly with like features, partly with heterogeneous ones, and both correspondences make attraction as well as repulsion possible. In their play and counter-play and in their combinations, the total relationship takes its course. The essential affinity of another individual, for instance, may release in us sympathetic feelings in one respect, and antipathetic feelings in another. A social power, therefore, favors similar powers in its own province not only because of the natural sympathy for ideal affinities, but because the strengthening of the principle common to all is necessarily beneficial to it, too. On the other hand, however, jealousy, competition, and the desire to be the *only* representative of the principle have the opposite effect. This is very notable in the relation between monarchy and nobility. The hereditary principle of nobility is intimately shared by monarchy. For this reason, monarchy sides with nobility, is supported by it, and hence favors it. Often, however, it cannot tolerate a class which is privileged by heredity, that is, in its own right, to exist side by side with it; it necessarily wishes for every individual to receive its privileges specifically from monarchy itself. Originally, the Roman Empire favored senatorial nobility and made it hereditary. But after Diocletian, senatorial nobility was overshadowed by office nobility in which each office holder attained a high post only through personal promotion. Whether in such cases the attraction or the repulsion of the similar element remains predominant, is a question evidently decided, not by utilitarian factors alone, but also by the deeper psychological readiness to value the like or else the unlike.

From the very general type of this sociological problem derives the specific problem here discussed. Innumerable times it is merely a sentiment, that cannot be rationalized, which decides whether one feels more humiliated by subordination to a closely related or to a more distant party. All medieval social instincts and life feelings are revealed by the fact that, when in the thirteenth century the guilds were endowed with public power, they demanded, at the same time, that all workers of the same craft be subordinated to them. The idea was that it would be unthinkable for a craft tribunal to judge somebody who was not himself a member of the judging court. The very opposite feeling, which can just as little be reduced to any particular utilities, moved some Australian hordes not to choose their chiefs by themselves, but to have them chosen for them by the leaders of adjacent tribes. In a similar fashion, some nature peoples do not manufacture their own currency but import it from the outside, so that occasionally we find a sort of industry which produces monetary symbols (shells, etc.) for export to other places where they are used as money.

In general, and reserving many modifications, we can say that the lower a group is as a whole and the more, therefore, every member of it is accustomed to subordination, the less will the group allow one of its members to rule it. And, inversely, the higher a group is as a whole, the more likely is it that it subordinates itself only to one of its peers. In the first case, domination by the member, the like person, is difficult because everybody is low; in the second case, it is easier because everybody stands high. The English House of Lords exhibits the most extreme intensification of this feeling. Not only did every Peer recognize it as his only judge, but once, in 1330, the House expressly rebutted the insinuation that it might adjudge people other than the Peers. Here the tendency to have oneself judged only by one's like is so decisive that it has a sort of inverse effect. In a logically false, but psychologically both profound and understandable fashion, the Peers argued that since the like of them were judged only by themselves, it followed that everybody they judged became, so to speak, the like of them.

In the last example, a decisive relationship of subordination, namely, the relation of the judged to his judge, is, in a certain sense, conceived as a coordinate relationship. But sometimes we find the reverse: that coordination is conceived as subordination. Here, again, is the dualism of reasons which can be indicated, and of dark instincts—and the two may be separated or fused. The rights of the medieval burgher were below those of the nobility, but above those of the peasant. Occasionally, the burgher rejected the idea of general legal equality because he feared that equalization would deprive him of *more* (in favor of the peasant) than it would give him (in his relation to the nobility). More than once we meet with this sociological type: an intermediate stratum can obtain its elevation to the level of a higher stratum only at the expense of permitting a lower stratum to become coordinate with itself; but it feels that this coordination is so degrading that it gives up that elevation for which it would have to pay such a stiff price. Thus, although the Creoles of Spanish America were violently jealous of European-born Spaniards, their contempt for Mulattoes, Mestizoes, Negroes, and Indians was even greater. In order to become the equals of the Spaniards they would have had to allow these other groups to become coordinate with themselves; but their racial feeling would have made this coordination such a degradation that, instead, they gave up their equality with the Spaniards. This formal combination is expressed even more abstractly or instinctively in a statement by H. S. Maine. The nationality principle, as it is often proclaimed, he said, seems to imply that people of one race are done wrong in case they have to have common political institutions with people of another race. That is, where there are two different social characters, A and B, A seems to be subordinate to B as soon as he has to live under the same constitution, even when this constitution, in its content, involves no lowering or subordination whatsoever.

Subordination under the more distant personality has, finally, the very important significance that it is the more suitable to the extent to which the subordinates are heterogeneous or mutually alien or opposed elements. The members of a collectivity who are subject to a higher personality resemble specific notions that are included in a general concept. This concept must be the more elevated and abstract—that is, it must be the more distant from the single ideas—the more different from one another the ideas to be covered by it. The most typical sociological case, whose identical form is represented in the most diverse fields, is that of conflicting parties which choose an arbitrator. This case has been discussed before. The more remote the arbiter is from the party interests of either of the two, the more willingly will the two parties submit to his decision. The analogy between the arbitrator and the higher concept consists in the fact that, what is common to both parties (the basis, that is, of their conflict as well as of their possible reconciliation), must somehow be inherent in the arbitrator, or must at least be accessible to him. There is a threshold of differences beyond which the meeting of conflicting parties becomes impossible, no matter how high the point of conciliation may be located. In regard to the history of English industrial courts of arbitration to date, it has been stressed that these courts perform excellent services in interpreting labor contracts and laws. These contracts and laws, however, are said to be only rarely the reason for large strikes and lockouts, which are the consequences, rather, of attempts, by workers or employers, to change working conditions. Here, where new bases of the relation between the two parties are at issue, the court of arbitration is not indicated: the cleavage between the interests has become so wide that arbitration would have to be infinitely high above them in order to include and balance them. Analogously, we can think of ideas of such heterogeneous contents that it is impossible to find a general concept which would cover their common features.

§ 12. *Coordination of Parties in Case of Arbitration*

In the case of conflicting parties which are to subject themselves to the higher tribunal of the arbitrator, it is, furthermore, a fact of decisive significance that these parties must be coordinate. If there exists some super-subordination relationship between them, this will easily affect the judge's attitude toward one of the two, and this attitude will disturb his impartiality.

The danger exists even where the arbitrator is equally remote from the objective interests of either party; for, in spite of this, he will be inclined to be prejudiced in favor of the superordinate party or, occasionally, of the subordinate one. Class sympathies are a case in point. They are often quite unconscious because they are inseparably interwoven with the totality of the individual's thoughts and feelings. They constitute the *a priori,* so to speak, which forms the apparently purely objective appraisal of the case. Class sympathies reveal their intimate integration with the very nature of the individual by the fact that his effort to avoid them usually does not lead to real objectivity and balance, but to falling into the opposite extreme.

Furthermore, where parties are in very different positions of elevation and power, the mere belief in the prejudicial character of the arbitrator (even if in actuality he is not prejudiced) is sufficient to make the whole procedure illusory. In conflicts between the workers and entrepreneurs, English courts of arbitration often call in an outside manufacturer as arbitrator. Yet every time his decision is against the workers, the workers accuse him of favoring his own class, no matter how impeccable his character may be. Inversely, if the arbitrator should be a parliamentarian, the manufacturers suspect him of weakness for the most numerous class of his constituents. Thus, a fully satisfactory situation will be the outcome only if the parties are in perfect coordination—be it only because, otherwise, the superordinate party usually also harvests the usurer's interest of its position, namely, that, for the decision between itself and the subordinate party, it will manage to obtain an arbitrator who is in its own favor. For this reason, it is also legitimate to make the inverse inference: the nomination of an impartial arbitrator is always a sign that the conflicting parties recognize a certain reciprocal coordination. In voluntary English arbitration, worker and entrepreneur must subject themselves, by contract, to the decision of the arbitrator, who can be neither an entrepreneur nor a worker. Evidently, only the entrepreneurs' recognition of the workers' coordination could make them renounce the participation of entrepreneurs in the settlement of a conflict, and make them entrust it to an outsider.

There is, finally, another, materially very different example which teaches us that the common relationship of several elements to a superordinate party presupposes, or effects, a coordination among these elements, irrespective of all other differences, indifferences, and contrasts; and that this coordination is the more necessary, the higher the tribunal is. It is obviously very important for the socializing significance which religion may have for large groups that God should be at a certain distance from the believers. The immediate, almost local nearness to the faithful, which is characteristic of the divine principles of all totemistic and fetishistic religions, as well as of the ancient Hebrew God, makes these religions entirely unsuitable to govern very large groups. Only the immense elevation of the idea of the Christian God permitted the equality-before-God of unequals. The distance to him was so immeasurable that differences among men were extinguished by it. This did not prevent the intimate relation of the individual from being very close to him, for in this respect, all differences among men were assumed to disappear. Yet this intimate, individual relation was crystallized in this purity and autonomy only under the impact of that highest principle and of the relationship to it. Perhaps, however, the Catholic Church could create a world religion only by interrupting even *this* immediacy: by interposing itself between man and God, it moved God to a height which even in *this* regard was inaccessible to the unaided individual.

Chapter 3

Subordination under a Plurality

§ 1. *Consequences for the Subordinates of Subordination under a Plurality*

CERTAIN SOCIETAL STRUC-
tures are characterized by the superordination of a plurality or
social collectivity over individuals or other collectivities. In
analyzing these structures, the first thing to be noted is that
their significance for the subordinate is very uneven. The highest aim of the Spartan and Thessalian slaves was to become slaves
of the state rather than of individuals. Prior to the emancipation
of the feudal peasants in Prussia, the peasants on the state
domains had a far better lot than private peasants had. In the
large modern enterprises and warehouses, which are not characterized by very individual management but either are joint-
stock companies or are administered as impersonally as if they
were, employees are better situated than in small businesses,
with their personal exploitation by the owner. This relationship
is repeated where the question is not the differential impact of
individuals as over collectivities, but of smaller *versus* larger
collectivities. India's fate is considerably more favorable under
British rule than under that of the East-India Company. In these
cases, it is irrelevant, of course, whether the larger collectivity
itself (for instance, England) is governed by a monarch—provided that the technique of the domination which it exercises
has, in the largest sense, the character of super-individuality.
Thus, the aristocratic regime of the Roman Republic oppressed
the provinces by far more than did the Roman Empire, which
was much more just and objective. Usually it is also more favor-

able for those who find themselves in a serving position to belong to a larger group. The great seigniories which developed in the seventh century in the Frankish realm often created a new, advantageous position for the subject population. The vast holdings permitted an organization and differentiation of the workers. They thus developed qualified, and therefore more highly esteemed, types of work which permitted the serf to rise socially within an individual seigniory. In the same sense, state criminal laws are often milder than those of smaller groups.

Yet, as has already been indicated, several phenomena run in exactly the opposite direction. The allies of Athens and Rome, as well as the territories which were once subject to particular Swiss cantons, were suppressed and exploited as cruelly as it would have hardly been possible under the tyranny of a single ruler. The same joint-stock company, which in consequence of the technique of its operation exploits its employees less than does the private entrepreneur, in many cases (for instance, in indemnifications and charities) *cannot* proceed as liberally as the private citizen, who owes nobody an account of his expenditures. And in regard to particular impulses: the cruelties committed for the pleasure of the Roman circus audiences—whose extreme intensification was often demanded by these audiences—would have hardly been committed by many, if the delinquent had faced them as an individual.

The basic reason for the difference in the results which the rule by a plurality has for its subordinates, lies, first of all, in its character of *objectivity*. This character excludes certain feelings, leanings, and impulses, which become effective only in the individual actions of the subjects, but not in their collective behavior. Within the given relationship and its particular contents, the situation of the subordinate may be influenced, favorably or unfavorably, by the objective or by the individually subjective character of this relationship; and, accordingly, differences result from this. Where the subordinate, in line with his situation, needs the tenderness, altruism, and favor of the superordinate, he will fare badly under the objective domination by a plurality. Inversely, under conditions where only legality, impartiality, and objectivity are favorable to his situation, the rule which has these features will be more desirable for him. It is characteristic of this phenomenon that the state, although it can legally condemn the criminal, cannot pardon him; and even in republics, the right to pardon is usually reserved for exercise by particular individuals. The principle is revealed most strikingly if we consider the material interests of communities. They are governed according to the profoundly objective axiom of greatest advantages and least sacrifices possible. This harshness and lack of consideration is by no means the same as the cruelty which individuals may commit for its own sake; but rather it is a wholly consistent objectivity. In a similar fashion, the brutality of a man purely motivated by monetary considerations and acting, to this extent, on the same axiom of greatest advantage and least sacrifice, often does not appear to him at all as a moral delinquency, since he is aware only of a rigorously logical behavior, which draws the objective consequences of the situation.

To be sure, this objectivity of collective behavior often merely implies something negative, namely, that certain norms to which the single individual ordinarily subjects himself, are suspended. Objectivity amounts to being a form that is designed to cover this suspension and to soothe the conscience. Every single individual who participates in a given decision can hide himself behind the fact, precisely, that it was a decision by the whole group. He can mask his own lust for gain and his brutality by maintaining that he only pursued the advantage of the totality. The idea that the possession of power—specifically, of rapidly acquired or long-lasting power—leads to its abuse, is true, for individuals, only with many and striking exceptions. By contrast, whenever it *cannot* be applied to social bodies and classes it is only because of especially fortunate circumstances.

It is very remarkable that the disappearance of the individual behind the totality serves, or even intensifies, the questionable character of this procedure, even in cases when also the subjugated party is a collectivity. The psychological re-creation of suffering—the essential vehicle of compassion and tenderness—fails easily if the sufferer is not a namable or visible individual but only a totality, which has no subjective states of mind, so to speak. It has been noted that English communal life has been characterized, throughout its history, by extraordinary justice toward persons and by equally great injustice toward groups.

In view of the strong feeling for individual rights, it is only this second psychological peculiarity which accounts for the manner in which Dissenters, Jews, Irishmen, Hindus, and, in earlier periods, Scotchmen, have been treated. The immersion of the forms and norms of personality in the objectivity of collective life determines not only the action, but also the suffering of the groups. Objectivity, to be sure, operates in the form of law; but, where law is not compulsory and, therefore, ought to be replaced by personal conscientiousness, it frequently appears that the latter is no trait of collective psychology. This is shown even more decisively when, because of its collective character, the object of the procedure does not even stimulate the development of this personal trait. The misuses of power, as, for instance, in American city administrations, would have hardly attained their enormous dimensions if the rulers were not corporations, and the ruled not collectivities. Characteristically, it is sometimes believed that these misuses can be reduced by greatly increasing the power of the mayor—so that there would be somebody who could personally be held responsible.

As a seeming exception to the objectivity of plurality action, which in reality, however, only anchors the rule more solidly, there is the behavior of the mass. It was already illustrated by the Roman circus audience. Two phenomena must be fundamentally distinguished here. On the one hand, there is the effect resulting from a plurality as a self-consistent and particular structure which, as it were, embodies an abstraction. Such a plurality may be an economic association, a state, a church—any grouping which in reality or by analogy has to be designated as a legal person. On the other hand, there is the plurality which is in fact physically present as a mass. Both are characterized by the suspension of individual-personal differences. But in the first case, this suspension causes features to come to the fore which lie, as it were, above the individual character; whereas, in the second case, those are activated which lie below. For within a mass of people in sensory contact, innumerable suggestions and nervous influences play back and forth; they deprive the individual of the calmness and autonomy of reflection and action. In a crowd, therefore, the most ephemeral incitations often grow, like avalanches, into the most disproportionate impulses, and thus appear to eliminate the higher, differentiated and critical functions of the individual. It is for this reason that, in the theatre and at assemblies, we laugh about jokes which in a room would "leave us cold"; that spiritualistic manifestations succeed best in "circles"; that social games usually reach the highest degree of gaiety at the lowest intellectual level. Hence the quick, objectively quite ununderstandable changes in the mood of a mass; hence the innumerable observations concerning the "stupidity" of collectivities.[7]

As I have said, I ascribe the paralyzation of higher qualities and the lack of resistance to being swept away, to the incalculable number of influences and impressions which cross back and forth in a crowd between everybody and everybody else, mutually strengthening, crossing, deflecting, and reproducing themselves. On the one hand, because of this tangle of minimal excitations below the threshold of consciousness, there develops a great nervous excitement at the expense of clear and consistent intellectual activity; it arouses the darkest and most primitive instincts of the individual, which ordinarily are under control. On the other hand, there emerges a hypnotic paralysis which makes the crowd follow to its extreme every leading, suggestive impulse. In addition, there are the power intoxication and irresponsibility of the individual, whereby the moral inhibitions of the low and brutal impulses are eliminated. This satisfactorily explains the cruelty of crowds—whether they be composed of Roman circus goers, medieval Jew baiters, or American Negro lynchers—and the dire lot of those who become their victims.

But here, too, the typical, twofold result of this sociological relationship of subordination clearly appears. For, the impulsiveness and suggestibility of the crowd occasionally allows it to follow suggestions of magnanimity and enthusiasm which the individual could not attain without it any more than he could commit those acts of cruelty. The ultimate reason for the contradictions within this configuration can be formulated as follows: between the individual with his situations and needs, on the one hand, and all the super-individual or sub-individual phenomena and internal and external situations involved in

[7] More on this in the chapter on self-preservation [of the group. Not contained in this volume].

collectivization, on the other, there is no fundamental and constant, but only a variable and contingent, relation. If, therefore, abstract social units proceed more objectively, coolly, and consistently than the individual; if, inversely, crowds in concrete physical proximity act more impulsively, senselessly, and extremely than each of its members alone; then, each of these two cases may be more favorable or more unfavorable for the person who is subject to such a plurality. There is, so to speak, nothing contingent about this contingency. It is the logical expression of the incommensurability between the specifically individual situations and claims at issue and the structures and moods that rule or serve the proximity and interaction of the many.

§ 2. *Subordination under a Heterogeneous Plurality*

In the preceding analyses of subordination under a plurality, the single elements forming the plurality were coordinated, or, in all relevant regards, they behaved as if they were. New phenomena result, however, as soon as the superordinate plurality does not act as a unit of homogeneous elements. In this case, the superordinates may be either opposed to one another, or they may form a scale on which some of them are subordinate to higher superordinates. I first consider the former case. Its various types can be shown in terms of the variety of consequences for the subordinate.

§ 3. *Subordination under Mutually Opposed Superordinates*

[a] TOTAL SUBORDINATION

If somebody is totally subject to several persons or groups, that is, subject in such a way that he has no spontaneity to contribute to the relationship but is entirely dependent on each superordinate, he will suffer severely from their opposition. For, everyone of them will claim him, his forces and services, wholly, while at the same time holding him responsible—as if he were free to be responsible—for whatever he does or neglects at the compulsory request of the other. This is the typical situation of the "servant of two masters." It is shown by children who stand between their conflicting parents; or by small states which are equally dependent on two powerful neighbors and hence, in case of their conflict, are often made responsible by each of the two for what their relationship of dependence upon the other forces them to do. If the conflict of such subordinate groups is wholly internalized and the superordinate elements operate as ideal moral forces which make their claim within the individual himself, then the situation appears as a "conflict of duties." While the more external conflict only appears in the person without originating there, as it were, this internal conflict breaks out of the individual because the moral conscience, internally, strives in two different directions, strives to obey two mutually exclusive powers. External conflict, therefore, in principle excludes the spontaneity of the subject; and would, as a rule, be quickly terminated if this spontaneity came to operate. By contrast, the conflict of duties is based on the fullest freedom of the subject, because only this freedom can embody the recognition of the two claims as morally obligatory claims. Yet, evidently, this contrast does not prevent the conflict between two powers, both of which request our obedience, from attaining the two forms simultaneously. As long as a conflict is purely external, it is worst if the personality is weak; but, if it becomes internalized, it is most destructive if the personality is strong.

The rudimentary forms of such conflicts pervade our lives at large, as well as in details. We are so adapted to them, we so instinctively come to terms with them through compromise and through the compartmentalization of our activities, that in most cases they do not even enter our consciousness as conflicts. But, where they do, the insolubility of this situation usually comes to the fore—merely on the basis of its sociological form, even if its contingent contents permit attenuation and conciliation. For as long as there is a conflict of elements, each of which makes full claim on the same individual, no partition of its forces will satisfy those claims. What is more, usually not even a relative solution by means of such a partition will be possible, because a definite stand must be taken, and every single action faces an inflexible *pro* or *contra*. There is no differentiating compromise for Antigone between the religiously clothed claim of the family group, which entails the burial of Polyneikes, and the law of the State, which forbids it. After her death, the contrasts, in their inner significance, face one another in exactly as harsh and unreconciled a manner as they did at the beginning of the tragedy. They demonstrate that no behavior or fate of the individual who is subject to them, can suspend the conflict which they project into him. And even where the collision does not occur between those forces themselves, but only within the subject which obeys both; where, therefore, it seems easier to settle the collision by dividing the subject's activities between them—even there, it is only the lucky accident following from the content of the situation which makes this solution possible. Here the type is: Render unto Caesar what is Caesar's, and unto God what is God's—but what, if one needs the coin claimed by Caesar for a deed in honor of God? The mere mutual strangeness and non-organization of the authoriites on both of which an individual depends at the same time, is sufficient to make his situation basically contradictory. And this is all the more the case, the more the conflict is internalized in the subject itself, and grows out of the ideal claims which live in the individual consciousness of duties. In the two examples given above, the subjectively moral accent lies essentially on *one* side of the contrast, while to the other side, the individual is subject only by some external inevitability. But where both claims have the same inner weight, it helps us little to use our best convictions for deciding in favor of one of them or for dividing our forces between them. For, the wholly or partially unmet claim still acts with all its weight; its unfilled quantum makes us fully responsible for it, even if externally it was impossible to satisfy it, and even if under the given circumstances our solution was morally the most correct one. Every really moral claim has something absolute that is not satisfied by any relative fulfillment—which nevertheless alone can be granted to it by virtue of the existence of another moral claim. Here, too, where we do not have to bow to any tribunal except our personal conscience, we fare no better than in the other case where neither of two external, contradictory bonds permits us any reservation in favor of the other. Internally, we cannot rest as long as a moral necessity remains unrealized, no matter whether or not we have a clean conscience in view of the fact that the existence of *another* necessity, which equally and in the same sense transcends its possibility of realization, forced us not to give more to the first than we actually did.

[b] RELATIVE SUBORDINATION

Subordination under external, mutually opposed or alien, powers certainly becomes entirely different if the subordinate possesses any spontaneity whatever, if he can invest in the relationship with some power of his own. This, in all its variations, is the situation of *duobus litigantibus tertius gaudet*,[8] which was discussed in the preceding chapter [part]. Here, only some of its applications to the case of *subordination* of the *tertius,* and of the possibility that the higher parties are not in conflict, but only strangers to one another, will be indicated.

In regard to the existing quantum of freedom on the part of the subordinates, the situation usually introduces a process of growth which sometimes reaches the point of dissolving the subordination itself. An essential difference between the medieval bondsman and the medieval vassal consisted in the fact that the former had, and could have, only one master, whereas the latter could take land from several lords and make the feudal vow to each of them. Through this possibility of entering several feudal service relations, the vassal gained solidity and independence in regard to the single feudal lord, and, thus, was compensated very considerably for the basic subordination of his position. A formally similar situation, in reference to the religious individual, is created by polytheism. Although the subject knows that he is ruled by a plurality of divine powers, he can—in a manner which logically, perhaps, is not wholly clear, but which psychologically is very real to him—turn from an inaccessible or powerless god to another god which gives him greater chances. Even in contemporary Catholicism, the believer often abandons a particular saint who has not rewarded him for his special adoration, in order to devote it to another saint—although, in principle, he cannot deny that the power which also the first has over him continues to hold. Inasmuch as the individual has at least *some* choice between the powers to which he is subject, he gains a certain independence in respect to each of them and,

8 "If two parties quarrel, the third has the advantage."—Tr.

as far as his intimate feelings are concerned, even, perhaps, in respect to their totality. But this independence is denied him where the same amount of religious dependency is concentrated inescapably, as it were, in the idea of a single God.

This also is the form, finally, in which modern man gains a certain independence in the field of economics. The modern individual, especially the resident of the large city, is infinitely more dependent on the sum of all his suppliers taken together than is man under conditions of a simpler economy. Nevertheless, since he has an almost unlimited possibility of changing or choosing among these suppliers, he has a freedom in regard to each one of them which cannot even be compared with the freedom of man under simpler or small-town conditions.

The same formal delimitation of the relationship results if the divergence among the superordinates develops successively, rather than simultaneously. According to historical contents and special conditions, the most varied transformations appear; but the same formal phenomenon operates in all of them. Formally, the Roman Senate greatly depended upon the high state officials. But since these officials had only short terms of office, whereas the Senate kept its members permanently, the power of the Senate actually became much greater than could be inferred from its legal relation to the government executives. Ever since the fourteenth century, the growth in power of the House of Commons, in comparison with the English Crown, resulted from basically the same motive. The dynastic parties were still capable of determining the elections in favor of Royalism or Reform, of York or of Lancaster. Yet under all these power demonstrations of the rulers, Commons persevered and, precisely because of the oscillations and changes of wind in the highest regions, attained a firmness, strength, and independence which it would perhaps never have gained if the highest regimes had always had the same direction. In a corresponding manner, the growth of the democratic consciousness in France has been derived (among other things) from the fact that, since the fall of Napoleon I, changing governmental powers followed one another in rapid succession. Each one of them was incompetent, uncertain, and trying to gain the favor of the masses—whereby every citizen was bound to become deeply aware of his own social significance. Although he was subject to every one of these governments, he nevertheless felt himself to be strong, because he formed the lasting element in all the change and contrast among the successive regimes.

There is a power which an element in a relationship acquires by the mere fact of its perseverance in comparison with its variable fellow elements. This power is such a general, formal consequence that its exploitation by an element which is subordinate in some relationship must be understood merely as a special case. For, the superordinate has this power, too. There is the prerogative which "the state" and "the church" have by virtue of their mere stability as over against the short-livedness of those that are ruled by them; and there is a whole range of other examples—down to the highly singular one, that the high frequency of puerperal fever during the Middle Ages greatly increased the sovereignty of the husband in the house. For, the result of this frequency was that most healthy men successively had several wives. Thus, the power of the lord of the house accumulated in one person, whereas that of the housewife was distributed among several persons in succession.

§ 4. *Subordination under Stratified Superordinates*

In all the cases discussed, the phenomena of superordination and subordination seemed to permit the most contradictory consequences for the subordinate. Yet everywhere, closer specification showed the reasons for these contradictions, without making it necessary to abandon the same general type: no matter what the contents, the common form remained the same. This similarity also holds true in regard to the second combination, which we must now discuss, namely, the case in which a number of superordinate authorities, instead of being mutually alien or hostile, themselves stand in superordinate and subordinate relationships toward one another.

[a] CONTACT BETWEEN TOP AND BOTTOM OF THE STRATIFICATION
SYSTEM

Here again, two very different constellations must be distinguished. The first is that the subordinate still stands in an immediate relation with the highest among his superordinates. The second is that the intermediate layer, which is superordinate to him but subordinate to the highest, completely separates him from the latter and thus alone, actually, represents the superordinate elements to him. Cases of the first kind were created by feudalism, where the person who was inferior to the more powerful vassal, nevertheless remained the subject of the reigning dynasty. English feudalism at the time of William the Conqueror is a very faithful portrayal of this. It is described by Stubbs as follows: "All men continued to be primarily the king's men and the public peace to be his peace. Their lords might demand their service to fulfill their own obligations, but the king could call them to his courts, and tax them without the intervention of their lords, and to the king they could look for protection against all foes." Thus, the position of the subordinate in regard to his superordinate is favorable if the latter, in his turn, is subordinate to a still higher authority in which the former finds support. This, in fact, is really a natural consequence of the underlying sociological configuration. In general, there is always some hostility or question of jurisdiction between contiguous elements of a hierarchy. The middle element, therefore, is often in conflict with both the higher and lower ones. Common hostility unites the most divergent sectors, that cannot be unified by any other means. This is one of the typical formal rules which is proved in all existing fields of social life.

A nuance of it becomes particularly important for the problem under discussion here. Even in the ancient Orient, it is the glory of the ruler to take up the cause of the weak who are oppressed by the strong—be it only, because in this fashion, the ruler emerges more powerful than the oppressor. In Greece it happened that an oligarchy previously in power branded the very same person with the name of tyrant whom the lower masses revered as their liberator from tyranny—as it occurred to Euphron of Sicyon. It is hardly necessary to re-emphasize the frequency, throughout history, of the motive of the lower masses which are supported by the ruler in their fight against the aristocracy. What is more, even where there is no such immediate relation between the highest and lowest steps of the social scale for the purpose of checking the intermediate layers;

where, on the contrary, the lowest and intermediate strata are equally suppressed by the highest; even there, the mere fact that the intermediate layer, too, experiences the fate of the lowest, offers it at least a psychological, emotional relief. Among certain African and Asiatic peoples, polygamy takes on a form in which only one of the wives is considered the proper, first, or legitimate spouse, while the others are in a subordinate or serving position in regard to her. But, in respect to the husband, even the superordinate wife is by no means better situated: for him, she is as much a slave as the other wives are. Such a situation, in which one of two superordinates is under the same pressure from above as is his inferior in regard to *him,* no doubt makes—in view of general human disposition—the pressure more bearable for the latter, too. Man usually draws some satisfaction from the suppression of his suppressor. He usually has some feeling of superiority if he can identify himself with his master's master, even where this sociological constellation does not involve any real relief from pressure.

[b] TRANSMISSION OF PRESSURE

The content or form of the sociological structure may exclude contact between the highest and lowest layer which could be used for a common hostility against the middle. Hence, the continuity of the structure runs from top to bottom, but not inversely. If these are the features of the structure, there is room for the emergence of a typical sociological process which may be designated as the transfer or transmission [*Abwälzung*] of pressure. If this occurs, we no longer have the case of a powerful person or party exploiting its position for the abuse of a weaker one. Rather, the superordinate here transmits the impairment of his position, against which he cannot defend himself, to some powerless person, and thus tries to maintain himself in the *status quo ante*. The retailer transfers the difficulties which arise for him from the pretensions and caprices of the public, to the wholesaler; the wholesaler, to the manufacturer; and the manufacturer to his workers.

In every hierarchy, a new pressure or imposition moves along the line of least resistance which, though not in its first stage, usually and eventually, runs in a descending direction. This is the tragedy of whoever is lowest in any social order. He not only has to suffer from the deprivations, efforts, and discriminations which, taken together, characterize his position: in addition, every new pressure on any point whatever in the superordinate layers is, if technically possible at all, transmitted downward and stops only at him. Irish agrarian conditions give a very pure example of this. The English lord who owned an estate in Ireland but never visited his property, leased it to a head farmer who in turn rented it out to smaller farmers, etc., so that the poor peasant often had to lease his small piece of land from a fifth or sixth middleman. This accounted for the fact, first, that he had to pay six pounds for a field, of which sum the owner received only ten shillings. But furthermore, every rise of the farm-rent by a shilling, which the owner imposed upon the farmer with whom he negotiated directly, reached the peasant not as a rise by a shilling, but by the twelvefold amount. For, evidently, the initial increase in pressure is not transferred in its absolute magnitude, but in its relative magnitude, which corresponds to the already existing measure of power of the superior over the inferior. Thus, the reprimand which an employee receives from his superior may be in the moderate phraseology of higher civilization; but this employee, perhaps, will already express his annoyance at the reprimand by crudely shouting at his subaltern, who angrily beats up his children on a perfectly trifling occasion.

[c] SEPARATION BETWEEN TOP AND BOTTOM OF THE
STRATIFICATION SYSTEM

The particularly unfavorable situation of the lowest element in a complex scale of super-subordination derives from the fact that the scale permits a certain continuous downward-gliding of the pressure. Another structure, which formally strikes us as quite different, leads to very similar results for the lowest stratum. It, too, destroys its connection with the highest element, which was its support against the intermediary layers. This intermediate layer may be such a broad and powerful stratum between the other two that all measures taken by the top in favor of the bottom must pass through it. Instead of a connection between above and below, this situation often effects their complete separation. As long as individuals were subject to particular manors, the nobility carried the administrative organization of the state and, in regard to its subjects, exercised judicial, economic, and tax functions, without which the state could not have existed. Thus, nobility did in fact link the subject masses to the general interest and to the supreme power. But, since the nobility also had private interests, in behalf of which it wanted to exploit the peasants for itself, it utilized its position as an administrative organ intermediate between the government and the bottom, and thus for a long time actually annulled the measures and laws designed by the government in behalf of the peasants. This was possible because, for a very long time, the government could act only through the medium of the nobility. It is obvious that the formation of such insulating layers harms not only the lowest, but also the highest link of the scale, by depriving it of forces which would accrue to it from below. Medieval German kingship, for instance, was extraordinarily weakened by the fact that the rising lower nobility was bound only to the higher nobility, because it was enfeoffed by it alone. The intermediate link of the high nobility eventually separated the lower nobility from the crown entirely.

For the rest, obviously, the effect of this structure and its separations and fusions upon the lowest element, depends on the attitude of the higher strata toward this element. Contrary to the cases observed thus far, modifications in this attitude may cause the separation through the intermediate layer to be favorable, and the circumvention of the intermediate layer, to be unfavorable. The first case has applied to England since Edward I, when the exercise of judiciary, financial, and police authority was gradually transferred, by legal order, to the propertied classes organized in county and city associations. These, as whole groups, took over the individual's protection against absolute force. The communal units, represented in Parliament, became the counterweight of the highest power which shielded the individual from illegal and unjust transgressions by the state government. In the France of the *Ancien Régime* the process was the reverse. Here, from the beginning, nobility was tied up intimately with the local group which it administered and ruled, and whose interests it represented in the central government. The state injected itself into this relation between nobleman and peasant, and gradually took away from the nobility the functions of government—administration of justice, care of the poor, police, and road construction. The nobility wanted no traffic with this centralized government, which was only interested in the collection of money, and, therefore, withdrew from its social duties, abandoning the peasant to the royal intendants and delegates who thought only of the cash box of the state, or of their own, and completely deprived the farmer of his original support by the nobility.

§ 5. *The Phenomenon of Outvoting*

A special form of subordination under a plurality lies in the principle of "outvoting" [*Überstimmung*] of minorities by majorities. Yet, beyond its significance for the sociology of superordination and subordination, outvoting roots itself in so many other interests of societal formation and branches out in so many of them, that it appears appropriate to discuss it in a special section.[9]

The essence of societal formation, which accounts for the incomparability of its results as much as for the unsolved state of its inner problems, is this: that out of closed units—such as human personalities more or less are—a new unit emerges. A painting cannot be made out of paintings, nor a tree out of trees: the autonomous whole does not grow out of wholes, but of dependent parts. Only society makes that which is whole and centered in itself into a mere member of a more comprehensive whole. Ultimately, all restless evolution of societal forms, in its bold outlines as in its minute details, is merely the ever renewed attempt at reconciling the individual's unity and totality (which are oriented inwardly) with his social role (which is only a part of society and a contribution to it). It is an attempt at saving the unity and totality of society from disruption by the autonomy of its parts. Every conflict among the members of a collectivity makes the continuance of this collectivity dubious. The signifi-

---

[9] "... *sie in einem besonderen Exkurs* [excursion, note] *zu behandeln*." Follows a five-page "*Exkurs über die Überstimmung*" in smaller type. This is translated as the present section.—Tr.

cance, therefore, of voting—of voting to the result of which the minority, too, agrees to yield—is the idea that the unity of the whole must, under all circumstances, remain master over the antagonism of convictions and interests. In its seeming simplicity, voting is one of the most outstanding means by which the conflict among individuals is eventually transformed into a uniform result.

But this has by no means always been so matter-of-course as it strikes us today. The form under discussion also includes the dissenter. Every person who participates in the voting practically accepts its result—unless he secedes from the group in anticipation of this result. There are two main factors which, in all kinds of groups, do not admit of the majority principle, but require unanimity for every decision. On the one hand, there is a certain intellectual clumsiness which makes it impossible to understand the creation of a social unit out of dissenting elements. On the other hand, there is a strong feeling of individuality on account of which one does not wish to yield to any decision without full consent. Thus, the decisions of the German mark associations had to be unanimous; what could not be done unanimously was not done at all. Until far into the Middle Ages, the English nobleman who dissented from the granting of a tax or was absent at the relevant deliberations, often refused to pay for it. The above-mentioned feeling of individuality operates where unanimity is required for the election of a king or leader: he who has not personally elected him is not expected or required to obey him. In the tribal council of the Iroquois, as well as in the Polish Diet, no decision was valid from which even a single voice had dissented.

Yet the contradiction between cooperating in a collective action and opposing it as an individual, does not, in itself alone, entail the logical consequence of unanimity. For if a proposal, for lack of a unanimous vote, is considered rejected, the minority (to be sure) is thereby prevented from being violated by the majority—but the majority is also violated by the minority. Moreover, the suspension of a measure which has been approved by a majority usually is something very tangible, something which has very positive consequences; and it is these consequences which the minority, with the help of the principle of compulsory unanimity, foists upon the majority. This "minor-ization" [10] of the majority by means of unanimity negates, in principle, the individual freedom which it is designed to save. But aside from this "minorization," historically and practically, the principle of unanimity has often enough had the same result. For the Spanish kings, there was no more favorable situation for suppressing the Aragonese *Cortes* than this very "freedom": until 1592, the *Cortes* could make no decision once even a single member of the four estates disagreed. This so paralyzed action that a less cumbersome substitute was required forthwith. Some-times—as in verdicts by juries—it is impossible to waive a pro-posal or to renounce a practical result, because it must be reached under all circumstances. In such cases, the requirement of unani-mity (found, for instance, in England and America) is based on the more or less unconscious assumption that the objective truth must always also be subjectively convincing, and that, inversely, the identity of subjective convictions is the criterion of objective truth. It is further assumed, therefore, that a mere majority decision probably does not yet contain the full truth because, if it did, it ought to have succeeded in uniting *all* votes. Here we have an apparently clear, but at bottom mystical, faith in the power of truth, in the ultimate coincidence of the logi-cally correct with the psychologically real. This faith brings about the solution of the basic conflict between individual con-victions and the claim on them to produce a uniform, over-all result. In its practical consequences, this faith leads to the oppo-site of its own tendency, as much as does the individualistic justification of unanimity: where the jury is locked up until it reaches a unanimous verdict, a potential minority is almost ir-resistibly tempted to join the majority against its own conviction, which it cannot hope to carry through—in order to avoid the senseless and possibly unbearable prolongation of the session.

On the other hand, in majority decisions, the subordination of the minority may be based on two motives, whose distinction is of the greatest sociological significance. The overpowering of the minority can, first, derive from the fact that the many are more powerful than the few. Although, or rather because, the voting individuals are considered to be equals, the majority has

[10] The original, by mistake, reads *"Majorisierung."*—Tr.

the physical power to coerce the minority, whether the majority is ascertained by preliminary vote or by representation. The voting serves the purpose of avoiding the immediate contest of forces and of finding out its potential result by counting votes, so that the minority may convince itself that its actual resistance would be of no avail. In the group, therefore, two parties confront one another like two independent groups, between which the decision is made by power relations, represented by votes. Voting has the same methodological function here as have, between parties, diplomatic or other negotiations designed to avoid the *ultima ratio* of fight. Aside from exceptions, here too, the individual after all gives in only if the adversary can make it clear to him that, in case of a serious contest, he would have to pay an (at least) equally severe penalty. Like those inter-group negotiations, voting, too, is a projection of real forces and of their proportions upon the plane of intellectuality; it anticipates, in an abstract symbol, the result of concrete battle and coercion. This symbol, at least, does represent the real power relations and the enforced subordination which they impose on the minority.

Sometimes, this enforced physical subordination is sublimated into an ethical form. In the later Middle Ages, we often find the principle that the minority ought to follow the majority. This principle, evidently does not only involve the suggestion that the minority should cooperate with the majority for practical reasons: it should also accept the will of the majority; it should recognize that the majority wants what is right. Unanimity is not a fact but a moral claim. The action taken against the will of the minority is legitimated by a unity of the will, which is produced retroactively. The old-German, real requirement of unanimity thus became a pale ideal requirement. But a wholly new factor is contained in it, namely, the majority's inner right, which goes beyond the numerical preponderance of votes and the external superiority symbolized by it. The majority appears as the natural representative of the totality. It shares in the significance of its unity, which transcends the mere sum of the component individuals, and has something of a superempirical or mystical note. If Grotius later maintained that the majority had *naturaliter jus integri* [by nature the right of the whole], he thus fixed this inner claim over the minority; for one not only *must* recognize a law, one also *ought* to do so.

The fact that the majority possesses the right of the whole according to "the nature" of things, that is, on grounds of inner, rational necessity, shows the transition from the nuance of the right to outvote which has just been noted, to its second important central motive. The voice of the majority now no longer is the voice of the greater power within the group, but is the sign that the homogeneous will of the group has decided in favor of this side. The requirement of unanimity initially derived entirely from an individualistic basis. The original sociological feeling of the Germanic peoples was that the unity of the common cause did not live outside the individuals but entirely within them. For this reason, the will of the group not only was not ascertained, but did not exist at all, as long as even a single member dissented. But even where outvoting is resorted to, it still has an individualistic basis as long as it operates on the idea that the many are more powerful than the few, and that the function of voting is merely to reach the result of the real contest of forces without engaging in this contest itself. In comparison with this conception, the principle of an objective group unit, with its own, homogeneous will, is a wholly new development, whether the assumption of this principle is a conscious act, or practice merely proceeds as if such an autonomous group will did exist. The will of the state, of the community, of the church, of the group based on a common interest, exists irrespective of any contrasts among individual wills contained in these groups, and it also exists outside the temporal succession of their members. Since the group will is one, it must act in a certain, homogeneous fashion. But this is in conflict with the fact that its bearers have antagonistic volitions. The contradiction, therefore, calls for a solution. It is found in the assumption that the majority knows or represents this will better than the minority.

Here, therefore, the subordination of the minority has a very different significance than before. For now, the minority is, in principle, not excluded but included; and the majority acts, not in the name of its own greater power, but in the name of the ideal unity and totality. It is only to the latter, speaking through the voice of the majority, that the minority subordinates itself: it has already belonged to it from the beginning. This is the inner principle of parliamentary elections. The representative feels himself to be the delegate of the whole people, rather than of particular interests, which ultimately are based on the individualistic principle of the contest of forces, or of local interests, which derive from the erroneous idea that their sum equals the interest of the whole.

The transition to this fundamental sociological principle can be observed in the development of the English Lower House. From the beginning, its members were considered the representatives neither of a particular number of citizens nor of the whole people, but of certain local political groups, communities and counties, which had the right to participate in forming the parliament. This local principle was so rigidly observed that, for a long time, every member of Commons had to reside in his electoral place. But, nevertheless, it was of a somehow ideal nature, since it rose above the notion of the mere sum of individual voters. It only took an increase and awareness of the interests which were common to all these groups; and the higher union to which all of them belonged, namely, the state unit, emerged as the proper subject of their mandate. Through the recognition of their essential solidarity, the individual localities represented grew together into the whole of the state in such a way that the localities came to have the only function of designating a delegate for the representation of this whole. Once such a homogeneous group will was assumed, the elements of the minority dissented, so to speak, only as individuals, not as group members.

This alone can be the deeper meaning of the Lockean theory of the original contract which is designed to establish the state. Since this contract is the absolute foundation of the group, it must be concluded with full unanimity. Yet the contract itself contains the clause that everybody considers the will of the majority as his own will. In entering into the social contract, the individual is still absolutely free, and therefore cannot be subjected to outvoting. But once he has entered it, he is no longer a free individual but a social being and, as such, only part of a unit whose will finds its decisive expression in the will of the majority. This idea is formulated in an explicit fashion by Rousseau, when he holds outvoting not to be any violation of the individual, for the reason that it can be provoked only by the dissenter's error: the dissenter took something, which actually was not the general will, to be the *volonté générale*. This idea of Rousseau is based on the conviction that, in the capacity of group member, one can want nothing else than the will of the group: and in regard to the will of the group, only the single individual, but not the majority, can be mistaken. For this reason, Rousseau made a very fine distinction between the formal fact of voting and the particular contents of voting; and he declared that one participated in the formation of the common will by the fact of voting itself. Rousseau's idea could be explicated by stating that, through the act of voting, the individual commits himself not to avoid the unity of this will, not to destroy it by pitting his own will against the majority. Subordination to the majority, thus, is only the logical consequence of belonging to the social unit to which the individual committed himself by his vote.

Practice is not entirely removed from this abstract theory. The best student of the federation of English trade unions says that their majority decisions are justifiable and practicable only insofar as the interests of the various confederates are homogeneous. As soon as differences of opinion between majority and minority result from real differences in interests, any compulsion produced by outvoting inevitably leads to a separation of the members. In other words, a vote makes sense only if the existing interests can fuse into a unity. If divergent tendencies preclude this centralization, it becomes a contradictory procedure to entrust a majority with the decision, since the homogeneous will, which ordinarily (to be sure) can be better ascertained by a majority than by a minority, is objectively nonexistent.

Here, we have this seeming contradiction, which in reality, however, profoundly illuminates the relationship: that, precisely where a super-individual unity exists or is assumed, outvoting is possible; but that, where this unity is lacking, it is necessary to have unanimity, which in practice, from case to case, replaces it by actual equality. It is entirely in this sense that the municipal law of Leiden determined, in 1266, that the permission of the eight city jurors was necessary for the admission of outsiders into the city, but that for court decisions, not their unanimity, but only a simple majority, was required. The law by which the judges decided was determined once for all, and the point was merely to *recognize* the relationship of the individual case, which the majority could presumably do more correctly than the minority. But the admission of a new citizen touched on all the varied and divergent interests within the citizenry so that this admission could not be granted on the basis of the abstract unit constituted by these interests, but only on the basis of the sum of all individual interests, that is, through unanimity.

The deeper justification of outvoting, then, is that it merely reveals, as it were, the will of a significant unit, a will which already existed ideally. This justification, however, does not remove the difficulty which inheres in the majority as a purely overwhelming power surplus. For often the conflict over the content of the will of that abstract unit will be no more easily solved than the conflict among the immediate, real interests. The violation of the minority is no less grave for occurring in this indirect way and under this different name. The idea of the majority needs, at least, an additional, entirely new dignity. For, it may be plausible, but it is by no means self-evident, that the more correct knowledge is, in fact, on the side of the majority. It is particularly dubious where knowledge, and action upon this knowledge, is based on the inner responsibility of the individual—as in the more profound religions. The whole history of Christianity has been characterized by the opposition of the individual conscience to the resolutions and actions of majorities. In the second century, when the Christian communities of a given area introduced assemblies with the purpose of deliberating on religious and external affairs, the resolutions of these assemblies were explicitly *not* obligatory for the dissenting minority. Yet the effort of the church toward the unity came into insoluble conflict with this individualism. The Roman state wished to recognize only one united church; the church itself sought to solidify itself by imitating the unity of the state. Thus, the originally autonomous Christian communities fused into a unitary total structure whose councils decided, by majority vote, on the contents of the faith. This was an unheard-of violation of the individual members—at least, of the communities—whose unity, previously, had consisted only in the equality of the ideals and hopes which each of them possessed for himself. A subordination in matters of faith might have been permissible for inner or personal reasons; but that the majority, as such, requested subjection and declared every dissenter a non-Christian, could be justified only, as I have already suggested, by accepting a wholly new significance of "majority": one had to assume that God was always with the majority. As an unconscious but fundamental feeling, or in some kind of formulation, this motive pervades the whole later development of voting forms. That an opinion, only because its exponents are more numerous than those of another opinion, should encompass the meaning of the super-individual unit, is an entirely undemonstrable dogma. In fact, it is so little justified that without an auxiliary, more or less mystical relation between that unit and the majority, it remains suspended in mid-air; or else it is based on the somewhat weak foundation that, after all, one has to act somehow and, even if one may not assume the majority as such to know what is right, there is the less reason for assuming it of the minority.

Thus, both the requirement of unanimity and the subordination of the minority are threatened by difficulties from various sides. All these difficulties are merely the expression of the fundamentally problematic character of the whole task of extracting the action of a homogeneous will from a totality which is composed of differently oriented individuals. The task is a calculation which cannot be solved without remainder, any more than one can make something out of black and white elements, on the condition that the result be either black or white. Even in the most favorable case of a group unity supposed to exist outside the individuals, where the counting of votes is merely a means for ascertaining the tendencies of this group unity—even in this case, there remains unsettled the question whether the objectively necessary decision is identical with that which is based on counting votes. What is more, provided even the elements of the minority really dissent only as individuals and not as elements of that group unity, nevertheless, they *exist* as individuals: after all, they belong to the group in the larger sense of the term; they are not simply obliterated by the whole. In some way or other, they enter the whole of the group even as dissenting individuals.

To be sure, the separation of man as a social being and as an individual is a necessary and useful fiction. But reality and its claims are by no means exhausted by it. The inadequacy and the feeling of inner contradiction in voting methods are characterized by the fact that, in various places, most recently probably in the Hungarian Parliament well into the 'thirties of the nineteenth century, the votes were not counted but weighed, so that the presiding officer could announce even the opinion of the minority as the result of the vote. It appears nonsensical that a man subjects himself to an opinion which he holds to be false, only because others hold it to be true—while, following from the very premise of the election, every one of these others has the same right and the same value as he does. But, on the other hand, the requirement of unanimity which is to meet this contradiction, shows itself to be no less contradictory and unfair. And this is not an accidental dilemma, not a merely logical difficulty. It is only one among the symptoms of the deep and tragic ambiguity which pervades the very roots of every societal formation, of every formation of a unit out of units. The individual who lives from his inner resources, who can answer for his actions only if they are directed by his own conviction, is supposed to orient his will toward the purposes of others. As something ethical, this remains always a matter of his own will; it flows from the innermost core of his personality. But what is more, he is also supposed to become, in his self-based existence, a member of a collectivity which has its center outside of him. We are not discussing here *particular* harmonies or collisions of these two claims. The point, rather, is that man *internally* stands under two, mutually alien norms; that our movement revolving around our own center (something totally different from egoism) claims to be as definitive as the movement around the social center; in fact, it claims to be the decisive meaning of life. Into the vote concerning the action of the group, the individual does not enter as an individual, but in his super-individual function of member. But still, the dissent of votes transplants upon this purely social soil a ray, a secondary form, of individuality and its unique character. And even this individuality, which merely desires to ascertain and represent the will of the super-individual group unit, is negated by the fact of outvoting. Even here, the minority must subordinate itself, although to belong to the minority forms the inalienable opportunity of every individual. And it must subordinate itself, not only in the simple sense in which ordinarily convictions and efforts are negated and made ineffectual by opposing forces, but in the more subtle and crafty sense that the loser, because he is part of the group, must positively participate in the action which was decided upon against his will and conviction. What is more, the uniform character of the eventual decision which contains no trace of his dissent, makes him, too, responsible for it. In this way, outvoting, far from being only the simple practical violation of the one by the many, becomes the most poignant expression of the dualism between the autonomous life of the individual and the life of society, a dualism which is often harmonized in experience, but which, in principle, is irreconcilable.

Chapter 4

Subordination under
a Principle

§ 1. *Subordination under a Principle vs. a Person*

I NOW COME, FINALLY, TO
the third typical form of subordination, subordination neither
to an individual nor to a plurality, but to an impersonal, objective principle. The fact that here a real interaction, at least
an immediate interaction, is precluded, seems to deprive this
form of the element of freedom. The individual who is subordinate to an objective law feels himself determined by it;
while he, in turn, in no way determines the law, and has no
possibility of reacting to it in a manner which could influence
it—quite in contrast to even the most miserable slave, who, in
some fashion at least, can still in this sense react to his master.
For if one simply does not obey the law, one is, to this extent,
not *really* subjected to it; and if one changes the law, one is not
subordinate to the old law at all, but is again, in the same entirely unfree manner, subject to the new law. In spite of this,
however, for modern, objective man, who is aware of the difference between the spheres of spontaneity and of obedience, subordination to a law which functions as the emanation of impersonal, uninfluenceable powers, is the more dignified situation.
This was quite different at a time when the personality could
preserve its self-esteem only in situations characterized by full
spontaneity, which even in case of complete subordination were
still associated with inter-personal effect and counter-effect. For
this reason, as late as in the sixteenth century, princes in France,
Germany, Scotland, and the Netherlands often met with considerable resistance, if they let their countries be ruled by ad-

ministrative bodies or erudite substitutes—that is, more nearly by laws. The ruler's order was felt to be something personal; the individual wanted to lend him obedience only from personal devotion; and personal devotion, in spite of its unconditional character, is always in the form of free reciprocity.

This passionate personalism of the subordination relationship almost becomes its own caricature in the following circumstance, reported from Spain at the beginning of the modern period. An impoverished nobleman who became a cook or lackey, did not thereby definitively lose his nobility: it only became latent and could be awakened again by a favorable turn of fate. But once he became a craftsman, his nobility was destroyed. This is entirely contrary to the modern conception, which separates the person from his achievement and, therefore, finds personal dignity to be preserved best if the content of subordination is as objective as possible. Thus, an American girl, who would work in a factory without the slightest feeling of humiliation, would feel wholly degraded as a family cook. Already in thirteenth-century Florence, the *lower* guilds comprised occupations in the immediate service of persons, such as cobblers, hosts, and school teachers; whereas the *higher* guilds were composed of occupations which, though still serving the public, were yet more objective and less dependent on particular individuals—for instance, clothiers and grocers. On the other hand, in Spain, where knightly traditions, with their engagement of the whole person in all activity, were still alive, every relationship which (in any sense) took place between person and person, was bound to be considered at least bearable; while every subordination to more objective claims, every integration into a system of impersonal duties (impersonal, because serving many and anonymous persons), was bound to be regarded as wholly disgraceful. An aversion to the objectivity of law can still be felt in the legal theories of Althusius: the *summus magistratus* legislates, but he does so, not because he represents the state, but because he is appointed by the people. The notion that the ruler could be designated as the representative of the state by appointment through law, not by personal appointment (actual or presumed) by the people—is still alien to Althusius.

In antiquity, on the contrary, subordination to law appeared thoroughly adequate, precisely because of the idea that law is free from any personal characteristics. Aristotle praised law as *"tó méson,"* that is, as that which is moderate, impartial, free from passions. Plato, in the same sense, had already recognized government by impersonal law as the best means for counteracting selfishness. His, however, was only a psychological motivation. It did not touch the core of the question, namely, the fundamental transition of the relationship of obedience from personalism to objectivism, a transition which cannot be derived from the anticipation of utilitarian consequence. Yet, in Plato, we also find this other theory: that, in the ideal state, the insight of the ruler stands above the law; and as soon as the welfare of the whole seems to require it of the ruler, he must be able to act even against the laws laid down by him. There must be laws which may not be broken under any circumstances, only if there are no true statesmen. The law, therefore, appears here as the lesser evil—but not, as in the Germanic feeling, mentioned before, because subordination under a person has an element of freedom and dignity in comparison with which all obedience to laws has something mechanical and passive. Rather, it is the rigidity of the law which is felt to be its weakness: in its rigidity, it confronts the changing and unforeseeable claims of life in a clumsy and inadequate way; and this is an evil from which only the entirely unprejudiced insight of a personal ruler can escape; and only where there is no such insight, does law become relatively advantageous. Here, therefore, it is always the *content* of the law, its physical state, as it were, which determines its value or disvalue as compared with subordination under persons. The fact that the relationship of obedience is totally different in its inner principle and in terms of the whole feeling of life, on the part of the obeyer, according to whether it originates in a person or in a law—this fact does not enter these considerations. The most general, or formal relation between government by law and government by person can (of course) be expressed in a preliminary, practical manner by saying that where the law is not forceful or broad enough, a person is necessary, and where the person is inadequate, the law is required. But, far beyond this, whether rule by man is considered as something provisional in lieu of rule by perfect law, or, inversely, rule by law is considered a gap-filler or an inferior substitute for government by a personality which is absolutely qualified to rule—this choice depends upon decisions of ultimate, indiscussable feelings concerning sociological values.

§ 2. *Subordination under Objects*

There is still another form in which an objective principle may become the turning point in the relationship between superordinates and subordinates, namely, when neither a law nor an ideal norm, but rather a concrete object governs the domination, as, for instance, in the principle of patrimony. Here—most radically under the system of Russian bondage— bonded subjects are only appurtenances of the land—"the air bonds the people." The terrible hardship of bondage at least excluded personal slavery which would have permitted the sale of the slave. Instead, it tied subordination to the land in such a way that the bondsman could be sold only along with the land. In spite of all contentual and quantitative differences, nevertheless, sometimes this same form occurs in the case of the modern factory worker, whose own interest, through certain arrangements, binds him to a given factory. For instance, the acquisition of his house was made possible for him, or he participated out of his own purse in certain welfare expenditures, and all these benefits are lost once he leaves the factory, etc. He is thus bound, merely by objects, in a way which in a very specific manner makes him powerless in respect to the entrepreneur. Finally, it was this same form of domination which, under the most primitive patriarchal conditions, was governed not by a merely spatial, but by a living object: children did not belong to the father because he was their progenitor, but because the mother belonged to him (as the fruits of the tree belong to the tree's owner); therefore, children begotten by other fathers were no less his property.

This type of domination usually involves a humiliatingly harsh and unconditional kind of subordination. For, inasmuch as a man is subordinate by virtue of belonging to a thing, he himself psychologically sinks to the category of mere thing. With

254 Subordination under a Principle

the necessary reservations, one could say that where law regulates domination, the superordinate belongs in the sphere of objectivity; while, where a *thing* regulates it, the *subordinate* does. The condition of the subordinate, therefore, is usually more favorable in the first case, and more unfavorable in the second, than in many cases of purely personal subordination.

§ 3. *Conscience*

Immediate sociological interest in subordination under an objective principle attaches to two chief cases of it. One case is when this ideal, superordinate principle can be interpreted as a psychological crystallization of an actual social power. The other is when, among those who are commonly subject to it, it produces particular and characteristic relationships. The first case must be taken into consideration, above all, when dealing with moral imperatives. In our moral consciousness, we feel subordinate to a command which does not seem to derive from any human, personal power. The voice of conscience we hear only in ourselves, although in comparison with all subjective egoism, we hear it with a force and decisiveness which apparently can stem only from a tribunal *outside* the individual. An attempt has been made, as is well-known, to solve this contradiction by deriving the contents of morality from social norms. What is useful to the species and the group, the argument runs, and what the group, therefore, requests of its members for the sake of its own maintenance, is gradually bred into the individual as an instinct. He thus comes to contain it in himself, as his own, autonomous feeling, in addition to his personal feelings properly speaking, and thus often in contrast to them. This, it is alleged, explains the dual character of the moral command: that on the one hand, it confronts us as an impersonal order to which we simply have to submit, but that, on the other, no external power, but only our most private and internal impulses, imposes it upon us. At any rate, here is one of the cases where the individual, within his own consciousness, repeats the relationships which exist between him, as a total personality, and the group. It is an old observation that the conceptions of the single individual, with all their relations of association and dissociation, differentiation, and unification, behave in the same way in which individuals behave in regard to one another. It is merely a peculiar case of this correspondence that those intra-psychological relations are repeated, not only between individuals in general, but also between the individual and his group. All that society asks of its members—adaptation and loyalty, altruism and work, self-discipline and truthfulness—the individual also asks of himself.

In all of this, several very important motives cut across one another. Society confronts the individual with precepts. He becomes habituated to their compulsory character until the cruder and subtler means of compulsion are no longer necessary. His nature may thereby be so formed or deformed that he acts by these precepts as if on impulse, with a consistent and direct will which is not conscious of any law. Thus, the pre-Islamic Arabs were without any notion of an objectively legal compulsion; in all instances, purely personal decision was their highest authority, although this decision was thoroughly imbued with tribal consciousness and the requirements of tribal life, which gave it its norms. Or else, the law, in the form of a command which is carried by the authority of the society, does live in the individual consciousness, but irrespective of the question whether society actually backs it with its compulsory power or even itself supports it solely with its explicit will. Here then, the individual represents society to himself. The external confrontation, with its suppressions, liberations, changing accents, has become an interplay between his social impulses and the ego impulses in the stricter sense of the word; and both are included by the ego in the larger sense.

But this is not yet the really objective lawfulness, indicated above, in whose consciousness of which no trace of any historical-social origin is left. At a certain higher stage of morality, the motivation of action lies no longer in a real-human, even though super-individual power; at this stage, the spring of moral necessities flows beyond the contrast between individual and totality. For, as little as these necessities derive from society, as little do they derive from the singular reality of individual life. In the free conscience of the actor, in individual reason, they only have their bearer, the locus of their efficacy.

Their power of obligation stems from these necessities themselves, from their inner, super-personal validity, from an objective ideality which we must recognize, whether or not we
want to, in a manner similar to that in which the validity of a
truth is entirely independent of whether or not the truth becomes real in any consciousness. The *content,* however, which
fills these forms is (not necessarily but often) the societal requirement. But this requirement no longer operates by means of its
social impetus, as it were, but rather as if it had undergone a
metapsychosis into a norm which must be satisfied for its own
sake, not for my sake nor for yours.

We are dealing here with differences which not only are
psychologically of the greatest delicacy, but whose boundaries
are also constantly blurred in practice. Yet this mixture of motivations in which psychic reality moves, makes it all the more
urgent that it be isolated analytically. Whether society and
individual confront one another like two powers and the individual's subordination is effected by society through energy
which seem to flow from an uninterrupted source and constantly seems to renew itself; or whether this energy changes into
a psychological impulse in the very individual who considers
himself a social being and, therefore, fights and suppresses those
of his impulses that lean toward his "egoistic" part; or whether
the Ought, which man finds above himself as an actuality as
objective as Being, is merely filled with the content of societal
life conditions—these are constellations which only begin to
exhaust the kinds of individual subordination to the group.
In them, the three powers which fill historical life—society,
individual, and objectivity—become norm-giving, in this order.
But they do so in such a way that each of them absorbs the
social content, the quantity of superordination of society over
the individual; in a specific manner, each of them forms and
presents the power, the will, and the necessities of society.

§ 4. *Society and "Objectivity"*

Among these three potencies, objectivity can be defined as
the unquestionably valid law which is enthroned in an ideal
realm above society and the individual. But it can also be de-

fined in still another dimension, as it were. Society often is the third element, which solves conflicts between the individual and objectivity or builds bridges where they are disconnected. As regards the genesis of cognition, the concept of society has liberated us from an alternative characteristic of earlier times, namely, that a cultural value either must spring from an individual or must be bestowed upon mankind by an objective power—as has been shown by some examples in Chapter 1.[11] Practically speaking, it is societal labor by means of which the individual can satisfy his claims upon the objective order. The cooperation of the many, the efforts of society as a unit, both simultaneously and successively, wrest from nature not only a greater quantity of need-satisfactions than can be achieved by the individual, but also new qualities and types of need-satisfactions which the labor of the individual alone cannot possibly attain. This fact is merely a symbol of the deeper and fundamental phenomenon of society standing between individual man and the sphere of general natural laws. As something psychologically concrete, society blends with the individual; as something general, it blends with nature. It is the general, but it is not abstract. To be sure, every historical group is an individual, as is every historical human being; but it is this only in relation to other groups; for its members, it is super-individual. But it is super-individual, not as a concept is in regard to its single, concrete realizations, where the concept synthesizes what is common to all of them. The group is super-individual, rather, in a specific manner of generality—similar to the organic body, which is "general" above its organs, or to "room furniture," which is "general" above table, chair, chest, and mirror. And this specific generality coincides with the specific objectivity which society possesses for its members as subjects.

But the individual does not confront society as he confronts nature. The objectivity of nature denotes the irrelevance of the question of whether or not the subject spiritually participates in nature; whether he has a correct, a false, or no conception of it. Its being exists, and its laws are valid, independently of

---

[11] This chapter is not contained in the present volume. See, however, Part One, Chapter 1, "The Field of Sociology," especially pp. 12–13.—Tr.

the significance which either of them may have for any subject. Certainly, society, likewise, transcends the individual and lives its own life which follows its own laws; it, too, confronts the individual with a historical, imperative firmness. Yet, society's "in front of" the individual is, at the same time, a "within." The harsh indifference toward the individual also is an interest: social objectivity needs general individual subjectivity, although it does not need any particular individual subjectivity. It is these characteristics which make society a structure intermediate between the subject and an absolutely impersonal generality and objectivity.

The following observation, for instance, points in this direction. As long as the development of an economy does not yet produce objective prices, properly speaking; as long as knowledge and regulation of demand, offer, production costs, amounts at risk, gain, etc., do not yet lead to the idea that a given piece of merchandise is worth so much and must have such and such a fixed price—so long is the immediate interference of society and its organs and laws with the affairs of commerce (particularly in regard to the price and stability of commerce) much more strong and rigorous than under other conditions. Price taxes, the surveillance of quantity and quality of production, and, in a larger sense, even sumptuary laws and consumers' obligations, often emerged at that stage of economic development at which the subjective freedom of commerce strove after stable objectivity, without, however, yet being able to attain any pure, abstract objectivity in determining prices. It is at this stage that the concrete generality, the living objectivity of society enters, often clumsily, obstructively, schematically, but yet always as a super-subjective power which supplies the individual with a norm before he derives this norm directly from the structure of the matter at issue and its understood regularity.

On a much larger scale, this same formal development, from subordination under society to subordination under objectivity, occurs in the intellectual sphere. All of intellectual history shows to what extent the individual intellect fills the content of its truth-concepts only with traditional, authoritative conceptions which are "accepted by all," long before he confronts the object directly and derives the content of the truth-concepts from its objectivity. Initially, the support and the norm of the inquiring mind are not the object, whose immediate observation and interpretation the mind is entirely unable to manipulate, but the general opinion of the object. It is this general opinion which mediates theoretical conceptions, from the silliest superstition to the subtlest prejudices, which almost entirely conceal the lacking independence of their recipient and the un-objective nature of their contents. It seems as if man could not easily bear looking the object in the eye; as if he were equal neither to the rigidity of its lawfulness nor to the freedom which the object, in contrast to all coercion coming from men, gives him. By comparison, to bow to the authority of the many or their representatives, to traditional opinion, to socially accepted notions, is something intermediate. Traditional opinion, after all, is more modifiable than is the law of the object; in it, man can feel some psychological mediation; it transmits, as it were, something which is already digested psychologically. At the same time, it gives us a hold, a relief from responsibility—the compensation for the lack of that autonomy which we derive from the purely intrinsic relationship between ego and object.

The concept of objective justice, no less than the concept of truth, finds its intermediate stage, which leads toward the objective sense of "justice," in social behavior. In the field of criminal law, as well as in all other regulations of life, the correlation between guilt and expiation, merit and reward, service and counter-service, is first, evidently, a matter of social expediency or of social impulses. Perhaps the equivalence of action and reaction, in which justice consists, is never an analytical equivalence directly resulting from these elements, but always requires a third element, an ideal, a purpose, a norm-setting situation, in which the first two elements create or demonstrate their mutual correspondence synthetically. Originally, this third element consists in the interests and forms of the general life which surrounds the individuals, that is, the subjects of the realization of justice. This general life creates, and acts on, the criteria of justice or injustice in the relation between action and reaction—of justice or injustice which cannot be ascertained in the action-and-reaction in isolation. Above this process, and mediated by it, there rises, at an objectively and historically later stage, the necessity of the "just" correspondence between action and reaction, a correspondence which emerges in the comparison of these two elements themselves. This higher norm, which perhaps even in this later phase continues to determine weight and counter-weight according to its own scale, is completely absorbed by the elements themselves; it has become a value which seems to originate with them and operates out of them. Justice now appears as an objective relationship which follows necessarily from the intrinsic significance of sin and pain, good deed and happiness, offer and response. It must be realized for its own sake: *fiat justitia, pereat mundus.* It was, by contrast, the very preservation of the world which, from the earlier standpoint, constituted the ground of justice. Whatever the ideal sense of justice may be (which is not the topic of discussion here), the *objective* law, in which justice, purely for its own sake, embodies itself, and which claims compliance in its own right, is historically and psychologically a later stage of development. It is preceded, prepared, and mediated by the claim to justice stemming from merely *social* objectivity.

This same development, finally, prevails within the moral sphere, in the stricter sense of this term. The original content of morality is of an altruistic-social nature. The idea is not that morality has its own life independent of this content and merely absorbs it. Rather, the devotion of the "I" to the "thou" (in the singular or plural) is the very idea, the definition, of the moral. Philosophical doctrines of ethics represent, by comparison, a much later phase. In them, an absolutely objective Ought is separated from the question of "I" and "thou." If it is important to Plato that the Idea of the Good be realized; to Kant, that the principle of individual action be suitable as a general law; to Nietzsche, that the human species transcend its momentary stage of development; then, occasionally, these norms may also refer to reciprocal relations among individuals. But, essentially this is no longer important. What is important is the realization of an objective law, which not only leaves behind the subjectivity of the actor but also the subjectivity of the individuals whom the action may concern. For, now, even the reference to the societal complex of the subjects is merely an accidental satisfaction of a much more general norm and obligation, which may legitimate socially and altruistically oriented action, but may also refuse to do so. In the development of the individual as of the species, ethical obedience to the claims of the "thou" and of society characterizes the first emergence from the pre-ethical stage of naïve egoism. Innumerable individuals never go beyond obedience to the "thou." But, in principle, this stage is preparatory and transitory to subordination under an objectively ethical law, which transcends the "I" as much as the "thou," and only on its own initiative admits the interests of the one or the other as ethical contents.

§ 5. *The Effect of Subordination under a Principle upon the Relations between Superordinates and Subordinates*

The second sociological question in regard to subordination under an impersonal-ideal principle concerns the effect of this common subordination upon the reciprocal relations among the subordinates. Here, also, it must above all be remembered that ideal subordination is often preceded by real subordination. We frequently find that a person or class exerts superordination in the name of an ideal principle to which the person or class themselves are allegedly subordinated. This principle, therefore, seems to be logically prior to the social arrangement; the actual organization of domination among people seems to develop in consequence of that ideal dependency. Historically, however, the road has usually run in the opposite direction. Superordinations and subordinations develop out of very real, personal power relations. Through the spiritualization of the superordinate power or through the enlargement and de-personalization of the whole relationship, there gradually grows an ideal, objective power over and above these superordinations and subordinations. The superordinate then exerts his power merely in the capacity of the closest representative of this ideal, objective force.

These successive processes are shown very distinctly in the development of the position of *pater familias* among the Aryans.

Originally—this is how the type is presented to us—his power was unlimited and wholly subjective. That is, the *pater familias* decided all arrangements by momentary whim and in terms of personal advantage. Yet this arbitrary power was gradually replaced by a feeling of responsibility. The unity of the family group, embodied (for instance) in the *spiritus familiaris,* became an ideal force, in reference to which even the master of the whole felt himself to be merely an executor and obeyer. It is in this sense that custom and habit, rather than subjective preference, determined his actions, his decisions, and judicial decrees; that he no longer behaved as the unconditional master of the family property, but rather as its administrator in the interest of the whole; that his position had more the character of an office than that of an unlimited right. The relation between superordinates and subordinates was thus placed upon an entirely new basis. Whereas, at the first stage, the subordinates constituted, so to speak, only a personal appurtenance of the superordinates, later there prevailed the objective idea of the family which stands above all individuals and to which the leading patriarch is as much subordinated as is every other member. The patriarch can give orders to the other members of the family only in the name of that ideal unit.

Here we encounter an extremely important form-type, namely, that the very commander subordinates himself to the law which he has made. The moment his will becomes law, it attains objective character, and thus separates itself from its subjective-personal origin. As soon as the ruler gives the law as law, he documents himself, to this extent, as the organ of an ideal necessity. He merely reveals a norm which is plainly valid on the ground of its inner sense and that of the situation, whether or not the ruler actually enunciates it. What is more, even if instead of this more or less distinctly conceived legitimation, the will of the ruler itself becomes law, even then the ruler cannot avoid transcending the sphere of subjectivity: for in this case, he carries the super-personal legitimation *a priori* in himself, so to speak. In this way, the inner form of law brings it about that the law-giver, in giving the law, subordinates himself to it as a person, in the same way as all others. Thus, the Privileges of the medieval Flemish cities stated expressly that the jurors must give everybody a fair trial, including even the Count who had bestowed this privilege upon the city. And such a sovereign ruler as the Great Elector introduced a head-tax without asking the estates for their consent—but then he not only made his court pay it, but he also paid it himself.

The most recent history gives an example of the growth of an objective power, to which the person, who is originally and subsequently in command, must subordinate himself in common with his subordinates. The example is formally related to the case cited from the history of the family. In modern economic production, objective and technical elements dominate over personal elements. In earlier times, many superordinations and subordinations had a personal character, so that in a given relationship, one person simply was superordinate, and the other subordinate. Many of these super-subordinations have changed in the sense that both superordinates and subordinates alike stand under an objective purpose; and it is only within this common relationship to the higher principle that the subordination of the one to the other continues to exist as a technical necessity. As long as the relationship of wage labor is conceived of as a rental contract (in which the worker is rented), it contains as an essential element the worker's subordination to the entrepreneur. But, once the work contract is considered, not as the renting of a person, but as the purchase of a piece of merchandise, that is, labor, then this element of personal subordination is eliminated. In this case, the subordination which the employer requests of the worker is only—so it has been expressed—subordination "under the cooperative process, a subordination as compulsive for the entrepreneur, once he engages in any activity at all, as for the worker." The worker is no longer subject as a person but only as the servant of an objective, economic procedure. In this process, the element which in the form of entrepreneur or manager is superordinated to the worker, operates no longer as a personal element but only as one necessitated by objective requirements.

The increased self-feeling of the modern worker must, at least partly, be connected with this process, which shows its purely sociological character also in the circumstance that it often has no influence upon the material welfare of the laborer.

He merely sells a quantitatively defined service, which may be smaller or larger than what was required of him under the earlier, personal arrangement. As a man, he thus frees himself from the relationship of subordination, to which he belongs only as an element in the process of production; and to this extent, he is coordinate with those who direct the production. This technical objectivity has its symbol in the legal objectivity of the contract relation: once the contract is concluded, it stands as an objective norm above *both* parties. In the Middle Ages, this phenomenon marked the turning point in the condition of the journeyman, which originally implied full personal subordination under the master: the journeyman was generally called "servant" [*Knecht*]. The gathering of journeymen in their own estate was centered upon the attempt at transforming the personal-service relationship into a contractual relationship: as soon as the organization of the "servants" was achieved, their name, most characteristically, was replaced by that of "journeymen." In general, it is relative coordination, instead of absolute subordination, which is correlated with the contractual form, no matter what the material content of the contract may be.

This form further strengthens its objective character if the contract is not concluded between individuals, but consists in collective regulations between a group of workers on the one side, and a group of employers on the other. It has been developed especially by the English Trade Unions, which in certain, highly advanced industries conclude contracts regarding wage rates, working time, overtime, holidays, etc., with associations of entrepreneurs. These contracts may not be ignored by any sub-contract that might be made between individual members of these larger categories. In this manner, the impersonality of the labor relationship is evidently increased to an extraordinary degree. The objectivity of this relationship finds an appropriate instrument and expression in the super-individual collectivity. This objective character, finally, is assured in an even more specific manner if the contracts are concluded for very brief periods. English Trade Unions have always urged this brevity, in spite of the increased insecurity which results from it. The explanation of the recommendation has been that the worker distinguishes himself from the slave by the right to leave his place of work; but, if he surrenders this right for a long time, he is, for the whole duration of this period, subject to all conditions which the entrepreneur imposes upon him, with the exception of those expressly stipulated; and he has lost the protection offered him by his right to suspend the relationship. Instead of the breadth, or comprehensiveness, of the bond which in earlier times committed the total personality, there emerges, if the contract lasts very long, the length, or duration, of the bond. In the case of short contracts, objectivity is guaranteed, not by something positive, but only by the necessity of preventing the objectively regulated contractual relationship from changing into a relationship determined by subjective arbitrariness—whereas in the case of long contracts there is no corresponding, sufficient protection.

In the condition of domestic servants—at least, on the whole, in contemporary central Europe—it is still the total individual, so to speak, who enters the subordination. Subordination has not yet attained the objectivity of an objectively, clearly circumscribed service. From this circumstance derive the chief inadequacies inherent in the institution of domestic service. This institution does approach that more perfect form when it is replaced by services of persons who perform only certain, objective functions in the house, and who are, to this extent, coordinated with the housewife. The earlier, but still existing, relationship involved them as total personalities and obliged them—as is most strikingly shown by the concept of the "all-around girl" ["*Mädchen für alles*"]—to "unlimited services": they became subordinate to the housewife as a person, precisely because there were no objective delimitations. Under thoroughly patriarchal (as contrasted with contemporary) conditions, the "house" is considered an objective, intrinsic purpose and value, in behalf of which housewife and servants cooperate. This results, even if there is a completely personal subordination, in a certain coordination sustained by the interest which the servant, who is solidly and permanently connected with the house, usually feels for it. The "thou," used in addressing him, on the one hand gives expression to his personal subordination, but on the other, makes him comparable to the children of the house and thus ties him more closely to its organization. Strangely enough, it thus appears that in some measure, obedience to an objective idea occurs at the extreme stages in the development of obedience: under the condition of full patriarchal subordination, where the house still has, so to speak, an absolute value, which is served by the work of the housewife (though in a higher position) as well as by that of the servant; and then, under the condition of complete differentiation, where service and reward are objectively pre-determined, and the personal attachment, which characterizes the stage of an undefined quantity of subordination, has become extraneous to the relationship. The contemporary position of the servant who shares his master's house, particularly in the large cities, has lost the first of these two kinds of objectivity, without having yet attained the second. The total personality of the servant is no longer claimed by the objective idea of the "house"; and yet, in view of the general way in which his services are requested, it cannot really separate itself from it.

Finally, this form-type may be illustrated by the relationship between officers and common soldiers. Here, the cleavage between subordination within the organization of the group, and coordination which results from common service in defense of one's country, is as wide as can be imagined. Understandably enough, the cleavage is most noticeable at the front. On the one hand, discipline is most merciless there, but on the other hand, fellowship between officers and privates is furthered, partly by specific situations, partly by the general mood. During peacetime, the army remains arrested in the position of a means which does not attain its purposes; it is, therefore, inevitable for its technical structure to grow into a psychologically ultimate aim, so that super-subordination, on which the technique of the organization is based, stands in the foreground of consciousness. The peculiar sociological mixture with coordination, which results from the common subordination under an objective idea, becomes important only when the changed situation calls attention to this idea, as the real purpose of the army.

Within the group organization of his specific content of life, the individual thus occupies a superordinate or subordinate position. But the group as a whole stands under a dominating idea which gives each of its members an equal, or nearly equal, position in comparison with all outsiders. Hence, the individual has a double role which makes his purely formal, sociological situation the vehicle for peculiarly mixed life-feelings. The employee of a large business may have a leading position in his firm, which he lets his subalterns feel in a superior and imperious way. But, as soon as he confronts the public, and acts under the idea of his business as a whole, he will exhibit serviceable and devout behavior. In the opposite direction, these elements are interwoven in the frequent haughtiness of subalterns, servants in noble houses, members of decimated intellectual or social circles, who actually stand at the periphery of these groups, but to the outsider represent all the more energetically the dignity of the whole circle and of its idea. For, the kind of positive relation to the circle which they have, gives them only a semi-solid position in it, internally and externally; and they seek to improve it in a negative way, by differentiating themselves from others. The richest formal variety of this type is offered, perhaps, by the Catholic hierarchy. Although every member of it is bound by a blind obedience which admits of no contradiction, nevertheless, in comparison with the layman, even the lowest member stands at an absolute elevation, where the idea of the eternal God rises above all temporal matters. At the same time, the highest member of this hierarchy confesses himself to be the "servant of servants." The monk, who within his order may have absolute power, dresses himself in deepest humility and servility in the face of a beggar; but the lowest brother of an order is superior to the secular prince by all the absolute sovereignty of church authority.

Chapter 5

Superordination and Subordination and Degrees of Domination and Freedom

THE CROSS-SECTION through the phenomena of superordination and subordination which has been presented, was arranged in terms of the question regarding the exercise of domination by one or by many, and by persons or by objective structures. But another cross-section can be made in addition. This second viewpoint focuses upon the sociological significance of the *degree* of domination, especially upon the correlation of varying degrees of it with freedom and its conditions. The following investigations are oriented along this second line.

§ 1. *Superordination without Subordinates*

A group may contain numerous and highly articulated superordinations and subordinations, either in a single hierarchical structure or in a variety of co-existing relationships of domination. In either case, the group, as a whole, will derive its character, essentially, from subordination; as is shown with particular clarity in states that are governed bureaucratically. For the social layers expand downward in quick progression. In other words, where super-subordination stands at all in the foreground of formal sociological consciousness, the quantitatively preponderant side of this relationship, that is, of subordination, will color the whole picture. On the basis of very special combinations, however, there may also emerge the impression and the feeling that the whole group is superordinate. Thus,

Spanish pride and contempt of labor stemmed from the fact that for a long time the Spaniards used the subjugated Moors as laborers. When they later destroyed the Moors (and expelled the Jews), they yet retained the air of superordinates, although there no longer were any corresponding subordinates. At the time of their highest splendor, it was explicitly stated among the Spaniards that, as a nation, they wished to occupy a position in the world such as is occupied by noblemen, officers, and officials within the single state. Something similar, but on a more solid basis, had already appeared in the Spartan warrior democracy. Sparta subjugated the neighboring tribes without enslaving them, but, instead, left them their land and only treated them as serfs. These subjects grew together into a low stratum in comparison with which the totality of the full citizens formed a lordly class, however much procedures within this class were democratic. This was not a simple aristocracy which, from the beginning, constituted a homogeneous group along with the less privileged elements. It was, in fact, the whole original state which, without changing its *status quo,* underpinned itself with a layer of conquered peoples, and thus made the totality of its members into a sort of nobility. The Spartans repeated this principle of general superordination even in a more special respect: their army was *graded* in such a way that, in large part, it consisted of commanding officers.

We encounter here a peculiar sociological form-type: where characteristics of an element can originate only in the relation between this and another element, and can derive their content and significance only from this relation; yet these characteristics come to be essential qualities of the element and no longer depend on any interaction. The fact that one is the ruler presupposes an object of one's domination; yet the psychological reality can, to a certain extent, evade this conceptual necessity. One of the motives, the inner motive which underlies this possibility, is already alluded to by Plato. Plato maintained that domination as such, as a function, is always the same, in spite of the innumerable differences in its extent and content. It is one and the same capacity to command which must be possessed by the *politikós* [statesman] and the *basileús* [king], by the *despótes* [master] and the *oikonómos* [house steward]. For this reason, according to Plato, the real statesman is not necessarily the executive of the highest state power, but he who possesses the "science of command"—no matter whether or not he actually has something to command. Plato thus goes back to the subjective ground of the relationship of domination. This ground is not created with the actual realization of a given case of domination, but exists irrespective of the existence of such a realization. The "born king" does not need a country, so to speak, he *is* king; he does not have to *become* king. If the Spartans did not develop a nobility among themselves and yet felt like noblemen, and if the Spaniards had the air of lords even though they no longer had any servants, these phenomena have their deeper significance in the fact that the reciprocal effects of the relationship of domination is the sociological expression or actualization of inner qualities of the subject. Whoever has these, is ruler by this very fact. One side of the two-sided relationship of domination has been taken out of it, as it were, and the reciprocal relation exists only in an ideal form; but the other side does not thereby lose its intrinsic significance for the relationship.

If this process occurs in *all* members of a larger group, it finds expression in their reciprocal designation as "equals," a designation which does not specifically stress with respect to *what* the equality exists. The citizens of Sparta who were entitled to vote, were simply called the *homoioi* [similar ones]. The aristocratic character of their political and economic position over that of the other strata was self-evident. To designate themselves, therefore, they used only their formal relation to one another and did not even mention their relationship to other strata, which, nevertheless, ought to have constituted the content of the rank designation. A similar feeling is at the bottom of the situation wherever aristocracies call themselves "peers." They exist, as it were, only for one another: others do not concern them even to the extent where the designation of the collectivity would express their superiority over them—and yet, it is for the sake of this superiority that such a designation is needed.[12]

[12] This is merely an example of a general sociological phenomenon. A number of elements, making up a group, often have the same relation in regard to a certain point which gives content and significance to the group interest in question. Some-

There is a second way in which the idea of superordination, without the logically required correlate of any corresponding subordination, may be realized. This is found when forms, which were developed in a large circle, are applied to a small group whose conditions themselves do not justify the forms. Certain positions within an extensive group involve a power, a quantity of superordination, a significance, all of which are lost as soon as these positions, without changing their form, are repeated in a smaller circle. Nevertheless, even into the smaller group, they introduce the note of superiority and command which they possessed in the larger organization. This note, as it were, has become a substantive quality of such a position; the quality no longer depends upon the relationship which engendered it originally. In this process, the mediating element is frequently a "title," which in narrow conditions is often left with hardly a trace of its power, but which retains the aplomb conferred upon it by its origin in a larger group. In the fifteenth century, the Dutch *Rederykers,* a sort of master-singers, had kings, princes, archdeacons, etc., in each of their many groups.

times, this decisive point on which the elements converge is absent in any designation of the group, perhaps even in the consciousness of the members; and, although they are equal only in regard to that one point, nevertheless, equality alone is stressed. It has already been mentioned that noblemen often designate themselves as "peers." In the twelfth and thirteenth centuries, many French cities called their jurymen and jurors by this same name. When the *"Gesellschaft für ethische Kultur"* [Society for Ethical Culture] was to be organized in Berlin, a brochure appeared which was entitled "Preparatory Communications of a Circle of Like-Minded Men and Women." Nothing indicated in regard to *what* their minds were alike. In 1905, or thereabouts, a party was formed in the Spanish Chamber which simply designated itself as the "Party of the Solidary." In the 'nineties, a faction of the Munich artists' association called itself "the group of the colleagues," without adding to this title, which they used quite officially, *what* constituted the content of the collegiate relationship and what distinguished this group from an organization of colleagues among school teachers, actors, agents, or editors. These trivial episodes contain the sociologically very striking fact that the formal relation among certain individuals may supersede the content and purpose of this relation. For, this could not occur in all these designations if they did not somehow reveal the direction of the sociological consciousness. The fact that the elements of a group have equal rights or like minds, or are colleagues, gains an extraordinary importance in comparison with any materials that are clothed in these sociological forms, although the forms make sense only on the basis of the materials. And however much the practical behavior is determined by the material not contained in the title, nevertheless (as a closer study of such groups shows), it is, in innumerable cases, also determined by the orientation toward these pure forms of relationship and toward these formal structures, and by the effect of them.

I call attention to the "officers" of the Salvation Army, and to the "high degrees" of Freemasonry: in 1756, a chapter of the French Freemasons declared its members "sovereign and born princes of the whole order"; another chapter, a little later, called itself the *"Conseil des Empereurs d'Orient et d'Occident."*

But it is, of course, not only a change in the purely extensive, numerical size of the groups that effects the application of an originally superordinate position to conditions which leave it with the stamp of superordination, while yet eliminating the logically required subordination. Contractions in the intensity of the group life also may bring this about. What destroyed the whole Hellenic existence during the Empire was the shrinkage of its range of significance, the loss of all deeper or far-reaching content. But yet, an ambition which borrowed its ideals from the great past, a feeling that it was possible or necessary to preserve some kind of superiority, did survive that lost past. Thus originated an empty ambition which eventually suggested a feeling of significance and prerogative, without any real superiority, to the victor in the Olympiads, to an insignificant community official, to the holder of a chair of honor or of a distinction (with perhaps a statue erected in his honor), or to the orator who had political influence, but was acclaimed with exultation only for his rhetoric, by a public of loiterers. On the basis of its *real* structure, the Greek society of the time could not have produced elevation above the average to which the social advantages and privileges of this class of persons were raised. Derived from the original significance of the community, which alone gave such superiorities a basis, they were now cut down to much smaller proportions, without changing their dimensions. Because of their very lack of content, they made possible a general mania for socially elevated positions which lacked all downward correlates.

Here we find, among other things, though in a certain sense inversely, a strange trait, which is interwoven with many human actions. It is shown in great purity by primitive "sympathetic magic." Man believes that he can evoke phenomena which lie outside the sphere of human power, by himself producing them on a smaller scale. Among many different peoples, the pouring of water is a strong rain magic. The power of the general idea is everywhere so pervasive that any minimal or one-sided realization of it seems to appropriate the idea; and, along with it, its reality on much higher levels of extensity and intensity. A certain aspect of "authority" shows us a special modification of the type of behavior at issue here. The inner preponderance which somebody has attained on the grounds of a particular achievement or quality, helps him very often gain "authority" in questions, matters, and directions which are entirely unrelated to his actually demonstrated superiority. Here too, therefore, the partially existing and partially justified "superordination" is transmitted to a *general* relationship, which lacks the correlate of a really "mastered" field. The paradoxical phenomenon of the stratum which has become superordinate in an absolute sense, and which lacks the logically required quantity of subordination—but has absorbed it, as it were, or possesses it only ideally —is seen here merely in another context.

§ 2. *Superordination in Lieu of Freedom*

I began by saying that a group as a whole may have the character of subordination without containing, in any practical and tangible way, a corresponding measure of superordination. The cases discussed form the counterpart of this phenomenon: in them, a superordination appears to exist as if it were an absolute quality, not based on any corresponding measure of subordination. Yet this is a rare form: the more general opposite of the first type is the *freedom* of all. If liberation from subordination is examined more closely, however, it almost always reveals itself as, at the same time, a gain in domination—either in regard to those previously superordinate, or in regard to a newly formed stratum that is destined to definitive subordination. Thus the greatest English constitutional historian notes at one point in reference to the "Quarrel of Puritanism": "Like every other struggle for liberty it ended in being a struggle for supremacy." This general schema, of course, does not often realize itself in pure form, but rather (for the most part) as one tendency among many others operating at the same time, in fragmentary, distorted, modified forms, in which, nevertheless, the fundamental will to substitute superordination for freedom can always be recognized. I now turn to the principal types of this tendency.

For the Greek citizen, in the field of politics, the two values, superordination and freedom, could not even be clearly separated. He lacked the sphere of individual law which would have protected him from the claims and the arbitrariness even of the community, that sphere which would have guaranteed him constitutional freedom even in regard to the state. Freedom, therefore, properly existed in only one form: as participation in state government itself. In its sociological type, this corresponds precisely to the communistic movements of antiquity, which did not aim at the abolition of private property but at the greater participation in it on the part of the disinherited. This basic form of behavior is repeated even in the lowest stratum, where it is impossible to speak of gaining any superiority: nevertheless, the Greek slave uprisings hardly ever aimed at breaking the slave fetters in general but, rather, at reducing their tightness and making them more bearable. The uprisings stemmed from rebellion against individual abuses of the institution of slavery, rather than from the desire to abolish the institution altogether.

It makes a characteristic difference whether the protection from dangers, the arrest of evils, or the winning of cherished values, is to be attained by means of abolishing the sociological form that bred these evils, or whether it is to be attained *within* this form, which is thereby preserved. Where the general conditions based on super-subordination are very solid, the liberation of the subordinates often does not entail general freedom—which would presuppose a fundamental change of the social form—but only the rise of the subordinates into the ruling stratum. The process contains a logical contradiction leading to practical contradictions—a point which will be discussed later. The outcome of the French Revolution for the Third Estate—in appearance only the liberation of that estate from the privileges of the privileged—involved the gain of superordination in the two senses of the term indicated. By means of its economic power, the Third Estate made the other, previously higher estates dependent upon itself; but, this effect, and the whole emancipation of the Third Estate, derived its rich content and its important consequences only because there existed (or, rather, there was formed in the same process) a Fourth Estate which the Third could exploit and above which it could rise. For this reason, one can by no means draw the simple analogy that today the Fourth Estate wishes to do what the Third had done at that earlier time.

Freedom here shows its connection with equality, even though, at the same time, the unavoidable breakdown of this connection. To the extent that general freedom prevails, there also prevails general equality. For, general freedom only entails the negative fact that there is no domination. This characteristic, because of its negativity, may be common to elements which in all other respects are highly differentiated. But equality, although appearing as the first consequence or accident of freedom, actually is only the point of transition through which human insatiability must pass once it seizes the oppressed masses. Typically speaking, nobody is satisfied with the position which he occupies in regard to his fellow creatures; everybody wishes to attain one which is, in some sense, more favorable. Thus, if the majority which got the worst of a situation feel a desire for a heightened style of life, the expression which most easily suggests itself to them will be the wish to have, and be, the same as the upper ten thousand. Equality with the superior is the first objective which offers itself to the impulse of one's own elevation. This is shown in any kind of small circle, in school classes, groups of merchants, or bureaucratic hierarchies. It is one of the reasons why the resentment of the proletarian usually does not turn against the highest classes, but against the bourgeois. For it is the bourgeois whom the proletarian sees immediately above himself, and who represents to him that rung of the ladder of fortune which he must climb first and on which, therefore, his consciousness and his desire for elevation momentarily concentrate.

As the first step, the inferior wants to be the equal of the superior. But a myriad of experiences show that once he is his equal, this condition, which previously was the essential aim of his endeavor, is merely a starting point for a further effort; it is the first station on the unending road toward the most favored position. Wherever an attempt is made at effecting equalization, the individual's striving to surpass others comes to the fore in all possible forms on the newly reached stage.

Equality, which is logically entailed by freedom as long as freedom operates in its pure and negative sense of mere not-being-dominated, is by no means the definitive intent of freedom. Yet man's inclination to take an immediately required or attainable step in realizing his aims for the ultimately satisfactory step, has often deluded him into believing this. In fact, a naive confusion places superiority directly alongside equality, although freedom pushes man far beyond it. Whether authentic or not, the remark which a woman coalheaver made to an elegantly dressed lady in 1848 is typically true: "Yes, Madam, now everything will become equal: I shall go dressed in silk, and you will heave coals!"

This is the inevitable result of what has already been mentioned before, namely, that one not only wants to have freedom, but also wants to use it for some purpose. Thus, the "freedom of the church" usually does not consist in the liberation from superordinate secular powers alone, but, through this liberation, in dominion over these powers. The church's liberty of teaching, for instance, means that the state obtains citizens who are inculcated by the church and stand under its suggestion; whereby the state comes often enough under the domination of the church. It has been said of medieval class privileges that they often were a means for helping to gain the freedom of all, including the non-privileged, under a condition of tyrannical pressure exerted upon all. But, once this freedom is attained, the continued existence of privilege operates in a sense which once more reduces general freedom. The freedom of the privileged produces a situation whose inner structure, to be sure, entails as its consequence or condition the freedom of all. But, latently, this freedom carries within itself the preferential treatment of the very elements from which it originated. Given the freedom of movement which has been gained in modern times, this preferential treatment is, eventually, actuated once more; that is, it again restricts the freedom of all others.

This complement of freedom, domination, attains a special form where the issue is the freedom of a group within a larger association, especially the state. Historically, such freedom often presents itself as the autonomous, more or less comprehensive jurisdiction of that group. Here, therefore, freedom refers to the fact that the group as a whole, as a super-individual unit, is master over its individual members. The decisive point is not that the group has the right to impose anything particularly arbitrary upon its members—this alone would not fundamentally subordinate them to it—but that it has the general right to have its own law. For, this right equalizes the group with the larger association which administers law in general and thus unconditionally subjects all who belong to it. Customarily, therefore, the narrower group makes sure with great rigor that its members subject themselves to its jurisdiction, because it knows that its own freedom is based on this subjection. In medieval Denmark, a guild brother could seek his right against his fellow only before a guild court. He was not prevented by external force from seeking such right, in addition, before the public court, the king's or the bishop's; but where the guild did not expressly permit this, it was considered wrong as regards both the guild and the guild brother concerned, and was thus sanctioned by fines to be paid to both. The city of Frankfort had received the privilege from the Emperors that no outside court would ever be resorted to against its citizens. In consequence of this privilege, a Frankfort citizen was arrested, in 1396, because he had sued fellow resident debtors before an outside court.

Freedom can always have the two aspects, of representing an esteem, a right, a power, on the one hand, and an exclusion and a contemptuous indifference on the part of the higher power, on the other. It is therefore no negative case to the argument presented here, if the autonomous jurisdiction enjoyed by medieval Jews in case of legal quarrels among one another, appears to have embodied a certain degradation and neglect. The situation of the Eastern Roman Jews under the Empire was quite different. Strabo, for instance, reports of the Alexandrian Jews that they had their own Chief Justice who decided their trials. This special legal position became a source of hatred against the Jews, because the Jews asserted that their religion claimed a particular jurisdiction possessed only by them. The tendency appears even more pointedly in the case reported from medieval Cologne where, for a short time, the Jews had the privilege of having a Jewish judge decide trials even against Christians.

In such situations, the individual member of the group was perhaps no freer than he would have been under the law of the land, but yet the totality of the group enjoyed a freedom which the other citizens of the state felt to be an ostentatious exemption. The privilege of a group with its own jurisdiction is by no means based on the peculiar content of the law administered by it; the fact that its members are subject only to *this* law is *formally* already a freedom. The heads of the guilds fought the collective jurisdiction of journeymen's organizations even where the content of this jurisdiction was slight—concerning, for instance, the maintenance of decency and good morals. But they knew very well that the moral censorship, which was codified and exercised by these organizations, gave the journeymen a consciousness of solidarity, of class honor, of organized independence, which constituted a support against the masters and made the journeymen feel that they firmly belonged together. The heads of the guilds knew that the essential point was this sociological form; and, that if they once conceded it, the further extension of its contents depended only on the power relations and economic conditions of the moment. The general content of this freedom of the whole is the subjection of the individual. It does not necessarily involve, therefore, his materially greater freedom (as has already been suggested). The doctrine of the people's sovereignty, as over against the prince's —a doctrine which emerged during the Middle Ages—by no means implied the freedom of the individual, but the freedom of the church, rather than that of the State, to reign over him. And when, in the sixteenth century, the Monarchomachists took over the idea of the sovereign people, and based government upon a sort of private legal contract between them and the ruler, they did not intend to liberate the individual but, on the contrary, to subject it to domination by religion and social rank.

In fact, the eminent interest of the subgroup, of the relatively closed circle, in dominion over its members, and the exposed position characteristic of such a prominent and privileged circle, often brings it about that special jurisdictions are more rigorous than the law of the larger association that permits the exemption of the subgroup. The Danish guilds, of which I have already spoken, decreed that, if a guild member broke a purchasing contract concluded with a guild brother, he, as the seller, had to pay a fine to the buyer that was twice the fine he would have had to pay to the king's officer if the buyer had not been a guild brother, and to all guild brothers a fine that was twice the fine to the city. The structure of the larger group permits it to give the individual more freedom than the smaller group can allow because the existence of the smaller circle depends more immediately upon the adequate behavior of every single member. Moreover, the small circle must demonstrate again and again, through the rigor of its jurisdiction, that it firmly and worthily exercises dominion over its members with which it has been entrusted, and that it gives the state power no occasion for any corrective interference. But this dominion over its members, in which consists the very freedom of the partial group, can become worse than legal harshness. To be sure, up to the sixteenth century, the relatively great autonomy of the German cities greatly promoted their development. But later, it produced an oligarchical government by classes and cousins which deeply oppressed all who did not participate in it. Only the developing state powers, in a battle lasting for almost two hundred years, eventually managed to halt this tyrannical exploitation of city freedom, and to guarantee, once more, the freedom of the individual in the face of it. Although, in principle, self-administration is a blessing, there is nevertheless the danger of local parliaments being dominated by egoistic class interests. It is this almost pathological exaggeration into which the correlation between the attainment of freedom and its complement and content (as it were), the attainment of domination, are transformed.

The type-process discussed here, then, is the development of the group's liberation—in which many participate in the same way and which entails no subordination of others—into the striving after superordination or the attainment of it. This type is realized in a direction quite different from those discussed thus far, that is, in the differentiation which usually occurs in low strata that rise to freer or generally better life conditions. The result of the process is very often this: certain elements of the group, which ascends as a whole, actually rise but thereby become part of the previously superordinate stratum, while the remainder stays subordinate. Naturally, this is most likely to occur where a distinction between superordinates and subordinates already exists within the upward-striving layers. In this case, after the rebellion against the generally superior stratum is ended, the difference among the rebels reappears. During the upward movement, this difference was relegated to the background; but now, with the uprising ended, those who previously had a higher position become assimilated to the highest stratum, while their erstwhile fellows-in-arms come to be pushed down all the more definitely.

In part, the 1830 revolution of English workers followed this type. In order to gain the right of parliamentary vote, the workers formed an alliance with the Reform party and the middle classes. The result was the enactment of a law which gave all classes the right to vote—except the workers. The class struggle in Rome, in approximately the fourth century B.C., took its course according to the same formula. The wealthy Plebeians who, in the interest of their class, desired connubiality and a democratic process of occupying office, joined the middle and lower classes. The success of the total movement was that those points of the program which predominantly concerned full citizens were achieved, whereas reforms designed to help the middle class and the small peasants soon came to nothing. The Bohemian revolution of 1848, in which the peasants abolished the last remnants of feudalism, developed in the same way. Once feudalism was eliminated, the differences in the positions among the peasants came again to the fore, while before and during the revolution, they had receded under the impact of the common subordination. The lower classes of the rural population demanded the partition of the community lands. This at once roused all the conservative instincts of the more well-to-do peasants. They fought the claims of the rural proletariat, although it was in alliance with them that they had just won a victory over the masters, who had fought *their* claims in the same way. It is very typical of the stronger element, which may, as a matter of fact, have achieved *most* of the victory, to wish to harvest its fruits alone: the *relatively* preponderant share in the success grows into the claim upon the *absolutely* preponderant share in the gain.

For the realization of this scheme, it is of great sociological help (as has been emphasized) that there already exist a broad class stratification, and that the more vigorous elements in the rising stratum join the higher layer which they previously fought. The originally relative difference between the better and worse situated elements of that class thereby becomes absolute, so to speak: for the privileged positions, the quantity of advantages gained reaches the point where this quantity changes into a new, advantageous quality. A procedure occasionally used in Spanish America shows a formal similarity. It was applied to the particularly gifted member of the colored population, who either inaugurated or threatened a freer and better position for his race in general. Such an individual was given a patent "that he should be considered white." By being assimilated into the ruling class, his superiority over his fellows was replaced by equality with the upper layer, an equality which he might otherwise have gained for his whole race, and thus only, for himself. It is out of a feeling for this sociological type that, for instance, in Austria, some politicians, *friendly* toward labor, raised objections to labor committees which, after all, were designed to attenuate the oppression of the workers. The fear was that these committees might develop into a workers' aristocracy; that, because of their privileged position which approached that of the entrepreneur, the entrepreneur might more easily assimilate them to his own interests; and that in this fashion, by this seeming progress, the remaining workers were actually more exposed than before. In the same way, generally, the chance of the best workers to rise into the propertied class seems to document the progress of the labor class as a whole. But this is only superficial; in reality, the rise is by no means favorable to the workers, because it deprives them of their best and leading elements. The absolute rise of certain members is, at the same time, their relative rise over their class, and thus their separation from it—a regular bleeding, depriving the class of its best blood. For this reason, if a mass rebels against an authority, the authority gains an immediate advantage if it succeeds in causing the mass to choose representatives who are to lead the negotiations. At least, the overwhelming, smashing onslaught of the mass, as such, is broken in this fashion; for the moment, the mass is checked by its own leaders in a way in which the authority itself can no longer succeed. The mass leaders exert the formal function of the authority, and thus prepare for the re-entrance of the authority into its dominating position.

§ 3. *The Sociological Error of Socialism and Anarchism*

All these phenomena lead into the most divergent directions, but they have the same sociological core: the fact, namely, that the quest for freedom and the attainment of freedom—in the various, negative and positive senses of this word—at the same time has, as its correlate or consequence, the quest for domination and the attainment of domination. Both socialism and anarchism deny the necessary character of this connection. In the discussion here presented, the dynamic equilibrium of the individuals—which may be designated as social freedom—appeared as a mere point of transition (real or only ideal), beyond which the balance sank once more on one side. By contrast, socialism and anarchism declare that the stability of this dynamic equilibrium is possible once the general social organization is articulated, no longer as super-subordination, but as the co-ordination of all elements.

The reasons *usually* advanced against this possibility are not at issue here. They may be summarized, however, as those of the *terminus a quo* and those of the *terminus ad quem*. No measure, it is argued, can eliminate natural differences among men, nor can any measure eliminate the expression of these differences through some upward-downward arrangement of commanding and obeying elements. The technique of civilized labor requires for its perfection a hierarchical structure of society, "one mind for a thousand hands," a system of leaders and executors. The constitution of individuals and the claims of objective achievement, as well as the workers and the realization of their aims—all coincide in the necessity of domination and subordination. It is urged by causality and teleology alike; and it is this which is the most definite and decisive justification of its indispensability.

Historical development, however, shows sporadic beginnings of a social form whose fundamental perfection could reconcile the continuation of super-subordination with the values of freedom. It is on behalf of this form that socialism and anarchism fight for the abolition of super-subordination. After all, the motivation of the endeavor lies exclusively in the feeling-states of individuals, in the consciousness of degradation and oppression, in the descent of the whole ego to the lowness of the social stratum, and, on the other hand, in the personal haughtiness into which self-feelings are transformed by externally leading positions. If some kind of social organization could avoid these psychological consequences of social inequality, social inequality could continue to exist without difficulties. Very often, one overlooks the purely technical character of socialism, the fact that it is a *means* for bringing about certain subjective reactions, that its ultimate source lies in men and in their life-feelings which are to be released by it. To be sure, the means—in accord with our psychological constitution—often becomes the end. The rational organization of society and the elimination of command and subjection appear as values not questioned beyond themselves, values claiming realization irrespective of those personal, eudaemonistic results. And yet, in these lies that real psychological power which socialism has at its disposal to inject into the movement of history. As a mere *means*, however, socialism succumbs to the fate of every means, namely, of never being, in principle, the *only* one. Since different causes may have the same effect, it is never impossible that the same purpose may be reached by different means. Insofar as socialism is considered an institution depending on the will of people, it is only the first proposal for eliminating those eudaemonistic imperfections which derive from historical inequality. For this reason, it is so closely associated with the need for abolishing these inequalities that it appears synonymous with it.

§ 4. *Super-Subordination without Degradation*

But if it were possible to dissolve the association between super-subordination and the feeling of personal devaluation and oppression, there is no logical reason why the all-decisive feeling of dignity and of a life which is its own master, should stand and fall only with socialism. Maybe this aim will be achieved if the individual feeling of life grows more psychologically independent of external activity in general and, in particular, of the position which the individual occupies within the sphere of this external activity. It could be imagined that, in the course of civilization, work in behalf of production becomes more and more a mere technique, more and more losing its consequences for the personality and its intimate concerns. As a matter of fact, we do find as the sociological type which underlies various developments, an approximation to this separation of personality and work. While originally the two were fused, division of labor and production for the market, that is, for completely unknown and indifferent consumers, have later permitted the personality increasingly to withdraw from work and to become based upon itself. No matter how unconditional the expected obedience may be, at this later stage it at least no longer penetrates into the layers that are decisive for life-feeling and personality-value. Obedience is merely a technical necessity, a form of organization which remains in the separate sphere of external matters, in the same way as manual labor itself.

This differentiation of objective and subjective life-elements, whereby subordination is preserved as a technical-organizational value which has no personally and internally depressing and degrading consequences, is, of course, no panacea for all the difficulties and sufferings that are everywhere produced by domination and obedience. In the present context, the differentiation is merely the principal expression of a tendency which is only partially effective and which in actuality never yields an undistorted and conclusive result. Voluntary military service, however, is one of its purest examples in our time. The intellectually and socially highest person may subordinate himself to a non-commissioned officer and actually tolerate a treatment which, if it really concerned his ego and feeling of honor, would move him to the most desperate reactions. But he is aware that he must bow before an objective technique, not as an individual personality, but only as an impersonal link requiring such discipline. This awareness, at least in many cases, prevents a feeling of degradation and oppression from arising. In the field of economics, it is particularly the transition from job work to machine work and from compensation in kind to compensation in wage which promote this objectification of super-subordination—as compared with the situation of the journeyman where the supervision and domination of the master extend to all aspects of the journeyman's life, quite beyond the prerogative which accrues to the master from the journeyman's role as a worker.

The same goal of development might be served by a further important type of sociological formation. It will be recalled that Proudhon wished to eliminate super-subordination by dissolving all dominating structures which, as the vehicles of social forces, have become differentiated out of individual interaction, and by once more founding all order and cohesion upon the direct interaction of free, coordinate individuals. But this co-ordination can perhaps be reached even if superordination and subordination continue to exist—provided they are reciprocal. We would then have an ideal organization, in which A is superordinate to B in one respect or at one time, but in which, in another respect or at another time, B is superordinate to A. This arrangement would preserve the organizational value of super-subordination, while removing its oppressiveness, one-sidedness, and injustice. As a matter of fact, there are a great many phenomena of social life in which this form-type is realized, even though only in an embryonic, mutilated, and covert way. A small-scale example might be the production association of workers for an enterprise for which they elect a master and foreman. While they are subordinate to him in regard to the technique of the enterprise, they yet are his superordinates with respect to its general direction and results. All groups in which the leader changes either through frequent elections or according to a rule of succession—down to the presidents of social clubs—transform the synchronous combination of superordination and subordination into their temporal alternation. In doing so, they gain the technical advantages of super-subordination while avoiding its personal disadvantages. All outspoken democracies try to attain this by means of brief office terms or by the prohibition of re-election, or both. In this fashion, the ideal of everybody having his turn is realized as far as possible. Simultaneous superordination and subordination is one of the most powerful forms of interaction. In its correct distribution over numerous fields, it can constitute a very strong bond between individuals, merely by the close interaction entailed by it.

§ 5. *Coordination and Reciprocal Super-Subordination*

In this, Stirner sees the essence of constitutionalism: "The ministers," he says, "reign over their lord, the prince; the deputies reign over theirs, the people." But it is in an even deeper sense that parliamentarism contains this form of correspondence. Modern jurisprudence divides all legal conditions into those of coordination and those of super-subordination. But it is likely that the former also are often of the super-subordinate type, which is practiced, however, reciprocally. The coordination of two citizens may consist in the fact that neither of them has a prerogative over the other. But inasmuch as each of them elects a representative, and inasmuch as this representative co-determines the laws which are also obligatory for the other, a relationship of reciprocal superordination and subordination originates; more precisely, it does so as the expression of coordination. This general form is of decisive significance for constitutional questions. Already Aristotle recognized this when he distinguished legal from factual participation in state power. The mere fact that a citizen (in contrast to a non-citizen) is a bearer of state power, is no guarantee that, within the organization of citizens he ever has any function other than simple obedience. The individual who in respect to the military privileges of the citizen is among the *oligoi* [the few who rule], the "haves," may, in respect to his share in the exercise of state power, belong among those who "have" less, among the mere *demos,* for the reason, perhaps, that only people of high esteem can be elected to office, while those of lower esteem are entitled only to participation in the *ekklesia* [popular assembly]. A state may be an oligarchy in regard to the first relationship, military privilege; but in regard to the second, state power, it may under certain circumstances be a democracy. Here the official is subject to the general state power whose bearers, in terms of practical organization, are in turn subject to him, the official.

This relationship has been expressed, both in a more refined and more general manner, by contrasting the people, as object of *imperium,* with the individual, as a link coordinate with all other individuals: in the first respect, the individual is an object of duty; in the second, a legal subject. This differentiation and concomitant consistency of group life, which is effected by the reciprocity of superordination and subordination, are further increased if certain contents are taken into consideration to which this form of group life applies. With full awareness of the paradox involved, the strength of democracy has been pointed out as being exemplified by the fact that everybody is a servant in matters in which he has the greatest specialized knowledge, but a master in things of general knowledge. That is, in professional matters, he must obey the wishes of the consumer or the regulations of the entrepreneur or of whoever else gives him orders. By contrast, like all others, he is master as regards the general, or political, interests of the collectivity, of which he has no special understanding but only that which he shares with the rest of the society. Where the ruler, it has further been argued, is also the expert, the absolute suppression of the lower classes is quite inevitable. If, in a democracy, the numerical majority also possessed the concentration of knowledge and power, they would exert a tyranny no less harmful than that of an autocracy. In order to make sure that it does not come to such a split between above and below but that, instead, the unity of the whole is preserved, that peculiar combination is necessary by which the highest power is entrusted to those who, in respect to expert knowledge, are mere subalterns.

This interlacing of alternating superordinations and subordinations among the same powers also sustained the unity of the idea of the state into which the parliamentary and ecclesiastic constitutions fused after the Glorious Revolution in England. The clergy had a deep antipathy for the parliamentary regime and, above all, for the prerogative which it claimed even in respect to the clergy. In its essential points, the truce came about by the church retaining special juridicial power over marriages and testaments, as well as sanctions concerning Catholics and persons not attending church. In exchange, it gave up its doctrine of unchangeable "obedience" and recognized that the divine world order had room for a parliamentary world order, to whose special regulations even the clergy was subjected. Yet, the church dominated the parliament because, in order to enter parliament, one had to take oaths which only members of the state church could take without difficulty, dissenters only by some devious route, and members of other faiths not at all. The ruling clerical and secular class was integrated in such a way that, in the Upper House, the archbishops retained their seats above the dukes; the bishops theirs above the lords; while all parsons subordinated themselves to the patronage of the secular ruling class. To compensate for this, the local cleric again received the direction of the local community meeting. This was the form of interaction which power factors, otherwise contradictory, could attain, so that the state church of the eighteenth century and a consistent organization of English life in general came about.

The relationship of marriage, too, owes its inner and outer firmness and unity, at least in part, to the fact that it comprises a large number of interest spheres in some of which the one part, and in others the other part, is superordinate. In this fashion, there results an interpenetration, a consistency and, at the same time, vitality of the relation which can hardly be atained in other sociological forms. Probably, what is called the "equal rights" of man and wife in marriage—as a fact or as a pious wish—is actually to a large extent such an alternating superordination and subordination. At least, this alternation would result in a more organic relationship than would mechanical equality in the literal sense of the term, especially if one recalls the thousand subtle relations of daily life which cannot be cast in the form of principles. The alternation also would make sure that momentary superordination does not appear as brute command. This form of relationship, finally, constituted one of the closest bonds in Cromwell's army. The same soldier who, in military matters, blindly obeyed his superior, in the hour of prayer often made himself into his moral preacher. A corporal could preside over the worship in which his captain participated in the same way as all privates. The army which unconditionally followed its leader once a political goal was accepted, beforehand made political decisions to which the leaders themselves had to bow. As long as it lasted, the Puritan army derived an extraordinary firmness from this reciprocity of superordination and subordination.

The favorable result of this societal form depends on the

fact that the sphere within which one social element is super-ordinate is very precisely and clearly separated from those spheres in which the other element is superordinate. As soon as this is not the case, constant conflicts over competencies develop; and the result is not the strengthening, but the weakening of the group. When a person, who in general is subordinate, occasionally attains superordination in the field of his normal subordination, the solidity of the group suffers greatly. It does so, in part because of the rebellious character which usually characterizes such a situation, in part because of the incapability for superordination in a field in which the person ordinarily is subordinate. While Spain was a world power, periodic rebellions broke out in the Spanish army, for instance, in the Netherlands. No matter how terrible the discipline by which the army was held together, nevertheless, it occasionally showed an insuppressible democratic force. The soldiers rebelled against the officers in certain, almost calculable intervals, demoting them and choosing their own. But these new officers were under the control of the soldiers, and could do nothing which was not approved of by all subordinates. The harm of such medley of superordination and subordination in the same field needs no comment.

In an indirect form, this harm also lies in the short office term of elected officials in many democracies. Certainly, by this method, as large as possible a number of citizens at one time or another comes into leading positions; but, on the other hand, long-range plans, continuous actions, consistently applied measures, and technical perfection, are often enough made impossible. In the ancient republics, this quick alternation was not yet harmful to the extent it is today, inasmuch as their administrations were simple and transparent, and most citizens had the knowledge and training necessary for office. The sociological form of the occurrences in the Spanish army—although the content was very different—show the same great evils which, at the beginning of the nineteenth century, appeared in the American Episcopal Church. The congregations were seized by a feverish passion to exercise control over their ministers—who were appointed, precisely, for the moral and ecclesiastical control of their congregations. In consequence of this refractoriness on the part of the congregations, clerics in Virginia were for a long time appointed for one year only.

In a slightly modified manner, which is yet formally the same in all essentials, this sociological process occurs in bureaucratic hierarchies, where the superior is technically dependent upon the subaltern. The higher official often lacks the knowledge of technical details or of the actual objective situation. The lower official usually moves in the same circle of tasks during all his life, and thus gains a specialized knowledge of his narrow field that a person who rapidly advances through various stages does not possess. Yet, the decisions of such a person cannot be executed without that knowledge of detail. Thus, under the Roman Empire, the knights' and senators' right to state service did not entail any theoretical training for it; the acquisition of the required knowledge was simply left to practice. But already in the last stages of the Republic, this procedure had resulted in the higher officials' dependence upon their subalterns who managed to produce a certain business routine since they did not constantly change. In Russia, this is a general characteristic, which is especially promoted by the particular manner in which offices are occupied there. Advancement is according to rank classes, but not only within the same department; rather, the official who has reached a certain class is often transferred—on his own or his superior's wish—into a very different department, but with the same rank. Thus, at least until recently, it was by no means rare for a graduated student to become an officer with no more training than six months of service at the front, and for an officer, by passing to the civil rank corresponding to his military position, to receive some office in the civil state service that he preferred. The way in which either of them came to terms with his new situation, for which his training had not prepared him, was his own affair. It is inevitable that such a situation often results in the technical ignorance of the higher official with respect to his position; and it is just as inevitable that this ignorance makes him depend upon his inferior with his expert knowledge. The reciprocity of superordination and subordination thus often lets the actual leader appear as the subordinate, and the actual mere-executor as the superordinate. As a consequence, this reciprocity damages the solidity of the organization as much as an expediently distributed alternation of superordination and subordination can strengthen it.

§ 6. *Super-Subordination as a Form of Social Organization and as an Expression of Individual Differences; Person vs. Position*

Beyond these special formations, the fact of domination poses the following quite general sociological problem. Superordination and subordination constitute, on the one hand, a form of the objective organization of society. On the other hand, they are the expression of differences in personal qualities among men. How do these two characteristics compare with one another, and how is the form of sociation influenced by the differences in this relationship?

In the beginning of societal development, the superordination of one personality over others must have been the adequate expression and consequence of personal superiority. There is no reason why, at a social stage with no fixed organization that would *a priori* allocate his place to the individual, anybody should subordinate himself to another, unless force, piety, bodily or spiritual or volitional superiority, suggestion—in brief, the relation of his personal being to that of the other—determined him to do so. Since the beginning of societal formation is historically inaccessible to us, we must, on methodological principles, make the simplest assumption, namely, that of approximate equilibrium. We thus proceed as we do in the case of cosmological deductions. Since the beginning stage of the world process is unknown, it was necessary to try the deduction of the origin and progress of manifold and differentiated phenomena from what was as simple as possible—the homogeneity and equilibrium of the world elements. There is, of course, no doubt that, if these assumptions are made in an absolute sense, no world process could ever have begun, since there was no cause for movement and specialization. We must, therefore, posit at the initial stage some differential behavior of elements, however minimal, in order to make subsequent differentiations understandable on its basis. In a similar way, we are forced, in the development of social variation, to start with a fictitious simplest stage; and the minimum of variation, which is needed as the germ of all later differentiations, will probably have to be placed into the purely personal differences among individual dispositions. Among men, differences in reciprocal positions that are directed toward the outside, will initially, therefore, have to be derived from such qualitative individualizations.

Thus, in primitive times, the prince is required or assumed to have perfections which are extraordinary in their extent or combination. The Greek king of the heroic period had to be, not only brave, wise, and eloquent, but also outstanding as an athlete and, if possible, an excellent carpenter, shipbuilder, and husbandman as well. It has been noted that the position of King David rested largely upon the fact that he was, at the same time, a singer and warrior, a layman and prophet, and that he had the capabilities needed for a fusion of secular state power with spiritual theocracy. This origin of superordination and subordination, of course, still operates constantly in society and continuously creates new situations. But out of it have developed, and are developing, fixed organizations of superordination and subordination. Individuals are either born into them or attain given positions in them on the basis of qualities quite different from those which originally founded the super-subordination in question.

This transition from the subjectivistic relationship of domination to an objective formation and fixation, is effected by the purely quantitative expansion of the sphere of domination. The connection between the increased quantity of elements and the objectivity of the norms which are valid for them, can be observed everywhere. Two, actually contradictory motives are significant in it. The increase of elements entails an increase in the qualitative characteristics existing among them. This greatly increases the improbability that any one element with a strong subjective individuality has identical or even generally satisfactory relations to all others. To the extent that there is an increase in the differences within the group over which domination or norm extend, the ruler or the norm must shed all individual character and adopt, instead, a general character, above subjective fluctuations.

On the other hand, this same expansion of the group leads

to the division of labor and differentiation among its leading elements. Unlike the Greek king, the ruler of a large group can no longer be the standard and leader of all their essential interests. What is required, rather, are manifold specialization and specialized division of the regime. But the division of labor is everywhere correlated with the objectification of actions and conditions. It moves the labor of the individual into a context which lies outside his proper sphere: the personality, as a whole and as something intimate, is placed beyond any one-sided activity. The results of activity, now circumscribed in purely objective terms, form a unit along with those of other personalities. It is probable that the totality of such causal chains has transformed the relation of domination, which originated from case to case and from person to person, into an objective form in which not the person, but the position, so to speak, is the superordinate element. The *a priori* elements of the relationship are no longer the individuals with their characteristics, out of which the social relation develops, but, rather, these relations themselves, as objective forms, as "positions," empty spaces and contours (as it were) which must merely be "filled" by individuals. The firmer and the more technically articulated the organization of the group, the more objectively and formally do the patterns of superordination and subordination present themselves. Individuals suited for the positions are sought only "afterwards," or else the positions are filled by the mere accidents of birth and other contingencies.

This by no means applies to hierarchies of governmental positions alone. Money economy creates a very similar societal formation in the spheres which are dominated by it. The possession or the lack of a particular sum of money entails a certain social position, an almost entire independence upon the personal qualities of the individual occupant. Money has carried to its extreme the separation emphasized a moment ago, between man as a personality and man as the instrument of a special performance or significance. Everyone who can conquer or somehow acquire the possession of money, thereby attains a power and a position which appear and disappear with the holding of this possession, but not with the personality and its characteristics. Men pass through positions associated with the possession of certain amounts of money in the way in which purely accidental "fillings" pass through rigid, solid forms.

It is obvious, however, that modern society does not everywhere exhibit this discrepancy between position and personality. In fact, the separation of the position with its objective content from the personality itself, frequently results in a certain elasticity in the allocation of persons, and thus in a new, often more rational basis for adequate proportioning. This is in addition to the immensely increased possibilities that liberal orders provide, in general, for the procurement of positions to which available qualifications are adequate. Nor is this altered by the fact that the relevant qualifications are often so specialized that the personality, in terms of its *over-all* value, nevertheless does not deserve the superordination attained through them. The discrepancy involved here occasionally reaches its maximum in certain intermediate structures, like estates and guilds. It has correctly been emphasized that the system of big industry gives the exceptionally gifted man more opportunity to excel than did anything prior to this system. The numerical proportion of foreman and supervisor to workers, the argument runs, is nowadays smaller than the proportion of petty masters to journeymen two hundred years ago; but the special talent now has a much greater chance of rising to a higher position. Here, the important point is only the peculiar *chance* of the discrepancy between the personal quality and its position in terms of ruling or being ruled. This chance has been brought about by the objectification of positions and by their differentiation from purely personal, individual factors.

However much socialism abhors this blindly contingent relationship between the objective scale of positions and the qualifications of persons, its organizational proposals nevertheless amount to the same sociological form. For, socialism desires a constitution and administration which are absolutely centralized and hence, by necessity, rigorously articulated and hierarchical; but, at the same time, it presupposes that all individuals are, *a priori*, equally capable of occupying any position whatever in this hierarchy. But, in this fashion, that circumstance of contemporary conditions which appeared senseless is, at least in one respect, elevated into a principle. For, the mere fact that in an ideally pure democracy those who are guided *choose* their guide, offers no guarantee against the accidental character of the relation between person and position. It does not for two reasons. The first is that, in order to choose the best expert, one himself must be an expert. The other reason is that, in all very large groups, the principle of choice from below produces entirely accidental results. An exception to this are pure party elections —where, however, the very factor whose meaningful or accidental nature is in question here, is eliminated. For, the party election as such is a vote for a person, not because of certain personal qualities, but because this person is the anonymous representative (to put it in extreme terms) of a certain objective principle.

The form of leader creation which socialism ought to espouse, if it seeks to be consistent, is the drawing of positions by lot. The lot expresses the ideal claim of everybody much more adequately than does the circulation of positions, which, besides, cannot be perfectly carried out under large-scale conditions. Yet, this by no means makes the lot itself democratic. In the first place, the lot may also be resorted to under a ruling aristocracy: as a purely formal principle, it has no connection with the contrast between democracy and aristocracy. In the second place, and above all, democracy implies the actual cooperation of all, whereas the drawing of leading positions by lot transforms actual cooperation into ideal cooperation, into the merely potential right of everybody to attain a leading position. The lottery principle completely severs the mediation between the individual and his position, the mediation which is represented by the individual's subjective qualification. With the lottery principle, super-subordination as a formal, organizational requirement, wholly overpowers personal qualities—from which, nevertheless, this requirement took its origins.

§ 7. *Aristocracy vs. Equality*

The problem of the relation between personal and mere positional superiority branches out into two important sociological forms. In view of the actual differences in the qualities of men—differences eliminable only in a utopia—certainly, "dominion by the best" is that constitution which most precisely and suitably expresses the inner and ideal relation among men in an external relation. This, perhaps, is the deepest reason why artists are so often aristocratically inclined. For, the attitude of the artist is based upon the assumption that the inner significance of things adequately reveals itself in their appearance, if only this appearance is seen correctly and completely. The separation of the world from its value, of appearance from its significance, is *the* anti-artistic disposition. This is so in spite of the fact that the artist must, of course, transform the *immediately* given so that it yields its true, super-contingent form—which, however, is at the same time the text of its spiritual or metaphysical meaning. Thus, the psychological and historical connection between the aristocratic and the artistic conceptions of life may, at least in part, be based on the fact that only an aristocratic order equips the inner value relations among men with a visible form, with their aesthetic symbol, so to speak.

But an aristocracy in this pure sense, as government by the best, such as Plato visualized, cannot be realized empirically. One reason is that, thus far, no procedure has been found by which "the best" could with certainty be recognized and given their positions. Neither the *a priori* method of breeding a ruling caste, nor the *a posteriori* method of natural selection in the free struggle for the favored position, nor the (as it were) intermediate method of electing persons, from below or from above, has proved adequate. But aside from these presuppositional difficulties, there are others. Men rarely are satisfied with the superiority of even the best among them, because they do not wish any superiority at all or, at least, none in which they cannot themselves participate. Furthermore, the possession of power, even of power which was originally acquired in a legitimate fashion, usually demoralizes, not always (to be sure) the individual, but almost always organizations and classes. In view of all these difficulties, it becomes understandable that Aristotle should have held the following opinion. From an abstract standpoint, he said, it befits the individual or family which in *areté* [virtue] excels all others to have absolute dominion over them. But on the basis of practical requirements, it is necessary to recommend a mixture of this domination with that of the mass;

the numerical preponderance of the mass must be combined with the qualitative preponderance of the particular individual or family.

But the above-mentioned difficulties of the "dominion by the best" may lead, rather than to these mediating notions, to the resigned proposition that general equality should be considered as the practical regulation. In this case, the argument is that in comparison with the disadvantages of aristocracy— which, logically, alone is justified—general equality represents the lesser *evil*. Since it is definitely impossible to express, certainly and permanently, subjective differences in objective relationships of domination, subjective differences should altogether be eliminated from the characteristics of the social structure, which ought to be regulated as if these differences did not exist.

But since, as a rule, the question of greater or lesser evil can be decided only by personal valuation, the same pessimistic mood may also lead to the exactly opposite conviction. One can argue that, in large as in small groups, there must be *some* government; and that, therefore, it is better that unsuited persons govern than that nobody does. Moreover, one can argue that the societal group must adopt the form of super-subordination, from inner and objective necessity, so that it would be merely a desirable accident if the place which is pre-formed by objective necessity were indeed filled by the subjectively adequate individual.

This formal consideration derives from quite primitive experiences and necessities. The most obvious is that the form of domination itself means or creates a social tie. More awkward periods, which did not have a variety of interactional forms at their disposal, often had no other means for effecting formal membership in the collectivity than that of subordinating the individuals, who were not immediately associated, to those who were members *a priori*. After the earliest constitution, of complete personal and property equality in the community, had ceased to exist in Germany, the landless man lacked all rights to any positive freedom. Therefore, if he did not wish to remain altogether without connection with the community, he had to join some lord, so that he could participate in this indirect fashion, as a denizen, in the public organizations. The community was interested in his doing this, for it could not tolerate any unattached individual in its territory. For this reason, Anglo-Saxon law made it expressly the duty of the landless person to subject himself to a lord [*sich "verherren"*]. In medieval England, too, the interest of the community required the stranger to subordinate himself to a patron. One belonged to the group if one owned a piece of its territory; those who lacked land and yet wished to belong were forced personally to belong to somebody who, in turn, was connected with the group in the original manner.

The general importance of leading personalities, combined with the relative irrelevance of their personal qualifications, is found, in a formally similar manner, in several early elaborations of the voting principle. The elections, for instance, of the medieval English parliament seem to have been conducted with astonishing negligence and indifference. The only important point seems to have been that each district designated a member of parliament; it was much less important *who* this member was. This indifference also applied to the qualification of the *voters* and, during the medieval period, was often striking. Whoever happened to be present voted; it seems that often no value was placed upon the legitimation of the voters, nor upon any particular number of them. This carelessness in regard to the electorate was only the expression, evidently, of the carelessness in regard to the qualitative and personal results of the election.

§ 8. *Coercion*

Finally, in the same sense, there operates quite generally the conviction that coercion is necessary for social organization. the idea is that human nature simply needs coercion lest human actions become completely purposeless and formless. For the general character of this postulate, it is irrelevant whether subordination be under a person and his arbitrariness, or under a law. There are, admittedly, certain extreme cases where the formal value of subordination no longer makes up for the senselessness of its content; but, aside from these, it is of only secondary interest whether the content of the law be a little better or a little worse—exactly, it will be remembered, as was the case concerning the quality of the ruling personality. Here one could refer to the advantages of hereditary despotism—a despotism which, obviously, is to a certain extent independent of the qualities of the person—particularly where it dominates the over-all political and cultural life of large territories, and has certain advantages over a free federation.

These advantages are similar to the prerogative of marriage over free love. Nobody can deny that the coercion of law and custom holds innumerable marriages together which, from the moral standpoint, ought to break apart. In these instances, the persons concerned subordinate themselves to a law which simply does not fit their case. But in other instances, this same coercion—however hard, momentarily and subjectively, it may be felt to be—is an irreplaceable value, because it keeps together those who, from the moral standpoint, ought to stay together but, for some momentary ill-temper, irritation, or vacillation of feeling, would separate if they only could, and thus would impoverish or destroy their lives irreparably. The content of marriage laws may be good or bad, may be or may not be applicable to a given case: the mere coercion of the law to stay together develops individual values of an eudaemonistic and ethical nature (not to mention values of social expediency) which, according to the pessimistic, perhaps one-sided standpoint presupposed here, could never be realized in the absence of all coercion. The mere consciousness of everyone that he is bound to the other by coercion may, in some cases, make the common life utterly unbearable. But in other cases, this consciousness will bring about a tolerance, self-discipline, and thorough psychological training which nobody would feel inclined to undergo if separation were possible at all times. These traits are produced, rather, only by the desire to make the unavoidable life in common at least as bearable as possible.

Occasionally, the consciousness of being under coercion, of being subject to a superordinate authority, is revolting or oppressive—whether the authority be an ideal or social law, an arbitrarily decreeing personality or an executor of higher norms. But, for the majority of men, coercion probably is an irreplaceable support and cohesion of the inner and outer life. In the inevitably symbolic language of all psychology: our soul seems to live in two layers, one of which is deeper, hard or impossible to move, carrying the real sense or substance of our life, while the other is composed of momentary impulses and isolated irritabilities. This second layer would be victorious over the first and even more often than it actually is; and, because of the onslaught and quick alternation of its elements, the second layer would give the first no opportunity to come to the surface, if the feeling of a coercion interfering from somewhere did not dam its torrent, break its vacillations and caprices, and thus, again and again, give room and supremacy to the persistent undercurrent.

In comparison with this functional significance of coercion as such, its particular content is of only secondary importance. Senseless coercion may be replaced by sensible coercion, but even the latter has its significance, which is relevant here, only in that which it shares with the former. Moreover, not only the toleration of coercion, but also opposition to it—both to unjust and to justified coercion—has for the rhythm of our surface life this same function of inhibition and interruption: to make conscious and effective the deeper currents of the most intimate and substantial life, which cannot be inhibited by any external means. Insofar as coercion is associated with some form of domination, the association reveals that element in domination which is, as it were, indifferent to the quality of the ruler and to any individual right to dominate, and which thus shows the deeper sense of the claim to authority as such.

§ 9. *The Inevitably Disproportionate Distribution of Qualifications and Positions*

It is, in fact, impossible in principle that, in the scale of super-subordination, personal qualification and social position correspond to one another throughout and without remainder—no matter which organization might be proposed for attaining such a correspondence. The reason is that there are always more people qualified for superordinate positions than there are such positions. Among the ordinary workers in a factory, there certainly are very many who could equally well be foremen or entrepreneurs; among common soldiers, many who are fully capable of being officers; among the millions of subjects of a prince, doubtless many who would be equally good or better princes. Rule "by the grace of God" gives expression to the fact that not any subjective quality, but a super-human criterion, decides who shall rule.

Moreover, the fraction of those who have attained leading positions among those who are qualified for them, must not be assumed to be greater than it is, merely on the recognition of the fact that (surely) there also are a great many persons in superordinate positions who are not qualified for them. For, this sort of disproportion between person and position appears, for several reasons, more considerable than it actually is. In the first place, incompetence in a given position of control is especially visible; it is obviously more difficult to conceal than very many other human inadequacies—particularly *because* so many other men, thoroughly qualified for this same position, stand aside as subordinates. Furthermore, this disproportion often results not from individual shortcomings at all, but from contradictory requirements of the office; nevertheless, the inevitable consequences of these requirements are easily ascribed to the office occupant as his subjective faults. The idea of modern "state government," for instance, connotes an infallibility which is the expression of its (in principle) absolute objectivity. Measured by this ideal infallibility, it is natural that its actual executives should often appear inadequate.

In reality, purely individual shortcomings of leading personalities are relatively rare. If one considers the senseless and uncontrollable accidents through which men obtain their positions in all fields, the fact that not a very much greater sum of incapabilities manifests itself in their occupancies would be an incomprehensible miracle, if one did not have to assume that the latent qualifications for the positions exist in very great diffusion. This very assumption underlies the phenomenon that, under republican constitutions, the candidate for office is sometimes investigated only for negative traits; that is, it is merely asked whether he has, in some way, made himself unworthy of the office. Thus, in Athens, appointment was by lot, and the only questions examined were whether the candidate treated his parents well, paid his taxes, etc., in other words, whether there was anything against him—the assumption being that everybody was *a priori* worthy of the office. This is the deeper justification of the proverb: "If God gives somebody an office, he also gives him the mind necessary for it." For, precisely, the "mind" required for the occupancy of higher positions exists in many men, but it proves, develops, reveals itself only once they occupy the position.

This incommensurability between the quantity of qualifications for superordination and the quantity of their possible applications, can perhaps be explained in terms of the difference between the character of man as a group member and as an individual. The group as such is low and in need of guidance. It develops qualities which all members have in common. But they are only those qualities which are securely inherited, that is, more primitive and undifferentiated traits or traits easily suggested—in short, "subordinate" qualities. Once a group of any size is formed, therefore, it is expedient that the whole mass organize itself in the form of subordination to a few. This, evidently, does not prevent any given individual member from having higher and finer qualities. But these are individual. They transcend in various respects what all have in common, and thus do not raise the low level of the qualities in which they coincide. From all this, it follows that the group as a whole needs a leader, and that, therefore, there can be many subordinates but only few superordinates—but that, on the other hand, every individual member of the group is more highly qualified than he is as a group element, that is, as a subordinate.

All social formations thus involve this contradiction between the just claim to a superordinate position and the technical impossibility of satisfying this claim. The arrangement by estates and the contemporary order come to terms with this contradiction by building the classes one on top of the other, with an ever smaller number of members in the upward direction, in the form of a pyramid, thereby limiting from the beginning the number of those "qualified" for leading positions. This selection is not based on the individuals available, but inversely, it prejudges these individuals. Out of a mass of equals, not everyone can be brought into the position he deserves. For this reason, the arrangements just mentioned may be considered as the attempt at training the individuals for predetermined positions, from the standpoint of these positions.

But instead of the slowness with which heredity and education, that is commensurate with rank, may succeed in this training, there also are acute procedures, so to speak. They serve, by means of authoritative or mystical edict, to equip the personality with the capability of leading and ruling, irrespective of his previous quality. For the tutelary state of the seventeenth and eighteenth centuries, the subject was incapable of any participation in public affairs; in political respects, he remained permanently in need of guidance. But the moment he occupied a state office, he at once attained the higher insights and the public spirit which enabled him to direct the collectivity—as if, by the sheer occupancy of office, there had emerged out of the immature person, through an inexplicable birth, not only the mature individual, but the leader equipped with all the prerequisites of intellect and character. This tension between everyone's *a priori* lack of qualification for a certain superiority and the absolute qualification which he acquires *a posteriori* through the interference of a higher authority, reaches its peak in Catholic clergy. Here, family tradition, or education from childhood on, play no role. Even the personal quality of the candidate is unimportant in comparison to the spirit which exists in mystical objectivity and which is bestowed upon him through consecration to priesthood. The superior position is not given to him because he alone is naturally predestined for it— although this may, of course, be of some importance and does form the basis for a certain differentiation among those admitted. Nor is it given to him on the greater chance of his being "called" rather than not. No, the consecration *creates* the special qualification for the position to which it calls the individual, because it transfers the *spirit* to him. The principle of God giving an office and the required competence along with it is here realized in the most radical fashion, in both of its two dimensions—unfitness prior to the occupancy, and subsequent fitness created by the "office" itself.

Part Four

The Secret and the
Secret Society

Chapter 1

Knowledge, Truth, and Falsehood in Human Relations

OBVIOUSLY, ALL RELATIONS
which people have to one another are based on their knowing
something about one another. The merchant knows that his
correspondent wants to buy at the lowest possible price, and to
sell at the highest possible price. The teacher knows that he can
tax the student with a certain kind and amount of learning
material. Within each social stratum, an individual knows how
much culture, approximately, he may expect of every other
individual. Without such knowledge, evidently, these and many
other kinds of interaction could not take place at all. One may
say (with reservations which easily suggest themselves) that in
all relations of a personally differentiated sort, intensity and
nuance develop in the degree in which each party, by words
and by mere existence, reveals itself to the other. How much
error and mere prejudice may be contained in all this knowledge, is another question. Yet, just as our apprehension of external nature, along with elusions and inadequacies, nevertheless attains the truth required for the life and progress of our
species, so everybody knows, by and large correctly, the other
person with whom he has to deal, so that interaction and relation
become possible.

§ 1. *Knowledge of One Another*

The first condition of having to deal with somebody at all
is to know with *whom* one has to deal. The fact that people
usually introduce themselves to one another whenever they
engage in a conversation of any length or meet on the same

social level, may strike one as an empty form; yet it is an adequate symbol of the mutual knowledge presupposed by every relationship. We are very often not conscious of this because, for a large number of relations, we need to know only that quite typical tendencies and qualities are present on both sides. The necessary character of these tendencies is usually noted only when, on occasion, they are absent. It would be worth a special investigation to find out the kind and degree of reciprocal knowledge required by various relations among people; to find out how the general psychological assumptions, with which everybody approaches everybody else, are interwoven with the special experiences in regard to the particular individual with whom we interact; how, in many fields, reciprocal knowledge does not have to be equal on both sides or is not permitted to be; to discover how the development of existing relations is determined merely by the growing knowledge, on both sides or on one side, about the other; finally, on the other hand, how our objectively psychological picture of the other individual is influenced by real, practical and sentimental, relations.

This last influence is by no means one of mere falsification. It is entirely legitimate that the theoretical conception we have of a particular individual should vary with the standpoint from which it is formed, a standpoint which is the result of the overall relation between knower and known. One can never know another person *absolutely*, which would involve knowledge of every single thought and mood. Nevertheless, one forms some personal unity out of those of his fragments in which alone he is accessible to us. This unity, therefore, depends upon the portion of him which our standpoint permits us to see. But such differences by no means arise from differences in the quantity of knowledge alone. No psychological knowledge is a mere stereotype of its object but depends, as does the knowledge of external nature, upon the forms which the cognizing mind brings to it and in which it receives the given. But where the knowledge of individuals is at issue, these forms differ very much individually. They do not attain the scientific generality and super-subjective power of conviction which can be reached with respect to external nature and to merely typical psychological processes.

§ 2. *Knowledge of External Nature vs.*
Knowledge of Persons

If A and B have different conceptions of M, this by no means necessarily implies incompleteness or deception. Rather, in view of the relation in which A stands to M, A's nature and the total circumstances being what they are, A's picture of M is true for him in the same manner in which, for B, a different picture is true. It would be quite erroneous to say that, above these two pictures, there is the objectively correct knowledge about M, and that A's and B's images are legitimated to the extent to which they coincide with this objective knowledge. Rather, the ideal truth which the picture of M in the conception of A approaches—to be sure, only asymptotically—is something different, even as an ideal, from that of B. It contains as an integrating, form-giving precondition the psychological peculiarity of A and the particular relation into which A and M are brought by their specific characters and destinies.

Every relationship between persons gives rise to a picture of each in the other; and this picture, obviously, interacts with the actual relation. The relation constitutes the condition under which the conception, that each has of the other, takes this or that shape and has its truth legitimated. On the other hand, the real interaction between the individuals is based upon the pictures which they acquire of one another. Here we have one of the deep-lying circuits of intellectual life, where an element presupposes a second element which yet, in turn, presupposes the first. While, in narrow fields, this is a fallacy that invalidates everything, in more general and fundamental fields it is the inevitable expression of the unity into which both elements fuse, a unity which, with our forms of thought, cannot be expressed otherwise than by saying that we build the first upon the second and, at the same time, the second upon the first. Our relationships thus develop upon the basis of reciprocal knowledge, and this knowledge upon the basis of the actual relations. Both are inextricably interwoven. In their alternation within sociological interaction, they reveal interaction as one of the points where being and conceiving make their mysterious unity empirically felt.

§ 3. *Truth, Error, and Social Life*

Our conduct is based upon our knowledge of total reality. But this knowledge is characterized by peculiar limitations and distortions. That "error alone is life, and knowledge, death" cannot, of course, be valid as a principle, because a person caught in continuous error would continuously act in an inexpedient fashion, and thus inevitably would perish. And yet, in view of our accidental and defective adaptations to our life conditions, there is no doubt that we preserve and acquire not only so much truth, but also so much ignorance and error, as is appropriate for our practical activities. We have only to think of the great insights which transform human life, but which fail to make their appearance or go unnoticed, unless the total cultural situation renders them possible and useful. Or we may think, on the other hand, of the *"Lebenslüge"* ["vital lie"] of the individual who is so often in need of deceiving himself in regard to his capacities, even in regard to his feelings, and who cannot do without superstition about gods and men, in order to maintain his life and his potentialities. In the sense that the expediency of the external as of the internal life sees to it that we obtain the exact amounts of error and truth which constitute the basis of the conduct required of us, error and truth are psychologically coordinate—although, of course, only by and large, and with a wide latitude for variations and defective adaptations.

§ 4. *The Individual as an Object of Knowledge*

But within the range of objects, which we may know correctly or about which we may be deceived, there is a section wherein both truth and deception can attain a character that is not found anywhere else. This is the inner life of the individual with whom we interact. He may, intentionally either reveal the truth about himself to us, or deceive us by lie and concealment. No other object of knowledge can reveal or hide itself in the same way, because no other object modifies its behavior in view of the fact that it is recognized. This modification, of course, does not occur always; very often, even the other individual is basically no more to us than a piece of nature which poses for our cognition, as it were. Insofar as this cognition goes by utterances made by the other, and particularly by utterances which are not modified by any thought of being utilized for our cognition but which are wholly spontaneous and immediate communications, there becomes apparent an element of fundamental importance for the determination of the individual by his environment. Our psychic process, which runs its course in a purely natural manner, is nevertheless, as far as its content is concerned, almost always, at the same time, in accordance with the norms of logic. This has been declared a problem; and the most far-reaching conclusions have been drawn from it.

§ 5. *The Nature of the Psychic Process and of Communication*

In fact, it is most remarkable that an event engendered exclusively by natural causes should proceed as if governed by the ideal laws of logic. For, it is exactly as if a tree branch, so connected with a telegraphic apparatus that its movements in the wind set the apparatus in motion, thereby caused signs in it that yield a rational meaning to us. The whole of this problem is not at issue here; but one remark must be made. Our actual psychological processes are governed by logic in a much slighter degree than their *expressions* make us believe. If we look closely at our conceptions as they pass our consciousness in a continuous temporal sequence, we find that there is a very great distance between any regulation by rational norms and the characteristics of these conceptions: namely, their flaring up, their zigzag motions, the chaotic whirling of images and ideas which objectively are entirely unrelated to one another, and their logically unjustifiable, only so-to-speak probative, connections. But we are only rarely conscious of this, because the accents of our interests lie merely on the "usable" portion of our imaginative life. Usually we quickly pass over, or "overhear," its leaps, its nonrationality, its chaos, in spite of their psychological factualness, in favor of what is logical or otherwise useful, at least to some extent.

All we communicate to another individual by means of words or perhaps in another fashion—even the most subjective, impulsive, intimate matters—is a selection from that psycholog-ical-real whole whose absolutely exact report (absolutely exact in terms of content and sequence) would drive everybody into the insane asylum—if a paradoxical expression is permissible. In a quantitative sense, it is not only fragments of our inner life which we alone reveal, even to our closest fellowmen. What is more, these fragments are not a representative selection, but one made from the standpoint of reason, value, and relation to the listener and his understanding. Whatever we say, as long as it goes beyond mere interjection and minimal communication, is never an immediate and faithful presentation of what really occurs in us during that particular time of communication, but is a transformation of this inner reality, teleologically directed, reduced, and recomposed. With an instinct automatically pre-venting us from doing otherwise, we show nobody the course of our psychic processes in their purely causal reality and—from the standpoints of logic, objectivity, and meaningfulness—com-plete incoherence and irrationality. Always, we show only a section of them, stylized by selection and arrangement. We sim-ply cannot imagine any interaction or social relation or society which are *not* based on this teleologically determined non-knowledge of one another. This intrinsic, *a priori,* and (as it were) absolute presupposition includes all relative differences which are familiar to us under the concepts of sincere revelations and mendacious concealments.

§ 6. The Lie

Every lie, no matter how objective its topic, engenders by its very nature an error concerning the lying *subject.* The lie consists in the fact that the liar hides his true idea from the other. Its specific nature is not exhaustively characterized by the fact that the person lied-to has a false conception about the topic or object; this the lie shares with common error. What is specific is that he is kept deceived about the private opinion of the *liar.*

Truthfulness and lie are of the most far-reaching significance for relations among men. Sociological structures differ pro-foundly according to the measure of lying which operates in them. In the first place, in very simple circumstances the lie is often more harmless in regard to the maintenance of the group than under more complex conditions. Primitive man who lives in a small group, who satisfies his needs through his own production or through direct cooperation, who limits his intellectual interests to his own experiences or to unilinear tradition, surveys and controls the material of his life more easily and completely than does the man of higher cultures. To be sure, the innumerable errors and superstitions in the life of primitive man are harmful enough to him, but far less so than are corresponding ones in advanced epochs, because the practice of his life is guided in the main by those few facts and circumstances of which his narrow angle of vision permits him to gain directly a *correct* view. In a richer and larger cultural life, however, existence rests on a thousand premises which the single individual cannot trace and verify to their roots at all, but must take on faith. Our modern life is based to a much larger extent than is usually realized upon the faith in the honesty of the other. Examples are our economy, which becomes more and more a credit economy, or our science, in which most scholars must use innumerable results of other scientists which they cannot examine. We base our gravest decisions on a complex system of conceptions, most of which presuppose the confidence that we will not be betrayed. Under modern conditions, the lie, therefore, becomes something much more devastating than it was earlier, something which questions the very foundations of our life. If among ourselves today, the lie were as negligible a sin as it was among the Greek gods, the Jewish patriarchs, or the South Seas islanders; and if we were not deterred from it by the utmost severity of the moral law; then the organization of modern life would be simply impossible; for, modern life is a "credit economy" in a much broader than a strictly economic sense.

These historical differences are paralleled by distances of other dimensions as well. The farther removed individuals are from our most intimate personality, the more easily can we come to terms with their untruthfulness, both in a practical and in an intimate psychological sense—while if the few persons closest to us lie, life becomes unbearable. This is a banality, but it must be noted in a sociological light, because it shows that the measures of truthfulness and mendacity which are compatible with the existence of certain conditions, constitute a scale on which the measures of intensity of these conditions can be read off.

In addition to this relative sociological *permissibility* of the lie under primitive circumstances, there is also its positive *expediency*. Where a first organization, arrangement, centralization of the group is at stake, this organization will take place through the subordination of the weak under the physically and intellectually superior. The lie which maintains itself, which is not seen through, is undoubtedly a means of asserting intellectual superiority and of using it to control and suppress the less intelligent. It is an intellectual club law as brutal, but on occasion as appropriate, as physical club law. It may operate as a selecting factor to breed intelligence or create leisure for the few for whom others must work; for the few who need the leisure for producing higher cultural goods or for giving a leader to the group forces. The more easily these aims can be reached by means whose incidental consequences are only slightly undesirable, the less is there need for lying, and the more is there room for being aware of its ethically objectionable character. Historically this process is by no means completed. Even today, retail trade believes that it cannot do without mendacious claims concerning certain merchandise, and therefore practices them with good conscience. But wholesale business and retail trade on a really large scale, have overcome this stage and can afford to proceed with complete sincerity when offering their goods. Once the business practice of the small and middle-sized merchant reaches the same perfection, the exaggerations and outright falsehoods of advertising and praising, for which it is not usually blamed today, will meet with the same ethical condemnation which already is meted out wherever these falsehoods are no longer required by practice. In general, intra-group interaction based on truthfulness will be the more appropriate, the more the welfare of the many, rather than of the few, constitutes the norm of the group. For, those who are lied-to, that is, those who are harmed by the lie, will always constitute the majority over the liars who find their advantage in lying. For this reason, "enlightenment," which aims at the removal of the untruths operating in social life, is entirely democratic in character.

Human interaction is normally based on the fact that the ideational worlds of men have certain elements in common, that objective intellectual contents constitute the material which is transformed into subjective life by means of men's social relations. The type, as well as the essential instrument, of these common elements is shared language. But, on closer examination, it appears that the basis discussed here, by no means consists only in what both of two interacting individuals know, or with what they are acquainted as the phychological content of one another. For, it must also be noted that all of this is interwoven with elements known to only one of the two. This limitation reveals significances even more basic than those which result from the contrast between the non-logical and contingent reality of the ideational process and the logical and teleological selection we make of it in order to show it to others. Human nature is dualistic: we feel that each of its expressions flows from a plurality of divergent sources; we consider each measure of it as great or small, according to its comparison with something smaller or greater.

This same dualism also causes sociological relationships to be determined in a twofold manner. Concord, harmony, co-efficacy, which are unquestionably held to be socializing forces, must nevertheless be interspersed with distance, competition, repulsion, in order to yield the actual configuration of society. The solid, organizational forms which seem to constitute or create society, must constantly be disturbed, disbalanced, gnawed-at by individualistic, irregular forces, in order to gain their vital reaction and development through submission and resistance. Intimate relations, whose formal medium is physical and psychological nearness, lose the attractiveness, even the content of their intimacy, as soon as the close relationship does not also contain, simultaneously and alternatingly, distances and intermissions. Finally, and this is the decisive point: although reciprocal knowledge conditions relationships positively, after all, it does not do this by itself alone. Relationships being what they are, they also presuppose a certain ignorance and a measure of mutual concealment, even though this measure varies im-

mensely, to be sure. The lie is merely a very crude and, ultimately, often a contradictory form in which this necessity shows
itself. However often a lie may destroy a given relationship, as
long as the relationship existed, the lie was an integral element
of it. The ethically negative value of the lie must not blind us
to its sociologically quite positive significance for the formation
of certain concrete relations. In regard to the elementary sociological fact at issue here—the restriction of the knowledge of the
one about the other—it must be remembered that the lie is only
one among all possible available means. It is the positive and,
as it were, aggressive technique, whose purpose is more often attained by mere secrecy and concealment. These more general
and more negative forms will be discussed in the following pages.

Types of Social Relationships by Degrees of Reciprocal Knowledge of Their Participants

BEFORE COMING TO THE secret in the sense of a consciously desired concealment, one must note the different degrees to which various relationships leave the reciprocal knowledge of the total personalities of their members outside their province.

§ 1. *Interest Groups*

Among the various groups still involving direct interaction, the most important is the association based on some particular interest [*Zweckverband*], more especially that which involves completely objective member contributions, determined by mere membership. The purest form here is monetary contribution. In this case, interaction, solidarity, and the pursuit of common purposes do not depend on everybody's psychological knowledge of everybody else. As a group member, the individual is only the executor of a certain function. Questions concerning those individual motives which determine this performance, or the sort of total personality in which his conduct is imbedded, are completely irrelevant. The association based on some particular interest is the discreet sociological form *par excellence.* Its members are psychologically anonymous. In order to form the association, all they have to know of one another is precisely this fact—that they form it. The increasing objectification of our culture, whose phenomena consist more and more of impersonal elements and less and less absorb the subjective totality of the individual (most simply shown by the contrast between handicraft and factory work), also involves sociological structures. Therefore, groups into which earlier man entered in his totality and individuality and which, for this reason, required reciprocal knowledge far beyond the immediate, objective content of the relationship—these groups are now based exclusively on this objective content, which is neatly factored out of the whole relation.

§ 2. *Confidence under More and Less Complex Conditions*

This development also gives a peculiar evolution to an antecedent or subsequent form of knowledge about a human being, namely, confidence in him. Confidence, evidently, is one of the most important synthetic forces within society. As a hypothesis regarding future behavior, a hypothesis certain enough to serve as a basis for practical conduct, confidence is intermediate between knowledge and ignorance about a man. The person who knows completely need not trust; while the person who knows nothing can, on no rational grounds, afford even confidence.[1] Epochs, fields of interest, and individuals differ, characteristic-

[1] There is, to be sure, also another type of confidence. But since it stands outside the categories of knowledge and ignorance, it touches the present discussion only indirectly. This type is called the *faith* of one man in another. It belongs in the category of religious faith. Just as nobody has ever believed in God on the basis of any "proof of the existence of God," since, on the contrary, these proofs are *post-festum* justifications or intellectual mirrors of a completely immediate, affective attitude, so one "believes" in a particular man without justifying this faith by proofs of his worthiness, and often even in spite of proofs to the contrary. This confidence, this inner unreservedness in regard to another individual, is mediated neither by experiences nor by hypotheses; it is a primary, fundamental attitude toward the other. In an entirely pure form, detached from any empirical consideration, this state of faith probably exists only within religion. In regard to men, it always, presumably, needs some stimulation or confirmation by the knowledge or expectation mentioned above. On the other hand, even in the social forms of confidence, no matter how exactly and intellectually grounded they may appear to be, there may yet be some additional affective, even mystical, "faith" of man in man. Perhaps what has been characterized here is a fundamental category of human conduct, which goes back to the metaphysical sense of our relationships and which is realized in a merely empirical, accidental, fragmentary manner by the conscious and particular reasons for confidence.

ally, by the measures of knowledge and ignorance which must mix in order that the single, practical decision based on confidence arise.

The objectification of culture has decisively differentiated the quanta of knowledge and ignorance necessary for confidence. The modern merchant who enters business with another; the scholar who together with another embarks upon an investigation; the leader of a political party who makes an agreement with the leader of another party concerning matters of election or the treatment of pending bills; all these know (if we overlook exceptions and imperfections) only exactly *that* and no more about their partner which they *have* to know for the sake of the relationship they wish to enter. The traditions and institutions, the power of public opinion and the definition of the position which inescapably stamps the individual, have become so solid and reliable that one has to know only certain external facts about the other person in order to have the confidence required for the common action. The question is no longer some foundation of personal qualities on which (at least in principle) a modification of behavior within the relation might be based: motivation and regulation of this behavior have become so objectified that confidence no longer needs any properly personal knowledge. Under more primitive, less differentiated conditions, the individual knows much more about his partner in regard to personal matters, and much less in regard to his purely objective competence. The two belong together: in order to produce the necessary confidence despite a lack of knowledge in objective matters, a much higher degree of knowledge in personal matters is necessary.

The purely general knowledge, which extends only to the objective elements of the person and leaves its secret—the personal-individual area—untouched, must be supplemented considerably by the knowledge of this very area, whenever the interest group is of essential significance to the total existence of its members. The merchant who sells grain or oil needs to know only whether his correspondent is good for the price. But if he takes him as his associate, he must not only know his financial standing and certain of his very general qualities, but he must have thorough insight into him as a personality; he must know whether he is decent, compatible, and whether he has a daring or hesitant temperament. Upon such reciprocal knowledge rest not only the beginning of the relationship, but also its whole development, the daily common actions, and the division of functions between the partners. Today the secret of the personality is sociologically more limited. In view of the large extent to which the interest in the common pursuit is borne by personal qualities, the personal element can no longer be so autonomous.

§ 3. *"Acquaintance"*

Aside from interest groups but aside, equally, from relationships rooted in the total personality, there is the sociologically highly peculiar relation which, in our times, among educated strata, is designated simply as "acquaintance." Mutual "acquaintance" by no means is *knowledge* of one another; it involves no actual insight into the individual nature of the personality. It only means that one has taken notice of the other's existence, as it were. It is characteristic that the idea of acquaintance is suggested by the mere mentioning of one's name, by "introducing oneself": "acquaintance" depends upon the knowledge of the *that* of the personality, not of its *what*. After all, by saying that one is acquainted, even well acquainted, with a particular person, one characterizes quite clearly the lack of really intimate relations. Under the rubric of acquaintance, one knows of the other only what he is toward the outside, either in the purely social-representative sense, or in the sense of that which he shows us. The degree of knowledge covered by "being well acquainted with one another," refers not to the other *per se;* not to what is essential in him, intrinsically, but only to what is significant for that aspect of him which is turned toward others and the world.

§ 4. *Discretion*

Acquaintance in this social sense is, therefore, the proper seat of "discretion." For, discretion consists by no means only in the respect for the secret of the other, for his specific will to conceal this or that from us, but in staying away from the knowledge of all that the other does not expressly reveal to us. It does not refer to anything particular which we are not permitted to know, but to a quite general reserve in regard to the total personality. Discretion is a special form of the typical contrast between the imperatives, "what is not prohibited is allowed," and "what is not allowed is prohibited." Relations among men are thus distinguished according to the question of mutual knowledge—of either "what is not concealed may be known," or "what is not revealed must not be known."

To act upon the second of these decisions corresponds to the feeling (which also operates elsewhere) that an ideal sphere lies around every human being. Although differing in size in various directions and differing according to the person with whom one entertains relations, this sphere cannot be penetrated, unless the personality value of the individual is thereby destroyed. A sphere of this sort is placed around man by his "honor." Language very poignantly designates an insult to one's honor as "coming too close": the radius of this sphere marks, as it were, the distance whose trespassing by another person insults one's honor.

Another sphere of the same form corresponds to what is called the "significance" of a personality. In regard to the "significant" ["great"] man, there is an inner compulsion which tells one to keep at a distance and which does not disappear even in intimate relations with him. The only type for whom such distance does not exist is the individual who has no organ for perceiving significance. For this reason, the "valet" knows no such sphere of distance; for him there is no "hero"; but this is due, not to the *hero,* but to the valet. For the same reason, all importunity is associated with a striking lack of feeling for differences in the significance of men. The individual who fails to keep his distance from a great person does not esteem him highly, much less too highly (as might superficially appear to be the case) ; but, on the contrary, his importune behavior reveals lack of proper respect. The painter often emphasizes the significance of a figure in a picture that contains many figures by arranging the others in a considerable distance from it. In an analogous fashion, the sociological simile of significance is the distance which keeps the individual outside a certain sphere that is occupied by the power, will, and greatness of a person.

The same sort of circle which surrounds man—although it is value-accentuated in a very different sense—is filled out by his affairs and by his characteristics. To penetrate this circle by taking notice, constitutes a violation of his personality. Just as material property is, so to speak, an extension of the ego,[2] and any interference with our property is, for this reason, felt to be a violation of the person, there also is an intellectual private-property, whose violation effects a lesion of the ego in its very center. Discretion is nothing but the feeling that there exists a right in regard to the sphere of the immediate life contents. Discretion, of course, differs in its extension with different personalities, just as the positions of honor and of property have different radii with respect to "close" individuals, and to strangers and indifferent persons. In the case of the above-mentioned, more properly "social" relations, which are most conveniently designated as "acquaintances," the point to which discretion extends is, above all, a very typical boundary: beyond it, perhaps there *are* not even any jealously guarded secrets; but conventionally and discreetly, the other individual, nevertheless, does not trespass it by questions or other invasions.

The question where this boundary lies cannot be answered in terms of a simple principle; it leads into the finest ramifications of societal formation. For, in an absolute sense, the right to intellectual private-property can be affirmed as little as can the right to material property. We know that, in higher civilizations, material private-property in its essential three dimensions —acquisition, insurance, increase—is never based on the individual's own forces alone. It always requires the conditions and forces of the social milieu. From the beginning, therefore, it is limited by the right of the whole, whether through taxation or through certain checks on acquisition. But this right is grounded more deeply than just in the principle of service and counter-service between society and individual: it is grounded in the much more elementary principle, that the part must sustain as great a restriction upon its autonomous existence and posses-

---

2 Property is that which obeys the will of the owner, as, for instance (with a difference of degree only), our body which is our first "property."

siveness as the maintenance and the purposes of the whole require.

This also applies to the inner sphere of man. In the interest of interaction and social cohesion, the individual *must* know certain things about the other person. Nor does the other have the right to oppose this knowledge from a moral standpoint, by demanding the discretion of the first: he cannot claim the entirely undisturbed possession of his own being and consciousness, since this discretion might harm the interests of his society. The businessman who contracts long-range obligations with another; the master who employs a servant (but also the servant before entering the service); the superior who advances a subordinate; the housewife who accepts a new member into her social circle: all these must have the right to learn or infer those aspects of the other's past and present, temperament, and moral quality on the basis of which they can act rationally in regard to him, or reject him. These are very crude instances of the case where the duty of discretion—to renounce the knowledge of all that the other does not voluntarily show us—recedes before practical requirements. But even in subtler and less unambiguous forms, in fragmentary beginnings and unexpressed notions, all of human intercourse rests on the fact that everybody knows somewhat more about the other than the other voluntarily reveals to him; and those things he knows are frequently matters whose knowledge the other person (were he aware of it) would find undesirable.

All this may be considered indiscretion in the individual sense: in the social sense, it is a condition necessary for the concrete density and vitality of interaction. Nevertheless, it is extremely difficult to trace the legal limit of this trespass into intellectual private-property. In general, man arrogates to himself the right to know all he can find out through mere observation and reflection, without applying externally illegitimate means. As a matter of fact, however, indiscretion practiced in this fashion can be just as violent and morally inadmissible as listening behind closed doors and leering at a stranger's letters. To the man with the psychologically fine ear, people innumerable times betray their most secret thoughts and qualities, not only *although,* but often *because,* they anxiously try to guard them. The avid, spying grasp of every inconsiderate word, the boring reflection on what this or that tone of voice might mean, how such and such utterances might be combined, what blushing on mentioning a certain name might betray—none of this transcends the limits of external discretion; it is entirely the work of one's own intellect and, for this reason, one's apparently indisputable right. And all the more so, since such an abuse of psychological superiority often occurs quite involuntarily: often we simply cannot check our interpretation of the other, our construction of his inner nature. No matter how much every decent person tells himself that he must not muse on what the other hides, that he must not exploit the slips and helplessnesses of the other; knowledge, nevertheless, occurs often so automatically, and its result confronts us with such striking suddenness, that mere good will has no power over it. Where the doubtlessly impermissible can yet be so inevitable, the boundary between what is allowed and what is not, is all the more blurred. How far discretion must refrain from touching even intellectually "all that is his"; how far, on the other hand, the interests of interaction and the interdependence of the members of society limit this duty—this is a question for whose answer neither moral tact nor knowledge of objective conditions and their requirements alone is sufficient, since *both* are needed. The subtlety and complexity of this question relegate it to the individual decision which cannot be prejudged by any general norm—to a much higher degree than does the question of private property in the material sense.

§ 5. *Friendship and Love*

In this pre-form or complementation of the secret, the point is not the behavior of the individual who keeps a secret, but the behavior of another individual: within the mixture of reciprocal knowledge or ignorance, the accent is more on the degree of knowledge than of ignorance. We now come to a totally different configuration. It is found in those relationships which, in contrast to the ones discussed, do not center around clearly circumscribed interests that must be fixed objectively, if only because of their "superficiality." Instead, they are built, at least in their idea, upon the person in its totality. The principal types here are friendship and marriage.

To the extent that the ideal of friendship was received from antiquity and (peculiarly enough) was developed in a romantic spirit, it aims at an absolute psychological intimacy, and is accompanied by the notion that even material property should be common to friends. This entering of the whole undivided ego into the relationship may be more plausible in friendship than in love for the reason that friendship lacks the specific concentration upon one element which love derives from its sensuousness. To be sure, by virtue of the fact that *one* among the total range of possible reasons for a relation takes the lead, these reasons attain a certain organization, as a group does through leadership. A particularly strong relational factor often blazes the trail on which the rest follow it, when they would otherwise remain latent; and undoubtedly, for most people, sexual love opens the doors of the total personality more widely than does anything else. For not a few, in fact, love is the only form in which they can give their ego in its totality, just as to the artist the form of his art offers the only possibility for revealing his whole inner life. Probably, this observation can be made especially often of women (although the very differently understood "Christian love" is also designed to achieve the same result). Not only because they love do women unreservedly offer the total remainder of their being and having; but all of this, so to speak, is chemically dissolved in love, and overflows to the other being exclusively and entirely in the color, form, and temperament of love. Yet, where the feeling of love is not sufficiently expansive, and the remaining psychological contents of the relationship are not sufficiently malleable, the preponderance of the erotic bond may suppress, as I have already suggested, the other contacts (practical-moral, intellectual), as well as the opening-up of those reservoirs of the personality that lie outside the erotic sphere.

Friendship lacks this vehemence, but also the frequent unevenness, of this abandon. It may be, therefore, more apt than love to connect a whole person with another person in its entirety; it may melt reserves more easily than love does—if not as stormily, yet on a larger scale and in a more enduring sequence. Yet such complete intimacy becomes probably more and more difficult as differentiation among men increases. Modern man, possibly, has too much to hide to sustain a friendship in the ancient sense. Besides, except for their earliest years, personalities are perhaps too uniquely individualized to allow full reciprocity of understanding and receptivity, which always, after all, requires much creative imagination and much divination which is oriented only toward the other. It would seem that, for all these reasons, the modern way of feeling tends more heavily toward differentiated friendships, which cover only one side of the personality, without playing into other aspects of it.

Thus a very special type of friendship emerges, which is of the greatest significance for our problem (the degrees of invasion and reserve within the friendship relation). These differentiated friendships which connect us with one individual in terms of affection, with another, in terms of common intellectual aspects, with a third, in terms of religious impulses, and with a fourth, in terms of common experiences—all these friendships present a very peculiar synthesis in regard to the question of discretion, of reciprocal revelation and concealment. They require that the friends do not look into those mutual spheres of interest and feeling which, after all, are not included in the relation and which, if touched upon, would make them feel painfully the limits of their mutual understanding. But the relation which is thus restricted and surrounded by discretions, may yet stem from the center of the total personality. It may yet be reached by the sap of the ultimate roots of the personality, even though it feeds only part of the person's periphery. In its idea, it involves the same affective depth and the same readiness for sacrifice, which less differentiated epochs and persons connect only with a common *total* sphere of life, for which reservations and discretions constitute no problem.

§ 6. *Marriage*

The measures of self-revelation and self-restraint, with their complements of trespass and discretion, are much more difficult to determine in the case of marriage. Their ratio here belongs in a very general problem area of extreme importance to the sociology of intimate relations. This problem area centers around the question whether the maximum of common values can be attained under the condition that the personalities reciprocally relinquish their autonomies altogether, or under the condition of reserve: the question whether, perhaps, they do not belong *more* to one another qualitatively if, quantitatively, they do so less. This question can be answered, of course, only along with the other question as to how, within the total communicability of man, one can draw the line where restraint and respect of the other begin. The advantage of modern marriage— which, certainly, can answer both questions only from case to case—is that this line is not fixed from the beginning, as it is in other and earlier civilizations. In earlier cultures particularly, marriage is not an erotic but, in principle, only a social and economic institution. The satisfaction of the desire for love is only accidentally connected with it; it is contracted (with exceptions, of course), not only on the basis of individual attraction, but on the ground of family connections, working conditions, and descendants. In this respect, the Greeks achieved a particularly clear differentiation—according to Demosthenes: "We have hetaerae for pleasure; concubines for our daily needs; and wives to give us legitimate children and take care of the interior of the house." In such a mechanical relationship, the psychic center is obviously put out of function. Nevertheless (incidentally), this kind of marriage is constantly illustrated, though with certain modifications, by history and by the observation of actual contemporary marriages. There probably exists in it neither the need for any intimate, reciprocal self-revelation, nor the possibility of it. On the other hand, there is probably an absence of certain reserves of delicacy and chastity which, in spite of their seemingly negative character, are yet the flower of a fully internalized and personal, intimate relation.

The same tendency to exclude, *a priori* and by superindividual decree, certain life-contents from the common features of marriage lies in the variety of marriage forms which may coexist among the same people. Prior to entering marriage, the prospective spouses must choose among these forms, which variously distinguish economic, religious, and domestic-legal interests in their bearing upon matrimony. We find this among many nature peoples, as well as among the Hindus and Romans. Nobody will deny, of course, that even in modern life, marriage is probably contracted overwhelmingly from conventional or material motives. Yet no matter how often it is actualized, the sociological *idea* of modern marriage is the commonness of *all* life-contents, insofar as they determine the value and fate of the personality, immediately or through their effects. Nor is the nature of this ideal requirement without results: often enough it allows, or even stimulates, an initially quite imperfect union to develop into an ever more comprehensive one. But, whereas the very interminability of this process is the instrument of the happiness and inner vitality of the relationship, its reversal usually entails grave disappointments—namely, when absolute unity is anticipated from the beginning, when neither demand nor revelation knows restraint, not even the restraint which, for all finer and deeper natures, remains locked in the obscurity of the soul even where it seems to pour itself out before the other entirely.

During the first stages of the relationship there is a great temptation, both in marriage and in marriage-like free love, to let oneself be completely absorbed by the other, to send the last reserves of the soul after those of the body, to lose oneself to the other without reservation. Yet, in most cases, this abandon probably threatens the future of the relationship seriously. Only those individuals can give themselves *wholly* without danger who *cannot* wholly give themselves, because their wealth consists in a continuous development in which every abandon is at once followed by new treasures. Such individuals have an inexhaustible reservoir of latent psychological possessions, and hence can no more reveal and give them away at one stroke than a tree can give away next year's fruits with those of the season. But other individuals are different. With every flight of feeling, with every unconditional abandonment, with every revelation of their inner life, they make inroads (as it were) into their capital, because they lack the mainspring of ever renewed psychic affluence which can neither be exhaustively revealed nor be separated from the ego. In these cases, the spouses have a good chance of coming to face one another with empty hands; and the Dionysian bliss of giving may leave behind it an impoverishment which, unjustly, but no less bitterly for that, belies in restrospect even past abandons and their happiness.

We are, after all, made in such a way that we need not only a certain proportion of truth and error as the basis of our lives (as was pointed out earlier), but also a certain proportion of distinctness and indistinctness in the image of our life-elements. The other individual must give us not only gifts we may accept, but the possibility of our giving *him*—hopes, idealizations, hidden beauties, attractions of which not even *he* is conscious. But the place where we deposit all this, which *we* produce, but produce for *him,* is the indistinct horizon of his personality, the interstitial realm, in which faith replaces knowledge. But it must be strongly emphasized that this is, by no means, only a matter of illusions and optimistic or amorous self-deceptions, but that portions even of the persons closest to us must be offered us in the form of indistinctness and unclarity, in order for their attractiveness to keep on the same high level.

It is in this way that the majority of people replace the attraction values, which the minority possess in the inexhaustibility of their inner life and growth. The mere fact of absolute knowledge, of a psychological having-exhausted, sobers us up, even without prior drunkenness; it paralyzes the vitality of relations and lets their continuation really appear pointless. This is the danger of complete and (in more than an external sense) shameless abandon, to which the unlimited possibilities of intimate relations tempt us. These possibilities, in fact, are easily felt as a kind of duty—particularly where there exists no absolute certainty of one's own feeling; and the fear of not giving the other enough leads to giving him too much. It is highly probable that many marriages founder on this lack of reciprocal discretion—discretion both in taking and in giving. They lapse into a trivial habituation without charm, into a matter-of-factness which has no longer any room for surprises. The fertile depth of relations suspects and honors something even more ultimate behind every ultimateness revealed; it daily challenges us to reconquer even secure possessions. But this depth is only the reward for that tenderness and self-discipline which, even in the most intimate relation that comprises the total individual, respects his inner private property, and allows the right to question to be limited by the right to secrecy.

Chapter 3

Secrecy

THE SOCIOLOGICAL CHAR-
acteristic of all these combinations is that the secret of a given
individual is acknowledged by another; that what is intentionally or unintentionally hidden is intentionally or unintentionally respected. The intention of hiding, however, takes on
a much greater intensity when it clashes with the intention of
revealing. In this situation emerges that purposive hiding and
masking, that aggressive defensive, so to speak, against the third
person, which alone is usually designated as secret.

§ 1. *The Role of the Secret in Social Life*

The secret in this sense, the hiding of realities by negative
or positive means, is one of man's greatest achievements. In
comparison with the childish stage in which every conception
is expressed at once, and every undertaking is accessible to the
eyes of all, the secret produces an immense enlargement of life:
numerous contents of life cannot even emerge in the presence of
full publicity. The secret offers, so to speak, the possibility of a
second world alongside the manifest world; and the latter is
decisively influenced by the former.

Whether there is secrecy between two individuals or groups,
and if so how much, is a question that characterizes every relation between them. For even where one of the two does not
notice the existence of a secret, the behavior of the concealer, and
hence the whole relationship, is certainly modified by it.[3] The

---

[3] In some cases, this hiding has a sociological consequence of a peculiar ethical
paradoxicalness. For however destructive it often is for a relation between two
if one of them has committed a fault against the other of which both are conscious,
it can, on the contrary, be very useful for the relation if the guilty one alone knows
of the fault. For, this causes in him a considerateness, a delicacy, a secret wish to
make up for it, a yieldingness and selflessness, none of which would ever occur
to him had he a completely untroubled conscience.

historical development of society is in many respects characterized by the fact that what at an earlier time was manifest, enters the protection of secrecy; and that, conversely, what once was secret, no longer needs such protection but reveals itself. This is comparable to that other evolution of the mind by which what originally was done consciously, sinks to the level of consciously mechanical *routine,* and, on the other hand, what at an earlier stage was unconscious and instinctive, rises to the clarity of consciousness. How this is distributed among the various formations of private and public life; how this evolution leads to ever more purposeful conditions inasmuch as, at the beginning, the range of secrecy is often extended much too far, in clumsy and undifferentiated fashion, and, on the other hand, the utility of secrecy is recognized only late with respect to many other items; how the quantum of secrecy is modified in its consequences by the importance or irrelevance of its contents—all this, even as mere question, illuminates the significance of the secret for the structure of human interaction.

This significance must not be overlooked in view of the fact that the secret is often ethically negative; for, the secret is a general sociological form which stands in neutrality above the value functions of its contents. It may absorb the highest values —as, for instance, in the case of the noble individual whose subtle shame makes him conceal his best in order not to have it remunerated by eulogy and other rewards; for, otherwise, he would possess the remuneration, as it were, but no longer the value itself. On the other hand, although the secret has no immediate connection with evil, evil has an immediate connection with secrecy: the immoral hides itself for obvious reasons even where its content meets with no social stigma as, for instance, in the case of certain sexual delinquencies. The intrinsically isolating effect of immorality as such, irrespective of all direct social repulsion, is real and important beyond the many alleged entanglements of an ethical and social kind. Among other things, the secret is also the sociological expression of moral badness, although the facts contradict the classical phrase that nobody is bad enough to want, in addition, to *appear* bad. For often enough, spite and cynicism do not even let it come to a concealment of badness; in fact, they may exploit badness in order to enhance the personality in the eyes of others—to the point where an individual sometimes brags about immoralities he has not even committed.

§ 2. *The Fascination of Secrecy*

The employment of secrecy as a sociological technique, as a form of action without which certain purposes—since we live in a social environment—can simply not be attained, is understandable immediately. Not quite so evident are the attractions and values of the secret beyond its significance as a mere means—the peculiar attraction of formally secretive behavior irrespective of its momentary content. In the first place, the strongly emphasized exclusion of all outsiders makes for a correspondingly strong feeling of possession. For many individuals, property does not fully gain its significance with mere ownership, but only with the consciousness that others must do without it. The basis for this, evidently, is the impressionability of our feelings through *differences*. Moreover, since the others are excluded from the possession—particularly when it is very valuable—the converse suggests itself psychologically, namely, that what is denied to many must have special value.

Inner property of the most heterogeneous kinds, thus, attains a characteristic value accent through the form of secrecy, in which the contentual significance of what is concealed recedes, often enough, before the simple fact that others know nothing about it. Among children, pride and bragging are often based on a child's being able to say to the other: "I know something that you don't know"—and to such a degree, that this sentence is uttered as a formal means of boasting and of subordinating the others, even where it is made up and actually refers to no secret. This jealousy of the knowledge about facts hidden to others, is shown in all contexts, from the smallest to the largest. British parliamentary discussions were secret for a long time; and, as late as under George III, press communications about them were prosecuted as criminal offenses—explicitly, as violations of parliamentary *privileges*. The secret gives one a position of exception; it operates as a purely socially determined attraction. It is basically independent of the content it guards but, of course, is increasingly effective in the measure in which the exclusive possession is vast and significant.

For this, a converse notion, analogous to the one mentioned above, is also responsible in part. For the average man, all superior persons and all superior achievements have something mysterious. All human being and doing, to be sure, flows from enigmatic forces. Yet among individuals of the same quality and value level, this does not yet make one a problem in the eyes of the other, particularly because the equality produces a certain direct understanding, not mediated by the intellect. Essential inequality, on the contrary, produces no such understanding, and any *particular* difference makes the *general* enigmatic character come to the fore at once. (This is similar to one's always living in the same landscape and thus never suspecting the problem of influence by scenery—a problem which impresses us, however, as soon as we change our surroundings, and a different life-feeling calls our attention to the causative role of the scenic milieu generally.) From secrecy, which shades all that is profound and significant, grows the typical error according to which everything mysterious is something important and essential. Before the unknown, man's natural impulse to idealize and his natural fearfulness cooperate toward the same goal: to intensify the unknown through imagination, and to pay attention to it with an emphasis that is not usually accorded to patent reality.

§ 3. *The Fascination of Betrayal*

Peculiarly enough, these attractions of secrecy are related to those of its logical opposite, betrayal—which, evidently, are no less sociological. The secret contains a tension that is dissolved in the moment of its revelation. This moment constitutes the acme in the development of the secret; all of its charms are once more gathered in it and brought to a climax—just as the moment of dissipation lets one enjoy with extreme intensity the value of the object: the feeling of power which accompanies the possession of money becomes concentrated for the dissipator, most completely and sensuously, in the very instant in which he lets this power out of his hands. The secret, too, is full of the consciousness that it *can* be betrayed; that one holds the power of surprises, turns of fate, joy, destruction—if only, perhaps, of self-destruction. For this reason, the secret is surrounded by the possibility and temptation of betrayal; and the external danger of being discovered is interwoven with the internal danger, which is like the fascination of an abyss, of giving oneself away. The secret puts a barrier between men but, at the same time, it creates the tempting challenge to break through it, by gossip or confession—and this challenge accompanies its psychology like a constant overtone. The sociological significance of the secret, therefore, has its practical extent, its mode of realization, only in the individual's capacity or inclination to keep it to himself, in his resistance or weakness in the face of tempting betrayal. Out of the counterplay of these two interests, in concealing and revealing, spring nuances and fates of human interaction that permeate it in its entirety. In the light of our earlier stipulation, every human relation is characterized, among other things, by the amount of secrecy that is in and around it. In this respect, therefore, the further development of every relation is determined by the ratio of persevering and yielding energies which are contained in the relation. The former rest on the practical interest in secrecy and its formal attraction. The latter are based on the impossibility of bearing the tension entailed by keeping a secret any longer, and on a feeling of superiority. Although this superiority lies in a latent form, so to speak, in secrecy itself, for our feelings it is fully actualized only at the moment of revelation or often, also, in the lust of confession, which may contain this feeling of power in the negative and perverted form of self-humiliation and contrition.

§ 4. *Secrecy and Individualization*

All these elements which determine the sociological role of the secret are of an individual nature; but the measure in which the dispositions and complications of personalities form secrets depends, at the same time, on the social structure in which their lives are placed. The decisive point in this respect is that the secret is a first-rate element of individualization. It is this in a typical dual role: social conditions of strong personal differentiation permit and require secrecy in a high degree; and, conversely, the secret embodies and intensifies such differentiation. In a small and narrow circle, the formation and preservation of secrets is made difficult even on technical grounds: everybody is too close to everybody else and his circumstances, and frequency and intimacy of contact involve too many temptations of revelation. But further, the secret is not even particularly needed, because this type of social formation usually levels its members, and the peculiarities of existence, activities, and possessions whose conservation requires the form of secrecy, militate against this social form and its leveling.

With the enlargement of the group, evidently, all this changes into its opposite. Here, as elsewhere, the specific traits of the *large* group are most clearly revealed by the conditions of a money economy. Ever since traffic in economic values has been carried on by means of money alone, an otherwise unattainable secrecy has become possible. Three characteristics of the monetary form of value are relevant here: its compressibility, which permits one to make somebody rich by slipping a check into his hand without anybody's noticing it; its abstractness and qualitylessness, through which transactions, acquisitions, and changes in ownership can be rendered hidden and unrecognizable in a way impossible where values are owned only in the form of extensive, unambiguously tangible objects; and finally, its effect-at-a-distance, which allows its investment in very remote and ever-changing values, and thus its complete withdrawal from the eyes of the immediate environment. These possibilities of dissimulation develop in the measure in which the money economy expands, and they are bound to show their dangers in economic action involving foreign moneys. They have led to a protective measure, namely, the public character of financial manipulations by joint-stock companies and governments.

This suggests a somewhat more exact phrasing of the evolutionary formula touched upon above. According to it, it will be recalled, the secret is a form which constantly receives and releases contents: what originally was manifest becomes secret, and what once was hidden later sheds its concealment. One could, therefore, entertain the paradoxical idea that under otherwise identical circumstances, human collective life requires a certain measure of secrecy which merely changes its topics: while leaving one of them, social life seizes upon another, and in all this alternation it preserves an unchanged quantity of secrecy.

But one can find a somewhat more precisely determined content for this general scheme. It seems as if, with growing cultural expediency, general affairs became ever more public, and individual affairs ever more secret. In less developed stages, as has already been noted, the individual and his conditions cannot, to the same extent, protect themselves against being looked into and meddled with as under the modern style of life, which has produced an entirely new measure of reserve and discretion, especially in large cities. In earlier times, functionaries of the public interests were customarily clothed with mystical authority, while, under larger and more mature conditions, they attain, through the extension of their sphere of domination, through the objectivity of their technique, and through their distance from every individual, a certainty and dignity by means of which they can permit their activities to be public. The former secrecy of public affairs, however, showed its inner inconsistency by at once creating the countermovements of betrayal, on the one hand, and of espionage, on the other. Even as late as in the seventeenth and eighteenth centuries, governments kept anxiously silent about the amounts of state debts, the tax situation, and the size of the army. Ambassadors, therefore, often knew no better than to spy, to intercept letters, and to make people who "knew something" talk, domestics not excluded.[4] In the nineteenth century, however, publicity invaded the affairs of state to such an extent that, by now, governments officially publish facts without whose secrecy, prior to the nineteenth century, no regime seemed even possible. Politics, administration, and jurisdiction thus have lost their secrecy and inaccessibility in the same measure in which the individual has gained the possibility of ever more complete withdrawal, and in the same measure in which modern life has

[4] This countermovement also occurs in the opposite direction. It has been said about English court history that the real court cabal, the secret whisperings, the organizations of intrigue, did not occur under despotism, but only once the king had constitutional counselors, that is, when the government was, to this extent, an openly revealed system. Only then, the king began—and this is supposed to have been noticeable particularly since Edward II—to form, against these co-rulers who somehow were foisted upon him, an inofficial quasi-subterranean circle of advisers, which in itself, as well as through the efforts to enter it, created a chain of concealments and conspiracies.

developed, in the midst of metropolitan crowdedness, a technique for making and keeping private matters secret, such as earlier could be attained only by means of spatial isolation.

The answer to the question of how far this development may be considered expedient depends on social value axioms. Every democracy holds publicity to be an intrinsically desirable situation, on the fundamental premise that everybody should know the events and circumstances that concern him, since this is the condition without which he cannot contribute to decisions about them; and every shared knowledge itself contains the psychological challenge to shared action. It is a moot question whether this conclusion is quite valid. If, above all individualistic interests, there has grown an objective governing structure which embodies certain aspects of these interests, the formal autonomy of this structure may very well entitle it to function secretly, without thereby belying its "publicity" in the sense of a material consideration of the interests of all. Thus, there is no *logical* connection which would entail the greater *value* of publicity. On the other hand, the general scheme of cultural differentiation is again shown here: what is public becomes ever more public, and what is private becomes ever more private. And this historical development is the expression of a deeper, objective significance: what is essentially public and what, in its content, concerns all, also becomes ever more public externally, in its sociological form; and what, in its inner meaning, is autonomous—the centripetal affairs of the individual—gains an ever more private character even in its sociological position, an ever more distinct possibility of remaining secret.

I pointed out earlier that the secret also operates as an adorning possession and value of the personality. This fact involves the contradiction that what recedes before the consciousness of the others and is hidden from them, is to be emphasized in their consciousness; that one should appear as a particularly noteworthy person precisely through what one conceals. But this contradiction proves, not only that the need for sociological attention may indeed resort to intrinsically contradictory means, but also that those *against* whom the means are actually directed in the given case, satisfy this need by bearing the cost of the superiority. They do so with a mixture of readiness and dislike;

but, in practice, they nevertheless supply the desired recognition. It may thus be appropriate to show that, although apparently the sociological counter-pole of secrecy, adornment has, in fact, a societal significance with a structure analogous to that of secrecy itself. It is the nature and function of adornment to lead the eyes of others upon the adorned. Although, in this sense, it is the antagonist of secrecy, not even the secret (it will be remembered) is without the function of personal emphasis. And this, adornment, too, exercises, by mixing superiority to others with dependence upon them, and their good will with their envy. It does so in a manner which, as a sociological form of interaction, requires its special investigation.

§ 5. *Adornment* [5]

Man's desire to please his social environment contains two contradictory tendencies, in whose play and counterplay in general, the relations among individuals take their course. On the one hand, it contains kindness, a desire of the individual to give the other joy; but on the other hand, there is the wish for this joy and these "favors" to flow back to him, in the form of recognition and esteem, so that they be attributed to his personality as values. Indeed, this second need is so intensified that it militates against the altruism of wishing to please: by means of this pleasing, the individual desires to *distinguish* himself before others, and to be the object of an attention that others do not receive. This may even lead him to the point of wanting to be envied. Pleasing may thus become a means of the will to power: some individuals exhibit the strange contradiction that they need those above whom they elevate themselves by life and deed, for they build their own self-feeling upon the subordinates' realization that they *are* subordinate.

The meaning of adornment finds expression in peculiar elaborations of these motives, in which the external and internal aspects of their forms are interwoven. This meaning is to single the personality out, to emphasize it as outstanding in some sense

[5] In the original, this section, printed in smaller type, is called *"Exkurs über den Schmuck"* (Note on Adornment).—According to the context, *"Schmuck"* is translated as "adornment," "jewels," or "jewelry."—Tr.

—but not by means of power manifestations, not by anything that externally compels the other, but only through the pleasure which is engendered in him and which, therefore, still has some voluntary element in it. One adorns oneself for oneself, but can do so only by adornment for others. It is one of the strangest sociological combinations that an act, which exclusively serves the emphasis and increased significance of the actor, nevertheless attains this goal just as exclusively in the pleasure, in the visual delight it offers to others, and in their gratitude. For, even the envy of adornment only indicates the desire of the envious person to win like recognition and admiration for himself; his envy proves how much he believes these values to be connected with the adornment. Adornment is the egoistic element as such: it singles out its wearer, whose self-feeling it embodies and increases at the cost of others (for, the same adornment of all would no longer adorn the individual). But, at the same time, adornment is altruistic: its pleasure is designed for the others, since its owner can enjoy it only insofar as he mirrors himself in them; he renders the adornment valuable only through the reflection of this gift of his. Everywhere, aesthetic formation reveals that life orientations, which reality juxtaposes as mutually alien, or even pits against one another as hostile, are, in fact, intimately interrelated. In the same way, the aesthetic phenomenon of adornment indicates a point within sociological interaction—the arena of man's being-for-himself and being-for-the-other—where these two opposite directions are mutually dependent as ends and means.

Adornment intensifies or enlarges the impression of the personality by operating as a sort of radiation emanating from it. For this reason, its materials have always been shining metals and precious stones. They are "adornment" in a narrower sense than dress and coiffure, although these, too, "adorn." One may speak of human radioactivity in the sense that every individual is surrounded by a larger or smaller sphere of significance radiating from him; and everybody else, who deals with him, is immersed in this sphere. It is an inextricable mixture of physiological and psychic elements: the sensuously observable influences which issue from an individual in the direction of his environment also are, in some fashion, the vehicles of a spiritual fulguration. They operate as the symbols of such a fulguration even where, in actuality, they are only external, where no suggestive power or significance of the personality flows through them. The radiations of adornment, the sensuous attention it provokes, supply the personality with such an enlargement or intensification of its sphere: the personality, so to speak, *is* more when it is adorned.

Inasmuch as adornment usually is also an object of considerable value, it is a synthesis of the individual's having and being; it thus transforms mere possession into the sensuous and emphatic perceivability of the individual himself. This is not true of ordinary dress which, neither in respect of having nor of being, strikes one as an individual particularity; only the fancy dress, and above all, jewels, which gather the personality's value and significance of radiation as if in a focal point, allow the mere *having* of the person to become a visible quality of its *being*. And this is so, not *although* adornment is something "superfluous," but precisely *because* it is. The necessary is much more closely connected with the individual; it surrounds his existence with a narrower periphery. The superfluous "flows over," that is, it flows to points which are far removed from its origin but to which it still remains tied: around the precinct of mere necessity, it lays a vaster precinct which, in principle, is limitless. According to its very idea, the superfluous contains no measure. The free and princely character of our being increases in the measure in which we add superfluousness to our having, since no extant structure, such as is laid down by necessity, imposes any limiting norm upon it.

This very accentuation of the personality, however, is achieved by means of an impersonal trait. Everything that "adorns" man can be ordered along a scale in terms of its closeness to the physical body. The "closest" adornment is typical of nature peoples: tattooing. The opposite extreme is represented by metal and stone adornments, which are entirely unindividual and can be put on by everybody. Between these two stands dress, which is not so inexchangeable and personal as tattooing, but neither so un-individual and separable as jewelry, whose very elegance lies in its impersonality. That this nature of stone and metal—solidly closed within itself, in no way alluding to any individuality; hard, unmodifiable—is yet forced to serve the person, this is its subtlest fascination. What is really elegant avoids pointing to the specifically individual; it always lays a more general, stylized, almost abstract sphere around man —which, of course, prevents no finesse from connecting the general with the personality. That new clothes are particularly elegant is due to their being still "stiff"; they have not yet adjusted to the modifications of the individual body as fully as older clothes have, which have been worn, and are pulled and pinched by the peculiar movements of their wearer—thus completely revealing his particularity. This "newness," this lack of modification by individuality, is typical in the highest measure of metal jewelry: it is always new; in untouchable coolness, it stands above the singularity and destiny of its wearer. This is not true of dress. A long-worn piece of clothing almost grows to the body; it has an intimacy that militates against the very nature of elegance, which is something for the "others," a social notion deriving its value from general respect.

If jewelry thus is designed to enlarge the individual by adding something super-individual which goes out to all and is noted and appreciated by all, it must, beyond any effect that its material itself may have, possess *style*. Style is always something general. It brings the contents of personal life and activity into a form shared by many and accessible to many. In the case of a work of art, we are the less interested in its style, the greater the personal uniqueness and the subjective life expressed in it. For, it is with these that it appeals to the spectator's personal core, too—of the spectator who, so to speak, is alone in the whole world with this work of art. But of what we call handicraft— which because of its utilitarian purpose appeals to a diversity of men—we request a more general and typical articulation. We expect not only that an individuality with its uniqueness be voiced in it, but a broad, historical or social orientation and temper, which make it possible for handicraft to be incorporated into the life-systems of a great many different individuals. It is the greatest mistake to think that, because it always functions as the adornment of an individual, adornment must be an individual work of art. Quite the contrary: *because* it is to serve the individual, it may not itself be of an individual nature—as little as the piece of furniture on which we sit, or the eating utensil which we manipulate, may be individual works of art. The work of art cannot, in principle, be incorporated into another life—it is a self-sufficient world. By contrast, all that occupies the larger sphere around the life of the individual, must surround it as if in ever wider concentric spheres that lead back to the individual or originate from him. The essence of stylization is precisely this dilution of individual poignancy, this generalization beyond the uniqueness of the personality—which, nevertheless, in its capacity of base or circle of radiation, carries or absorbs the individuality as if in a broadly flowing river. For this reason, adornment has always instinctively been shaped in a relatively severe style.

Besides its formal stylization, the *material* means of its social purpose is its *brilliance*. By virtue of this brilliance, its wearer appears as the center of a circle of radiation in which every close-by person, every seeing eye, is caught. As the flash of the precious stone seems to be directed at the other—like the lightning of the glance the eye addresses to him—it carries the social meaning of jewels, the being-for-the-other, which returns to the subject as the enlargement of his own sphere of significance. The radii of this sphere mark the distance which jewelry creates between men—"I have something which you do not have." But, on the other hand, these radii not only let the other participate: they shine in *his* direction; in fact, they exist only for his sake. By virtue of their material, jewels signify, in one and the same act, an increase in distance and a favor.

For this reason, they are of such particular service to vanity— which needs others in order to despise them. This suggests the profound difference which exists between vanity and haughty pride: pride, whose self-consciousness really rests only upon itself, ordinarily disdains "adornment" in every sense of the word. A word must also be added here, to the same effect, on the significance of "genuine" material. The attraction of the "genuine," in all contexts, consists in its being more than its immediate appearance, which it shares with its imitation. Unlike its falsification, it is not something isolated; it has its roots in a soil that lies beyond its mere appearance, while the unauthentic is only what it can be taken for at the moment. The "genuine" individual, thus, is the person on whom one can rely even when he is out of one's sight. In the case of jewelry, this more-than-appearance is its *value,* which cannot be guessed by being looked at, but is something that, in contrast to skilled forgery, is *added* to the appearance. By virtue of the fact that this value can always be realized, that it is recognized by all, that it possesses a relative timelessness, jewelry becomes part of a super-contingent, super-personal value structure. Talmi-gold and similar trinkets are identical with what they momentarily *do* for their wearer; genuine jewels are a value that goes beyond this; they have their roots in the value ideas of the whole social circle and are ramified through all of it. Thus, the charm and the accent they give the individual who wears them, feed on this super-individual soil. Their genuineness makes their aesthetic value—which, too, is here a value "for the others"—a symbol of general esteem, and of membership in the total social value system.

There once existed a decree in medieval France which prohibited all persons below a certain rank to wear gold ornaments. The combination which characterizes the whole nature of adornment unmistakably lives in this decree: in adornment, the sociological and aesthetic emphasis upon the personality fuses as if in a focus; being-for-oneself and being-for-others become reciprocal cause and effect in it. Aesthetic excellence and the right to charm and please, are allowed, in this decree, to go only to a point fixed by the individual's social sphere of significance. It is precisely in this fashion that one adds, to the charm which adornment gives one's whole appearance, the *sociological* charm of being, by virtue of adornment, a representative of one's group, with whose whole significance one is "adorned." It is as if the significance of his status, symbolized by jewels, returned to the individual on the very beams which originate in him and enlarge his sphere of impact. Adornment, thus, appears as the means by which his social power or dignity is transformed into visible, personal excellence.

Centripetal and centrifugal tendencies, finally, appear to be fused in adornment in a specific form, in the following information. Among nature peoples, it is reported, women's private property generally develops later than that of men and, originally, and often exclusively, refers to adornment. By contrast, the personal property of the male usually begins with weapons. This reveals his active and more aggressive nature: the male enlarges his personality sphere without waiting for the will of others. In the case of the more passive female nature, this result—although formally the same in spite of all external differences—depends more on the others' good will. Every property is an extension of personality; property is that which obeys our wills, that in which our egos express, and externally realize, themselves. This expression occurs, earliest and most completely, in regard to our body, which thus is our first and most unconditional possession. In the *adorned* body, we possess *more;* if we have the adorned body at our disposal, we are masters over more and nobler things, so to speak. It is, therefore, deeply significant that bodily adornment becomes private property above all: it expands the ego and enlarges the sphere around us which is filled with our personality and which consists in the pleasure and the attention of our environment. This environment looks with much less attention at the unadorned (and thus as if less "expanded") individual, and passes by without including him. The fundamental principle of adornment is once more revealed in the fact that, under primitive conditions, the most outstanding possession of women became that which, according to its very idea, exists only for others, and which can intensify the value and significance of its wearer only through the recognition that flows back to her from these others. In an aesthetic form, adornment creates a highly specific synthesis of the great convergent and divergent forces of the individual and society, namely, the elevation of the ego through existing for others, and the elevation of existing for others through the emphasis and extension of the ego. This aesthetic form itself stands above the contrasts between individual human strivings. They find, in adornment, not only the possibility of undisturbed simultaneous existence, but the possibility of a reciprocal organization that, as anticipation and pledge of their deeper metaphysical unity, transcends the disharmony of their appearance.

Chapter 4

The Secret Society

THE SECRET IS A SOCIOLOG-
ical determination characteristic of the reciprocal relations between group elements; or, rather, together with other relational
forms, it constitutes their relationship as a whole. But it may
also characterize a group in its totality: this applies to the case
of "secret societies." As long as the existence, the activities, and
the possessions of an individual are secret, the general sociological significance of the secret is isolation, contrast, and egoistic
individualization. The sociological significance of the secret is
external, namely, the relationship between the one who has
the secret and another who does not. But, as soon as a whole
group uses secrecy as its form of existence, the significance becomes internal: the secret determines the reciprocal relations
among those who share it in common. Yet, since even here there
is the exclusion (with its specific nuances) of the non-initiates,
the sociology of the secret society is confronted with the complicated problem of ascertaining how intra-group life is determined by the group's secretive behavior toward the outside. I do
not preface this discussion by a systematic classification of secret
societies, which would have only an external, historical interest;
even without it, essential categories will emerge by themselves.

§ 1. *Protection and Confidence*

The first internal relation typical of the secret society is the
reciprocal *confidence* [6] among its members. It is required to
a particularly great extent, because the purpose of secrecy is,
above all, *protection*. Of all protective measures, the most radical
is to make oneself invisible. In this respect, the secret society

[6] *"Vertrauen,"* i.e., both "confidence" and "trust." Both terms are used in this
translation, according to context.—Tr.

differs fundamentally from the individual who seeks the protection of secrecy. The individual can properly do so only in regard to particular undertakings or situations; as a whole, he can, to be sure, hide for certain periods of time, but his existence, except for very abstruse combinations, cannot itself be a secret. This is quite possible, however, for a societal unit. Its elements may live in the most frequent interactions; but the fact that they form a society—a conspiracy or a gang of swindlers, a religious conventicle or an association for engaging in sexual orgies —can essentially, as well as permanently, be a secret.

In this type, then, it is not the individuals, but the group they form, which is concealed. It must be distinguished from another type, where the formation of the group is completely known, while the membership, the purpose, or the specific rules of the association remain secret. Examples are many secret orders among nature peoples; also the Freemasons. Secrecy protects this type less than it does the former, since what is known always offers points of attack for further penetration. On the other hand, such relatively secret societies often have the advantage of a certain elasticity. Since their existence is manifest to a certain extent from the beginning, they can bear further revelations more easily than can those societies whose very life is secret, and whose mere discovery frequently spells destruction—their secret usually rests on the radical alternatives of All or Nothing.

The fact that secrets do not remain guarded forever is the weakness of the secret society. It is therefore said quite correctly that the secret known by two is no longer a secret. The protection which secret societies offer is thus absolute, but only temporary. In fact, for contents of a positve social value to be lodged in secret societies is only a transition which, after a certain period of growing strength, they no longer need. Secrecy, therefore, eventually comes to resemble the mere protection which is gained by resisting disturbances; and it is appropriate for it to yield to the other kind of protection, namely, strength, which is capable of coping with disturbances. Under these conditions, the secret society is the suitable social form for contents which still (as it were) are in their infancy, subject to the vulnerability of early developmental stages. A new insight, a young religion, morality, or party, is often still weak and needs protection, and for this reason conceals itself.

Periods in which new contents of life develop against the resistance of existing powers are predestined, therefore, to witness the growth of secret societies. This is shown, for instance, by the eighteenth century. At that time—merely to give an example—the elements of the liberal party already existed in Germany, but their appearance in the form of a permanent structure was still prevented by political conditions. The secret order was the form under whose protection the germs could be preserved and strengthened—a service rendered particularly by the order of the Illuminati.

But the secret society protects the decaying as well as the growing development. The flight into secrecy is a ready device for social endeavors and forces that are about to be replaced by new ones. In these cases, secrecy constitutes a sort of transitional stage between being and not-being. When, by the end of the Middle Ages, the German communal associations began to be suppressed by the strengthened central powers, they developed a far-flung secret life through hidden assemblies and compacts and through the secret exercise of law and violence—like animals seek the protection of a hiding-place when they go to their death. This double function of the secret order as a form of protection—as in an interim arrangement for rising as well as for sinking forces—is perhaps most evident in religious developments. As long as the Christian communities were prosecuted by the state, they were often forced to seek refuge for their assemblies, their worship, their whole existence, in concealment. But, once Christianity became a state religion, it was the adherents of the persecuted, dying paganism who had to resort to the same concealment of their cultural associations into which they had previously forced the now dominant religion. In general, the secret society emerges everywhere as the counterpart of despotism and police restriction, as the protection of both the defensive and the offensive in their struggle against the overwhelming pressure of central powers—by no means of political powers only, but also of the church, as well as of school classes and families.

Corresponding to this protective character as an external

quality, there is in the secret society, as already noted, the internal quality of reciprocal confidence among its members—the very specific trust that they are capable of keeping silent. According to their content, associations rest upon premises of various kinds of confidence: confidence in business ability, in religious conviction, in courage, love, decency, or—in the case of criminal groups—in the radical break with moral concerns. But as soon as the society becomes secret, it adds to the trust determined by its particular purpose, the formal trust in secrecy. This, evidently, is faith-in-the-person of a sociologically more abstract character than any other, since every possible common content may be subject to it. Furthermore (but for exceptions), no other kind of confidence needs such uninterrupted subjective renewal. For, in the cases of faith in affection, energy, morality, intelligence, decency, or tact, it is more likely that there are certain facts which, once for all, justify the faith and its extent, and which reduce to a minimum the probability of deceit. By contrast, the chance of "talking" rests on momentary imprudence, on the tenderness or excitement of a mood, or on the nuance, perhaps unconscious, of some emphasis. The preservation of the secret is something so unstable; the temptations of betrayal are so manifold; the road from discretion to indiscretion is in many cases so continuous, that the unconditional trust in discretion involves an incomparable preponderance of the subjective factor.

For this reason, secret societies offer a very impressive schooling in the moral solidarity among men. Their rudimentary forms begin with any two persons who share a secret; their diffusion in all places and at all times is immense and has hardly ever been appreciated even quantitatively. For, in the confidence of one man in another lies as high a moral value as in the fact that the trusted person shows himself worthy of it. Perhaps it is even more free and meritorious, since the trust we *receive* contains an almost compulsory power, and to betray it requires thoroughly positive meanness. By contrast, confidence is "given"; it cannot be *requested* in the same manner in which we are requested to honor it, once we are its recipients.

§ 2. *Silence*

It is natural that secret societies should seek means for promoting the secrecy psychologically, since it cannot be directly enforced. Above all, there are the oath and the threat of punishment, which need no discussion. More interesting is a technique that is sometimes encountered, namely, the systematic instruction of the novice in the art of silence. In view of the above-mentioned difficulties of wholly guarding one's tongue and, particularly, in view of the easy connection between thought and utterance that exists in the more primitive stages (among children and many nature peoples, thinking and speaking are almost the same), it is necessary, above all, to learn how to be silent, before silence regarding any particular item may be expected.[7] Thus it is reported of a secret order in the Moluccan Island of Ceram that the young man who seeks admittance, not only is enjoined to keep silent concerning everything he experiences on entering, but also is not permitted for weeks to say a word to anybody, not even to his family. Certainly not merely the educational factor of thoroughgoing silence operates here; it is in line with this psychologically undifferentiated stage that, during a period when something particular must be kept secret, speaking altogether should be prohibited. This is the same radicalism in which primitive peoples often use the death penalty in cases where later a partial sin is met with a partial punishment; or in which, if this is their inclination, they pay for some-

---

[7] If human sociation is *conditioned* by the capacity to speak, it is *shaped* by the capacity to be silent, although this becomes obvious only upon occasion. Where all conceptions, feelings, and impulses gush forth in speech without inhibition, they produce a chaotic helter-skelter, instead of an organic coordination. We rarely realize how necessary this capacity for silence is in the development of any regulated interaction; we rather take it for granted. Nevertheless, it undoubtedly has a historical development, which begins with the chatter of the child and of the Negro for whom ideas gain some sort of concreteness and self-assurance only in the very process of chattering. Correspondingly, this developmental process also begins with the clumsy commands of silence mentioned above. It culminates in the urbanity of high societal culture, among whose noblest possessions is the secure feeling of knowing where one must speak, and where one must be silent. Thus, at a social party (for instance), the host must refrain from talk as long as the guests carry the conversation among themselves; but he must seize on it immediately, once it lags. An intermediate case is perhaps presented by the medieval guilds which, by statute, punished everybody who interrupted the alderman in his speech.

thing momentarily attractive with a wholly disproportionate part of their possessions.

In all this, there is manifested a specific "lack of skill" whose essence seems to consist in the incapability of engendering the particular innervation needed for a particular purposive movement: the clumsy person moves the whole arm where, for his purpose, he should move only two fingers, or the whole body where a precisely articulated movement of the arm would be appropriate. In the cases quoted, the preponderance of psychological association immensely intensifies the danger of indiscretion and, at the same time, allows its prohibition to grow beyond its particular, teleologically determined content and, instead, to cover the whole function that includes this content. If, on the other hand, the secret order of the Pythagoreans prescribed several years' silence for the novices, the intention, probably here too, went beyond mere education for guarding the secrets of the order—but not because of that "lack of skill" but, on the contrary, because the differentiated purpose itself was enlarged in its own direction: the adept had to learn, not only to keep silent about particular matters, but to master himself generally. The order aimed at a rigorous self-discipline and a stylized purity of life; and, whoever managed to be silent over years, was also able, presumably, to resist temptations other than talkativeness.

Another means for placing discretion upon an objective basis was applied by the secret order of the Gallic Druids. The content of their secrets lay, particularly, in spiritual songs which every Druid had to memorize. But this was so arranged—above all, probably, because of the prohibition to write the songs down —that it required an extraordinary long time, even up to twenty years. By means of this long period of learning before there was anything essential that could have been betrayed, a gradual habituation to silence was developed. The fascination of disclosure did not assail the undisciplined mind all at once, as it were; the young mind was allowed to adapt itself slowly to resisting this fascination. The rule according to which the songs could not be written down, however, was more than a mere protective measure against the revelation of the secrets—it is part of much more comprehensive sociological phenomena. The individual's dependence upon personal instruction, and the fact that the exclusive source of the teaching was within the secret order—not deposited in any objective piece of writing—these facts tied every single member with incomparable closeness to the group, and made him constantly feel that, if he were severed from this substance, he would lose his own and could never find it again anywhere.

It has perhaps not been sufficiently noted how much, in more mature cultures, the objectification of the spirit promotes the growing independence of the individual. So long as immediate tradition, individual teaching, and, above all, establishment of norms through persons in authority, determine the individual's intellectual life, he is wholly integrated with his surrounding, living group. It alone gives him the possibility of a fulfilled and spiritual existence; the direction of all channels, through which his life-contents flow to him, runs only between his social milieu and himself; and he feels this at every moment. But, once the labor of the species capitalizes its results in the form of writing, in visible works, in enduring examples, this immediate, organic flow between the actual group and its individual member is interrupted. The life process of the individual no longer continuously binds him to the group without competition from any other quarter: it can now feed on objective sources which need not be personally present. The fact that this supply actually orginates in processes of the social mind, is relatively irrelevant. These processes are not only quite remote, having occurred in generations which are no longer connected with the present feeling of the individual, although his supply is the crystallization of actions by these past generations. Above all, however, it is the objective form of this supply, its separateness from subjective personality, that opens a super-social source of food to the individual. His spiritual content, both in degree and kind, thus comes to depend much more markedly upon his capacity to absorb, than upon any allotted offering. The particularly close association within the secret society (to be discussed later in greater detail), which has its affective category, so to speak, in specific "trust," thus suggests that, where the secret society has as its core the transmission of intellectual contents, it is fit for it to avoid the written fixation of these matters.

§ 3. *Written Communication* [8]

Some remarks on the sociology of the letter are appropriate here, since the letter, evidently, represents a very peculiar constellation even under the category of secrecy. In the first place, writing is opposed to all secrecy. Prior to its general use, every legal transaction, however simple, had to be concluded before witnesses. The written form replaced this necessity, inasmuch as it involves an unlimited, even if only potential, "publicity": not only the witnesses, but everybody in general, may know of the business concluded.

Our consciousness has a peculiar form at its disposal, which can only be designated as "objective spirit." Natural laws and moral imperatives, concepts and artistic creations lie ready, as it were, for everybody able and willing to use them; but, in their timeless validity, they are independent of whether, when, and by whom they are thus used. Truth, as an intellectual phenomenon, is something quite different from its passing, actual object: it remains true, no matter whether or not it is known and acknowledged. The moral and juridical law is valid, whether lived by or not. Writing is a symbol, or visible vehicle, of this immeasurably important category. In being written down, the intellectual content receives an objective form, an existence which, in principle, is timeless, a successively and simultaneously unlimited reproducibility in the consciousness of individuals. But its significance and validity are fixed, and thus do not depend on the presence or absence of these psychological realizations. Writing, thus, possesses an objective existence which renounces all guarantees of remaining secret.

The letter, more specifically, is likewise wholly unprotected against anybody's taking notice of it. It is for this reason, perhaps, that we react to indiscretion concerning *letters* as to something particularly ignoble—so that, for subtler ways of feeling, it is the very defenselessness of the letter which protects its secrecy. The mixture of these two contrasts—the objective elimination of all warranty of secrecy, and the subjective intensification of this warranty—constitutes the letter as a specific sociological

[8] In the original, this section, printed in smaller type, is called *"Exkurs über den schriftlichen Verkehr"* (Note on Written Communication).—Tr.

phenomenon. The form of expression by letter is an objectification of its content, which involves, on the one hand, the letter's being addressed to one particular person and, on the other hand, the correlate of this first fact, namely, the personal and subjective character in which the letter writer (in contrast to the writer of literature) presents himself. It is particularly in this second respect that the letter is a unique form of communication. Individuals in physical proximity give each other more than the mere content of their words. Inasmuch as each of them *sees* the other, is immersed in the unverbalizable sphere of his mood, feels a thousand nuances in the tone and rhythm of his utterances, the logical or the intended content of his words gains an enrichment and modification for which the letter offers only very poor analogies. And even these, on the whole, grow only from the memories of direct personal contact between the correspondents.

It is both the advantage and the disadvantage of the letter that it gives, in principle, only the pure, objective content of our momentary ideational life, while being silent concerning what one is unable, or does not wish, to say. But the characteristic of the letter is that it is, nevertheless, something wholly subjective, momentary, solely-personal (except for cases where it is a treatise in unprinted form)—and, by no means, only when it is a lyrical outburst, but also when it is a perfectly concrete communication. This objectification of the subjective, this stripping of the subjective element of everything pertaining to the matter at issue and to oneself which one does not (as it happens) want to reveal at the moment, is possible only in periods of high culture. It is then that one adequately masters the psychological technique which enables one to give a permanent form to momentary moods and thoughts, and to consider and receive them with the understanding that they *are* momentary, commensurate with the requirements of the situation. Where an inner production has the character of a "work," this permanent form is entirely adequate; but, in the letter, there lies a contradiction between the character of its content and that of its form. Only a sovereign objectivity and differentiation can produce, come to terms with, and utilize, this contradiction.

This synthesis finds its further analogy in the mixture of determinateness and ambiguity which is characteristic of written expressions and to, the highest extent, of the letter. Determinateness and ambiguity are sociological categories of the first rank in regard to *all* utterances between man and man; evidently, all of the discussions in this chapter [part] belong in their general area. Yet here the point is not simply the more-or-less, which the one lets the other know about himself; but, rather, the fact that, what he does give, is only more or less *clear* to its recipient, and that this lack of clarity is as if compensated for by a corresponding plurality of possible interpretations. It is almost certain that there exists no enduring relation between individuals in which the changing proportions of clarity and interpretability of utterances do not play an essential role, although we usually become aware of this role only through its practical results. Superficially, the written utterance appears to be safer in the sense that it seems to be the only one from which "no iota can be taken away." Yet this prerogative of the written word is only the consequence of a lack of all those accompaniments—sound of voice, tone, gesture, facial expression—which, in the *spoken* word, are sources of both obfuscation and clarification. As a matter of fact, however, the recipient does not usually content himself with the purely logical sense of the words which the letter surely transmits much less ambiguously than speech; innumerable times, indeed, the recipient *cannot* do so, because even to grasp the mere logical sense, more than the logical sense is required. For this reason, the letter is much more than the spoken word the locus of "interpretations" and hence of misunderstandings—despite its clarity, or more correctly, because of it.

Corresponding to the cultural level at which a relationship (or period of relationship) based on written communication is possible, the qualitative characteristics of such a relation are, likewise, sharply differentiated: what in human utterances is clear and distinct, is more clear and distinct in the letter than in speech, and what is essentially ambiguous, is more ambiguous. Expressed in terms of the categories of freedom and unfreedom on the part of the recipient of the utterance: his understanding, in regard to its logical core, is less free; but, in regard to its deeper and personal significance, his understanding is freer in the case of the letter than in that of speech. One may say that, whereas speech reveals the secret of the speaker by means of all that surrounds it—which is visible but not audible, and which also includes the imponderables of the speaker himself—the letter conceals this secret. For this reason, the letter is clearer than speech where the secret of the other is *not* the issue; but where it *is* the issue, the letter is more ambiguous. By the "secret of the other" I understand his moods and qualities of being, which cannot be expressed logically, but on which we nevertheless fall back innumerable times, even if only in order to understand the actual significance of quite concrete utterances. In the case of speech, these helps to interpretation are so fused with its conceptual content that both result in a wholly homogeneous understanding. This is, perhaps, the most decisive instance of the general fact that man is quite incapable of distinguishing what he actually sees, hears, and experiences from what his interpretation makes of it through additions, subtractions, and transformations. It is one of the intellectual achievements of written communication that it isolates one of the elements of this naïve homogeneity, and thus makes visible the number of fundamentally heterogeneous factors which constitute our (apparently so simple) mutual "understanding."

§ 4. *Secrecy and Sociation*

In these questions concerning techniques of keeping secrets, it must not be forgotten that the secret is not only a means under whose protection the material purposes of a group may be furthered: often, conversely, the very formation of a group is designed to guarantee the secrecy of certain contents. This occurs in the special type of secret societies whose substance is a secret doctrine, some theoretical, mystical, or religious *knowledge*. Here, secrecy is its own sociological purpose: certain insights must not penetrate into the masses; those who know form a community in order to guarantee mutual secrecy to one another. If they were a mere sum of unconnected individuals, the secret would soon be lost; but sociation offers each of them psychological support against the temptation of disclosure. Sociation counterbalances the isolating and individualizing effect of the secret which I have emphasized. All sorts of sociation shift the needs for individualization and socialization back and forth within their forms, even within their contents—as if the requirement of an enduring mixture were met by the employment of elements constantly changing in quality. The secret society compensates for the separating factor inherent in every secret by the simple fact that it is a *society*.

Secrecy and individualization are so closely associated that sociation may play two wholly different roles in regard to secrecy. Sociation may be directly sought, as has just been emphasized, in order to compensate, in part, for the isolating consequences of continuing secrecy—in order to satisfy *within* secrecy the impulse toward communion which the secret destroys in regard to the outside. On the other hand, secrecy greatly loses in significance whenever, for reasons of content, individualization is fundamentally excluded. The Freemasons stress their wish of being the *most general* society, "the union of unions," the only group which rejects all particularistic elements and wants to appropriate only what is common to *all* good men. Hand in hand with this ever more decisive tendency, there has developed among them the growing indifference toward the secret character of the lodges, which have come to be limited to mere external formalities. It is thus not contradictory for secrecy to be sometimes favored, sometimes dissolved, by sociation—these are merely different forms in which the relation between secrecy and individualization finds expression. An analogy is the connection between weakness and fear, which shows itself in the weak person's seeking sociation for protection, as well as in his avoiding it for fear of greater dangers from sociation than from isolation.

§ 5. *Hierarchy*

The gradual initiation of the member into the secret society, which was touched upon above, belongs in a very comprehensive area of sociological forms, within which secret societies are marked in a particular way. This area is the principle of hierarchy, or graduated differentiation, of the elements in a society. Secret societies, above all others, carry through the division of labor and the gradation of their members with great finesse and thoroughness. This is related to a characteristic of them, to be discussed later, namely, the highly developed *consciousness* of their life. By virtue of it, organically instinctive forces are replaced by a constantly regulating will; and growth from within is exchanged for constructive purposiveness. This rationalistic nature of their organization finds no more visible expression than in its clear-cut and well-balanced structure. An example is the Czech secret society "Omladina," mentioned earlier,[9] which was formed on the model of a group of the Carbonari and became known, in 1893, through a legal process. The directors of the "Omladina" were divided into "thumbs" and "fingers." The "thumb," chosen by the members in secret session, chose four "fingers," who again chose a thumb. This second thumb introduced himself to the first, chose four fingers who chose a thumb; and thus the process of organization continued. The first thumb knew all thumbs, but they did not know one another. Among all fingers, only those four knew one another who were subordinated to a common thumb. All transactions of the "Omladina" were conducted by the first thumb, the "dictator." He informed the other thumbs of all intended actions; the thumbs then issued orders to their subordinate fingers, who relayed the orders to the ordinary members assigned to them.

Evidently, the fact that the secret society must be built up from its basis by means of a conscious, reflective will, gives free reign to the peculiar passion engendered by such arbitrarily disposing, organizational activities of planning important schemata. All system-building, whether of science, conduct, or society, involves the assertion of power: it subjects material outside of thought to a form which thought has cast. If this is true of all attempts at organizing a group according to principles, it is especially true of the secret society, which does not grow but is built, and which can count on fewer pre-formed parts than can any despotic or socialistic system. In addition to making plans, in addition to the constructive impulse, both of which, themselves, are expressions of a will to power, there is here the special challenge of completely controlling a large, potentially and ideally subordinated group of human beings, by developing

[9] Cf. pp. 171–172 above.—Tr.

a scheme of positions with their rank interrelations. Occasionally, this passion is quite characteristically severed from all purposiveness, and revels in wholly fantastic hierarchy constructions, as, for instance, in the "high degrees" of degenerate Freemasonry. I shall only cite some typical details of the organization of the "Order of African Master Builders." It came into existence in Germany and France after the middle of the eighteenth century. Although itself constructed on Masonic principles, it aimed at the destruction of Freemasonry. The administration of the society (which was very small) lay in the hands of fifteen officers: *Summus Magister, Summi Magistri Locum Tenens, Prior, Subprior, Magister,* etc. There were seven degrees of the order: the Scotch Apprentice, Scotch Brother, Scotch Master, Scotch Knight, *Eques Regii, Eques de Secta Consueta, Eques Silentii Regii,* etc.

§ 6. *Ritual*

The growth of ritual in secret societies stands under the same developmental conditions as does hierarchy. The extraordinary freedom and wealth of forms here, too, derives from the characteristic fact that the organization of the society is not predetermined by historical precedent, but is built up from its own basis. There are perhaps no other external traits, which are so typical of the secret society, and so sharply distinguish it from the open society, than the high valuation of usages, formulas, and rites, and their peculiar preponderance over the purposive contents of the group, if not their contrast with them. Sometimes, in fact, the contents are less anxiously guarded than is the secret of the ritual. Progressive Freemasonry maintains explicitly that it is not a secret association, that it has no reason for concealing membership, intentions, and actions; that the vow of secrecy refers exclusively to the form of the Masonic ritual. At the end of the eighteenth century, the student order of the Amicists decreed, in typical fashion, in the first paragraph of its statutes: "The most sacred duty of every member is to keep the deepest silence regarding such matters as concern the welfare of the order. Among these are: signs of the order and of recognition, names of the brothers, ceremonies, etc." Later in the same statute, the purpose and nature of the order are indicated in detail and without any concealment. In a slim book describing the constitution and the nature of the Carbonari, the enumeration of the formulas and usages at the initiation of new members and at meetings covers seventy-five printed pages. Further examples are unnecessary. The role of the ritual in secret societies is sufficiently well known, from the religio-mystical orders of antiquity down to the eighteenth-century Rosicrucians, on the one hand, and, on the other, to the most dastardly criminal gangs. The sociological motivations of the connection between ritual and secret society are approximately as follows.

The striking feature in the treatment of ritual is not only the rigor of its observance but, above all, the anxiousness with which it is guarded as a secret. Its disclosure appears to be as detrimental as that of the purposes and actions, or perhaps of the very existence, of the society. The teleological aspect of this is, probably, that the total action and interest sphere of the secret society becomes a well rounded unity only through inclusion, in the secret, of a whole complex of external forms. Under its characteristic categories, the secret society must seek to create a sort of life totality. For this reason, it builds round its sharply emphasized purposive content a system of formulas, like a body round a soul, and places both alike under the protection of secrecy, because only thus does it become a harmonious whole in which one part protects the other. The particular emphasis with which the secrecy of the *external* element is thereby stressed, is necessitated by the fact that this secrecy is not required so obviously and so much by sheer, immediate interest as is the secrecy of the objective group purpose.

This is not different from (for instance) the military organization and the religious community. In both, schematism, formulas, and the precise determination of conduct, play an important role which, quite generally, can be explained in terms of the fact that both of them claim the individual wholly. That is, each projects the totality of life upon a specific plane; each, from a particular viewpoint, fuses a plurality of forces and interests into a closed unit. This, usually, is also the aim of the secret society. To be sure, it may seize upon its members only in regard to partial interests; and, in terms of its content, it may be a purely purposive association. But even in these cases, it quite characteristically claims to a greater extent the whole individual, connects its members in more of their totality, and mutually obligates them more closely, than does an open society of identical content. Through the symbolism of the ritual, which excites a whole range of vaguely delimited feelings beyond all particular, rational interests, the secret society synthesizes those interests into a total claim upon the individual. By means of the ritual form, the particular purpose of the secret society is enlarged to the point of being a closed unit, a whole, both sociological and subjective.

It must be added that, through such formalism, as well as through the hierarchical organization itself, the secret society makes itself into a sort of counter-image of the official world, to which it places itself in contrast. Here we find the ubiquitous sociological norm: that structures which resist larger, encompassing structures through opposition and separation, nevertheless themselves repeat the forms of these structures. Only a structure that somehow can be considered a whole is capable of strongly tying its members to itself. The *kind* of organic self-sufficiency by virtue of which the same stream of life flows through all group members, is borrowed by the group from the larger whole, to whose forms the members had been adapted. The smaller structure can meet this whole most viably, precisely by imitating it.

§ 7. *Freedom*

The same conditions, finally, involve still another motive in the sociology of the ritual in secret societies. Every secret society contains a measure of *freedom,* which the structure of the society at large does not have. Whether the secret society, like the *fehme,* supplements the inadequate judicature of the political community; or like the conspiratory or criminal band, rebels against its law; or like the Mysteries, stands beyond the commands and prohibitions of the general society—the singling-out, so characteristic of the secret society, always has a note of freedom: the society lives in an area to which the norms of the environment do not extend.

The essence of the secret society, as such, is autonomy. But this autonomy approaches anarchy: the consequences of leaving the general normative order easily are rootlessness and the absence of a stable life-feeling and of a norm-giving basis. The fixed and minute character of the ritual helps to overcome this lack. In this, we see once more how much man needs a certain ratio between freedom and law; and how, when he does not receive it from *one* source, he seeks to supplement what he obtains of the one by the missing quantity of the other, no matter from what additional source, until he has the ratio he needs. In ritual, the secret society voluntarily imposes upon itself a formal coercion, a complement required by its material separateness and autonomy. It is characteristic that, among the Freemasons, precisely those who enjoy the greatest political freedom, namely, the Americans, request of all their lodges the most rigorous uniformity of work procedure and ritual, whereas in Germany the practice involves a greater autonomy of the individual lodge: here, Freemasonry is so integrated with the general society that it does not demand such freedoms as would easily lead to the counterclaim of their being curtailed. In short, in the secret society the nature of ritual—objectively often quite senseless and schematically coercive—is by no means inconsistent with that group freedom which resembles anarchy, with severance from the norms of the inclusive society. On the contrary: just as the widespread diffusion of secret societies is usually a proof of public un-freedom, of a tendency toward police regimentation, and of political oppression, in short, just as it is a reaction stemming from the need for freedom—so, conversely, the internal, ritual regimentation of secret societies reflects a measure of freedom and severance from society at large which entails the counter-norm of this very schematism, in order to restore the equilibrium of human nature.

§ 8. *Features of the Secret Society as*
  Quantitative Modifications of
  General Group Features

These last considerations suggest the methodological principle on the basis of which I wish to analyze those traits of the secret society which have not yet been discussed. The question is, to what extent can they be shown to be essentially quantitative modifications of the typical features of sociation in general? The justification of this conception of the secret society leads once more to a consideration of its position in the whole complex of sociological forms.

The secret element in societies is a primary sociological fact, a particular kind and shading of togetherness, a formal quality of relationship. In direct or indirect interaction with other such qualities, it determines the shape of the group member or of the group itself. Yet, from a historical standpoint, the secret society is a secondary phenomenon; that is, it always develops only within a society already complete in itself. To put it differently: the secret society is characterized by its secrecy in the same way in which other societies (or even secret societies themselves) are characterized by their superordination and subordination, or by their aggressive purposes, or by their imitative character; but, that it can develop with these characteristics is possible only on the condition that a society already exists. Within this larger circle, it opposes it as a narrower one; whatever the purpose of the society, this opposition has, at any rate, the sense of exclusion. Even the altruistic secret society, which merely wants to render a certain service to the total group and intends to disband after achieving it, evidently considers temporary separation from this total group a technique unavoidable in view of its purpose.

[a] SEPARATENESS, FORMALITY, CONSCIOUSNESS

Among the many smaller groups which are included in larger ones, there is none whose sociological constellation forces it to emphasize its formal self-sufficiency to the same extent as it does the secret society. Its secret surrounds it like a boundary outside of which there is nothing but materially, or at least formally, opposite matter, a boundary which therefore fuses, within itself, the secret society into a perfect unity. In groups of every other sort, the *content* of group life, the actions of the members in terms of rights and duties, can so occupy the members' consciousness that, normally, the formal fact of sociation plays scarcely any role at all. The secret society, on the other hand, cannot allow its members to forget the distinct and emphatic consciousness that they form a *society*. In comparison with other associations, it here is the passion of secrecy—always felt and always to be preserved—which gives the group-form, depending on it, a significance that is far superior to the significance of content. The secret society completely lacks organic growth, instinctive expansions, and, on the part of its members, all naïve, matter-of-fact feeling of belonging together and forming a unit. However irrational, mystical, or emotional its contents may be, the way in which it is formed is thoroughly conscious and intentional. In its *consciousness* of being a society— a consciousness which is constantly emphasized during its formative period and throughout its lifetime—it is the opposite of all spontaneous groups, in which the joining is only the expression, more or less, of elements which have grown together like roots. Its social-psychological form clearly is that of the interest group [*Zweckverband*]. This constellation makes it understandable why the formal characteristics of group formation in general are specifically pointed up in the secret society, and why some of its essential sociological traits develop as mere quantitative intensifications of very general types of relationship.

[b] SECLUSION: SIGNS OF RECOGNITION

One of these has already been indicated, namely, the characterization as well as the cohesion of the secret society by means of seclusion against the social environment. This is the function of the often complicated signs of recognition through which the individual legitimates himself as a member. It should be noted that, prior to the more general diffusion of writing, these signs were more indispensable than later, when their other sociological uses became more important than those of mere legitimation. As long as there were no credentials of acceptance, notifications, or written descriptions of persons, an association with branches in several different places, had nothing but such signs for excluding unauthorized persons, and for having only individuals entitled to them receive its benefits or communications. These signs were revealed only to the legitimate members who, by means of them, were able to legitimate themselves wherever the group existed, and who had the duty to keep them secret.

The *purpose of seclusion* is clearly illuminated by the development of certain secret orders among nature peoples, especially in Africa and among the Indians. These orders are composed only of men. Their essential purpose is to emphasize the differentiation of men from women. Whenever their members act in this capacity, they appear in masks, and women are usually forbidden on severe penalty to approach them. Yet sometimes women succeed in discovering the secret that the horrible apparitions are not ghosts but their husbands. When this happens, the orders often lose their whole significance and become harmless mummeries. The man of nature with his undifferentiated, sensuous conception, cannot imagine a more perfect separateness, such as he wants to emphasize, than for those who wish it and are entitled to it to *hide* themselves, to make themselves invisible. This is the crudest and, externally, most radical manner of concealment: not only a particular act of man, but all of man at once, is concealed—the group does not do something secret, but the totality of its members makes *itself* into a secret. This form of the secret society is perfectly in line with that primitive stage of mind in which the whole personality is still absorbed in every particular activity, and in which the activity is not yet sufficiently objectified to have any character that the whole personality does not automatically share. It is also understandable, therefore, why the whole separateness becomes invalid once the secret of the mask is broken, and why, then, the secret society loses its inner significance along with its means and its expression.

[c] THE ARISTOCRATIC MOTIVE; ARISTOCRACY

The separateness of the secret society expresses a value: people separate from others because they do not want to make common cause with them, because they wish to let them feel their superiority. This motive leads everywhere to group formations, which evidently are very different from those undertaken for objective purposes. By joining one another, those who want to distinguish themselves give rise to the development of an aristocracy, which strengthens and (so to speak) enlarges their position and self-consciousness by the weight of their own sum. Separation and group formation are thus connected through the aristocratizing motive. In many cases, this connection gives separation itself the stamp of something "special," in an honorific sense. Even in school classes, it can be observed how small, closely integrated cliques of classmates think of themselves as the elite over against the others who are not organized—merely because of the formal fact of constituting a special group; and the others, through their hostility and envy, involuntarily acknowledge this higher value. In these cases, secrecy and mystification amount to heightening the wall toward the outside, and hence to strengthening the aristocratic character of the group.

This significance of the secret society as the intensification of sociological exclusiveness in general, is strikingly shown in political aristocracies. Secrecy has always been among the requisites of their regime. In the first place, by trying to conceal the numerical insignificance of the ruling class, aristocracies exploit the psychological fact that the unknown itself appears to be fearsome, mighty, threatening. In Sparta, the number of warriors was kept secret as much as possible. In Venice, the same end was intended by the decree that all *nobili* [noblemen] had to wear a simple black costume: no striking dress was to call the small number of men in power to the attention of the people. This was even carried to the point where the group of the highest elite was concealed completely: the names of the three state inquisitors were unknown to everybody except the council of ten who elected them. In some Swiss aristocracies, one of the most important authorities was simply called "the Secret Ones"; and in Freiburg, the aristocratic families were known as "the secret lineages" [*die heimlichen Geschlechter*]. The democratic principle, on the contrary, is associated with the principle of publicity and, in the same sense, with the tendency toward general and basic laws. For, these laws apply to an unlimited number of subjects and are, therefore, public in their very essence. Conversely, the use of secrecy by aristocratic regimes is only the extreme intensification of the social exclusiveness and exemption which, ordinarily, make aristocracies opposed to general, fundamentally fixed legislations.

Where the aristocratic idea does not characterize the policies of a group but the disposition of an individual, the relation between exclusiveness and secrecy manifests itself on a very different plane. The morally and intellectually distinguished person despises all concealment, because his inner certainty makes him indifferent to what others know or do not know of him, and to the question whether he is appraised correctly or falsely by them, or held in high or low esteem. For him, secrecy is a concession to outsiders; secrecy is dependence of conduct upon regard for others. For this reason, the "mask" which many consider sign and proof of an aristocratic personality that is turned away from the multitude, on the contrary proves the importance of the multitude to the wearer of the mask. The "mask" of the truly noble person is that even when he shows himself without disguise, the many do not understand him, do not even see him, so to speak.

[d] DEGREES OF INITIATION: FORMAL AND MATERIAL SEPARATION
FROM THE OUTSIDE

This exclusion of everything outside the group is a general formal-sociological fact, which merely uses secrecy as a more pointed technique. It attains a particular nuance in the plurality of degrees in which it is customary for initiation into the secret society, down to its last mysteries, to take place. The existence of such degrees threw light earlier upon another sociological feature of the secret society. As a rule, before he is even accepted into the first degree, the novice must give a solemn promise of secrecy concerning everything he may experience, whereby the absolute, *formal* separation, achievable by secrecy, is effected. Yet, inasmuch as the actual content or purpose of the society becomes accessible to the neophyte only gradually—whether this purpose is the perfect purification and sanctification of the soul through the consecration of the mysteries, or the absolute suspension of every moral barrier, as among the Assassins and other criminal societies—the *material* separation is achieved differently, in a more continuous, relative manner. In this material respect, the neophyte is still closer to the status of non-participant, from which testing and education eventually lead him to grasp the totality or core of the association. This core, evidently, thus gains a protection and isolation from the outside far beyond those by means of the oath upon entrance. It is seen to (as has already been shown in the example of the Druids) that the still untried neophyte does not have much he could betray: within the general secrecy that encompasses the group as a whole, the graduated secrecy produces an elastic sphere of protection (as it were) around its innermost essence.

The contrast between exoteric and esoteric members, such as is attributed to the Pythagorean order, is the most poignant form of this protective measure. The circle composed of those only partially initiated formed a sort of buffer region against the non-initiates. It is everywhere the dual function of the "middler" to connect and to separate, or, actually, rather to play only one role which, according to our perceptual categories and our viewpoint, we designate as connecting or as separating. In the same way, the real unity of superficially contradictory activities is here seen in its clearest light: precisely because the lower grades of the order mediate the transition to the center of the secret, they create a gradual densification of the sphere of repulsion which surrounds this center and which protects it more securely than could any abrupt and radical alternative between total inclusion and total exclusion.

[e] GROUP EGOISM

In practice, sociological autonomy presents itself as group egoism: the group pursues its own purposes with the same inconsiderateness for all purposes outside itself which, in the case of the individual, is precisely called egoism. Usually, to be sure, this inconsiderateness is morally justified in the consciousness of the individual members by the fact that the group purposes themselves have a super-individual, objective character; that it is often impossible to name any particular individual who profits from the group's egoistic behavior; and that, as a matter of fact, this behavior often requires the group members' selflessness and sacrifice. But the point here is not to make any ethical valuation, but only to stress the group's separation from its environment, which is brought about or characterized by the egoism of the group. However, in the case of a small circle, which intends to preserve and develop itself within a larger one, this egoism has certain limits as long as it exists publicly. An open association, no matter how violently it fights against other associations within the same larger society, or against the general foundations of this society itself, must always maintain that the realization of its own ultimate purposes is to the advantage of the whole; and the necessity of this outward assertion somewhat restricts the actual egoism of its actions. This necessity does not exist in the case of secret societies, which always therefore, at least potentially, can afford to be hostile to other groups or to the whole. Non-secret groups cannot admit such a hostility, and, therefore, cannot unconditionally practice it. Nothing symbolizes, or possibly promotes, the separation of the secret society from its social environment as decisively as the elimination of the hypocrisy, or of the actual condescension, by means of which the non-secret society is inevitably integrated with the teleology of its environment.

[f] INCLUSIVENESS AND EXCLUSIVENESS AS GROUP PRINCIPLES

In spite of the actual quantitative delimitation of every true community, there exists a considerable number of groups whose inner tendency is to include all those who are not explicitly excluded. Within certain political, religious, and status limits, everybody is considered immediately as "belonging" so long as he satisfies certain external conditions, which are usually not a matter of his will, but are given with his existence itself. All people, for instance, who are born within the territory of a given state, are members, unless particular circumstances make exceptions of them, of the (often very complex) civic society. The member of a given social class is included, as a matter of course, in the social conventions and forms of connection of this class, unless he becomes a voluntary or involuntary outsider. The extreme case is the claim of a church that it includes all mankind; and that, if any individuals are excluded from the religious association, which, ideally, is valid also for them, it is only through historical accident, sinful stubbornness, or God's special intention.

We note here the distinction of two principles, which clearly indicate a basic differentiation of the sociological significance of groups generally, no matter how much practice may mix them and make the difference lose some of its sharpness. On the one hand, there is the principle of including everybody who is not explicitly excluded; and, on the other, there is the principle of excluding everybody who is not explicitly included. The second type is represented in greatest purity by the secret society. The unconditional character of its separation, which is borne by the consciousness of it at every step of the group's development, causes, and is caused by, the fact that those who are not explicitly accepted, are for this simple reason explicitly excluded. The Masonic order could no better have supported its recent emphatic assertion that it is not a "secret order," properly speaking, than by simultaneously professing its ideal of including *all* men, of representing humanity.

[g] SECLUSION AGAINST THE OUTSIDE AND INTERNAL COHESION

Here, as everywhere else, the intensified seclusion against the outside is associated with the intensification of cohesion internally: we have here two sides, or external forms, of the same sociological attitude. A purpose which occasions an individual to enter into secret association with others, excludes almost always such an overwhelming part of his general social circle from participation, that the potential and real participants gain rarity value. He must keep on good terms with them because it is much more difficult to replace them here than (other things being equal) in a legitimate association. Furthermore, every discord inside the secret society brings danger of betrayal, which usually both the self-preservation of the individual and that of the group are interested in avoiding.

Finally, the isolation of the secret society from the surrounding social syntheses removes a number of occasions for conflict. Among all the bonds of the individual, the bond of secret sociation always has an exceptional position. In comparison with it, the official bonds—familial, civic, religious, economic, through rank and friendship—no matter how varied their contents, touch contact surfaces of a very different kind and measure.

Only the contrast with the secret societies makes it clear that their claims criss-cross one another, because they lie (so to speak) in the same plane. Since these claims openly compete for the individual's strength and interests, individuals collide within any one of these circles: each individual is simultaneously claimed by the interests of other groups.

The sociological isolation of the secret society greatly limits such collisions. In accordance with its purpose and operation, competing interests of open-society origin are shut out. Every secret society—if only because it usually fills its own sphere alone (the same individual hardly ever belongs to more than one secret society)—exercises over its members a sort of absolute dominion, which gives them little opportunity to engage in conflicts such as result from the coordination of the plurality of spheres that represent open groups. The "king's peace," which really ought to reign within every association, is promoted, in a formally unsurpassable manner, by the peculiar and exceptional conditions of the secret society. In fact, it seems as if, aside from the more realistic reason in favor of the "king's peace," the mere form of secrecy itself kept the members freer from other influences and disturbances, and thus facilitated their accord. A certain English politician found the basis for the strength of the English cabinet in the secrecy which surrounds it: everybody who has ever been active in public life, he suggested, knows that a small number of people can be brought to agree the more easily, the more secret are its negotiations.

[h]   CENTRALIZATION

Corresponding to the outstanding degree of cohesion within the secret society is the thoroughness of its centralization. The secret society offers examples of unconditional and blind obedience to leaders who—although, naturally, they may also be found elsewhere—are yet particularly remarkable in view of the frequent anarchic character of the secret society that negates all other law. The more criminal its purposes, the more unlimited, usually, is the power of the leaders and the cruelty of its exercise. The Assassins in Arabia; the Chauffeurs, a predatory band with a widely ramified organization which raged, particularly, in eighteenth-century France; the Gardunas in Spain, a criminal society that had relations with the Inquisition from the seventeenth to the beginning of the nineteenth century— all these, whose very nature was lawlessness and rebellion, unconditionally and without any criticism submitted to chiefs whom they themselves (as least in part) appointed.

The interrelation between the needs for freedom and for a bond operates here; it appears in the rigor of ritual, which combines the extremes of both: for the sake of a balanced life-feeling, the excess of freedom from all otherwise valid norms must be brought into equilibrium by a similarly excessive submission and renunciation of the will. Yet more essential, probably, is the necessity of centralization, which is the life condition of the secret society. It is especially important for that type— for instance, the criminal band—which lives off surrounding groups, interferes with them through all kinds of radiations and actions, and thus is gravely threatened by treason and the distraction of interests, once it is no longer governed by the most intransigent cohesion with its point of origin in its own center.

Secret societies which, for whatever reasons, fail to develop a tightly solidifying authority are, therefore, typically exposed to very grave dangers. Originally, the Waldenses were not a secret society; they became one in the thirteenth century, only because of external pressure to keep themselves hidden. This made it impossible for them to meet regularly, which in turn deprived their doctrine of its unity. A number of branches arose, which lived and developed separately, and were often hostile to one another. The order declined because it lacked the necessary complement of the secret society: uninterruptedly effective centralization. Freemasonry, probably, owes the evident lag in its power behind its diffusion and means, to the considerable autonomy of its parts, which have neither a unified organization nor a central authority. Their common features merely cover principles and signs of recognition, and thus are traits of equality and of relations between person and person only, not of centralization, which holds the energies of the members together and is the complement of separation.

It is merely an exaggeration of this formal motive of centralization that secret societies are often directed by *unknown* leaders: the lower echelons are not to know whom they obey. To be sure, this occurs, above all, for the sake of preserving the secret. With this intention, it was developed to an extraordinary degree in the organization of an early nineteenth-century Italian secret society, the Welfic Knights, which worked for the liberation and unification of Italy. At each of their various branches, the Knights had a highest council of six persons, who did not know one another and communicated only by means of an intermediary, called "The Visible One." But the preservation of secrecy is by no means the only purpose of unknown leaders. Instead, they exemplify the most extreme and abstract sublimation of dependence upon a center: the tension between dependent and leader reaches the highest degree when the leader becomes invisible. All that remains then, is the pure fact of obedience—merciless, as it were, and unmodified by any personal nuances—out of which the superordinate as a subject has vanished. If obedience to impersonal authority, to mere office, to the executor of an objective law, has the character of invincible strength, it is intensified to the point of an uncanny absoluteness when the ruling personality remains, in principle, hidden. For if, with the visibility and familiarity of the ruler, the individual suggestion and the power of personality are removed from the relationship of domination, domination also loses all attenuations, all relative and "human" elements inherent in the empirical, unique personality. Obedience is thus colored by the feeling of subjection to an intangible power, whose limits cannot be traced, and which can nowhere be seen, but must, for this reason, be suspected everywhere. In the secret society with an unknown leader, the general sociological cohesion of a group through the unity of its ruling authority is transferred, as it were, into an imaginary focus, and thus attains its purest, most intense form.

[i] DE-INDIVIDUALIZATION

De-individualization is the sociological character which, in the individual member, corresponds to this centralistic subordination. Where the immediate concern of the society is not the interests of its elements; where the society rather transcends itself (as it were) by using its members as means for purposes and actions extraneous to them—the secret society shows, once more, a heightened measure of leveling of the individuality, of "de-selfing" [*Entselbstung*]. *Some* measure of this is characteristic of everything social, generally. But the secret *society* uses de-individualization to compensate for the above-mentioned indi-vidualizing and differentiating character of the *secret*. This be-gins with the secret orders of nature peoples, whose appearance and activities are accompanied almost everywhere by the wear-ing of masks—so that an outstanding expert suggested that the presence of masks among a nature people should at once make one suspect the existence of secret societies. It is, of course, in the nature of the secret order for its members to conceal them-selves. But, when a particular individual appears and acts unam-biguously as a member of a secret order, and merely does not show what individuality (which is normally well known) is associated with him, the disappearance of personality behind its role is most strongly emphasized. In the Irish conspiracy which was organized under the name of Clan-na-gael in America in 1870, the individual members were never designated by their names, but only by numbers. This, too, of course, was done for the practical purpose of secrecy; but, at the same time, it proves how much this purpose suppresses individuality. Leadership can proceed with much greater inconsiderateness and indifference to individual wishes and capacities of persons who appear only as numbers and who may not be known by their personal names even to the other members (which at least occurred in groups similar to the Clan-na-gael), than it can if the group includes each member as a personal entity. No less effective, toward the same end, is the comprehensive role and strength of ritual, which always indicates the fact that the ob-jective organization has overcome the personal element in the members' activities and contributions to the group. The hier-archical order admits the individual only as the discharger of a predetermined role; for each member, it holds ready a stylized garb in which his personal outlines disappear.

[j] EQUALITY OF MEMBERS

It is merely another name for this elimination of the differentiated personality if secret societies practice great relative equality among their members. This does not contradict the despotic character of their organization: in all kinds of other groups, too, despotism is correlated with the leveling of the ruled. Within the secret society, there often is a brotherly equality among the members, which constitutes a sharp and tendentious contrast to their differences in their other life situations. Characteristically, this is most noticeable in secret societies of a religio-ethical nature—which strongly accentuate brotherhood —and, on the other hand, in those of an illegal character. In his memoirs, Bismarck writes of a pederastic organization, widespread in Berlin, with which he became acquainted as a young justiciary; he stresses "the *equalizing* effect throughout all strata of the collective practice of the forbidden."

This de-personalization, wherein the secret group exaggerates in a one-sided manner a typical relationship between individual and society, appears, finally, as characteristic *irresponsibility*. Here, too, the mask is the most primitive phenomenon. Most African secret orders are represented by a man disguised as a spirit of the woods, who commits all violations, including robbery and murder, against anyone he happens to meet. He is not held responsible for his crimes—obviously, only because of his mask. The mask is the somewhat clumsy form in which these groups let the personalities of their members disappear, and without which the members would undoubtedly be overtaken by revenge and punishment. But responsibility is so immediately connected with the ego (philosophically, too, the whole problem of responsibility belongs in the problem of the ego), that, for such naïve feeling, the disguise of the person suspends all responsibility.

This connection is used no less in political finesse. In the North American House of Representatives, actual decisions are made in the standing committees, with which the House is almost always in agreement. But the transactions of these committees are secret; thus, the most important part of legislative activity is hidden from the public. In large measure, this seems to extinguish the political responsibility of the delegates, since nobody can be held responsible for uncontrollable procedures. Inasmuch as individual contributions toward a particular decision remain hidden, the decision appears to be made by some super-individual authority. Here, too, irresponsibility is the consequence or the symbol of the intensified sociological deindividualization, which corresponds to the secrecy of group action. This also holds for all directorates, faculties, committees, administrations, etc., whose transactions are secret: the individual, as a person, disappears as the quasi-nameless group member, and with his disappearance as a person disappears the responsibility that cannot be imagined to inhere in a being whose concrete activities are intangible.

[k] THE SECRET SOCIETY AND THE CENTRAL GOVERNMENT

This one-sided intensification of general sociological features is confirmed, finally, by the danger with which society at large believes, rightly or wrongly, secret societies threaten it. Where the over-all aim of the general society is strong (particularly political) centralization, it is antagonistic to all special associations, quite irrespective of their contents and purposes. Simply by being units, these groups compete with the principle of centralization which alone wishes to have the prerogative of fusing individuals into a unitary form. The preoccupation of the central power with "special associations" runs through all of political history—a point which is relevant in many respects to the present investigations and has already been stressed. A characteristic type of this preoccupation is suggested, for instance, by the Swiss Convention of 1481, according to which no separate alliances were permitted between any of the ten confederated states. Another example is the persecution of apprentices' associations by the despotism of the seventeenth and eighteenth centuries. A third is the tendency to disenfranchise local political communities which is so often demonstrated by the modern state.

The secret society greatly increases this danger which the special association presents to the surrounding totality. Man has rarely a calm and rational attitude toward what he knows only little or vaguely. Instead, his attitude consists in part in levity, which treats the unknown as if it did not exist, and in part in anxious fantasy, which, on the contrary, inflates it into immense dangers and terrors. The secret society, therefore, appears dangerous by virtue of its mere secrecy. It is impossible to know whether a special association might not one day use its energies for undesirable purposes, although they were gathered for legitimate ones: this fear is the main source of the basic suspicion which central powers have of all associations among their subjects.

In regard to groups which make it their principle to conceal themselves, the suspicion that their secrecy hides dangers is all the more readily suggested. The Orange Societies which were organized in England, in the beginning of the nineteenth century, for the suppression of Catholicism, avoided all public discussion, working only in secret, through personal connections and correspondence. But this very secrecy let them appear as a public danger: the suspicion arose "that men, who shrank from appealing to public opinion, meditated a resort to force." Purely on the grounds of its secrecy, the secret order thus appears dangerously close to a conspiracy against the reigning powers. How much this is only an intensification of the general political questionability of special associations is clearly shown in a case like the following. The oldest German guilds offered their members effective legal protection, and thus replaced the protection of the state. For this reason, the Danish kings promoted them, since they saw in them a support of the public order. But, on the other hand, for the very same reason, the guilds also were considered to be *competitors* of the state: they were condemned in this capacity by the Frankish capitularies—more particularly, because they were designated as *conspiracies*. The secret society is so much considered an enemy of the central power that, even conversely, every group that is politically rejected, is called a secret society.

Faithfulness and Gratitude; Negativity of Collective Behavior; the Stranger; Metropolis

Chapter 1

Faithfulness and Gratitude

FAITHFULNESS IS ONE OF those very general modes of conduct that may become important in all interactions among men, no matter how different they may be materially or sociologically. In superordinations, subordinations, coordinations; in collective hostilities toward third parties as in collective friendships; in families and in regard to the state; in love as well as in one's relation to one's occupational group—in all these structures, examined purely in their sociological constellations, faithfulness and its opposite become important. But faithfulness is significant as a sociological form of the second order, as it were, as the instrument of relations which already exist and endure. In its general form, the connection between faithfulness and the sociological forms it supports is, in a certain sense, like the connection between these forms and the material contents and motives of social life.

Without the phenomenon we call faithfulness, society could simply not exist, as it does, for any length of time. The elements which keep it alive—the self-interest of its members, suggestion, coercion, idealism, mechanical habit, sense of duty, love, inertia —could not save it from breaking apart if they were not supplemented by this factor. Its measure and significance, however, cannot be determined in the given case, because its practical effect always consists in replacing some other feeling, which hardly ever disappears completely. The contribution of this feeling is inextricably interwoven with that of faithfulness itself, in a composite result that resists quantitative analysis.

Because of the supplementary character of faithfulness, such a term as "faithful love," for instance, is somewhat misleading. If love continues to exist in a relationship between persons, why does it need faithfulness? If the partners are not, from the beginning, connected by it but, rather, by the primary and genuine psychological disposition of love, why must faithfulness, as the guardian of the relationship, be added after ten years if, by definition, love remains identical even then, and still on its own strength has its initial binding power? If linguistic usage understands by *faithful* love what is simply *enduring* love, there is no objection, of course. Words do not concern us here; what is important is the existence of a specific psychic and sociological state, which insures the continuance of a relationship beyond the forces that first brought it about; which survives these forces with the same synthesizing effect they themselves had originally; and which we cannot help but designate as faithfulness, although this term also has a very different meaning, namely, the perseverance of these forces themselves. Faithfulness might be called the inertia of the soul. It keeps the soul on the path on which it started, even after the original occasion that led it onto it no longer exists.[1]

It is a fact of the greatest sociological importance that innumerable relationships preserve their sociological structure unchanged, even after the feeling or practical occasion, which originally gave rise to them, has ended. That destruction is easier than construction, is not unqualifiedly true of certain human relations, however indubitable it is otherwise. The rise of a relationship, to be sure, requires certain positive and negative conditions, and the absence of even one of them may, at once, preclude its development. Yet once started, it is by no means always destroyed by the subsequent disappearance of that condition which, earlier, it could not have overcome. An erotic relation, for instance, begun on the basis of physical beauty, may well survive the decline of this beauty and its change into ugliness. What has been said of states—that they are maintained only by the means by which they were founded—is only a very incomplete truth, and anything but an all-pervasive principle of sociation generally. Sociological connectedness, no matter what its origin, develops a self-preservation and autonomous

[1] It goes without saying that I always speak here of faithfulness only as a purely psychic disposition operating from "inside out," not as behavior such as marital faithfulness in the legal sense, for instance, which refers to nothing positive at all, but only to the non-occurrence of unfaithfulness.

existence of its form that are independent of its initially connecting motives. Without this inertia of existing sociations, society as a whole would constantly collapse, or change in an unimaginable fashion.

The preservation of social units is psychologically sustained by many factors, intellectual and practical, positive and negative. Faithfulness is the *affective* factor among them; or better, faithfulness in the form of feeling, in its projection upon the plane of feeling, is this affective factor. The quality of this feeling will be ascertained here only in its psychic reality, whether or not one accepts it as an adequate definition of the idea of faithfulness. Every beginning relationship is accompanied by a specific feeling, interest, impulse, directed toward it by its participants. If the relation continues, there develops a particular feeling in interaction with this continuance—or, better, often, though not always, the original psychic states change into a particular form which we call faithfulness. It is a psychological reservoir, as it were, an over-all or unitary mold for the most varied interests, affects, and motives of reciprocal bonds. In spite of all variety of origin, the original psychic states attain, in the form of faithfulness, a certain similarity, which understandably promotes the permanence of faithfulness itself. In other words, the discussion here does not concern so-called "faithful love," "faithful attachment," etc., which refer to certain modes or temporal quantities of feelings already defined: what I mean is that faithfulness itself is a specific psychic state, which is directed toward the continuance of the relation as such, independently of any particular affective or volitional elements that sustain the content of this relation. This psychic state of the individual is one of the *a priori* conditions of society which alone make society possible (at least as we know it), in spite of the extraordinary differences of degree in which this psychic state exists. It can probably never reach zero: the absolutely unfaithful person—the person for whom it is impossible to transform feelings that engender relationships into the feeling designed to preserve the relationship—is not a thinkable phenomenon.

Faithfulness, thus, might be called "induction by feeling." At such and such a moment a relation existed. In formal analogy to theoretical induction, feeling concludes that, therefore, the relation also exists at a later moment. And, just as in intellectual induction, the later instance need no longer be ascertained as fact, so to speak (because induction precisely means that we may do without this ascertainment), so here, very often, the later moment no longer shows a real feeling or interest, but only the inductively developed state called faithfulness. In the consideration of a great many relations and connections among men, one must count with the fact (a fundamental sociological fact) that mere habitual togetherness, the mere existence of a relation over a period of time, produces this induction by feeling.

This broadens the concept of faithfulness by adding a very important element. The external sociological situation of togetherness appropriates the particular feelings that properly correspond to it, as it were, even though they did not justify the beginnings of the relationship. In a certain sense, the process of faithfulness here runs backward. The psychical motives which produced the relation allow the specific feeling of faithfulness toward this relation to develop, or they transform themselves into this feeling. Although the relationship may have been brought about for external reasons (or at best, for intimate ones that are extrinsic to its meaning), it nevertheless develops its own faithfulness which, in turn, gives rise to deeper and more adequate feeling states: the relation is legitimated, so to speak, *per subsequens matrimonium animarum* [through the subsequent marriage of the souls].

The banal wisdom one often hears in reference to marriages that were concluded on conventional or other external grounds —that love will come later, during the marriage—is sometimes actually quite apt. For once the existence of the relationship has found its psychological correlate, faithfulness, then faithfulness is followed, eventually, also by the feelings, affective interests, and inner bonds that properly belong to the relationship. Only, instead of appearing at the beginning, as we should "logically" expect, they reveal themselves as its end product. But this development cannot come to pass without the mediation of faithfulness, of the affect which is directed toward the preservation of the relationship as such. In psychological association in general, once imagination B is tied to imagination A, there also develops the opposite effect: A is called into consciousness wherever B is. Analogously, the sociological form of a given relationship produces, in the manner indicated, the inner state of feeling that corresponds to it, although ordinarily the process runs in the opposite direction.

An example will illustrate this. In order to restrict, as much as possible, the exposing of children and their being given over to foundlings' homes, France introduced, in the middle of the nineteenth century, the *"secours temporaires,"* that is, fairly adequate subsidies for unmarried mothers who kept their children under their own care. On the basis of abundant observational material, the originators of this measure pointed out in favor of it that, in the overwhelming majority of cases, once the mother could be persuaded to keep the child for any length of time, there was no danger any longer of her giving it up. The natural emotional tie between mother and child should make her wish to keep it, but obviously does not always. Yet, if she can be swayed to do so even for a while, if only for external reasons, to secure the advantage of that temporary subsidy, this external relationship creates its own emotional underpinning.

These psychological constellations appear especially intensified in the phenomenon of the *renegade*. He exhibits a characteristic loyalty to his new political, religious, or other party. The awareness and firmness of this loyalty (other things being equal) surpass those of persons who have belonged to the party all along. In sixteenth- and seventeenth-century Turkey, this went so far that very often born Turks were not allowed to occupy high government positions, which were filled only by Janizaries, that is, born Christians, either voluntarily converted to Islam or stolen from their parents as children and brought up as Turks. They were the most loyal and energetic subjects. The special loyalty of the renegade seems to me to rest on the fact that the circumstances, under which he enters the new relationship, have a longer and more enduring effect than if he had naïvely grown into it, so to speak, without breaking with a previous one.

As far as it concerns us here, faithfulness or loyalty is the emotional reflection of the autonomous life of the relation, unperturbed by the possible disappearance of the motives which originally engendered the relation. But the longer these motives survive, and the less seriously the power of pure form alone (of the relationship itself) is put to test, the more energetic and certain is the effect of faithfulness. This is particularly true of the renegade because of his sharp awareness that he cannot go back: the old relationship, with which he has irrevocably broken, remains for him, who has a sort of heightened discriminatory sensitivity, the background of the relation now existing. It is as if he were repelled by the old relationship and pushed into the new one, over and over again. Renegade loyalty is so strong because it includes what loyalty in general can dispense with, namely, the conscious continuance of the motives of the relationship. This continuance here fuses more permanently with the formal power of the relationship itself than in cases without contrasting past and without absence of alternative paths, of return, or in other directions.

The very conceptual structure of faithfulness shows that it is a sociological, or (if one will) a sociologically oriented, feeling. Other feelings, no matter how much they may tie person to person, have yet something more solipsistic. After all, even love, friendship, patriotism, or the sense of social duty, essentially occur and endure in the individual himself, immanently—as is perhaps revealed most strikingly in Philine's question: "In what way does it concern *you* that I love you?" In spite of their extraordinary sociological significance, these feelings remain, above all, subjective states. To be sure, they are engendered only by the intervention of other individuals or groups, but they do so even before the intervention has changed into interaction. Even where they are directed toward other *individuals,* the *relation* to these individuals is, at least not *necessarily,* their true presupposition or content.

But precisely this is the meaning of faithfulness—at least as here discussed, although linguistic usage also gives it other meanings. Faithfulness refers to the peculiar feeling which is not directed toward the possession of the other as the possessor's eudaemonistic good, nor toward the other's welfare as an extrinsic, objective value, but toward the preservation of the *relationship* to the other. It does not engender this relationship; therefore, unlike these other affects, it cannot be pre-sociological:

it pervades the relation once it exists and, as its inner self-preservation, makes the individuals-in-relation hold fast to one another. This specific sociological character is connected with the fact that faithfulness, more than other feelings, is accessible to our moral intentions. Other feelings overcome us like sunshine or rain, and their coming and going cannot be controlled by our will. But *un*faithfulness entails a more severe reproach than does absence of love or social responsibility, beyond their merely obligatory manifestations.

Moreover, its particular sociological significance makes faithfulness play a unifying role in connection with a basic dualism that pervades the fundamental form of all sociation. The dualism consists in the fact that a relation, which is a fluctuating, constantly developing life-process, nevertheless receives a relatively stable external form. The sociological forms of reciprocal behavior, of unification, of presentation toward the outside, cannot follow, with any precise adaptation, the changes of their inside, that is, of the processes that occur in the individual in regard to the other. These two layers, relation and form, have different tempi of development; or it often is the nature of the external form not to develop properly at all.

Evidently, the strongest external measure for fixing internally variable relations is law. Examples are the marital form, which unyieldingly confronts changes in personal relationship; the contract between two associates, which continues to divide business profit evenly between them, although one of them does all the work, and the other none; membership in an urban or religious community that has become completely alien or antipathetic to the member. But even beyond these obvious cases, inter-individual as well as inter-group relations, which have hardly begun, can constantly be observed to have an immediate tendency toward solidifying their form. The form thus comes to constitute a more or less rigid handicap for the relation in its further course, while the form itself is incapable of adapting to the vibrating life and the more or less profound changes of this concrete, reciprocal relation.

But this is only the repetition of a discrepancy within the individual himself. Our inner life, which we perceive as a stream, as an incessant process, as an up and down of thoughts and moods, becomes crystallized, even for ourselves, in formulas and fixed directions often merely by the fact that we verbalize this life. Even if this leads only rarely to specific inadequacies; even if, in fortunate cases, the fixed external form constitutes the center of gravity or indifference above and below which our life evenly oscillates; there still remains the fundamental, formal contrast between the essential flux and movement of the subjective psychic life and the limitations of its forms. These forms, after all, do not express or shape an ideal, a contrast with life's reality, but this life itself.

Whether they are the forms of individual or social life, they do not flow like our inner development does, but always remain fixed over a certain period of time. For this reason, it is their nature sometimes to be ahead of the inner reality and sometimes to lag behind it. More specifically, when the life, which pulsates beneath outlived forms, breaks these forms, it swings into the opposite extreme, so to speak, and creates forms ahead of itself, forms which are not yet completely filled out by it. To take an instance from the field of personal relations: among friends, the *Sie* [polite form of address] is often felt to be a stiffness that is incommensurate with the warmth of the relation; but when it finally comes to the *Du* [intimate form of address], this too, at least in the beginning, strikes them just as often as something slightly "too much," as the anticipation of full intimacy which has yet to be achieved. Another example is the change of a political constitution, by which obsolete forms that have become unbearably oppressive are replaced by freer and larger ones, while the reality of the political and economic forces is not always ripe for them: an overly narrow frame is replaced by one which, for the time being, is still too wide.

In regard to these conditions of social life, faithfulness (in the sense discussed) has the significance that, by virtue of it, for once the personal, fluctuating inner life actually adopts the character of the fixed, stable form of a relation. Or vice versa: this sociological fixity, which remains outside life's immediacy and subjective rhythm, here actually becomes the content of subjective, emotionally determined life. Irrespective of the innumerable modifications, deflections, intermixtures of concrete destinies, faithfulness bridges and reconciles that deep and essential dualism which splits off the life-form of individual internality [*Innerlichkeit*] from the life-form of sociation that is nevertheless borne by it. Faithfulness is that constitution of the soul (which is constantly moved and lives in a continuous flux), by means of which it fully incorporates into itself the stability of the super-individual form of relation and by means of which it admits to life, as the meaning and value of life, a content which, though created by the soul itself, is, in its form, nevertheless bound to contradict the rhythm or un-rhythm of life as actually lived.

Although in the feeling called *gratitude* the sociological character emerges much less directly, its sociological importance can hardly be overestimated. Only the external insignificance of its concrete acts—which contrasts, however, with the immense sphere of its application—has thus far apparently concealed the circumstance that the life and the cohesion of society would be unforeseeably changed without this phenomenon.

Gratitude, in the first place, supplements the legal order. All contacts among men rest on the schema of giving and returning the equivalence. The equivalence of innumerable gifts and performances can be enforced. In all economic exchanges in legal form, in all fixed agreements concerning a given service, in all obligations of legalized relations, the legal constitution enforces and guarantees the reciprocity of service and return service—social equilibrium and cohesion do not exist without it. But there also are innumerable other relations, to which the legal form does not apply, and in which the enforcement of the equivalence is out of the question. Here gratitude appears as a supplement. It establishes the bond of interaction, of the reciprocity of service and return service, even where they are not guaranteed by external coercion. Gratitude is, thus, a supplementation of the legal form in the same sense that I showed *honor* to be.[2]

In order to appraise the specific nature of this connection correctly, it is necessary (above all) to realize that personal action

---

[2] On pp. 403-406 of the same chapter of *Soziologie* from which the present *"Exkurs"* is taken (VIII, *"Die Selbsterhaltung der sozialen Gruppe,"* The Self-Preservation of the Social Group). The chapter itself is not included in this volume.—Tr.

among men by means of things—as, for instance, in robbery and gift, the primitive forms of property exchange—becomes objectified in *exchange*. Exchange is the objectification of human interaction. If an individual gives a thing, and another returns one of the same value, the purely spontaneous character [*Seelenhaftigkeit*] of their relation has become projected into objects. This objectification, this growth of the relationship into self-contained, movable things, becomes so complete that, in the fully developed economy, personal interaction recedes altogether into the background, while goods gain a life of their own. Relations and value balances between them occur automatically, by mere computation: men act only as the executors of the tendencies toward shifts and equilibriums that are inherent in the goods themselves. The objectively equal is given for the objectively equal, and man himself is really irrelevant, although it goes without saying that he engages in the process for his own interest. The relation among men has become a relation among objects.

Gratitude likewise originates from interaction, and in interaction, between men. But it does so in the same manner, toward the inside, as the relation of things originates from it, toward the outside. While interaction is lifted out of the spontaneous act of correlation through the exchange of things, this act in its consequences, subjective meanings, and psychic echoes, sinks into the soul through gratitude. Gratitude, as it were, is the moral memory of mankind. In this respect, it differs from faithfulness by being more practical and impulsive: although it may remain, of course, something purely internal, it may yet engender new actions. It is an ideal bridge which the soul comes across again and again, so to speak, and which, upon provocations too slight to throw a *new* bridge to the other person, it uses to come closer to him.

Beyond its first origin, all sociation rests on a relationship's effect which survives the emergence of the relationship. An action between men may be engendered by love or greed of gain, obedience or hatred, sociability or lust for domination alone, but this action usually does not exhaust the creative mood which, on the contrary, somehow lives on in the sociological situation it has produced. Gratitude is definitely such a continuance. It is an ideal living-on of a relation which may have ended long ago, and with it, the act of giving and receiving. Although it is a purely personal affect, or (if one will) a lyrical affect, its thous-andfold ramifications throughout society make it one of the most powerful means of social cohesion. It is a fertile emotional soil which grows concrete actions among particular individuals. But much more: although we are often unaware of its funda-mentally important existence, and although it is interwoven with innumerable other motivations, nevertheless, it gives human actions a unique modification or intensity: it connects them with what has gone before, it enriches them with the element of personality, it gives them the continuity of inter-actional life. If every grateful action, which lingers on from good turns received in the past, were suddenly eliminated, society (at least as we know it) would break apart.[3]

All external and internal motives that bind individuals to-gether may be examined with respect to their implementation of the exchange which not only holds society together once it is formed but, in large measure, forms it. From such an exami-nation, gratitude emerges as the motive which, for inner reasons, effects the return of a benefit where there is no external neces-sity for it. But "benefit" is not limited to a person's giving things to another: we also thank the artist or poet who does not even know us. This fact creates innumerable connections, ideal and concrete, loose and firm, among those who are filled with grati-tude toward the same giver. In fact, we do not thank somebody only for what he *does:* the feeling with which we often react to the mere existence of a person, must itself be designated as gratitude. We are grateful to him only because he exists, because we experience him. Often the subtlest as well as firmest bonds among men develop from this feeling. It is independent of any

---

[3] Giving, itself, is one of the strongest sociological functions. Without constant giving and taking within society—outside of exchange, too—society would not come about. For, giving is by no means only a simple effect that one individual has upon another: it is precisely what is required of all sociological functions, namely, interaction. By either accepting or rejecting the gift, the receiver has a highly specific effect upon the giver. The manner of his acceptance, gratefully or ungrate-fully, having expected the gift or being surprised by it, being satisfied or dis-satisfied, elevated or humiliated—all this keenly acts back upon the giver, although it can, of course, not be expressed in definite concepts and measures. Every act of giving is, thus, an interaction between giver and receiver.

particular act of receiving; it offers our whole personality to the other, as if from a duty of gratitude to *his* total personality.

The concrete content of gratitude, that is, of the responses it induces, calls forth modifications of interaction whose delicacy does not lessen their significance for the structure of our relationships. The intimate character of these relations receives an extraordinary wealth of nuances when the psychological situation makes it necessary for a gift received to be returned with a gift of an essentially different kind. Thus an individual, perhaps, gives "spirit," that is, intellectual values, while the other shows his gratitude by returning affective values. Another offers the aesthetic charms of his personality, for instance, and the receiver, who happens to be the stronger nature, compensates him for it by injecting will power into him, as it were, or firmness and resoluteness. There is, probably, not a single interaction in which the things that go back and forth, in the reciprocity of giving and taking, are exactly equal, although the examples given are extreme intensifications of this inevitable difference between gifts and return gifts among men.

If this difference is striking and is accompanied by its own awareness, it constitutes a problem for what might be called "inner sociology," a problem which is equally difficult ethically and theoretically. For, when an individual offers his intellectual possessions, but is not very emotionally involved in the relation, while the other can return nothing but his love, there often is a slight note of inner incommensurateness; in fact, for our feelings, all cases of this sort have something fatal: they somehow resemble a purchase. Purchase—and this distinguishes it from exchange in general—implies that the exchange, which actually takes place under its name, concerns two entirely heterogeneous things that can be juxtaposed and compared only by means of a common monetary value. Thus, if earlier, prior to the use of metal money, some handiwork was purchased with a cow or goat, these wholly heterogeneous things were juxtaposed and became exchangeable by virtue of the economic, abstract-general value contained in each of them.

This heterogeneity reaches its peak in modern money economy. Because money expresses the general element contained in all exchangeable objects, that is, their exchange value, it is incapable of expressing the individual element in them. Therefore, objects insofar as they figure as salable things, become degraded: the individual in them is leveled down to the general which is shared by everything salable, particularly by money itself. Something of this basic heterogeneity occurs in the cases I mentioned. Two individuals offer one another different parts of their inner lives. Gratitude for the gift is realized in a different coin, as it were, and thus injects something of the character of purchase into the exchange, which is inappropriate in principle. One buys love with what one gives of spirit. One buys the charm of a person one wants to enjoy, and pays for it with one's superior power of suggestion or will, which the other either wishes to feel over himself or by which he allows himself to be inspired.

This feeling of a certain inadequacy or indignity, however, arises only if the reciprocal offerings appear as isolated objects of exchange, if the mutual gratitude concerns only the benefits, the exchanged contents themselves, so to speak. But man is not the merchant of himself; and particularly not in the relationships discussed here. His qualities, the powers and functions which emanate from him, do not simply lie before him like merchandise on a counter. It is most important to realize that, even if an individual gives only a particular item, offers only one side of his personality, he may yet wholly *be* in this side, may yet give his personality completely in the form of this single energy, or attribute, as Spinoza would say. This disproportion appears only if the relation has become differentiated to a point where the gift is severed from the giver's total personality. If this is *not* so, however, it is precisely in these cases that a wonderfully pure instance of a phenomenon emerges which is, otherwise, not very frequent: of gratitude as the reaction equally to the benefit and to the benefactor. Man's plasticity allows him both to offer and to accept, by means of the apparently objective response to the gift which consists in another gift, all of the subjectivity of gift and giver.

The most profound instance of this kind occurs when the whole inner mood, which is oriented toward the other person in the particular manner called gratitude, is *more* than an enlarged projection (as it were) of the actually well-defined reaction of thankfulness upon our total psychic disposition: but when, instead, the goods and other obligations we receive from the other, merely strike us as an occasion upon which our relation to him, predetermined as it is in our inner nature, is realized. What we usually call gratitude and what has given this feeling its name in terms of single benefits, here goes much below the ordinary form of thanks for gifts. One might say that here gratitude actually consists, not in the return of a gift, but in the consciousness that it cannot be returned, that there is something which places the receiver into a certain permanent position with respect to the giver, and makes him dimly envisage the inner infinity of a relation that can neither be exhausted nor realized by any finite return gift or other activity.

This touches upon a further deep-lying incommensurability, which is an essential characteristic of the relationships subsumed under the category of gratitude. Once we have received something good from another person, once he has preceded us with his action [*"vorgeleistet"*], we no longer can make up for it completely, no matter how much our own return gift or service may objectively or legally surpass his own. The reason is that his gift, because it was first, has a voluntary character which no return gift can have. For, to return the benefit we are obliged ethically; we operate under a coercion which, though neither social nor legal but moral, is still a coercion. The first gift is given in full spontaneity; it has a freedom without any duty, even without the duty of gratitude. By his bold identification of doing one's duty with freedom, Kant ruled this character of duty out of court, but thereby confused the negative side of freedom with its positive side. We are apparently free to do or not to do the duty we feel above us as an ideal; but, actually, complete freedom exists only in regard to *not* doing it, since to do it follows from a psychic imperative, from a coercion which is the inner equivalent of the legal coercion of society. Complete freedom does not lie on the side of doing, but only on that of not-doing, for, to *do* I am obligated because it is a duty—I am caused to return a gift, for instance, by the mere fact that I received it. Only when we give first are we free, and this is the reason why, in the first gift, which is not occasioned by any gratitude, there lies a beauty, a spontaneous devotion to the other, an opening up and flowering from the "virgin soil" of the soul, as it were, which cannot be matched by any subsequent gift, no matter how superior its content. The difference involved here finds expression in the feeling (apparently often unjustified in regard to the concrete *content* of the gift) that we *cannot* return a gift; for it has a freedom which the return gift, because it is *that,* cannot possibly possess.

This, perhaps, is the reason why some people do not like to accept, and try to avoid as much as possible being given gifts. Their attitude would be ununderstandable if gift and gratitude concerned objects only: for, merely by returning the gift, everything could be balanced and the inner obligation redeemed. Actually, however, these people act on the instinct, perhaps, that the return gift cannot possibly contain the decisive element of the original, namely, freedom; and that, in accepting it, therefore, they would contract an irredeemable obligation.[4] As a rule, such people have a strong impulse to independence and individuality; and this suggests that the condition of gratitude easily has a taste of bondage, that it is a moral *character indelebilis* [inextinguishable element]. A service, a sacrifice, a benefit, once accepted, may engender an inner relation which can never be eliminated completely, because gratitude is perhaps the only feeling which, under all circumstances, can be morally demanded and rendered. If by itself or in response to some external reality, our inner life has made it impossible for us to continue loving, revering, esteeming a person (aesthetically or ethically or intellectually), we can still be grateful to him, since he once gained our gratitude. To *this* demand we are (or could be) unconditionally subject: in regard to no fault of feeling is an unmitigated sentence as appropriate as in regard to ingratitude.

Even intimate faithfulness is more remissible. There are relationships which, from their very beginning, operate only with a limited capital of feeling (so to speak) and, after a time, inevitably use it up. Thus their termination does not involve any unfaithfulness, properly speaking. In their initial stages, how-

---

[4] This, of course, is an extreme statement, but its remoteness from reality is inevitable in analyses which try to isolate, and thus make visible, elements of phychic reality that actually are mixed in a thousand ways, are constantly deflected, and exist almost exclusively in embryonic forms.

ever, it is difficult to distinguish these from other relations, which (continuing the metaphor) live off interest only and in which no passionate and unreserved giving makes inroads into the capital. It is certainly one of the most common errors of man to think that something which actually is capital is only interest, and, for this reason, so to construct a relationship that its breach does become an act of unfaithfulness. But this act is not then a delinquency committed in full freedom, but only the logical outcome of a development based all along on erroneous factors. Nor does unfaithfulness appear any more avoidable where not the discovery of a mistake, but an actual change in the individuals, alters the presuppositions of their relationship. Perhaps the greatest tragedy of human conditions springs from (among other things) the utterly unrationalizable and constantly shifting mixture of the stable and variable elements of our nature. Even when we have entered a binding relationship with our whole being, we may yet remain in the same mood and inclination as before with some of our aspects—perhaps with those that are turned outward, but possibly even with some internal ones. But other aspects develop into entirely new interests, aims, capacities, and thus come to throw our total existence into new directions. In doing so, they turn us away from earlier conditions [5] with a sort of unfaithfulness, which is neither quite innocent, since there still exist some bonds which must now be broken, nor quite guilty, since we are no longer the persons we were when we entered the relationship; the subject to whom the unfaithfulness could be imputed has disappeared.

When our feeling of gratitude gives out, our sentiments admit of no such exoneration on inner grounds. For, gratitude seems to reside in a point in us which we do not allow to change; of which we demand constancy with more right, than we do of more passionate, even of deeper, feelings. Gratitude is peculiarly irredeemable. It maintains its claim even after an equal or greater return gift has been made, and it may, in fact, claim both parties to the relation, the first and the second giver (a possibility which is indirectly due, perhaps, to that freedom of the initial gift which is missing in the return gift with only its

---

[5] By conditions, of course, only purely internal ones are understood here, not those of external duty.

moral necessity). This irredeemable nature of gratitude shows it as a bond between men which is as subtle as it is firm. Every human relationship of any duration produces a thousand occasions for it, and even the most ephemeral ones do not allow their increment to the reciprocal obligation to be lost. In fortunate cases, but sometimes even in cases abundantly provided with counter-instances, the sum of these increments produces an atmosphere of generalized obligation (the saying that one is "obliged" ["*verbunden*"] to somebody who has earned our thanks is quite apt), which can be redeemed by no accomplishments whatever. This atmosphere of obligation belongs among those "microscopic," but infinitely tough, threads which tie one element of society to another, and thus eventually all of them together in a stable collective life.

Chapter 2

The Negative Character of Collective Behavior

THE RESULT OF [COLLEC-tive] phenomena is achieved, in several respects, only through negation. More precisely, often they develop their negative character as the groups, which are their instruments, increase in size. In mass actions, individual motives are frequently so different that their unification is the more easily possible, the more their content is merely negative, even destructive. The discontent that leads to great revolutions always feeds on so many, often contradictory, sources, that their unification in favor of a positive goal is impossible. The construction of this positive goal, therefore, is usually the task of smaller groups and of innumerable individual contributions of divergent forces which, if unified in mass action, would have only dispersing and destructive consequences. In this respect, one of the greatest historians said that the multitude is always ungrateful because, even if the whole is brought to flourish, the single individual nevertheless feels, above all, what he still lacks personally. The heterogeneity of individuals, which leaves negation [6] as the only common denominator, is shown very clearly, for instance, in earlier Russian revolutionism. The immense space, the cultural differences, the number of varying aims that dominated the movement, actually made *nihil*ism, the mere an*nihil*ation of whatever was at issue, the correct name for the features common to all of its elements.

The same trait emerges in the results of great plebiscites which, so often and almost ununderstandably, are negative. In

[6] This must be taken, of course, with a grain of salt; it does not consider at all what society does to overcome this particular fate of its forces.

Switzerland, in 1900, for instance, a referendum simply rejected a federal sickness and accident insurance bill, which had been passed unanimously by both popular *representations,* the National Council and the Council of States; and this, also, was the fate of most other bills subjected to the referendum. Negation is after all simplest; and, for this reason, the elements of a mass can agree on it where they can reach no consent concerning a positive aim. The various groups which rejected the law on the basis of very different standpoints—particularlistic, ultramontane, agrarian, capitalistic, technical, party-political—could only have negation in common.

For the same reason, however, the sharing of, at least, negative characteristics by many small groups may suggest or prepare their unity. Thus it has been pointed out that the Greeks showed great cultural differences among one another, but that both Arcadians and Athenians, as compared with contemporary Carthaginians, Egyptians, Persians, or Thracians, nevertheless had many *negative* common features: nowhere in historical Greece were there human sacrifices, intentional mutilations, polygamy, the sale of children into slavery, or unlimited obedience to an individual. In spite of all positive differences, this commonness of the merely negative was bound to make all Greeks conscious of belonging to a culture that transcended the individual Greek state.

The negative character of the bond that unifies the large group is revealed, above all, in its norms. It should be remembered that obligatory rules of *every* sort must be the simpler and the less voluminous (other things being equal), the larger the sphere of their application. There are much fewer rules of international courtesy, for instance, than there are courtesy rules which have to be observed within every smaller circle; or, the larger the states of the German Reich, the briefer, usually, are their constitutions. To put it in the form of a principle: as the size of the group increases, the common features that fuse its members into a social unit become ever fewer. For this reason (although at first glance it sounds paradoxical), a smaller minimum of norms can, at least, hold together a large group more easily than a small one. Qualitatively speaking, the larger the group is, usually the more prohibitive and restrictive the kinds of conduct which it must demand of its participants in order to maintain itself: the positive ties, which connect individual with individual and give the life of the group its real content, must (after all) be given over to these individuals.[7] The variety of persons, interests, events becomes too large to be regulated by a center; the center is left only with a prohibitive function, with the determination of what must not be done under any circumstances, with the restriction of freedom, rather than its direction. All this, of course, merely indicates the trend of a development which is always crossed and deflected by other tendencies.

The same problems arise in connection with the unification of a number of groups with divergent religious feelings or interests. Allah emerged as the general idea of God as such, so to speak, out of the decay of Arab polytheism. Polytheism necessarily engenders a split among its adherents since, according to their different tendencies (internal as well as practical), they espouse the various gods in different ways. Initially, therefore, Allah's abstract and unifying character was negative: its original nature was "to hold men back from evil," not to urge them to do good—he was only the "restrainer." Although, in comparison with all dispersing polytheisms and a-social monisms (as in India), the Hebrew God effected or expressed a consistency of the religio-social content unheard of in antiquity, he, too, delivered his most emphatic practical norms in the form of "Thou shalt not."

In Germany, the *positive* life relations underlying civil law were unified in the Civil Code only some thirty years after the Reich was founded, whereas the Criminal Code, with its *negative* rules, has been uniformly in force ever since 1872. The particular circumstance which makes prohibitions especially well suited for expanding smaller groups into large ones, is that the

[7] For this reason an English proverb says: "The business of everybody is the business of nobody." The peculiar fact that actions become negative once a plurality engages in them, is also shown in the motive in terms of which an attempt has been made at explaining the forbearance and indolence, in regard to public evils, of the (otherwise so energetic) North Americans. Public opinion there, the explanation runs, is supposed to bring about everything. Hence the fatalism which, "making each individual feel his insignificance, disposes him to leave to the multitude the task of setting right what is every one else's business just as much as his own."

opposite of prohibition is by no means always command, but often only permission. Thus, when in group A, *a* must not occur, but *b* and *c* are permitted; in B, not *b*, but *a* and *c*; and, in C, not *c*, but *a* and *b*, etc.; then the comprehensive structure composed of A and B and C may well be founded upon the prohibition of all the three *a*, *b*, and *c*. This unity, however, is possible only if, in A, *b* and *c* are not commanded, but only permitted, so that they also may *not* be done. If, instead, *b* and *c* are as positively commanded as *a* is prohibited (and correspondingly for B and C), a unity cannot be brought about, because, in such a case, what is explicitly commanded in one group, is explicitly prohibited in another.

This scheme is illustrated in the following example. Originally, every Egyptian was prohibited to eat of a particular animal species, which was sacred to his district. Later, as the result of the political fusion of a number of local cults into a national religion which was headed by a priesthood reigning throughout the nation, this developed into the doctrine that holiness demands abstention from *all* flesh food. The unification could be brought about only as the synthesis or generalization of all the particular prohibitions: had the eating of all animals permitted (but not enjoined) in every district been a positive command, evidently there would have been no possibility of combining the particular rules of the various districts into a more comprehensive unity.

The more general the norm and the larger the group in which it prevails, the less does the *observance* of the norm characterize the individual and the less important is it for him—whereas its *violation,* on the whole, has consequences which are especially grave, which single out the individual from his group. This is quite obviously so, above all, in the intellectual field. Theoretical communication [mutual understanding], without which human society could not exist at all, rests on a small number of generally agreed-on norms, which we call the norms of logic—although, of course, not everybody is conscious of them in their abstractness. They constitute the minimum of what must be acknowledged by all who want, in any way, to communicate with one another. On them rests the briefest agreement between strangers and the common daily life of the closest persons. Thought would never coincide with empirical reality without obeying these elementary norms: its adherence to them is the most indispensable, the most general condition of all sociological life. Logic, thus, cuts through the variety of world views, profound and shallow, and creates a certain common ground whose neglect would abolish all intellectual community in every sense of the term.

Yet, if we look closely, we find that logic gives us no positive possession at all: it is only a norm against which we must not sin—while we derive no distinction, no specific good or quality, from its observance. All attempts at gaining particular knowledge by means of logic alone have failed; and its sociological significance, therefore, is as negative as that of the criminal code: in both cases, only the *violation* of the norm creates particular and exposed situations, while staying in the norm produces no more for the individual than the possibility of remaining within (respectively) theoretical and practical generality. To be sure, because of a thousand contentual divergences, intellectual contact may not come forth even if logic is rigorously observed; but, if it is violated, communication is *bound* to fail—just as moral and social cohesion may collapse, for all avoidance of the prohibitions in the criminal code, while it *must* do so if its laws are disobeyed.

All this also applies to societal forms in the stricter sense, insofar as they *are* general within a given group. In this case, their observance is not characteristic of anybody, but their transgression certainly is: the most general norms of a group merely must not be transgressed, whereas (in the measure of their specialization) the particular norms, that hold smaller groups together, positively give their members character and distinction. On this situation rests the practical utility of social courtesy forms, which are so empty. Even from their most punctilious observance, we must not infer any positive existence of the esteem and devotion they emphasize; but their slightest violation is an unmistakable indication that these feelings do *not* exist. Greeting somebody in the street proves no esteem whatever, but failure to do so, conclusively proves the opposite. The forms of courtesy fail as symbols of positive, inner attitudes, but they are most useful in documenting negative ones, since even the

slightest omission can radically and definitely alter our relation
to a person. And they both fail and succeed to the extent to
which they are general and conventional, that is, characteristic
of the large circle.

Chapter 3

The Stranger

IF WANDERING IS THE LIB-
eration from every given point in space, and thus the concep-
tional opposite to fixation at such a point, the sociological form
of the "stranger" presents the unity, as it were, of these two
characteristics. This phenomenon too, however, reveals that
spatial relations are only the condition, on the one hand, and
the symbol, on the other, of human relations. The stranger is
thus being discussed here, not in the sense often touched upon
in the past, as the wanderer who comes today and goes tomor-
row, but rather as the person who comes today and stays to-
morrow. He is, so to speak, the *potential* wanderer: although
he has not moved on, he has not quite overcome the freedom
of coming and going. He is fixed within a particular spatial
group, or within a group whose boundaries are similar to spatial
boundaries. But his position in this group is determined, essentially, by the fact that he has not belonged to it from the beginning, that he imports qualities into it, which do not and
cannot stem from the group itself.

The unity of nearness and remoteness involved in every
human relation is organized, in the phenomenon of the stranger,
in a way which may be most briefly formulated by saying that
in the relationship to him, distance means that he, who is close
by, is far, and strangeness means that he, who also is far, is
actually near. For, to be a stranger is naturally a very positive
relation; it is a specific form of interaction. The inhabitants
of Sirius are not really strangers to us, at least not in any sociologically relevant sense: they do not exist for us at all; they
are beyond far and near. The stranger, like the poor and like
sundry "inner enemies," is an element of the group itself. His
position as a full-fledged member involves both being outside

it and confronting it. The following statements, which are by no means intended as exhaustive, indicate how elements which increase distance and repel, in the relations of and with the stranger produce a pattern of coordination and consistent interaction.

Throughout the history of economics the stranger everywhere appears as the trader, or the trader as stranger. As long as economy is essentially self-sufficient, or products are exchanged within a spatially narrow group, it needs no middleman: a trader is only required for products that originate outside the group. Insofar as members do not leave the circle in order to buy these necessities—in which case *they* are the "strange" merchants in that outside territory— the trader *must* be a stranger, since nobody else has a chance to make a living.

This position of the stranger stands out more sharply if he settles down in the place of his activity, instead of leaving it again: in innumerable cases even this is possible only if he can live by intermediate trade. Once an economy is somehow closed, the land is divided up, and handicrafts are established that satisfy the demand for them, the trader, too, can find his existence. For in trade, which alone makes possible unlimited combinations, intelligence always finds expansions and new territories, an achievement which is very difficult to attain for the original producer with his lesser mobility and his dependence upon a circle of customers that can be increased only slowly. Trade can always absorb more people than primary production; it is, therefore, the sphere indicated for the stranger, who intrudes as a supernumerary, so to speak, into a group in which the economic positions are actually occupied—the classical example is the history of European Jews. The stranger is by nature no "owner of soil"—soil not only in the physical, but also in the figurative sense of a life-substance which is fixed, if not in a point in space, at least in an ideal point of the social environment. Although in more intimate relations, he may develop all kinds of charm and significance, as long as he is considered a stranger in the eyes of the other, he is not an "owner of soil." Restriction to intermediary trade, and often (as though sublimated from it) to pure finance, gives him the specific character of *mobility*. If mobility takes place within a closed group, it embodies that synthesis of nearness and distance which constitutes the formal position of the stranger. For, the fundamentally mobile person comes in contact, at one time or another, with every individual, but is not organically connected, through established ties of kinship, locality, and occupation, with any single one.

Another expression of this constellation lies in the objectivity of the stranger. He is not radically committed to the unique ingredients and peculiar tendencies of the group, and therefore approaches them with the specific attitude of "objectivity." But objectivity does not simply involve passivity and detachment; it is a particular structure composed of distance and nearness, indifference and involvement. I refer to the discussion (in the chapter on "Superordination and Subordination"[8]) of the dominating positions of the person who is a stranger in the group; its most typical instance was the practice of those Italian cities to call their judges from the outside, because no native was free from entanglement in family and party interests.

With the objectivity of the stranger is connected, also, the phenomenon touched upon above,[9] although it is chiefly (but not exclusively) true of the stranger who moves on. This is the fact that he often receives the most surprising openness—confidences which sometimes have the character of a confessional and which would be carefully withheld from a more closely related person. Objectivity is by no means non-participation (which is altogether outside both subjective and objective interaction), but a positive and specific kind of participation—just as the objectivity of a theoretical observation does not refer to the mind as a passive *tabula rasa* on which things inscribe their qualities, but on the contrary, to its full activity that operates according to its own laws, and to the elimination, thereby, of accidental dislocations and emphases, whose individual and subjective differences would produce different pictures of the same object.

8 Pp. 216–221 above.—Tr.

9 On pp. 500–502 of the same chapter from which the present *"Exkurs"* is taken (IX, *"Der Raum und die räumlichen Ordnungen der Gesellschaft,"* Space and the Spatial Organization of Society). The chapter itself is not included in this volume.—Tr.

Objectivity may also be defined as freedom: the objective individual is bound by no commitments which could prejudice his perception, understanding, and evaluation of the given. The freedom, however, which allows the stranger to experience and treat even his close relationships as though from a bird's-eye view, contains many dangerous possibilities. In uprisings of all sorts, the party attacked has claimed, from the beginning of things, that provocation has come from the outside, through emissaries and instigators. Insofar as this is true, it is an exaggeration of the specific role of the stranger: he is freer, practically and theoretically; he surveys conditions with less prejudice; his criteria for them are more general and more objective ideals; he is not tied down in his action by habit, piety, and precedent.[10]

Finally, the proportion of nearness and remoteness which gives the stranger the character of objectivity, also finds practical expression in the more *abstract nature* of the relation to him. That is, with the stranger one has only certain *more general* qualities in common, whereas the relation to more organically connected persons is based on the commonness of specific differences from merely general features. In fact, all somehow personal relations follow this scheme in various patterns. They are determined not only by the circumstance that certain common features exist among the individuals, along with individual differences, which either influence the relationship or remain outside of it. For, the common features themselves are basically determined in their effect upon the relation by the question whether they exist only between the participants in this particular relationship, and thus are quite general in regard to this relation, but are specific and incomparable in regard to everything outside of it—or whether the participants feel that these features are common to them because they are common to a group, a type, or mankind in general. In the case of the second alternative, the effectiveness of the common features becomes

10 But where the attacked make the assertion falsely, they do so from the tendency of those in higher position to exculpate inferiors, who, up to the rebellion, have been in a consistently close relation with them. For, by creating the fiction that the rebels were not really guilty, but only instigated, and that the rebellion did not really start with *them,* they exonerate themselves, inasmuch as they altogether deny all real grounds for the uprising.

diluted in proportion to the size of the group composed of members who are similar in this sense. Although the commonness functions as their unifying basis, it does not make *these* particular persons interdependent on one another, because it could as easily connect everyone of them with all kinds of individuals other than the members of his group. This too, evidently, is a way in which a relationship includes both nearness and distance at the same time: to the extent to which the common features are general, they add, to the warmth of the relation founded on them, an element of coolness, a feeling of the contingency of precisely *this* relation—the connecting forces have lost their specific and centripetal character.

In the relation to the stranger, it seems to me, this constellation has an extraordinary and basic preponderance over the individual elements that are exclusive with the particular relationship. The stranger is close to us, insofar as we feel between him and ourselves common features of a national, social, occupational, or generally human, nature. He is far from us, insofar as these common features extend beyond him or us, and connect us only because they connect a great many people.

A trace of strangeness in this sense easily enters even the most intimate relationships. In the stage of first passion, erotic relations strongly reject any thought of generalization: the lovers think that there has never been a love like theirs; that nothing can be compared either to the person loved or to the feelings for that person. An estrangement—whether as cause or as consequence it is difficult to decide—usually comes at the moment when this feeling of uniqueness vanishes from the relationship. A certain skepticism in regard to its value, in itself and for them, attaches to the very thought that in their relation, after all, they carry out only a generally human destiny; that they experience an experience that has occurred a thousand times before; that, had they not accidentally met their particular partner, they would have found the same significance in another person.

Something of this feeling is probably not absent in any relation, however close, because what is common to two is never common to them alone, but is subsumed under a general idea which includes much else besides, many *possibilities* of commonness. No matter how little these possibilities become real and how often we forget them, here and there, nevertheless, they thrust themselves between us like shadows, like a mist which escapes every word noted, but which must coagulate into a solid bodily form before it can be called jealousy. In some cases, perhaps the more general, at least the more unsurmountable, strangeness is not due to different and ununderstandable matters. It is rather caused by the fact that similarity, harmony, and nearness are accompanied by the feeling that they are not really the unique property of this particular relationship: they are something more general, something which potentially prevails between the partners and an indeterminate number of others, and therefore gives the relation, which alone was realized, no inner and exclusive necessity.

On the other hand, there is a kind of "strangeness" that rejects the very commonness based on something more general which embraces the parties. The relation of the Greeks to the Barbarians is perhaps typical here, as are all cases in which it is precisely general attributes, felt to be specifically and purely human, that are disallowed to the other. But "stranger," here, has no positive meaning; the relation to him is a non-relation; he is not what is relevant here, a member of the group itself.

As a group member, rather, he is near and far *at the same time,* as is characteristic of relations founded only on generally human commonness. But between nearness and distance, there arises a specific tension when the consciousness that only the quite general is common, stresses that which is not common. In the case of the person who is a stranger to the country, the city, the race, etc., however, this non-common element is once more nothing individual, but merely the strangeness of origin, which is or could be common to many strangers. For this reason, strangers are not really conceived as individuals, but as strangers of a particular type: the element of distance is no less general in regard to them than the element of nearness.

This form is the basis of such a special case, for instance, as the tax levied in Frankfort and elsewhere upon medieval Jews. Whereas the *Beede* [tax] paid by the Christian citizen changed with the changes of his fortune, it was fixed once for all for every single Jew. This fixity rested on the fact that the

Jew had his social position as a *Jew,* not as the individual bearer
of certain objective contents. Every other citizen was the owner
of a particular amount of property, and his tax followed its
fluctuations. But the Jew as a taxpayer was, in the first place,
a Jew, and thus his tax situation had an invariable element.
This same position appears most strongly, of course, once even
these individual characterizations (limited though they were by
rigid invariance) are omitted, and all strangers pay an altogether
equal head-tax.

In spite of being inorganically appended to it, the stranger
is yet an organic member of the group. Its uniform life includes
the specific conditions of this element. Only we do not know
how to designate the peculiar unity of this position other than
by saying that it is composed of certain measures of nearness
and distance. Although some quantities of them characterize
all relationships, a *special* proportion and reciprocal tension
produce the particular, formal relation to the "stranger."

Chapter 4

The Metropolis and Mental Life

THE DEEPEST PROBLEMS OF modern life derive from the claim of the individual to preserve the autonomy and individuality of his existence in the face of overwhelming social forces, of historical heritage, of external culture, and of the technique of life. The fight with nature which primitive man has to wage for his *bodily* existence attains in this modern form its latest transformation. The eighteenth century called upon man to free himself of all the historical bonds in the state and in religion, in morals and in economics. Man's nature, originally good and common to all, should develop unhampered. In addition to more liberty, the nineteenth century demanded the functional specialization of man and his work; this specialization makes one individual incomparable to another, and each of them indispensable to the highest possible extent. However, this specialization makes each man the more directly dependent upon the supplementary activities of all others. Nietzsche sees the full development of the individual conditioned by the most ruthless struggle of individuals; socialism believes in the suppression of all competition for the same reason. Be that as it may, in all these positions the same basic motive is at work: the person resists to being leveled down and worn out by a social-technological mechanism. An inquiry into the inner meaning of specifically modern life and its products, into the soul of the cultural body, so to speak, must seek to solve the equation which structures like the metropolis set up between the individual and the super-individual contents of life. Such an inquiry must answer the question of how the personality accommodates itself in the adjustments to external forces. This will be my task today.

The psychological basis of the metropolitan type of individuality consists in the *intensification of nervous stimulation* which results from the swift and uninterrupted change of outer and inner stimuli. Man is a differentiating creature. His mind is stimulated by the difference between a momentary impression and the one which preceded it. Lasting impressions, impressions which differ only slightly from one another, impressions which take a regular and habitual course and show regular and habitual contrasts—all these use up, so to speak, less consciousness than does the rapid crowding of changing images, the sharp discontinuity in the grasp of a single glance, and the unexpectedness of onrushing impressions. These are the psychological conditions which the metropolis creates. With each crossing of the street, with the tempo and multiplicity of economic, occupational and social life, the city sets up a deep contrast with small town and rural life with reference to the sensory foundations of psychic life. The metropolis exacts from man as a discriminating creature a different amount of consciousness than does rural life. Here the rhythm of life and sensory mental imagery flows more slowly, more habitually, and more evenly. Precisely in this connection the sophisticated character of metropolitan psychic life becomes understandable—as over against small town life which rests more upon deeply felt and emotional relationships. These latter are rooted in the more unconscious layers of the psyche and grow most readily in the steady rhythm of uninterrupted habituations. The intellect, however, has its locus in the transparent, conscious, higher layers of the psyche; it is the most adaptable of our inner forces. In order to accommodate to change and to the contrast of phenomena, the intellect does not require any shocks and inner upheavals; it is only through such upheavals that the more conservative mind could accommodate to the metropolitan rhythm of events. Thus the metropolitan type of man—which, of course, exists in a thousand individual variants—develops an organ protecting him against the threatening currents and discrepancies of his external environment which would uproot him. He reacts with his head instead of his heart. In this an increased awareness assumes the psychic prerogative. Metropolitan life, thus, underlies a heightened awareness and a predominance of intelligence in metropolitan man. The reaction to metropolitan phenomena is shifted to that organ which is least sensitive and quite remote from the depth of the personality. Intellectuality is thus seen to preserve subjective life against the overwhelming power of metropolitan life, and intellectuality branches out in many directions and is integrated with numerous discrete phenomena.

The metropolis has always been the seat of the money economy. Here the multiplicity and concentration of economic exchange gives an importance to the means of exchange which the scantiness of rural commerce would not have allowed. Money economy and the dominance of the intellect are intrinsically connected. They share a matter-of-fact attitude in dealing with men and with things; and, in this attitude, a formal justice is often coupled with an inconsiderate hardness. The intellectually sophisticated person is indifferent to all genuine individuality, because relationships and reactions result from it which cannot be exhausted with logical operations. In the same manner, the individuality of phenomena is not commensurate with the pecuniary principle. Money is concerned only with what is common to all: it asks for the exchange value, it reduces all quality and individuality to the question: How much? All intimate emotional relations between persons are founded in their individuality, whereas in rational relations man is reckoned with like a number, like an element which is in itself indifferent. Only the objective measurable achievement is of interest. Thus metropolitan man reckons with his merchants and customers, his domestic servants and often even with persons with whom he is obliged to have social intercourse. These features of intellectuality contrast with the nature of the small circle in which the inevitable knowledge of individuality as inevitably produces a warmer tone of behavior, a behavior which is beyond a mere objective balancing of service and return. In the sphere of the economic psychology of the small group it is of importance that under primitive conditions production serves the customer who orders the good, so that the producer and the consumer are acquainted. The modern metropolis, however, is supplied almost entirely by production for the market, that is, for entirely unknown purchasers who never personally enter the producer's actual field of vision. Through this anonymity the interests of each party acquire an unmerciful matter-of-factness; and the intellectually calculating economic egoisms of both parties need not fear any deflection because of the imponderables of personal relationships. The money economy dominates the metropolis; it has displaced the last survivals of domestic production and the direct barter of goods; it minimizes, from day to day, the amount of work ordered by customers. The matter-of-fact attitude is obviously so intimately interrelated with the money economy, which is dominant in the metropolis, that nobody can say whether the intellectualistic mentality first promoted the money economy or whether the latter determined the former. The metropolitan way of life is certainly the most fertile soil for this reciprocity, a point which I shall document merely by citing the dictum of the most eminent English constitutional historian: throughout the whole course of English history, London has never acted as England's heart but often as England's intellect and always as her moneybag!

In certain seemingly insignificant traits, which lie upon the surface of life, the same psychic currents characteristically unite. Modern mind has become more and more calculating. The calculative exactness of practical life which the money economy has brought about corresponds to the ideal of natural science: to transform the world into an arithmetic problem, to fix every part of the world by mathematical formulas. Only money economy has filled the days of so many people with weighing, calculating, with numerical determinations, with a reduction of qualitative values to quantitative ones. Through the calculative nature of money a new precision, a certainty in the definition of identities and differences, an unambiguousness in agreements and arrangements has been brought about in the relations of life-elements—just as externally this precision has been effected by the universal diffusion of pocket watches. However, the conditions of metropolitan life are at once cause and effect of this trait. The relationships and affairs of the typical metropolitan usually are so varied and complex that without the strictest punctuality in promises and services the whole structure would break down into an inextricable chaos. Above all, this necessity is brought about by the aggregation of so many people with such differentiated interests, who must integrate their relations and activities into a highly complex organism. If all clocks and watches in Berlin would suddenly go wrong in different ways, even if only by one hour, all economic life and communication of the city would be disrupted for a long time. In addition an apparently mere external factor: long distances, would make all waiting and broken appointments result in an ill-afforded waste of time. Thus, the technique of metropolitan life is unimaginable without the most punctual integration of all activities and mutual relations into a stable and impersonal time schedule. Here again the general conclusions of this entire task of reflection become obvious, namely, that from each point on the surface of existence—however closely attached to the surface alone—one may drop a sounding into the depth of the psyche so that all the most banal externalities of life finally are connected with the ultimate decisions concerning the meaning and style of life. Punctuality, calculability, exactness are forced upon life by the complexity and extension of metropolitan existence and are not only most intimately connected with its money economy and intellectualistic character. These traits must also color the contents of life and favor the exclusion of those irrational, instinctive, sovereign traits and impulses which aim at determining the mode of life from within, instead of receiving the general and precisely schematized form of life from without. Even though sovereign types of personality, characterized by irrational impulses, are by no means impossible in the city, they are, nevertheless, opposed to typical city life. The passionate hatred of men like Ruskin and Nietzsche for the metropolis is understandable in these terms. Their natures discovered the value of life alone in the unschematized existence which cannot be defined with precision for all alike. From the same source of this hatred of the metropolis surged their hatred of money economy and of the intellectualism of modern existence.

The same factors which have thus coalesced into the exactness and minute precision of the form of life have coalesced into a structure of the highest impersonality; on the other hand, they have promoted a highly personal subjectivity. There is perhaps no psychic phenomenon which has been so unconditionally reserved to the metropolis as has the blasé attitude. The blasé attitude results first from the rapidly changing and closely compressed contrasting stimulations of the nerves. From this, the enhancement of metropolitan intellectuality, also, seems originally to stem. Therefore, stupid people who are not intellectually alive in the first place usually are not exactly blasé. A life in boundless pursuit of pleasure makes one blasé because it agitates the nerves to their strongest reactivity for such a long time that they finally cease to react at all. In the same way, through the rapidity and contradictoriness of their changes, more harmless impressions force such violent responses, tearing the nerves so brutally hither and thither that their last reserves of strength are spent; and if one remains in the same milieu they have no time to gather new strength. An incapacity thus emerges to react to new sensations with the appropriate energy. This constitutes that blasé attitude which, in fact, every metropolitan child shows when compared with children of quieter and less changeable milieus.

This physiological source of the metropolitan blasé attitude is joined by another source which flows from the money economy. The essence of the blasé attitude consists in the blunting of discrimination. This does not mean that the objects are not perceived, as is the case with the half-wit, but rather that the meaning and differing values of things, and thereby the things themselves, are experienced as insubstantial. They appear to the blasé person in an evenly flat and gray tone; no one object deserves preference over any other. This mood is the faithful subjective reflection of the completely internalized money economy. By being the equivalent to all the manifold things in one and the same way, money becomes the most frightful leveler. For money expresses all qualitative differences of things in terms of "how much?" Money, with all its colorlessness and indifference, becomes the common denominator of all values; irreparably it hollows out the core of things, their individuality, their specific value, and their incomparability. All things float with equal specific gravity in the constantly moving stream of money. All things lie on the same level and differ from one another only in the size of the area which they cover. In the individual case this coloration, or rather discoloration, of things through their money equivalence may be unnoticeably minute. However, through the relations of the rich to the objects to be had for money, perhaps even through the total character which the mentality of the contemporary public everywhere imparts to these objects, the exclusively pecuniary evaluation of objects has become quite considerable. The large cities, the main seats of the money exchange, bring the purchasability of things to the fore much more impressively than do smaller localities. That is why cities are also the genuine locale of the blasé attitude. In the blasé attitude the concentration of men and things stimulate the nervous system of the individual to its highest achievement so that it attains its peak. Through the mere quantitative intensification of the same conditioning factors this achievement is transformed into its opposite and appears in the peculiar adjustment of the blasé attitude. In this phenomenon the nerves find in the refusal to react to their stimulation the last possibility of accommodating to the contents and forms of metropolitan life. The self-preservation of certain personalities is brought at the price of devaluating the whole objective world, a devaluation which in the end unavoidably drags one's own personality down into a feeling of the same worthlessness.

Whereas the subject of this form of existence has to come to terms with it entirely for himself, his self-preservation in the face of the large city demands from him a no less negative behavior of a social nature. This mental attitude of metropolitans toward one another we may designate, from a formal point of view, as reserve. If so many inner reactions were responses to the continuous external contacts with innumerable people as are those in the small town, where one knows almost everybody one meets and where one has a positive relation to almost everyone, one would be completely atomized internally and come to an unimaginable psychic state. Partly this psychological fact, partly the right to distrust which men have in the face of the touch-and-go elements of metropolitan life, necessitates our reserve. As a result of this reserve we frequently do not even know by sight those who have been our neighbors for years. And it is this reserve which in the eyes of the small-town people makes us appear to be cold and heartless. Indeed, if I do not deceive myself, the inner aspect of this outer reserve is not only indifference but, more often than we are aware, it is a slight aversion, a mutual strangeness and repulsion, which will break into hatred and fight at the moment of a closer contact, however caused. The whole inner organization of such an extensive communicative life rests upon an extremely varied hierarchy of sympathies, indifferences, and aversions of the briefest as well as of the most permanent nature. The sphere of indifference in this hierarchy is not as large as might appear on the surface. Our psychic activity still responds to almost every impression of somebody else with a somewhat distinct feeling. The unconscious, fluid and changing character of this impression seems to result in a state of indifference. Actually this indifference would be just as unnatural as the diffusion of indiscriminate mutual suggestion would be unbearable. From both these typical dangers of the metropolis, indifference and indiscriminate suggestibility, antipathy protects us. A latent antipathy and the preparatory stage of practical antagonism effect the distances and aversions without which this mode of life could not at all be led. The extent and the mixture of this style of life, the rhythm of its emergence and disappearance, the forms in which it is satisfied— all these, with the unifying motives in the narrower sense, form the inseparable whole of the metropolitan style of life. What appears in the metropolitan style of life directly as dissociation is in reality only one of its elemental forms of socialization.

This reserve with its overtone of hidden aversion appears in turn as the form or the cloak of a more general mental phenomenon of the metropolis: it grants to the individual a kind and an amount of personal freedom which has no analogy whatsoever under other conditions. The metropolis goes back to one of the large developmental tendencies of social life as such, to one of the few tendencies for which an approximately universal formula can be discovered. The earliest phase of social formations found in historical as well as in contemporary social structures is this: a relatively small circle firmly closed against neighboring, strange, or in some way antagonistic circles. However, this circle is closely coherent and allows its individual members only a narrow field for the development of unique qualities and free, self-responsible movements. Political and kinship groups, parties and religious associations begin in this way. The self-preservation of very young associations requires the establishment of strict boundaries and a centripetal unity. Therefore they cannot allow the individual freedom and unique inner and outer development. From this stage social development proceeds at once in two different, yet corresponding, directions. To the extent to which the group grows—numerically, spatially, in significance and in content of life—to the same degree the group's direct, inner unity loosens, and the rigidity of the original demarcation against others is softened through mutual relations and connections. At the same time, the individual gains freedom of movement, far beyond the first jealous delimitation. The individual also gains a specific individuality to which the division of labor in the enlarged group gives both occasion and necessity. The state and Christianity, guilds and political parties, and innumerable other groups have developed according to this formula, however much, of course, the special conditions and forces of the respective groups have modified the general scheme. This scheme seems to me distinctly recognizable also in the evolution of individuality within urban life. The small-town life in Antiquity and in the Middle Ages set barriers against movement and relations of the individual toward the outside, and it set up barriers against individual independence and differentiation within the individual self. These barriers were such that under them modern man could not have breathed. Even today a metropolitan man who is placed in a small town feels a restriction similar, at least, in kind. The smaller the circle which forms our milieu is, and the more restricted those relations to others are which dissolve the boundaries of the individual, the more anxiously the circle guards the achievements, the conduct of life, and the outlook of the individual, and the more readily a quantitative and qualitative specialization would break up the framework of the whole little circle.

The ancient *polis* in this respect seems to have had the very character of a small town. The constant threat to its existence at the hands of enemies from near and afar effected strict coherence in political and military respects, a supervision of the citizen by the citizen, a jealousy of the whole against the individual whose particular life was suppressed to such a degree that he could compensate only by acting as a despot in his own household. The tremendous agitation and excitement, the unique colorfulness of Athenian life, can perhaps be understood in terms of the fact that a people of incomparably individualized personalities struggled against the constant inner and outer pressure of a de-individualizing small town. This produced a tense atmosphere in which the weaker individuals were suppressed and those of stronger natures were incited to prove themselves in the most passionate manner. This is precisely why it was that there blossomed in Athens what must be called, without defining it exactly, "the general human character" in the intellectual development of our species. For we maintain factual as well as historical validity for the following connection: the most extensive and the most general contents and forms of life are most intimately connected with the most individual ones. They have a preparatory stage in common, that is, they find their enemy in narrow formations and groupings the maintenance of which places both of them into a state of defense against expanse and generality lying without and the freely moving individuality within. Just as in the feudal age, the "free" man was the one who stood under the law of the land, that is, under the law of the largest social orbit, and the unfree man was the one who derived his right merely from the narrow circle of a feudal association and was excluded from the larger social orbit—so today metropolitan man is "free" in a spiritualized and refined sense, in contrast to the pettiness and prejudices which hem in the small-town man. For the reciprocal reserve and indifference and the intellectual life conditions of large circles are never felt more strongly by the individual in their impact upon his independence than in the thickest crowd of the big city. This is because the bodily proximity and narrowness of space makes the mental distance only the more visible. It is obviously only the obverse of this freedom if, under certain circumstances, one nowhere feels as lonely and lost as in the metropolitan crowd. For here as elsewhere it is by no means necessary that the freedom of man be reflected in his emotional life as comfort.

It is not only the immediate size of the area and the number of persons which, because of the universal historical correlation between the enlargement of the circle and the personal inner and outer freedom, has made the metropolis the locale of freedom. It is rather in transcending this visible expanse that any given city becomes the seat of cosmopolitanism. The horizon of the city expands in a manner comparable to the way in which wealth develops; a certain amount of property increases in a quasi-automatical way in ever more rapid progression. As soon as a certain limit has been passed, the economic, personal, and intellectual relations of the citizenry, the sphere of intellectual predominance of the city over its hinterland, grow as in geometrical progression. Every gain in dynamic extension becomes a step, not for an equal, but for a new and larger extension. From every thread spinning out of the city, ever new threads grow as if by themselves, just as within the city the unearned increment of ground rent, through the mere increase in communication, brings the owner automatically increasing profits. At this point, the quantitative aspect of life is transformed directly into qualitative traits of character. The sphere of life of the small town is, in the main, self-contained and autarchic. For it is the decisive nature of the metropolis that its inner life overflows by waves into a far-flung national or international area. Weimar is not an example to the contrary, since its significance was hinged upon individual personalities and died with them; whereas the metropolis is indeed characterized by its essential independence even from the most eminent individual personalities. This is the counterpart to the independence, and it is the price the individual pays for the independence, which he enjoys in the metropolis. The most significant characteristic of the metropolis is this functional extension beyond its physical boundaries. And this efficacy reacts in turn and gives weight, importance, and responsibility to metropolitan life. Man does not end with the limits of his body or the area comprising his immediate activity. Rather is the range of the person constituted by the sum of effects emanating from him temporally and spatially. In the same way, a city consists of its total effects which extend beyond its immediate confines. Only this range is the city's actual extent in which its existence is expressed. This fact makes it obvious that individual freedom, the logical and historical complement of such extension, is not to be understood only in the negative sense of mere freedom of mobility and elimination of prejudices and petty philistinism. The essential point is that the particularity and incomparability, which ultimately every human being possesses, be somehow expressed in the working-out of a way of life. That we follow the laws of our own nature—and this after all is freedom—becomes obvious and convincing to ourselves and to others only if the expressions of this nature differ from the expressions of others. Only our unmistakability proves that our way of life has not been superimposed by others.

Cities are, first of all, seats of the highest economic division of labor. They produce thereby such extreme phenomena as in Paris the renumerative occupation of the *quatorzième*. They are persons who identify themselves by signs on their residences and who are ready at the dinner hour in correct attire, so that they can be quickly called upon if a dinner party should consist of thirteen persons. In the measure of its expansion, the city offers more and more the decisive conditions of the division of labor. It offers a circle which through its size can absorb a highly diverse variety of services. At the same time, the concentration of individuals and their struggle for customers compel the individual to specialize in a function from which he cannot be readily displaced by another. It is decisive that city life has transformed the struggle with nature for livelihood into an inter-human struggle for gain, which here is not granted by nature but by other men. For specialization does not flow only from the competition for gain but also from the underlying fact that the seller must always seek to call forth new and differentiated needs of the lured customer. In order to find a source of income which is not yet exhausted, and to find a function which cannot readily be displaced, it is necessary to specialize in one's services. This process promotes differentiation, refinement, and the enrichment of the public's needs, which obviously must lead to growing personal differences within this public.

All this forms the transition to the individualization of mental and psychic traits which the city occasions in proportion to its size. There is a whole series of obvious causes underlying this process. First, one must meet the difficulty of asserting his own peronality within the dimensions of metropolitan life. Where the quantitative increase in importance and the expense of energy reach their limits, one seizes upon qualitative differentiation in order somehow to attract the attention of the social circle by playing upon its sensitivity for differences. Finally, man is tempted to adopt the most tendentious peculiarities, that is, the specifically metropolitan extravagances of mannerism, caprice, and preciousness. Now, the meaning of these extravagances does not at all lie in the contents of such behavior, but rather in its form of "being different," of standing out in a striking manner and thereby attracting attention. For many character types, ultimately the only means of saving for themselves some modicum of self-esteem and the sense of filling a position is indirect, through the awareness of others. In the same sense a seemingly insignificant factor is operating, the cumulative effects of which are, however, still noticeable. I refer to the brevity and scarcity of the inter-human contacts granted to the metropolitan man, as compared with social intercourse in the small town. The temptation to appear "to the point," to appear concentrated and strikingly characteristic, lies much closer to the individual in brief metropolitan contacts than in an atmosphere in which frequent and prolonged association assures the personality of an unambiguous image of himself in the eyes of the other.

The most profound reason, however, why the metropolis conduces to the urge for the most individual personal existence—no matter whether justified and successful—appears to me to be the following: the development of modern culture is characterized by the preponderance of what one may call the "objective spirit" over the "subjective spirit." This is to say, in language as well as in law, in the technique of production as well as in art, in science as well as in the objects of the domestic environment, there is embodied a sum of spirit. The individual in his intellectual development follows the growth of this spirit very imperfectly and at an ever increasing distance. If, for instance, we view the immense culture which for the last hundred years has been embodied in things and in knowledge, in institutions and in comforts, and if we compare all this with the cultural progress of the individual during the same period—at least in high status groups—a frightful disproportion in growth between the two becomes evident. Indeed, at some points we notice a retrogression in the culture of the individual with reference to spirituality, delicacy, and idealism. This discrepancy results essentially from the growing division of labor. For the division of labor demands from the individual an ever more one-sided accomplishment, and the greatest advance in a one-sided pursuit only too frequently means dearth to the personality of the individual. In any case, he can cope less and less with the overgrowth of objective culture. The individual is reduced to a negligible quantity, perhaps less in his consciousness than in his practice and in the totality of his obscure emotional states that are derived from this practice. The individual has become a mere cog in an enormous organization of things and powers which tear from his hands all progress, spirituality, and value in order to transform them from their subjective form into the form of a purely objective life. It needs merely to be pointed out that the metropolis is the genuine arena of this culture which outgrows all personal life. Here in buildings and educational institutions, in the wonders and comforts of space-conquering technology, in the formations of community life, and in the visible institutions of the state, is offered such an overwhelming fullness of crystallized and impersonalized spirit that the personality, so to speak, cannot maintain itself under its impact. On the one hand, life is made infinitely easy for the personality in that stimulations, interests, uses of time and consciousness are offered to it from all sides. They carry the person as if in a stream, and one needs hardly to swim for oneself. On the other hand, however, life is composed more and more of these impersonal contents and offerings which tend to displace the genuine personal colorations and incomparabilities. This results in the individual's summoning the utmost in uniqueness and particularization, in order to preserve his most personal core. He has to exaggerate this personal element in order to remain audible even to himself. The atrophy of individual culture through the hypertrophy of objective culture is one reason for the bitter hatred which the preachers of the most extreme individualism, above all Nietzsche, harbor against the metropolis. But it is, indeed, also a reason why these preachers are so passionately loved in the metropolis and why they appear to the metropolitan man as the prophets and saviors of his most unsatisfied yearnings.

If one asks for the historical position of these two forms of individualism which are nourished by the quantitative relation of the metropolis, namely, individual independence and the elaboration of individuality itself, then the metropolis assumes an entirely new rank order in the world history of the spirit. The eighteenth century found the individual in oppressive bonds which had become meaningless—bonds of a political, agrarian, guild, and religious character. They were restraints which, so to speak, forced upon man an unnatural form and outmoded, unjust inequalities. In this situation the cry for liberty and equality arose, the belief in the individual's full freedom of movement in all social and intellectual relationships. Freedom would at once permit the noble substance common to all to come to the fore, a substance which nature had deposited in every man and which society and history had only deformed. Besides this eighteenth-century ideal of liberalism, in the nineteenth century, through Goethe and Romanticism, on the one hand, and through the economic division of labor, on the other hand, another ideal arose: individuals liberated from historical bonds now wished to distinguish themselves from one another. The carrier of man's values is no longer the "general human being" in every individual, but rather man's qualitative uniqueness and irreplaceability. The external and internal history of our time takes its course within the struggle and in the changing entanglements of these two ways of defining the individual's role in the whole of society. It is the function of the metropolis to provide the arena for this struggle and its reconciliation. For the metropolis presents the peculiar conditions which are revealed to us as the opportunities and the stimuli for the development of both these ways of allocating roles to men. Therewith these conditions gain a unique place, pregnant with inestimable meanings for the development of psychic existence. The metropolis reveals itself as one of those great historical formations in which opposing streams which enclose life unfold, as well as join one another with equal right. However, in this process the currents of life, whether their individual phenomena touch us sympathetically or antipathetically, entirely transcend the sphere for which the judge's attitude is appropriate. Since such forces of life have grown into the roots and into the crown of

424 *The Metropolis and Mental Life*

the whole of the historical life in which we, in our fleeting existence, as a cell, belong only as a part, it is not our task either to accuse or to pardon, but only to understand.[11]

[11] The content of this lecture by its very nature does not derive from a citable literature. Argument and elaboration of its major cultural-historical ideas are contained in my *Philosophie des Geldes* [The Philosophy of Money; München und Leipzig: Duncker und Humblot, 1900].

Index

Index

cal features of, 311-312; written, 352-355

Compromise, impossible between conflicting moral claims, 230-231

Concept, analogy to group, 96-97, 220-221, 254-255, 257

Conciliation, boards of, 147, 149

Concubines, 327

Confession, 334

Confidence: and types of social conditions, 318-320; as faith, 318n., 348; characteristic of modern life, 313; characteristic of secret societies, 345, 347-348; vs. worthiness of confidence, 348

Conflict, deadliness of, among homogeneous elements, 168, 195

Conflict of duties, 230

Conscience, 100, 101n., 231-232, 254; and social and objective ideal, 255-256; vs. majority vote, 246-247

Contempt for mass, 32-33

Contents: of social life, 40-43; psychological, idealization of, 99-100

Contract: as objective norm above contracting parties, 264; social, 182, 187, 188, 244-245, 278

Conventicle Act, 175

Conversation, 51-53

Coordination: and reciprocal super-subordination, 286-291; as subordination, 219-220; of parties in arbitration, 221-223

Coquetry, 50-51

Corinth, 91

Cosmos, beginning of, 291

Court cabal and monarchy, 336n.

Courtesy, 49, 397, 400-401

Courts of arbitration, 221, 222

Cowardice, 153

"Credit economy," 313

Criminal code, analogy to logic, 399-400

Criminology, 14, 259-260

Cromwell, Oliver, 215, 288

Crowd cruelty, 228-229

Culture: and general affairs vs. individual affairs, 335-337; objective vs. individual, 422

Custom, law, and morality, relations among, 99-104

D

Darwin, Charles, 30

David, King, 292

Death, 124

Decimal principle of group subdivision, 171-174

"Decimation," 172

Delegation of responsibility to group, 226-227

Democracy, 47-48, 93-94, 110-111, 143n., 188, 205, 285, 286, 287, 295, 337, 365

Demosthenes, 327

Denunciation, 166

Despotism: and equalization, 198-199, 374; and individualization, 204; and secret societies, 347, 361; hereditary, 299

Determinateness: a sociological

438 *Index*

things, 16, 41; realms vs. society, 62, 99-100, 255-256; significance, as an interpretive category, 16-17; "spirit," 352, 421; values, 60-61, 99-100, 127, 147-148, 173-174, 255-256, 352; vs. subjective life-elements, 284-285; vs. "subjective spirit," disproportionate development of, 421-422

Objectivity: and cognition, 258-259; and morality, 260-261; as freedom from commitments, 405; as structure composed of distance and nearness, 404; definitions of, 256-257; in Kant, 69-70; of rule by plurality, 225-226; prerequisite of written communication, 353; vs. social norms, 256-258

Objects, 17, 41, 69

Old and new, esteem of, 29-30

Omladina, 171-172, 357

Orange Societies, 376

Organization, as exercise of power, 357

Organizations, splitting up of, 31

Outvoting: 239-249; as expression of irreconcilable dualism between individual and society, 248-249; group unity prerequisite for, 245-246

"Owner of soil," 403

P

Parents and children, 204, 383

Paris, 420

Parties, political, 34, 93, 94, 141-143, 157-158, 165, 205, 213, 233, 295; secret, 346-347

Pater familias, 114, 261-262

Patrimony, 253

Permissibility vs. expediency of lie, 313-314

Persians, 5

Personality: and work, separation of, 283-285; containability of, in one side of it, 391; decomposition of, through interaction, 202-203; qualitative character of, 202; radiation through adornment, 339-340, 342; secret of, 320, 322; "significance" of, 321-322, 339

Peru, 165-166, 172-173

Philip the Fair, 175;—the Good, 201

Philosophical areas, surrounding social science, 23

Philosophie des Geldes (Simmel), 424n.

Philosophische Kultur (Simmel), 50n.

Physics, 24

Physiocrats, 64

Plato, 91, 252, 260, 269-270, 296

Play, 42-43

Plebiscites, negative results of, 396-397

Pliny the Younger, 163

Poland, 91, 240

Polis, 417

Political organizations, prohibitions against, 163

Polyandry, 92

Polygamy, 236

Polyneikes, 231